Psychology

and
the National Institute
of Mental Health

Psychology

and

the National Institute of Mental Health

A Historical Analysis of
Science, Practice,
and Policy

Edited by
Wade E. Pickren *and*
Stanley F. Schneider

American Psychological Association • Washington, DC

Published by
American Psychological Association
750 First Street, NE
Washington, DC 20002
www.apa.org

To order
APA Order Department
P.O. Box 92984
Washington, DC 20090-2984
Tel: (800) 374-2721
Direct: (202) 336-5510
Fax: (202) 336-5502
TDD/TTY: (202) 336-6123
Online: www.apa.org/books/
E-mail: order@apa.org

In the U.K., Europe, Africa, and the Middle East, copies may be ordered from
American Psychological Association
3 Henrietta Street
Covent Garden, London
WC2E 8LU England

Typeset in Goudy by World Composition Services, Inc., Sterling, VA

Printer: Book-Mart Press, Inc., North Bergen, NJ
Cover Designer: Naylor Design, Washington, DC
Technical/Production Editor: Gail B. Munroe

The opinions and statements published are the responsibility of the authors, and such opinions and statements do not necessarily represent the policies of the American Psychological Association.

Library of Congress Cataloging-in-Publication Data

Psychology and the National Institute of Mental Health : a historical analysis of science, practice, and policy / Wade E. Pickren & Stanley F. Schneider, editors.
    p. cm.
  Includes bibliographical references and index.
  ISBN 1-59147-164-8
  1. National Institute of Mental Health (U.S.)—History. 2. Mental health policy—United States—History. 3. Psychology—Research—United States—History.
4. Psychiatry—Research—United States—History. 5. Psychologists—Training of—United States—History. I. American Psychological Association. II. Pickren, Wade E. III. Schneider, Stanley F.

RA790.6.P77 2004
362.2'0973—dc22   2004012361

British Library Cataloguing-in-Publication Data
A CIP record is available from the British Library.

Printed in the United States of America
First Edition

This volume is dedicated to the memory of Stanley F. Schneider (1922–2002). Stan embodied the wonderful ideals of the original mission of the National Institute of Mental Health and was the quintessential psychologist of the post-World War II era.

CONTENTS

CONTRIBUTORS

George W. Albee, University of Vermont, Vermont Conference on Primary Prevention, Burlington, and Florida Mental Health Institute, Tampa

David B. Baker, University of Akron, Akron, OH

Ludy T. Benjamin, Jr., Texas A&M University, College Station

Donald A. Dewsbury, University of Florida, Gainesville

Ingrid G. Farreras, Hood College, Frederick, MD

James G. Kelly, University of California, Davis

F. Vincent Mannino, independent practice and consultation, Silver Spring, MD

Wade E. Pickren, American Psychological Association, Washington, DC

Charles E. Rice, George Washington University, Washington, DC

Rachael I. Rosner, The Danielsen Institute, Boston University, MA

Stanley F. Schneider (1922–2002), National Institute of Mental Health, Bethesda, MD

Milton F. Shore, independent practice, Silver Spring, MD

James W. Stockdill, Western Interstate Commission for Higher Education, Boulder, CO

ACKNOWLEDGMENTS

A volume on such a complex subject as psychology and the National Institute of Mental Health (NIMH) necessarily entails the contributions of many people. First, and foremost, the chapter authors are to be thanked for their scholarship and for their patience. In each case, they devoted themselves to the project and spent many hours collecting the resources needed for their chapters. Each chapter required careful collection of facts and the checking and rechecking of those facts. Then, each author developed a narrative to tell his or her story in an interesting manner. I thank all of them for making this a useful volume.

My coeditor, the late Stanley F. Schneider, deserves special thanks. Stan spent many hours explaining the intricacies of NIMH. He also graciously introduced me to many key figures in late 20th-century American psychology. These were men and women with whom he had developed special relationships in his role as chief of Psychology Training at NIMH. Because of Stan, they were willing to talk openly and candidly with me about their research and their relationships with NIMH. I thank them as well.

My two research assistants, Sarah Kopelovich and Jung Ah Kim, also deserve my thanks. Both spent many hours checking facts, reading manuscripts, developing data tables, and helping prepare the manuscript for publication. I deeply appreciate their contributions.

Last, several people at the American Psychological Association Books Department have generously supported the research that went into developing the book. I especially thank Gary VandenBos, Susan Reynolds, and Phuong Huynh for their support, guidance, and encouragement.

I

INTRODUCTION AND HISTORICAL OVERVIEW

1

SCIENCE, PRACTICE, AND POLICY: AN INTRODUCTION TO THE HISTORY OF PSYCHOLOGY AND THE NATIONAL INSTITUTE OF MENTAL HEALTH

WADE E. PICKREN

Many factors were involved in the transformation of psychology after World War II (WWII). Perhaps no factor has been as important as the role played by several agencies of the federal government. The Veterans Administration (VA; now the Department of Veterans Affairs), the Department of Defense (especially the Office of Naval Research), the National Science Foundation, and the National Institute of Mental Health (NIMH) have provided funding and employment opportunities for psychologists that have shaped the direction and identity of psychology. This influence has been reciprocal: Psychologists, both individually and through organizations such as the American Psychological Association (APA), have been active participants in the development and transformation of these organizations as well.

This volume is a historical analysis of the reciprocal relationship of psychology and the NIMH. As a historical volume, the book provides important insights into the remarkable expansion of psychology since WWII and illuminates the role of government in shaping the lives and practices of its citizens through its funding of research, training, and service. It is also meant to serve as a resource for scholars who wish to write more specialized histories of post-WWII psychology and government.

There has been little historical work that offers a compelling analysis of the forces that have given such a psychological cast to the last 50 years. This volume fills a significant gap in our understanding of the development of current psychological science and practice, and it links that development to the emergent relationship of psychology and government.

PSYCHOLOGY AND THE NIMH: A BRIEF PREHISTORY

The changes in the disciplinary and professional boundaries of psychology that occurred after WWII had their origin in the two decades before the war (Pickren, 1995). In 1937, psychologists involved in application, including mental health work, were finally able to form their own organization, the American Association of Applied Psychologists. This group was successful enough to force APA to reorganize in a manner friendlier to the practice of psychology (Pickren & Dewsbury, 2002).

World War II was a transformative experience for American psychology (Capshew, 1999; Herman, 1995; Hoffman, 1992). The focus on real life problems became even sharper. Psychologists also took advantage of the opportunities provided by wartime needs to advance their personal and disciplinary causes. Their involvement on such a large scale in the war effort had unforeseen effects. One such effect was the receipt of large-scale government support of both basic and applied psychological science. For the first time, the federal government became the principal supporter of American science, and that support continued after the war (e.g., Appel, 2000; Darley, 1957; Sapolsky, 1990).

At the end of WWII, the reorganized APA seemed prepared to take advantage of its wartime experiences. Organizationally, psychologists were apparently more united than in the years just before the war. Their discipline was a science with seemingly unlimited possibilities for usefulness. Psychologists touted this utility to a public that was increasingly ready to believe them. The convergence of a number of factors exerted a powerful, disciplinary-bending force on American psychology. The specter of atomic weaponry, the provision of funds for education under the aegis of the GI Bill, and sharpened awareness of mental health problems all contributed to key changes in the role of psychology in American life. The most pressing demands were for assistance in caring for the mentally ill.

Above all, the war brought recognition of the prevalence of mental disorders. Almost 2 million men were rejected by the Selective Service for psychiatric problems or mental deficiencies, and another 500,000+ men were discharged because of mental disorders. The incidence of mental disorder was estimated at 6% of the population in the first few years after the war (see Brand & Sapir, 1964), and the lack of mental health personnel increased in salience to policymakers after the war. The shortage of trained mental health workers in the VA alone was critical. Veterans with psychiatric disorders occupied 60% of VA hospital beds in 1946 (Brand & Sapir, 1964). It was also clear that the United States as a whole did not have enough adequately trained personnel and that its medical schools were not prepared to produce enough psychiatrists to meet the need. The government turned to the professions of psychiatric nursing, social work, and clinical psychology for help. For the first time, the federal government became involved in the large-scale support of training, research, and service in the mental health field (see chap. 6, this volume).

In 1946, the VA began working with APA and several leading universities to develop a clinical psychology program (Miller, 1946). Clinical psychology was a diffuse subdiscipline without a clear identity. As Molly Harrower stated in March 1947, "We have, at the present time, no discipline of clinical psychology in the same sense that we have medicine, law, dentistry, or teaching" (Harrower, 1948, p. 11). This lack of identity placed clinical psychology in a weak position to negotiate with federal agencies.

On July 3, 1946, President Harry Truman signed into law the National Mental Health Act (NMHA). The basis for the act was the proposal prepared in 1944 by public health psychiatrist Robert Felix for a comprehensive mental health program. The NMHA provided for research, training, and service functions. It authorized research to determine the etiology of mental disorders through both an intramural and an extramural research program. Training in mental health professions was authorized through grants to institutions and individuals; research fellowships were also part of this authorization. Prevention, diagnosis, and treatment of psychiatric disorders formed the third part of the mandate. In this function, the U.S. Public Health Service was expected to assist the states in implementing mental health services. The NMHA thus greatly increased the role of the federal government in the daily lives of its citizens. It also altered the direction, size, and practice of American psychology.

The Division of Mental Hygiene of the U.S. Public Health Service began implementing the mandate of the NMHA in 1946. The division was abolished when the NIMH was formally established in April 1949. Robert Felix became the first director of the institute. By 1960, the NIMH was the dominant force in mental health in the United States.

As other historians have noted (e.g., Grob, 1991), psychologists were tapped by the NIMH for the leading role in mental health research. Felix held the view that a multidisciplinary research effort was vital and that the behavioral sciences were critical in that effort. Archival research and interviews with former staff members reveal that this influence was not just in the direction of the NIMH recruiting from psychology; psychologists, both clinical and scientific, began to play a major role in the work of the NIMH from its very beginning. First, psychologists were vastly overrepresented on the professional staff of the Institute: as research scientists in the Intramural Research Program, as branch and division chiefs, as deputy directors of the entire Institute, and as members of the superordinate National Advisory Mental Health Council. In these positions of power, psychologists influenced the implementation of national mental health policy, shaped models for training in both research and practice, and gave direction to mental health research through their roles as executive secretaries of study sections. Psychologists perhaps had their greatest influence in this last role. The study sections, or review committees, were responsible for recommending grantees, both institutional and individual, to the National Advisory Mental Health Council.

The rapid development of psychotherapy and the emergence of psychologists as primary mental health professionals in the eyes of the public is an example of profound change given impetus by NIMH policies (Cook, 1958). Psychologists' desire for independent practice led to friction between them and psychiatrists. What ensued was a battle over cultural and professional authority and legitimacy, not over who was more scientifically qualified to practice psychotherapy, because no sound scientific basis for the efficacy of therapy had been established (Buchanan, 2003). That battle had many nuances and contained multiple implications for the psychologically minded U.S. society. The emergence of psychotherapy as a social, personal, and purchasable commodity has never been entirely about professional turf wars; it has also reflected enduring themes in American life, and its emergence in the 1950s reflected the important social and cultural milieu in which NIMH and the transformation of psychology were embedded.

THE CULTURAL CONTEXT OF CLINICAL PSYCHOLOGY AND THE NIMH

The rapid growth of psychology as a mental health profession occurred in a convergence of policy initiatives and cultural changes that reinforced each other. In this section, I trace the outlines of that convergence: the large infusion of funds from federal agencies, Cold War fears, the cultural opening for psychotherapy created by the popularity of psychoanalysis, the rapid growth of suburbs and the rampant consumerism that accompanied that growth, and the felt superficiality of middle-class life.

The establishment of the NIMH and its consequences for mental health professions and the public had its origins in the New Deal policies of President Franklin Delano Roosevelt. These policies reflected a belief that government could and should play a positive role in the health and well-being of its citizens. In 1937, the National Cancer Institute became the first entity established in what became the National Institutes of Health (Strickland, 1972). After the war, the National Heart Institute, the NIMH, the National Institute for Dental Sciences, and the National Institute for Neurological Diseases and Blindness were established.

For approximately 20 years, the Congressional appropriations for the National Institutes of Health rose steadily, at times even spectacularly. It was typical for Congress to appropriate more money for the institutes than was requested by the executive branch (Strickland, 1972). It was in this period of grand largesse that monies for the training of clinical psychologists and for research related to mental health grew the fastest. The concerns of national policymakers with the nation's health included mental health.

Although a proximal stimulus for the establishment of the NIMH came from the wartime experience of a high incidence of mental disorders among soldiers, the fears of widespread morbidity in the general population were high—and for just cause. Within months of the use of atomic weaponry on the citizens of Nagasaki and Hiroshima, a cloud of anxiety settled over many Americans. Fears of the proliferation of nuclear weapons and their potential use led some to suggest the possibility of an epidemic of psychiatric disorders that could result in the collapse of civilization (Meerloo, 1946; Thompson, 1945; S. H. Walker, 1945). Franz Alexander, of the Chicago Institute for Psychoanalysis, suggested that the H-bomb would have a deadening effect on the American psyche and would lead to a mindless emphasis on work and consumption as a way to deal with the threat of nuclear war (Alexander, 1946). Michael Amrine, then the managing editor of the *Bulletin of Atomic Scientists*, wrote in *The New York Times Magazine* that the threat of nuclear war was shattering the American faith in progress and would end American optimism (Amrine, 1950). By any measure, the immediate effect of Hiroshima was to infuse Americans' psyches with anxiety about the future.

Suburbia and the Citizen–Consumer

In addition to widespread anxiety over the development of atomic weaponry, the end of WWII brought an economic resurgence and the beginning of the population growth now called the "baby boom." The boom, both population and economic, had profound effects on the patterns of American life. Suburbs were not new to America, but their growth in this era was phenomenal (K. T. Jackson, 1985; Marsh, 1990). After years of economic depression and war-related rationing of consumer goods, postwar prosperity brought new demands for an array of consumer goods, chief among them housing. The returning soldiers and their new brides' demands for housing led to a construction boom like none before it. The "good life," which itself is a term that became popular in these years, was represented by the individual home in a neighborhood, often far from the cramped urban spaces of the previous generation (Johns, 2003; Samuelson, 1995). Builders such as Levitt and Sons developed huge tracts of near-identical housing on pastureland.

Of course, the suburban home had to be filled. It is in this context that one sees the final transformation of middle-class identity as citizen to a new identity as consumer. The amplification of desire, begun on a large scale by Alfred P. Sloan in 1927 to sell more GM cars, reached its first peak in the postwar suburbs (Gartman, 1994). Gadgets of every kind were created and marketed to the middle class. It was a design for better living through the possession of more things (Bird, 1999; Marling, 1994). Toasters, portable toasters, vacuum cleaners (both uprights and sweepers), mixers, steam irons, percolators, electric frying pans, radios (console and transistor), refrigerators and freezers in amazing colors; power tools of every kind for the do-it-yourself-er, and above all, the television, represented modernity: The American family had a sense of technological mastery and everyday convenience greater than any society before it. "Better living through consumption" was the unstated motto, and American corporate success depended on it.

Karal Marling (1994), in her book *As Seen on TV*, pointed out that the 1950s was a period that emphasized the outside of things. This was the era, in her words, of "those who looked for their own reflections in the era's glittering surfaces" (p. 14). In other words, in an era of prosperity, and with the horrors of the war so close to mind and the deprivations of the Depression still a strong memory, most of the middle class did not want to examine life too closely. Along with television and household gadgets, design and fashion helped direct the middle-class gaze away from the recent horrors.

The New Look in art, architecture, fashion design, and furniture design in the late 1940s through the 1950s represented the emphasis on the exterior. Examples of the design include Eero Saarinen's design of the Dulles airport terminal in Virginia, the furniture of Charles Eames, the Guggenheim Museum, and the atomic clock, as well as ceramics by Pablo Picasso. The emphasis was on form and organic expression. In fashion, the exaggeration of female curves, with the hips padded to exaggerate the slenderness of the waist and the bustline emphasized by skintight tailoring, characterized the New Look (L. Jackson, 1998). The overall emphasis was on playfulness, color, amusement, and excitement. The new trends found their greatest expression in the applied arts, and many items were within reach of the middle class. Eames chairs, for example, were affordable, as were the wall-paper designs of Lucienne Day.

The New Look was part of the focus on the visual that came to dominate American cultural and social life at almost every level in the 1950s. It was design that was fun; it was meant to help people forget the war and the nuclear threat under which they lived. Like television and the suburban tract home, it was a haven from the pervasive threat of nuclear annihilation that now formed the constant backdrop of daily life. The anxiety posed by the possibility of nuclear war was too much to face directly.

Anxious Times

I turn now to another view of postwar America. There was intense anxiety and fear about the future in the aftermath of the use of atomic weapons. Popular literature after the war is filled with articles that raise the question of human survival. Beyond survival, questions of the meaningfulness of life and entrenched social customs were questioned. Government agencies stepped into this social breach with attempts to soothe the population. By 1950, the prospects of peaceful uses of the atom were touted by the Atomic Energy Commission. Paul Boyer (1994), in his excellent book *By the Bomb's Early Light*, documented the government's role in planting stories in the press and orchestrating a public information campaign to downplay alarmist views about atomic power. Academic institutions, radio networks, television, and even some filmmakers cooperated in this disinformation project, the goal of which was to allay public fears.

These developments must be seen in the context of the emerging Cold War. Military planners believed they needed secrecy as they led America into an increasingly dangerous arms race. An alarmed public would raise questions about the development of more powerful weapons. As part of the attempt to soothe the public, outright lies were told about the dangers of radiation and the stockpiling of hydrogen bombs (Whitfield, 1996).

During the Cold War, talk about atomic threat or social survival was enmeshed in a complex discourse that included patriotism, loyalty, and the evils of Communism. The political paranoia evident in the McCarthy era indicates how deeply threatened many people felt. The impact of the Communist witch hunt was felt in the NIMH, resulting in the barring of several prominent psychologists from serving as staff members or on review panels (see chap. 2, this volume).

In the mid-1950s, the fear of radiation poisoning re-emerged as a major concern of the American people. In 1955, radioactive rain fell on Chicago. One way to understand American fear is to examine science fiction and horror movies of the period. In "Them!" (1954), giant mutant ants emerge from a New Mexico atomic bomb test site and threaten citizens. "The

Thing," "The Day the Earth Stood Still," "Invasion of the Body Snatchers," and many other films all reflect Cold War fears. "The Incredible Shrinking Man" (1957) features fears of radiation as the protagonist, after passing through a radioactive cloud, shrinks and eventually disappears.

On the one hand, middle-class White Americans in the 1950s were living the good life. The new suburbs had given them purchase on privacy and property; television had created opportunities for togetherness; appliances of every kind promised freedom from drudgery; and the New Look had made fashion and design interesting, fun, and affordable. On the other hand, Americans were worried about many things, even worrying that they were watching too much television (Spigel, 1992). In Marling's (1994) memorable phrase, Americans got the "suburban jitters," and physicians became alarmed that their patients were frustrated and stressed by the demands of keeping up with the Joneses (pp. 254–255). The 1950s were the decade when middle-class fears about juvenile delinquency first peaked (see Bandura & Walters, 1959). Many parents worried that their children would become social deviants because of television messages and the emphasis on consumption (Spigel, 1992). Family life, far from being a haven in a heartless world, was often experienced as oppressive and mind numbing (May, 1988).

It is not surprising that this is the time when psychotherapy was incorporated into middle-class consumption (Gurin, Veroff, & Feld, 1960). Mental health became a purchasable commodity. Housewives in particular found that the "pushbutton way to leisure often led straight to the psychiatrist's couch" (Marling, 1994, p. 266)—except that it was very likely to be the psychologist's couch rather than the psychiatrist's.

Psychoanalysis, Psychotherapy, and Psychologists

Psychoanalysis reached the peak of its popularity and cultural influence in the immediate post-WWII years (Hale, 1995). Popular culture was saturated with psychoanalytic ideas in movies (e.g., "Spellbound"), magazines, literature, and even comic books (J. Walker, 1993). The American middle class, anxious about the Cold War, anxious even about its own consumerism, was primed for the commodification of mental health. Talking about one's problems to a professional became glamorous—and, perhaps more important, accessible—to the reinvigorated American middle class. The popularization of psychoanalysis was critical in the creation of a normalization of the use of mental health professionals.

However, psychoanalysis did not prove to be a good fit with mainstream, middle-class culture, White or Black (Lal, 2002). The rather bleak view of human nature and the inexorability of psychic conflict, combined with the demands on the analysand, were typically too great for most members of the middle class. So, although the popularity of psychoanalysis helped create a cultural space for talk therapy, it was soon superseded by psychotherapy. The public did not necessarily differentiate psychoanalysis and psychology, with the result that new professions were able to take advantage of the public's eagerness for psychological expertise. This new desire for therapeutic experiences was exploited by psychologists, newly trained in the new clinical psychology with new psychotherapies, who were able to move into public prominence as science-based mental health professionals (Cook, 1958).

The new psychotherapies, like that of Carl Rogers (1942), were easier to understand than psychoanalysis. Much of the content was not radically different from what was heard in church on Sunday, and most of it was positive, with a focus on conscious mental processes and practical real life problems. The new psychotherapies were imbued with American optimism and were more appealing than psychoanalysis, which only held out the hope that the patient would move from misery to common unhappiness. With the waning of religious influence, psychologists offering such therapies stepped in as alternative guides to the good life.

This is the immediate context for the rapid emergence of psychotherapy in postwar America (see also chap. 5, this volume). NIMH funding for training stipends and faculty recruitment provided the bulk of the support that made possible the training of clinical psychologists adept in these new psychotherapies. At the end of WWII, few psychologists were psychotherapists; even fewer made their living from its practice. Before the end of the 1950s, "psychologist" had come to mean "mental health professional" to most North Americans (Cook, 1958). Conversations with psychologists who were among the first cohort of postwar clinical students reveal that the majority did not consider a career in private practice as a desirable option (e.g., G. W. Albee, personal communication, June 4, 1999; C. A. Stenger, personal communication, July 19, 1999). By the early 1960s, vociferous complaints were being made that graduate training in clinical psychology did not prepare students well enough for private practice (Pottharst & Kovacs, 1964). The NIMH grant program for clinical training had made the training of more clinical psychologists possible, but it had also brought with it an increased desire on the part of trainees for autonomy of practice.

It is interesting that a series on psychology was published in *Life* magazine in the first four issues of 1957 (Havemann, 1957). In many ways, the content of the series was unremarkable. What the author highlighted was that whatever the problems facing Americans in the 1950s, psychologists and other mental health professionals were there to ameliorate personal problems and soothe the anxious brows of the public.

This is the milieu in which post-WWII psychology was transformed. No one factor can account for this transformation. Large-scale government funding, policymakers' concerns, changing patterns of living, Cold War fears, and trends in popular culture, among many others, are the factors that contributed to these changes. Movements within psychology were also important; some of them are discussed in the following chapters. Psychology, like other sciences and other professions, is inextricable from the society of which it is a part.

OVERVIEW OF THE BOOK

This volume focuses on issues of mental health policy, support of research through the extensive grants programs, training for research and practice, and the expanded support of mental health services by the federal government, each of which had important consequences for the discipline of psychology. In turn, government policy and practices were changed by the involvement of psychologists as science administrators. The chapters are arranged in four sections: "Part I: Introduction and Historical Overview," "Part II: NIMH Support of Psychological Science," "Part III: Training Psychologists for Science and Practice," and "Part IV: Psychologists on Site: Practice and Community." Thus, each of the main functions of NIMH are examined for their influence on psychology. There are many gaps in this volume, some unavoidable. Stanley F. Schneider, my coeditor, had planned to write two chapters: one on NIMH training philosophy and one to update the institute's organizational history. Regrettably, he became seriously ill and died just as he was preparing the materials, and he was unable to complete the chapters. Space limitations do not permit an account of the NIMH Intramural Research Program; fortunately, Ingrid Ferraras is preparing a volume on this. Perhaps the most serious gap is the lack of analysis of the NIMH study sections. Many scientists with whom I spoke commented that their service on the study sections was among the best experiences of their lives. Serious scholarship on the study sections will yield valuable insights about scientific communications in this country.

The various chapters in this book give an indication of the range of impact of the NIMH on psychology and the key roles that psychologists played at NIMH. However, the subject is simply too large for one volume, so this book stands as a first word on the subject, not the last. For readers who wish to pursue particular topics presented in the book, the copious references and tables should be a valuable resource.

Interviews conducted with NIMH staff members and grant recipients are available: A list appears in Exhibit 1.1. A number of archives were consulted by the editors and the chapter authors. Among those archives are the National Archives II in College Park, Maryland; the National Library of Medicine; the National Institutes of Health Office of History; the APA Archives; the Archives of the History of American Psychology at the University of Akron; the Harvard University Archives; and many personal archival

EXHIBIT 1.1
National Institute of Mental Health Oral Histories

Interviewer: Wade E. Pickren

Interviewees:

Interviewees:	Interviewees:
Nancy Adler	Ann Masten
George Albee	Wilbert McKeachie
Irving Alexander	Allan Mirsky
Harold Basowitz	Len Mitnick
Lyle Bivens	K. Patrick Okura
Jack Block	Suzanne Ouellette
Robert Cairns	Lucy Ozarin
Robert Callahan	Morris Parloff
Robert Cohen	David Pearl
John Coie	James Pittman
Robert Czeh	Tom Plaut
Bruce Dohrenwend	Al Raskin
Will Edgerton	Eli Rubinstein
Paul Ekman	Phil Sapir
Susan Folkman	Seymour Sarason
Robert Freeman and Tom Magoun	Stanley Schneider
David Galinsky	Milt Shore
John Gardner	Rae Silver
Stephen Goldston	Sam Silverstein
David Hamburg	Marianne Simmel
Les Hicks	Ralph Simon
Steve Hyman	Brewster Smith
Marty Katz	Jerome Singer
Herb Kelman	James Stockdill
Charles Kiesler	Henry Tomes
John Kihlstrom	Hussein Tuma
Ruth Knee and Jessie Dowling-Smith	Forrest Tyler
Ron Kurz	Wilse B. Webb
Marie Jahoda	Sheldon White
Peter Lang	Lou Wiencowski
Jack Maser	Ted Zahn

collections of former NIMH staff members. Research for this volume revealed many gaps in the archival record and helped fill some of them. Future historians of psychology and government will undoubtedly find records and other historical materials that will shed new light on the events described in this volume. It is hoped that the resources provided here will prove invaluable to those future scholars.

REFERENCES

Alexander, F. (1946). Mental hygiene in the Atomic Age. *Mental Hygiene, 30,* 532–537.

Amrine, M. (1950, August 6). What the Atomic Age has done to us. *The New York Times Magazine*, 27–30.

Appel, T. A. (2000). *Shaping biology: The National Science Foundation and American biological research, 1945–1975*. Baltimore: Johns Hopkins University Press.

Bandura, A., & Walters, R. H. (1959). *Adolescent aggression: A study of the influence of child-training practices and family interrelationships*. New York: Wiley.

Bird, W. L. (1999). *Better living: Advertising, media, and the new vocabulary of business leadership, 1935–1955*. Evanston, IL: Northwestern University Press.

Boyer, P. (1994). *By the bomb's early light: American thought and culture at the dawn of the Atomic Age*. Chapel Hill: University of North Carolina Press.

Brand, J., & Sapir, P. (1964). An historical perspective on the National Institute of Mental Health. In D. E. Woolridge (Ed.), *Biomedical science and its administration*. Unpublished manuscript.

Buchanan, R. (2003). Legislative warriors: American psychiatrists, psychologists, and competing claims over psychotherapy in the 1950s. *Journal of the History of the Behavioral Sciences, 39*, 225–249.

Capshew, J. H. (1999). *Psychologists on the march: Science, practice, and professional identity, 1929–1959*. New York: Cambridge University Press.

Cook, S. W. (1958). The psychologist of the future: Scientist, professional, or both. *American Psychologist, 13*, 635–644.

Darley, J. G. (1957). Psychology and the Office of Naval Research: A decade of development. *American Psychologist, 12*, 305–323.

Gartman, D. (1994). *Auto-opium: A social history of American automobile design*. New York: Routledge.

Grob, G. N. (1991). *From asylum to community: Mental health policy in modern America*. Princeton, NJ: Princeton University Press.

Gurin, G., Veroff, J., & Feld, S. (1960). *Americans view their mental health*. New York: Basic Books.

Hale, N. G. (1995). *The rise and crisis of psychoanalysis in the United States: Freud and the Americans, 1917–1985*. New York: Oxford University Press.

Harrower, M. R. (1948). The evolution of a clinical psychologist. *Journal of Clinical Psychology* (Monograph Suppl. No. 3), 11–15.

Havemann, E. (1957, January 7). The age of psychology in the U.S. *Life, 42*, 68–82.

Herman, E. (1995). *The romance of American psychology: Political culture in the age of experts*. Berkeley: University of California Press.

Hoffman, L. E. (1992). American psychologists and wartime research on Germany, 1941–1945. *American Psychologist, 47*, 264–273.

Jackson, K. T. (1985). *Crabgrass frontier: The suburbanization of the United States*. New York: Oxford University Press.

Jackson, L. (1998). *The new look: Design in the fifties*. New York: Thames & Hudson.

Johns, M. (2003). *Moment of grace: The American city in the 1950s.* Berkeley: University of California Press.

Lal, S. (2002). Giving children security: Mamie Phipps Clark and the racialization of child psychology. *American Psychologist, 57,* 20–28.

Marling, K. A. (1994). *As seen on TV: The visual culture of everyday life in the 1950s.* Cambridge, MA: Harvard University Press.

Marsh, M. (1990). *Suburban lives.* New Brunswick, NJ: Rutgers University Press.

May, E. T. (1988). *Homeward bound: American families in the Cold War era.* New York: Basic Books.

Meerlo, A. M. (1946). *Aftermath of peace: Psychological essays.* New York: Holt.

Miller, J. G. (1946). Clinical psychology in the Veterans Administration. *American Psychologist, 1,* 181–189.

National Mental Health Act of 1946, Pub. L. No. 79-487.

Pickren, W. E. (1995). Psychologists and physicians in the borderlands of science, 1900–1942. *Dissertation Abstracts International, 56,* 11B. (UMI No. 6373)

Pickren, W. E., & Dewsbury, D. A. (2002). Psychology between the world wars. In W. E. Pickren & D. A. Dewsbury (Eds.), *Evolving perspectives on the history of psychology* (pp. 349–352). Washington, DC: American Psychological Association.

Pottharst, K. E., & Kovacs, A. (1964). The crisis in training viewed by clinical alumni. In L. Blank & H. P. David (Eds.), *Sourcebook for training in clinical psychology* (pp. 278–300). New York: Springer.

Rogers, C. R. (1942). *Counseling and psychotherapy.* Boston: Houghton Mifflin.

Samuelson, R. J. (1995). *The good life and its discontents: The American dream in the age of entitlement, 1945–1995.* New York: Times Books.

Sapolsky, H. M. (1990). *Science and the Navy: The history of the Office of Naval Research.* Princeton, NJ: Princeton University Press.

Spigel, L. (1992). *Make room for TV: Television and the family ideal in postwar America.* Chicago: University of Chicago Press.

Strickland, S. P. (1972). *Politics, science, and dread disease: A short history of United States medical research policy.* Cambridge, MA: Harvard University Press.

Thompson, D. (1945, October). Atomic science and world organization. *Ladies Home Journal, 62,* 5–7.

Walker, J. (1993). *Couching resistance: Women, film, and psychoanalytic psychiatry.* Minneapolis: University of Minnesota Press.

Walker, S. H. (1945). *The first one hundred days of the Atomic Age.* New York: Woodrow Wilson Foundation.

Whitfield, S. J. (1996). *The culture of the Cold War* (2nd ed.). Baltimore: Johns Hopkins University Press.

2

REFLECTIONS ON PSYCHOLOGY AND THE NATIONAL INSTITUTE OF MENTAL HEALTH

STANLEY F. SCHNEIDER (1922–2002)

The National Institute of Mental Health (NIMH) was a burgeoning institute within the National Institutes of Health (NIH) when I joined it in September 1963. Although the law creating the institute was signed in 1946, it remained part of a division of the U.S. Public Health Service until 1949, when it became the fourth national institute of health, after those concerned with cancer (1938), heart disease (1948), and dental research (1948). In 1950, NIMH had fewer than 200 staff and a budget of $11 million. By 1964, it had a staff of more than 1,200 and a budget of $171 million.

Psychologists played key roles in NIMH. Joe Bobbitt was the first director's right hand (the director was Bob Felix, a psychiatrist, who held the position longer than any of the others, from 1946 to 1964). John Eberhart, another psychologist, was the first director of training for psychology, then

These reflections are based on preinterview notes made by Stanley F. Schneider prior to an interview with James G. Kelly on June 30, 2000. Copies of the entire transcript are available.

Schneider was for many years Chief, Psychology Section, Behavioral Sciences Training Branch, Division of Manpower and Training Programs at the National Institute of Mental Health.

the head of the entire extramural research program (1949–1954) before becoming NIMH deputy director (1961–1967) and then director (1967–1981) of the intramural research program, that is, NIMH's own laboratories within the NIH. Hal Hildreth, Jerry Carter, and David Shakow were other famous psychologists active in the NIMH's early days. Shakow became the head of the intramural laboratory of psychology, which at one time contained 80 people. Hildreth and Carter were concerned mainly with services, although Hildreth also assisted Felix on policy. In training, Norm Garmezy and Max Levin followed Eberhart, and they in turn were followed by Ken Little, later Executive Officer of the American Psychological Association; Irv Alexander; Hal Basowitz; and Joe Speisman. Eli Rubinstein was another psychologist who held high-level positions.

The pecking order among the mental health disciplines was characteristic of NIMH from its earliest days; probably it was most apparent in the area of training programs. There was never any doubt that a psychiatrist would be director of NIMH (in the one instance where it seemed a psychologist might get the job, the push was quickly repelled), nor was there much doubt that psychiatrists, and especially academic departments of psychiatry, considered NIMH to be their institute. The four *core disciplines*, as they were called in clinical training, were (in descending order of clout) psychiatry, clinical psychology, psychiatric social work, and psychiatric nursing. It is my own impression that, as a group, psychologists and social workers were much more oriented toward community approaches than the others, although some psychiatrists and nurses were notable leaders in the movement. The rivalry among the disciplines, which reflected the intense struggles over status, practice, and legal issues that went on outside the institute, was for the most part counterproductive within NIMH. However, given the history of these relationships, especially that between psychology and psychiatry, there was almost no way to avoid this.

I came into the NIMH during a period of fantastic growth and genuine regard for public service. New programs were being created and, in addition to our central jobs, many of us were involved in evaluating state plans for comprehensive community mental health centers (CMHCs), an effort that had strong support from Congress and the executive branch. NIMH was a place that also contained the seeds of new institutes. One of the first things I was involved in when I arrived was the transfer of all training programs in mental deficiency and gerontology to a new NIH institute, the National Institute of Child Health and Human Development. Later, the gerontology programs were spun off into the National Institute of Aging.

Psychologists have been the major professional group in the extramural NIMH programs; psychologists have also been the group that has received the greatest number of research grants and the largest number of research dollars from the institute, which has been the largest federal supporter of the field. However, the NIMH has never had a psychologist as director, although four psychologists have been deputy directors. The NIMH differed from all other NIH institutes in providing major support for clinical training (see Table 2.1 for details regarding training expenditures), in having a major program in mental health services, and in the importance of the behavioral sciences in its programs. It was the services portion of NIMH in particular that prompted its separation from the rest of the NIH in 1967. Soon after that departure, two additional institutes, concerned with alcoholism and with drug abuse, both of which had been part of NIMH, became sister institutes in a new agency: the Alcohol, Drug Abuse, and Mental Health Administration. NIMH rejoined the NIH in 1992, as did the National Institute on Alcohol Abuse and Alcoholism and the National Institute on Drug Abuse, as research institutes.

IDENTIFICATION WITH ALL OF PSYCHOLOGY

Something that profoundly changed in my outlook as I began my work at NIMH was an increasing identification with all of psychology. At the University of Michigan, I was very committed to the clinical enterprise and focused on diagnosis, psychotherapy, and psychopathology. I supervised and taught not only graduate students in psychology but also psychiatric residents. Because the NIMH training programs supported training in almost all areas of psychology (including even industrial mental health), it was necessary to learn something about them and to try to understand them on their own terms. There were not many clinical students in my graduate school days who did not harbor questions about the importance of "rat learning" or similar areas considered remote from human or societal concerns. I had graduate minors in social psychology and personality, but I was much less familiar with other areas of the field.

NIMH training programs always included site visits, frequently with a member or members of the training review committee, when a new or competing renewal (i.e., applying for another term of support) application was considered. My colleagues and I covered the entire country; we lacked training grants in only three states. I felt it incumbent on us to learn as much as we could about departments; the organization, culture, and politics of universities and their colleges; field training centers (and their relations with academic programs) and, increasingly, the milieu in which these enterprises took place. I became as familiar as I could with communities, the culture of regions, cities, states, and particular districts. With an active attempt to increase the representation of ethnic minorities, it was also necessary to understand their goals, aspirations, and institutions, such as the historically Black colleges.

TABLE 2.1

Support for Clinical Training, Division of Manpower and Training Programs (DMTP), National Institute of Mental Health, 1948–1986

Year	DMTP clinical training	Psychiatry[a]	Psychology (clinical)	Social work	Nursing
1948	1,140	483(69)	210(40)	212(50)	212(54)
1949	1,633	625(74)	359(51)	324(65)	280(74)
1950	3,098	1,425(109)	510(87)	543(109)	463(145)
1951	3,587	1,730(161)	595(103)	596(127)	544(160)
1952	4,199	2,000(205)	698(136)	701(145)	628(178)
1953	4,072	1,915(189)	698(124)	681(145)	627(187)
1954	4,398	1,965(208)	863(183)	686(165)	741(179)
1955	4,610	2,037(225)	749(153)	754(189)	639(172)
1956	6,206	3,012(300)	932(187)	961(194)	952(210)
1957	11,327	5,415(485/294)	1,687(368)	1,844(522)	1,755(360)
1958	13,827	6,139(571/424)	1,973(362)	2,133(576)	2,473(394)
1959	18,456	8,728(760/749)	2,880(551)	3,118(818)	2,195(283)
1960	21,137	10,289(908/749)	3,262(525)	3,709(800)	2,563(292)
1961	26,120	13,077(1,109/797)	3,880(631)	4,495(952)	2,841(311)
1962	35,523	18,111(1,547/832)	4,748(795)	5,959(1,150)	4,289(487)
1963	44,609	22,626(1,912/859)	5,747(956)	7,505(1,394)	5,489(683)
1964	59,353	28,878(2,188/939)	6,454(1,066)	8,996(1,668)	7,342(1,079)
1965	68,075	32,150(2,307/1,221)	7,202(1,144)	10,225(1,727)	8,443(1,338)
1966	77,314	35,670(2,464/1,290)	8,137(1,242)	11,712(1,799)	9,574(1,450)
1967	79,975	40,282(2,795/1,315)	9,095(1,382)	13,382(1,936)	11,196(1,827)
1968	83,577	39,989(2,462/1,362)	9,757(1,438)	14,628(1,901)	11,453(1,681)
1969	93,146	46,047(2,540/1,425)	11,932(1,476)	15,220(1,770)	12,061(1,630)
1970	89,947	43,700(2,364/1,406)	12,071(1,528)	14,068(1,596)	12,032(1,432)
1971	88,393	42,671(2,194/1,439)	11,790(1,510)	12,784(1,492)	11,579(1,363)
1972	87,209	38,525(2,050/1,323)	12,633(1,611)	13,053(1,476)	11,254(1,287)
1973	85,499	37,173(2,096/755)	12,414(1,640)	12,024(1,400)	9,788(1,190)

1974	79,630	32,417(1,786/656)	12,183(1,625)	13,992(1,310)	10,584(1,490)
1975	73,865	31,872(853/1,349)	11,550(1,662)	11,883(1,073)	9,370(1,169)
1976	68,558	26,630(402/1,300)	10,614(1,582)	10,356(767)	8,950(1,268)
1977	66,158	24,376(273/1,001)	10,276(1,565)	10,596(843)	8,339(1,092)
1978	67,225	22,826(230/930)	9,974(1,619)	10,060(787)	7,931(907)
1979	72,375	24,267(223/885)	10,445(1,497)	11,507(809)	8,459(874)
1980	69,706	23,147(155/739)	10,088(1,134)	10,884(787)	8,163(797)
1981	57,323	19,774(105)	8,302(894)	9,500(711)	7,070(802)
1982	30,886	12,884(36)	5,781(706)	6,945(574)	5,276(610)
1983	17,981	5,447(22)	2,536(270)	2,497(241)	2,079(236)
1984	16,238	6,711(45)	3,372(371)	2,995(304)	2,516(176)
1985	14,148	5,763(7)	3,028(341)	2,957(318)	2,279(179)
1986	9,888	3,225(28)	1,914(172)	2,138(194)	1,224(97)
Total training funds($)	1,660,411,000	724,001,000	231,339,000	266,543,000	213,653,000
Total no. stipends		36,457(24,039)	32,727	32,884	28,143

Note. All table values are in thousands of dollars. Numbers in parentheses represent total numbers of stipends.
[a]For psychiatry, beginning in 1957, the first stipend figure represents residency stipends; the second indicates medical school stipends. For psychiatry 1981 through 1986, figures for medical student support are unavailable; stipend numbers for these years represent only those requiring payback.

My colleagues and I had multiple coexisting priorities that kept things exciting and stimulating. For example, one of our purposes was an encouragement of rural mental health training, as was the development of training programs in what we called "have-not" states. It is important to understand that research grants, the gold standard of the institutes, went predominantly to prestigious research universities, so people knew something about Boston, New York City (but not much about the Bronx or Staten Island), Durham–Chapel Hill, Berkeley, Los Angeles, Chicago, Minneapolis, and even Iowa City and such, but not much about Pullman, Washington; Laramie, Wyoming; North or South Dakota; Arkansas; West Virginia; or Maine. I or one of my colleagues might be found visiting Emory University and Morehouse College in the same trip, and my meetings with the Black student psychological associations were often more interesting and meaningful than those with the chairs of graduate departments of psychology or the directors of clinical training programs. It is quite probable that, with the exception of my colleague Fred Elmadjian, who ran the Biological Sciences Training Program at NIMH, I had more contact with my research grant counterparts than anyone else in the training division. (See Table 2.1 for a listing of training grant funding during these years.)

I think the issue that in time became the most overriding one for me was the effect of psychologists' training, knowledge, and mental health centers on the people "out there." My colleagues and I placed a major emphasis on evaluation research for several years, in an effort to stimulate the field to think about this issue (see chap. 10, this volume). I knew, of course, that we were able to recruit outstanding students in psychology and that they equaled or surpassed the best students in most universities. Also, an abiding principle for me was to make sure in any way you can that you will be transcended—that the individuals who inherit anything you have been able give them will be wiser and better for the world than you were.

I do not know how many times, in my writings or talks, I have come back to George Miller's 1969 recommendation to "give psychology away." When I asked Miller at a 1983 symposium whether he still believed in what he said, his answer was characteristically succinct: "Yes, but nobody wants it." I do not agree with him. I think lots of people want it, for lots of different reasons, but psychologists have always had a problem about how to give it away and whether they really wish to do so. One reason is that they are not trained to communicate with the public in ways that can facilitate their understanding A more important reason has to do with whether they take Miller seriously. He claimed that everyone needed psychology but that psychologists needed less to assume the role of experts and more to learn how to help people help themselves. I read these statements as a call to empower people, but I think that psychologists are very ambivalent about that—if they think about it at all. Psychologists have spent considerable capital on defining, preserving, expanding, and protecting their expertise. Entire areas of psychology are devoted to these ends. How many people in our practice areas would even concede the possibility, let alone the desirability, of the practice of valid psychology by nonpsychologists? It would drive many of them up the wall. As for the scientists, they are generally much more interested in having their expertise impress other scientists than troubling to convey it meaningfully to the general public. I welcome every sign of change in these attitudes, but I am not terribly hopeful.

IMPACT OF POLITICAL CONSIDERATIONS ON PSYCHOLOGY TRAINING AND RESEARCH

During the Kennedy and Johnson administrations, budgets increased by large amounts. In 1963, Kennedy asked Congress to pass the legislation that led to the development of CMHCs. Psychologists played critical roles in this movement (see chap. 9, this volume). Most of the NIMH extramural professional staff were psychologists. We all worked on and critiqued state plans for CMHCs. Psychologists were influential in making certain that they as well as psychiatrists could be appointed directors of CMHCs. Training budgets doubled during my first 5 years at the NIMH.

Under President Nixon, attempts were made to decentralize activities with increased central (i.e., White House) control—give it to the states, but call the shots from the Oval Office. Nixon impounded training funds for a year, so that no awards were made, with the sole exception of a small postdoctoral program known as the "Weinberger awards" (Caspar Weinberger was then Nixon's head of the Department of Health, Education, and Welfare; he later became Secretary of Defense under President Reagan). The impoundment was ruled illegal, and by the time training support started again, Nixon had other things to worry about, because the Watergate controversy was about to erupt.

Before the Nixon years, the United States enjoyed a positive relationship with higher education. This had begun to erode with the onset of the Vietnam war, but the effects became much more general and profound under Nixon, who basically distrusted the academic establishment. In the case of psychology, the impoundment of training funds for a year caused significant hardship. At the same time, concomitant policies surfaced that foretold directions that were taken later. Nixon's economic advisors strongly advocated programs of student loans in place of stipends. The suggestions were accompanied by arguments about how student loans would help low-income and ethnic–minority students in particular.

I personally felt that low-income and ethnic–minority students would not be helped, because the deprivation of funds to institutions of higher education would mean increases in tuition, dormitory, and other fees, and the requirement to repay the loans would put these students in debt. The educational philosophy, based on market economy principles and geared toward technology education, would seriously undermine a liberal education, would favor a moneyed elite, and would curtail the type of dissent and disagreement with administration policy that was cresting in the country.

Another feature of the Nixon years was an emphasis on postdoctoral education, which was pushed in subsequent years on psychology (which did not have, and members of the field did not feel it needed, strong postdoctoral traditions, except in certain areas such as physiological psychology), and which remained in effect—to the field's detriment, in my opinion—until the National Academy of Sciences reversed its former recommendations of 30% predoctoral funding support to 70% postdoctoral, to 64% predoctoral to 36% postdoctoral, with an additional 50 minority students supported in undergraduate research training programs.

Perhaps the most enduring legacy of the Nixon administration, however, was the decline of respect for public service, an attribute that had become inextricably interwoven with higher education over the years since World War II. At times when regard for public service is high, good people come into such service, with a concomitant benefit to the nation. When regard for such service is low, there is generally a price to be paid. The Nixon years marked the really intense beginning of the politicization of the government–higher education relationship.

Under President Ford, things were much less confrontational. Under President Carter, early hopes were soon known to be too high, but Rosalynn Carter was very active in the President's Commission on Mental Health, which recommended a continuation and increased support for the CMHC program.

The Reagan years were not favorable to academic psychology. The administration began with a reduction in force that eliminated many government positions and reduced the grades of others; it was the greatest single morale crusher during my entire years with NIMH. When the NIMH was created, it was known as the agency that resembled a three-legged stool: one leg for support of research; a second leg for the support of training; and the third leg representing interest in and support of services, placing it in a lonely position in the NIH. During the Reagan administration, training and other programs deemed "undesirable" suffered greatly.

Early in the Reagan years, the service programs were moved to the states under block grants (the loss of one leg of the stool), and support for clinical training was seriously enough eroded to guarantee the imminent end of that program (the loss of a second leg). In addition, the Reagan administration was adamant about restrictions on the support of social research, feeling that too much of it centered on the relationship of factors such as poverty and immigration to mental health; support for social research (and in research training in areas such as social psychology) was severely curtailed. The abortion issue made for excruciating delays in agreements on budgets, so that people couldn't know whether they had funds in a timely fashion. President Bush was more permissive, but the 1994 Congressional election, had it continued on course, would have done in behavioral and social research across the board.

HIGH AND LOW POINTS IN MY EXPERIENCES AT NIMH

The high points throughout my time at NIMH were almost continual. I had wonderful mentors, an excellent staff, incredibly fine review committees, and interesting and accessible colleagues. I thoroughly enjoyed what I was doing: learning about educational institutions and programs throughout the country, learning about almost all areas of psychology, and meeting stimulating people in the field, being particularly impressed with students who bolstered my optimism about psychology and society. I was particularly fortunate to be able to be of some assistance in helping to diversify the field, not only through relations with psychologists from underrepresented ethnic groups but also in my ability to encourage the development of new areas (community psychology being one of them), new research emphases, and underdeveloped institutions and areas of the country as well.

When the training division was eliminated, I was able to direct a fair amount of energy to work in the nascent AIDS research and training program, whose director, Ellen Stover, is the daughter of one of my long-time colleagues in training. This was one of the most exciting and provocative periods in my professional life.

The high regard for public service that characterized my early years at NIMH was a real plus. We had increasing support (especially through the 1960s), minimal bureaucratic interference with our programs (it was assumed that the professional staff knew what they were doing), political support, and the upbeat feeling that we were doing things to benefit the field of mental health and the nation in general.

As I have mentioned, the Nixon years coincided with (and possibly encouraged) a decreasing regard for public service, although the general restiveness about the war in Vietnam cannot be discounted in this. This problem of decreasing regard has continued to the present. Support for clinical training began to be questioned during these years at the NIH (NIMH was not a part of NIH from 1967 to 1992), because most physicians entered practice rather than research. The National Research Act of 1974 created a new program of support for research training, with many new restrictions in grant mechanisms and, especially and predictably unfortunate for psychology, it "separated" research and clinical training. This later led to inane restrictions applied to the language that could be used in our announcements for clinical training, for which the word *research* was forbidden (one can begin to sense the bureaucratization of the process as well). During this entire period, the increased attention to, and emphasis on, psychiatry and "primary care" was medicalizing the enterprise to the extent that I proposed leaving NIMH.

In 1979, there was a separation of program and review, meaning that the function of selecting review committees went to a separate organizational component, entirely removed from program staff. Applications were still reviewed by outside reviewers, and pay decisions were still made by program staff and advisory councils, but in the past I acted as chief of the branch and executive secretary of the review committee (a position now titled *scientific review administrator*). This created an entirely new bureaucratic entity that required skilled professional and support staff. The appearance, or possibility, of a conflict of interest was the reason for this separation, and although this sort of conflict must be avoided, I have seen no compelling evidence that there is less of it since the change (and in our own programs we were especially careful about this possibility). It was also during this period that social research was attacked (it still has not recovered completely—many social psychology training programs became health psychology programs, and in others, attention to social problems has decreased).

The training division of NIMH was eliminated in 1985. The remaining research training programs are run out of the reconstituted research branches. The institute, which used to have a three-pronged purpose (research, training, and services), now lives solely under the banner of research, and its return to the NIH in 1992 fulfilled that aim.

There are additional low points that are very troubling. One of the worst, representing a bureaucratic attitude that was incapable of self-correction, was the refusal of NIMH officials to consider the appointment to our initial review committee of several superb and highly regarded social psychologists who were on a blacklist remaining from the McCarthy era. Recall that Sen. Joseph McCarthy of Wisconsin specialized in ferreting suspected subversives out of government, frequently without any real proof. We were never told the reasons for the refusals, and it wasn't revealed until much later that the McCarthy blacklists were still a factor. (McCarthy had left the scene in disgrace fully 20 years earlier.)

Not quite as outrageous, but related in its essence to the McCarthy incident, was a reaction of the NIMH director to a postdoctoral training grant we supported in the Mental Health, Health, and Science Policy division. The program was conducted during its 1st year at Duke University, with exposure to the Science Roundtable, and experience in the North

Carolina legislature, and during the 2nd year the trainees spent their entire time with a Congressperson or on a Congressional committee. This program, which had been supported for 5 years, was awarded the highest priority score by the review committee at the time it reapplied for continued funding, which was shortly after the Reagan presidency began. I was told that the director would not pay the award. I went to see him immediately to ask for an explanation. I was told we couldn't pay this grant because we didn't know whether the students were working for Republicans or Democrats. I could not believe what I heard. It so happened that I had a good deal of information about the program, and I pointed out that one of the postdocs was working for a New Hampshire senator who would have made most of the right wing seem liberal (and the postdoc was very valuable to the senator), another was working for a very liberal Congressman from New York, and the remainder of the students were on the entire spectrum between these two. This incident reflects a lack of spine that I found troubling indeed. It is fortunate that such incidents did not occur frequently.

Despite these low points, they were far outweighed by the positive elements in the work my colleagues and I did and the joy and feeling of accomplishment we had in doing it.

I was training branch chief from 1969 to 1985, but I began a history of this time a bit prior to 1968 and go beyond 1985. Changes in psychology mirrored those in general U.S. society. Perhaps the most important change of this kind had to do with diversity in the field. Even in the late 1960s, it was still common to ignore ethnic minorities and to regard women as persons who would "marry and contribute little to the field," as one of my professors once said. It was also common to have research populations that were exclusively White and male. The un-self-conscious integration of ethnic minorities into psychology still requires work, although things are vastly better than they were in the late 1960s. By now, women represent the majority of incoming university students, and they are certainly taken more seriously as contributors. Of course, the increasing diversity of people also led directly to an increased diversity of substance in the field. Research issues affecting women and minorities are now much more prevalent. It is interesting, for example, to review the lists of recipients of the distinguished scientific awards from the American Psychological Association to see how little attention was paid to diversity before the 1980s.

There were many additional developments, changes, and crises during this period. The cognitive revolution resulted in a major change in the way psychologists view learning. The emergence of emotion as a major research area, and the relationship of emotion and cognition, are more recent developments (the latter still requires a lot of work). The ascendancy of biological, neural, and genetic concepts has altered the strong environmental, individual, and social orientation that was characteristic of psychology at least since World War II. These approaches tend to be molecular rather than molar, and they require technological and methodological changes.

A subsidiary example of this change has to do with the shift from interpersonal to pharmacologic treatments and the current agendas that surround this issue. These may, of course, be viewed as additional aspects of diversity, and the problem of how to integrate nature and nurture and understand the relationships between them is not entirely different from what I have mentioned thus far. Another major substantive change has been the adoption of ecological and developmental perspectives in the way problems, particularly the exploration of life course development, are viewed. In recent years there has been greater confidence in programs for prevention, and the increased attention to psychological wellness and to what has been called *positive psychology* is related to this development, although it is absolutely necessary to understand these developments as quite distinct from prevention of mental health problems—indeed, as an attempt to get away from the limiting perspective of the NIMH psychopathology model.

Mention must be made also of the growth of psychology's contributions and roles in general health and especially of the importance of its contribution to the AIDS epidemic. AIDS research and training have become big-budget items at NIMH, and its AIDS prevention program, largely a creation of psychologists, is recognized internationally as a model for successful prevention.

KEEPING THE FAITH

I tend to be optimistic, and I was convinced that what my colleagues and I were doing at NIMH was worthwhile. I felt about it the way I felt about the GI Bill: that it was an inexpensive program that had the aims of helping people, of contributing to society, and of increasing the positive effects of psychology. My affection for psychology, which I once described as reflecting a combination of compassion and tough-mindedness, was also important in sustaining me.

II

NIMH SUPPORT OF
PSYCHOLOGICAL SCIENCE

3

COMPARATIVE PSYCHOLOGY: A CASE STUDY OF DEVELOPMENT OF SUPPORT FOR BASIC RESEARCH BY A FEDERAL AGENCY WITH AN APPLIED MISSION, 1948–1963

DONALD A. DEWSBURY

Prior to World War II, the primary sources for funding basic research in the United States were private foundations. Shortly after the war, however, several sources of federal funding became available. The amounts were generally larger than those from private foundations and, at least for a period, many applications were funded. This shift in support for research had great impact on many fields, including comparative psychology. Although there was some postwar funding from military sources, the two primary sources of support in comparative psychology were from the National Institute of Mental Health (NIMH) and the National Science Foundation (NSF).

The primary purpose of this chapter is to explore funding from the NIMH for research in comparative psychology during the period from 1948 through 1963. There are several reasons for singling out comparative psychology for analysis. First, the NIMH supported research in a wide range of health-related fields. A comprehensive analysis of the nature and consequences of such funding would be a very difficult task. The field of comparative psychology is among the smaller of the disciplines covered, and thus an analysis of its funding patterns presents problems that are more tractable than if a larger field were chosen.

Second, whereas the mission of the NIMH concerns human mental health, the field of comparative psychology is oriented toward basic research with nonhuman species. Indeed, it might be argued that the field of comparative psychology is among the more esoteric of the basic research areas supported in the name of progress related to mental health concerns. It is thus an ideal vehicle for examination of the support of basic research by a mission-oriented agency.

In addition, the postwar period was a time of great development and reorientation in comparative psychology. This corresponds with the time of the development of NIMH programs. Thus, NIMH support came at a time that was especially ripe for rapid development of the field.

However, NIMH policy also was being formulated during this critical period, making it one of special importance. The period corresponds to the "second transition period" of government funding for science as defined by Reingold (1994). By limiting the time period for analysis to 1948–1963, it is possible to choose a period (a) that is limited and thus more tractable than would be the whole life of the agency, (b) that covers the critical period of founding of support programs and thus for the development of policy at the NIMH, and (c) for which relevant data are readily available.

The nature of the NIMH support program can best be understood in comparison with the other federal program that provided support for research in comparative psychology: the Psychobiology Program of the NSF. Therefore, throughout the chapter I present parallel analyses of NSF support and contrast them with the NIMH data.

Furthermore, because comparative psychology represents just one part of the broad field of animal behavior studies, I also consider support from these agencies for animal behaviorists who were not comparative psychologists.

In an effort to assess the impact of postwar NIMH and NSF funding from the perspective of the recipients, in addition to that of the granting agency, I single out one facility—the Yerkes Laboratories of Primate Biology (YLPB)—for intensive analysis as a case study.

THE MISSION OF THE NIMH AND BASIC RESEARCH

The NIMH was established by the National Mental Health Act, which was signed by President Harry S. Truman on July 3, 1946. The mission of the agency included the following:

the improvement of the mental health of the people of the United States through the conducting of researches, investigations, experiments, and demonstrations relating to the cause, diagnosis, and treatment of psychiatric disorders; assisting and fostering such research activities by public and private agencies, and promoting the coordination of all such researches and activities and the useful application of results. (Grob, 1991, p. 53)

The portion of the mission statement of immediate concern here relates to the extramural research program, the funding of research programs related to mental health. Early in its existence, NIMH authorities decided that, because the etiology of mental illness was so poorly understood, "it is wisest to support the best research in any and all fields related to mental illness" (Brand & Sapir, 1964, p. 27).

It was recognized that advances in application were likely to come from a combination of targeted research aimed at solving specific problems and from scientists addressing issues of basic research and theoretical interest with little regard for application. The case for such a strategy was made persuasively by Comroe and Dripps (1976). Surely comparative psychologists were beneficiaries of this broad approach because much of their work was directed at understanding the bases of behavior, but the relationship to mental health issues often required a bit of a stretch.

One of the innovative aspects of the new institute was the inclusion of the behavioral and social sciences in its program of support (Grob, 1991; Rubinstein & Coelho, 1970). This may be attributed to the appointment of psychiatrist Robert H. Felix as the first NIMH director. Most of the testimony leading to the National Mental Health Act was provided by psychiatrists. Felix, however, although he was a psychiatrist, had ties with both psychodynamic and biological models of mental health and worked to foster both broad approaches (Grob, 1991).

In 1948, the first year of grants, the NIMH awarded 62 grants with a total budget of $1,140,079 (Grob, 1991, p. 65). The first grant (RO1-MH-00001 01) was awarded to psychologist Winthrop Kellogg for a project on the "Basic Nature of the Learning Process" (Program Analysis Section, Division of Extramural Research Programs, NIMH, 1964; Schneider, 2000). According to Schneider (2000), "psychologists have received the greatest number of NIMH research grants and the largest percentage of research dollars each year" (p. 394). Thus, in 1963, 55% of all research projects were awarded to psychologists, 14% were awarded to psychiatrists, 21% were awarded to biologists, and 10% were awarded to social scientists (Brand & Sapir, 1964). According to Grob (1991), 55% of all principal investigators for 1964 were psychologists; sociologists, anthropologists, and epidemiologists made up another 7%.

THE PSYCHOBIOLOGY PROGRAM OF THE
NATIONAL SCIENCE FOUNDATION

The NSF was founded slightly later than the NIMH, when President Truman signed the National Science Foundation Act of 1950 on May 10. Congressional consideration of legislation that would lead to the NSF began in 1942. Spearheading the effort to establish the foundation was electrical engineer Vannevar Bush. Bush (1945/1990) had written his classic *Science—The Endless Frontier* in response to a 1944 request from President Franklin D. Roosevelt for a report on how the federal government might further the development of science in the United States. His solution was the establishment of a national research foundation. Psychologists E. Lowell Kelly, Willard L. Valentine, and Dael Wolfle also played a role in bringing the foundation into existence (Wolfle, 1950).

There was much disagreement about such issues as the extent to which the foundation should be purely scientific, insulated from political concerns, or given a more applied mission so as to serve as an instrument for social change, and the possibility of inclusion of support for the social sciences (Lomask, 1975; Lyons, 1969; Wang, 1995). Many people wanted to remove the bulk of government support for science away from the military, where it had resided. Several versions of the bill had been considered by the Congress; the first to pass was vetoed by Truman. The foundation that was approved would be run by an entity called the National Science Board and a director; Alan T. Waterman was the first director appointed.

The delays and political wrangling resulted in a substantial decrease in the budget allocated to the new foundation. In 1945, Bush (1945/1990) had envisaged an NSF budget of $33.5 million in the 1st year, rising to $122.5 million in the 5th year (Appel, 2000, p. 19). The actual startup funds approved in 1950 were just $225,000. The first full budget, that for 1952, was for just $3.5 million, well below the $14 million requested and what Bush had earlier proposed (Lomask, 1975; Wilson, 1952). The NSF program followed the program at the NIMH; by the time the NSF program was established, the NIMH had already been funding grants for several years. As I show later, budgets for grants from the NSF generally remained substantially below those from the NIMH for the entire period covered in this chapter.

It was clear from the beginning that, unlike the NIMH, the NSF would have support of basic research as its primary mission. Just which basic sciences would be included was more problematic. Bush's vision was for the agency to support "the natural sciences, including biology and medicine" (Lomask, 1975, p. 205). Bush later agreed to a proposal that would permit, although not mandate, inclusion of the social sciences. The final charter was written to "support basic scientific research . . . in the mathematical, physical, medical, biological, engineering, and other sciences" (Lomask,

1975, p. 205). "It is as if Congress had said 'We won't tell the Foundation that it must support the social sciences, but we will fix things so that it can whenever it wants to'" (Wolfle, 1950, p. 206). A Sociology and Social Psychology Program was established later (Hicks, 1969).

A psychology program was immediately established, with John T. Wilson, formerly of the Office of Naval Research, as its director, to deal with (a) the assessment of the current status of psychology as a science; (b) provision of research grants; and (c) collateral activities, such as support for symposia and foreign travel (Wilson, 1953). The decision was made to emphasize research grants in the fields of physiological and experimental psychology, with some support for measurement theory and research. These fields could be fit within the Biological and Medical Sciences program. An advisory panel, consisting of Frank Beach, Lyle Lanier, Donald Lindsley, Donald Marquis, and Quinn McNemar, was established to assist in evaluating proposals. Wilson first referred to the Psychology Program as the "Psycho-biology Program" in his annual report of 1956.

A matter of concern was the support of individual scientists versus institutional grants (Wilson, 1954). The decision to support institutions, as well as individual investigators, would be important for comparative psychology with grants to such groups as the YLPB and the Jackson Laboratories.

By May 1953, Wilson could point to 29 proposals that had been received, with nine grants funded. It was somewhat ironic, but an omen of things to come, that the first grant funded by the Psychology Program was to zoologist Howard Evans for research on "behavior patterns of solitary Hymenoptera" (wasps). The first support for a comparative psychologist, as defined below, was for T. C. Schneirla in 1954. With a slight revision of the early data, Odbert and Cheatham (1963) traced the growth of the program from 1953 to 1963, noting increases in the number of proposals from 27 to 237 per year, the dollars requested from $500,000 to $14,208,100, the number of proposals supported from 8 to 118, and the dollar value supported from $100,000 to $3,313,300. For 1963, the mean grant size was $28,100, with an average duration of 1.8 years.

Writing of the NSF, Wilson (1952) concluded that "the importance of science in national affairs has been given a recognition never before achieved, and it should be of particular significance to psychologists that their science has a place in this scheme of things" (p. 501).

DEFINING COMPARATIVE PSYCHOLOGY

Because this analysis is limited to the field of comparative psychology, the definition used will have a critical effect on the results obtained. Unlike some other areas of psychology, there is no universally agreed-on definition of the field. Although most comparative psychologists are in general agreement about what constitutes comparative psychology, they disagree about the definition. I use the definition that I have developed and used repeatedly (e.g., Dewsbury, 1984). It must be emphasized that some decisions about which grants do and do not qualify as comparative psychology are fully determined by the definition adopted and that a different set would be selected by each student of the field attempting analysis. Some decisions must be somewhat arbitrary; however, although the specific grants included would vary with the definition chosen, it is unlikely that the broad conclusions to be drawn would be greatly affected by the definition adopted.

Comparative Psychology in Relation to the Rest of Psychology

Comparative psychology must be defined in relation to both the rest of psychology and studies of animal behavior outside of psychology. I use the term *animal psychology* to refer to all studies by psychologists using nonhuman animal subjects. Although there is appreciable overlap among them, it is possible to differentiate three major subfields within animal psychology. *Physiological psychology*, or behavioral neuroscience, is concerned with the physiological substrates of behavior. The emphasis is generally on the underlying mechanisms rather than the behavior itself; behavior is often used as a means to study the mechanisms. *Process-oriented learning* studies are designed to analyze the mechanisms of learning and some effects of motivational processes on the phenomena of learning. Both of these fields are regarded as worthwhile but differentiated from comparative psychology.

In essence, *comparative psychology* includes the remainder of the field of animal psychology. This generally includes studies of species other than the popular laboratory subjects or behavioral patterns other than learning and a few basic motivation systems. Although there is overlap among the fields, this approach can be used for some reasonable differentiation among them. Comparative studies of learning or studies of learning in species other than such common subjects as laboratory rats and white Carneaux pigeons would fall within comparative psychology. Studies aimed at the learning process using common laboratory species would not. Studies of physiological mechanisms designed to understand naturally occurring behavior might fall within comparative psychology, although most physiological studies would not be included.

One operational way to approach this differentiation is relation to the journals published by the American Psychological Association, which publishes one journal in each of these three fields. Studies in physiological psychology would generally appear in *Behavioral Neuroscience*. Process-oriented learning studies would generally appear in the *Journal of Experimental*

Psychology: Animal Behavior Processes. The concern in the present chapter is with research that would generally appear in the *Journal of Comparative Psychology*.

To qualify as comparative psychology, research need not include overt comparisons among species. The aim of the field is to elucidate general principles of behavior, not comparison per se. As formulated by Tinbergen (1963), the principles relate to the immediate control, development, evolutionary history, and adaptive functions of behavior. The term *zoological psychology*, used by some authors in the early development of the field (e.g., Morgan, 1894), might be more appropriate than *comparative psychology*.

Comparative Psychology as a Part of Animal Behavior Studies

In addition to overlap with several subfields of psychology, comparative psychology fits within the broad field of *animal behavior studies*, which includes research by many scientists outside of psychology. The field is the joint venture of psychologists, zoologists, anthropologists, animal scientists, and representatives from a host of related disciplines. Indeed, during the period under study in this chapter, comparative psychology was greatly affected by the interactions of comparative psychologists with the European ethologists of the time.

There is no hard-and-fast boundary between comparative psychology and the rest of animal behavior studies. Research in comparative psychology is that work on animal behavior done by psychologists. This, of course, raises the question of who qualifies as a psychologist. Ideally, psychologists are individuals who have completed PhD degrees in psychology departments, are employed in departments of psychology, and are members of the American Psychological Association. It is unfortunate that, for purposes of analysis, some individuals share some, but not all, of these characteristics, so that judgment again must be used. For purposes of the present analysis, I include as comparative psychologists a number of scientists, such as Karl Lashley, John Paul Scott, and John L. Fuller, who received their PhD degrees within other disciplines but spent significant parts of their careers associated with psychology (cf. Dewsbury, 1984). I include data concerning NIMH support for other animal behaviorists who are not psychologists, but I analyze those data separately.

Animal behaviorists have formed the Animal Behavior Society in North America and the Association for the Study of Animal Behavior, which includes the rest of the world. Yet another way to conceptualize the domains of comparative psychology and animal behavior is to include such work as might be presented at the meetings of one of these organizations or appear in the journal that they jointly sponsor, *Animal Behaviour*, or in similar journals, such as *Ethology* or *Behaviour*.

Application in the Present Analyses

It is clear that some arbitrary decisions had to be made. In most cases, the topics of grants were assessed only on the basis of their titles; full text was unavailable. Because many of these titles are vague, many decisions based on judgment were made. In some cases, individuals clearly identified as comparative psychologists did work at the boundaries of the field; in others, individuals not primarily identified as comparative psychologists conducted work that falls within its realm. These should be borne in mind when interpreting the results.

NIMH SUPPORT FOR COMPARATIVE PSYCHOLOGY

Analyses are based on data summarized by the NIMH (Program Analysis Section, Division of Extramural Research Programs, NIMH, 1964). The program in comparative psychology began with a grant of $5,750 to Karl Lashley, Director of the YLPB, in 1948 and continued with grants of $8,600 to John Paul Scott, of the Jackson Laboratories in Bar Harbor, ME, in 1949 and 1950. According to my analysis, the NIMH awarded researchers in the broad field of animal behavior 147 grants totaling $6,987,292 during 1948 through 1963 (see Table 3.1). Comparative psychologists received 117 of these grants, totaling $5,634,034, or approximately 80% of the total. The mean grant was approximately $48,000 for a period of 2.5 years with a mean annual budget of just under $20,000.

Growth of Support for Comparative Psychology

As can be seen in Table 3.2, both funding for comparative psychology and the overall budget for the NIMH grew over the 16-year period covered here. The data shown reflect the total budget, not that for just extramural research grants. Although complete data are not available at this time, for 1952, approximately half of the NIMH budget went to all 165 of its research grants; for 1963, the percentage sank to approximately one quarter (Brand & Sapir, 1964). Because many grants were intended to cover multiple years, there are more years of support shown in the table than there were grants awarded. The overall NIMH budget grew by a factor of 41 from 1948 to 1963; the expenditures for comparative psychology increased by a factor of 257. By 1963, the NIMH was spending nearly $1,500,000 annually on comparative psychology. However, in only 1 year, 1955, did the funds spent in support of comparative psychology reach 1% of the total budget.

TABLE 3.1
National Institute of Mental Health (NIMH) and National Science
Foundation (NSF) Support for All Animal Behavior Projects, 1948–1963

Category	NIMH	NSF
All animal behaviorists		
No. grants	147	165
No. grantees	102	92
Total dollars	6,987,292	3,516,300
Mean grant size ($)	47,532	21,311
Comparative psychologists		
No. grants	117	72
No. grantees	78	40
Total dollars	5,634,034	1,433,600
Mean grant size ($)	48,154	19,911
Mean duration (years)	2.5	1.8
Mean annual budget ($)	19,563	11,200
Other animal behaviorists		
No. grants	30	93
No. grantees	24	52
Total dollars	1,353,208	2,082,700
Mean grant size ($)	45,106	22,395
Mean duration (years)	2.1	2.1
Mean annual budget ($)	21,479	10,768
Percentages to comparative psychologists		
No.	79.6	43.6
Total dollars	80.6	40.8

Note. Data for NIMH from Program Analysis Section, Division of Extramural Research Programs, NIMH (1964). Date for NSH obtained through F. Stollnitz (personal communication, September, 1989).

Support by State and Institution

Grants were spread over 29 states and the District of Columbia. Nine states received 5 or more awards. New York led the list, with 15 grants, followed by Florida with 9 and California and Ohio, each with 7. Seven grants were made to comparative psychologists in other countries, including Canada, England, India, and Sweden.

Among institutions, the YLPB received the most grants: 9. They were followed by the Jackson Laboratories, with 6, and both the City College of New York and the University of Oklahoma, with 5 each. A somewhat different pattern is apparent when dollar amounts are analyzed. The University of Wisconsin was the leader, receiving $924,944, followed by Rutgers University, with $515,444; the YLPB, with $473,043; and the Jackson Laboratories, with $433,119. These four institutions received approximately 42% of all NIMH funds allocated to comparative psychologists during this period. It seems there was some advantage for these multi-investigator institutions rather than single-investigator laboratories.

TABLE 3.2
National Institute of Mental Health (NIMH) Grant Funding (Grants in Place) in Comparative Psychology by Year

Year	Comparative psychology No. grants	Total amount ($)	Total NIMH appropriation ($)	Percentage of total
1948	1	5,750	4,250,000	0.135
1949	1	8,600	9,128,000	0.094
1950	1	8,600	11,612,000	0.074
1951	3	14,788	9,505,000	0.156
1952	3	23,166	10,561,737	0.219
1953	4	32,574	10,895,000	0.299
1954	10	114,517	12,095,000	0.947
1955	13	158,892	14,147,500	1.112
1956	11	159,847	18,001,000	0.888
1957	19	269,042	35,197,000	0.764
1958	19	310,757	39,217,000	0.792
1959	24	502,575	52,419,000	0.959
1960	31	603,432	68,090,000	0.886
1961	44	919,786	100,900,000	0.912
1962	45	1,022,417	143,599,000	0.712
1963	59	1,479,291	176,374,000	0.839

Note. The data for comparative psychology are from *Mental Health Research Grant Awards: Fiscal Years 1948–63* (Table 8), by the Program Analysis Section, Division of Extramural Research Programs, National Institute of Mental Health, 1964, Chevy Case, MD: National Institute of Mental Health. In the public domain. The data for the NIMH budget are from "An Historical Perspective on the National Institute of Mental Health," by J. L. Brand and P. Sapir, 1964, unpublished manuscript.

Support of Individual Comparative Psychologists

The $5,634,034 of NIMH support was spread over 117 grants to 78 individual comparative psychologists. The data for individual comparative psychologists are presented in Table 3.3; those for the top 10 grant recipients are presented in Table 3.4. Harry Harlow of the University of Wisconsin, Daniel Lehrman of Rutgers, John Paul Scott of the Jackson Laboratories, and Henry Nissen and William Mason of the YLPB were responsible for major portions of the funding garnered for those institutions. The numbers are somewhat deceptive in that some grants, such as those to Harlow, Lehrman, Scott, and Nissen, appear to have been for support of institutional programs involving a number of investigators. It is obviously unfair to compare such grants with those for individual principal investigators conducting their own programs.

Most comparative psychologists would agree that the top 10 grantees were a very distinguished group. In an effort to assess the eminence of the leading grantees, the data for the top 10 grantees were compared with those for the next 10. Five of the top 10 (Frank Beach, Harlow, Lehrman, Nissen, and Curt Richter) were elected to the National Academy of Sciences of

TABLE 3.3
Individual Comparative Psychologists Who Received Grants From the National Institute of Mental Health

Principal investigator	No. years	Amount ($)
Adams, Donald K.	1	70,552
Angermeier, William F.	2	6,000
Beach, Frank A.	5	222,026
Berlyne, Daniel E.	2	53,924
Bernstein, Irwin S.	1	4,010
Best, Jay Boyd	2	90,996
Bitterman, Morton E.	1	151,910
Broadhurst, Peter L.	1	15,377
Bruell, Jan H.	1	2,300
Cairns, Robert B.	1	9,690
Campbell, Byron A.	2	136,876
Candland, Douglas K.	1	12,207
Carr, William J.	2	41,803
Church, Russell M.	2	66,090
D'Amato, Michael R.	1	29,405
Davis, Roger T.	2	33,283
Denenberg, Victor H.	2	57,708
Denniston, Rollin H.	2	42,043
Fantz, Robert L.	2	79,365
Feldman, Robert S.	1	68,708
Finger, Frank	1	47,076
Fischer, Gloria J.	5	23,451
Fowler, Harry	1	46,564
Fredericson, Emil	1	2,300
Fuller, John L.	1	24,000
Furchgott, Ernest	1	52,490
Garcia, John	1	26,087
Gardner, Beatrice Tugendhat	1	9,493
Gerall, Arnold	1	32,236
Gottlieb, Gilbert	1	14,278
Gray, Philip	1	21,216
Halas, Edward S.	1	30,074
Hall, John F.	1	2,300
Harlow, Harry F.	3	924,944
Hayes, Keith J.	1	16,632
Hebb, Donald O.	1	103,830
Held, Richard M.	1	43,211
Henderson, Norman D.	1	3,335
Hess, Eckhard	1	257,394
Hirsch, Jerry	1	2,300
Jensen, Gordon D.	2	22,233
Jerison, Harry J.	1	776
Kaufman, Charles I.	1	87,937
Kinder, Elaine F.	1	20,402
Klugh, Henry E.	1	2,300
Larsson, Knut	1	27,738
Lashley, Karl S.	1	7,750
Lehrman, Daniel S.	1	442,174
Levine, Seymour	3	114,903

(continued)

TABLE 3.3   *(Continued)*

Principal investigator	No. years	Amount ($)
Littman, Richard A.	3	37,819
Lockard, Robert B.	2	21,908
Longo, Nicholas	1	4,025
Mason, William A.	2	153,688
McConnell, James V.	1	51,663
Meier, Gilbert W.	1	30,169
Menzel, Emil W.	1	12,685
Moltz, Howard	3	48,958
Newton, Grant	2	24,557
Nissen, Henry W.	1	231,768
Pastore, Nicholas	1	15,580
Peacock, Lelon J.	2	32,603
Rice, George E.	2	7,742
Richter, Curt P.	1	296,464
Riopelle, Arthur J.	1	52,152
Rosenblatt, Jay S.	1	73,270
Royce, Joseph R.	1	3,500
Schneirla, Theodore C.	2	151,001
Schrier, Allan M.	1	126,097
Scott, John Paul	5	409,119
Singh, Sheo D.	2	4,600
Tidd, Charles W.	1	2,300
Tugendhat, Beatrice	1	975
Uyeno, Edward T.	1	17,103
Walk, Richard D.	1	3,630
Warren, John M.	1	26,108
Woods, Paul	1	56,089
Zeigler, H. Philip	1	16,990
Zimmerman, Robert	2	117,774
N	78	
Sum		$5,634,034
M		$7,231

Note. From Program Analysis Section, Division of Extramural Research Programs, National Institute of Mental Health (1964).

the USA (NAS). Only 1 psychologist in the second 10—Canadian D. O. Hebb—was elected. Grantees John Garcia and Karl Lashley also were elected.

I consulted the *Social Sciences Citation Index* for 1956–1965 (Institute for Scientific Information, 1989) in an effort to estimate the impact of the work of these comparative psychologists. Because of the large number of citations for some authors, only estimates were made. Harlow and Hebb have more than 7 columns in the print version and more than 1,000 citations during this period. Beach, M. E. Bitterman, Seymour Levine, Richter, and Scott each had more than 200 citations. My estimate is that the top 10 received more than 2,500 citations; the second 10 received approximately

TABLE 3.4
Top 10 Grant-Receiving Comparative Psychologists at the National Institute of Mental Health (NIMH) and the National Science Foundation (NSF)

Name	No. awards	Total value ($)
NIMH		
Harlow, Harry F.	3	924,944
Lehrman, Daniel S.	1	442,174
Scott, John Paul	5	409,119
Richter, Curt P.	1	296,464
Hess, Eckhard	1	257,394
Nissen, Henry W.	1	231,768
Beach, Frank A.	5	222,026
Mason, William A.	2	153,688
Bitterman, Morton E.	1	151,910
Schneirla, Theodore C.	2	151,001
NSF		
Nissen, Henry W.	2	160,000
Adler, Helmut E.	3	114,600
Schneirla, Theodore C.	6	102,600
Campbell, Byron A.	4	100,300
Thompson, William. R.	4	87,100
Bunnell, Bradford N.	2	67,800
Bernstein, Irwin S.	2	67,100
Walk, Richard D.	3	66,400
Richter, Curt P.	1	61,200
Levine, Seymour	1	47,800

Note. Data for NIMH from Program Analysis Section, Division of Extramural Research Programs, National Institute of Mental Health (1964). Data for NSH obtained through F. Stollnitz (personal communication, September, 1989).

1,700. The data would show a much more dramatic difference if Hebb were eliminated from the second 10. As a Canadian, he had other sources of funding and probably requested and received much less support than he would have had he been an American. It is difficult to determine whether this difference in impact between the top and second 10s was a factor in individuals receiving grants or the grants were a factor in increasing productivity. The former would provide an example of the expanded, macro-social version of the "Matthew Effect" described by Merton (1968), according to which those already judged to be eminent get a disproportionate share of credit and resources. Most likely, this was a two-way, positive feedback interaction.

Topics of Research Supported

Classification of grants by topic is even more risky than other analyses, because many titles are ambiguous and many grants cover more than one category. For example, a grant on "Psychophysiology of Reproductive

TABLE 3.5
Percentages of National Institute of Mental Health (NIMH) and National Science Foundation (NSF) Comparative Psychology Funding for 1948–1963, Allocated for Various Research Categories

Category	NIMH		NSF	
	No.	$	No.	$
Behavior genetics	1.7	0.3	0.0	0.0
Development	38.5	38.1	15.3	15.0
Reproductive behavior	6.8	6.3	1.4	0.7
Social behavior	12.0	11.8	6.4	11.3
Learning and cognition	10.2	9.1	13.9	11.1
Motivation	12.0	4.6	12.5	10.3
Physiological analyses	6.0	7.0	5.6	6.6
Primatology	3.4	12.3	8.3	13.8
Sensation and perception	6.0	2.4	18.0	18.9
General	3.4	8.1	18.0	12.1

Note. Data for NIMH from Program Analysis Section, Division of Extramural Research Programs, National Institute of Mental Health (1964). Data for NSH obtained through F. Stollnitz (personal communication, September, 1989).

Behavior" was classified as dealing with reproductive behavior but could have been counted as physiology. Nevertheless, an analysis is instructive. As can be seen in Table 3.5, the research projects supported dealt with a wide range of topics. The largest portion of NIMH funding of comparative psychology went to studies of development. This reflected the broader NIMH strategy of support for research on developmental disorders "in an effort to learn how to prevent, control and ameliorate emotional disorders in children . . . [and to gain] a gradual understanding of factors making for normal and abnormal development" (Brand & Sapir, 1964, p. 32). Although it was believed that a child's early environment affected his or her adult personality and behavior, clear evidence of this belief was sought. Within comparative psychology, this was a period of great explosion of research in imprinting and other forms of early experience, perhaps reflecting these funding priorities. The period led up to the initiation of the federal government's Head Start program in 1965. It might be argued that research in development was likely to have had the most direct impact on human health of any of the fields of comparative psychology supported by the NIMH.

Studies of motivation were also prevalent at this time, as there was much interest in drive theory, exploratory behavior, and other systems beyond basic drives. There were also numerous studies of social behavior, including altruism, cooperation, competition, imitation, and dominance. Although there were relatively few grants in general primatology, they tended to be large and thus account for a disproportionate percentage of the available funds relative to their number. It should be remembered, however, that some research classified as reproductive behavior, social behavior, learning, and in other categories was conducted with nonhuman primates.

NIMH Support for Other Animal Behaviorists

According to my analysis, the NIMH awarded animal behaviorists other than comparative psychologists 30 grants totaling $1,353,208 during the period from 1948 to 1963 (see Table 3.1). The mean grant size was approximately $45,000 for a duration of 2.1 years with a mean annual budget of just over $21,000. Thus, the sizes of the typical grants to comparative psychologists and other animal behaviorists were roughly comparable. However, comparative psychologists received approximately 80% of the grants and research dollars from the NIMH.

Data for individual animal behaviorists are presented in Table 3.6. The biggest recipient was William C. Young for his program on early hormones and reproductive behavior. He was followed by Benson Ginsburg, who studied drug effects on animal behavior, and anthropologist Sherwood Washburn, for his program in primatology. No animal behaviorist received more than two NIMH grants during this period. Washburn and Peter Marler were the two among the top 10 grant awardees on this list who got elected to the NAS; Clarence Little, the head of the Jackson Laboratories, also was elected.

The main conclusion to be drawn from these comparisons is that, when funding research in the broad field of animal behavior, the NIMH tended to favor psychologists rather than various biologists and anthropologists. This would appear to be a reflection of the mission of the NIMH in relation to problems of human health and the kinds of research emphasized in the different disciplines.

NATIONAL SCIENCE FOUNDATION SUPPORT FOR COMPARATIVE PSYCHOLOGY AND ANIMAL BEHAVIOR STUDIES

National Science Foundation Support for Comparative Psychologists

The NSF grants program did not begin until 1952. During the period from 1952 through 1963, comparative psychologists received just 72 grants from the NSF, compared with 117 NIMH grants. Furthermore, the mean size of the NSF grants was less than half that of the NIMH awards, they were for slightly shorter durations, and they had annual budgets slightly over half those of the NIMH grants.

TABLE 3.6
Individual Other Animal Behaviorists Who Received Grants From the
National Institute of Mental Health

Principal investigator	No. years	Amount ($)
Alland, Alexander	1	3,473
Altmann, Stuart A.	1	3,440
Aronson, Lester R.	1	37,149
Banks, Edwin M.	2	37,772
Collias, Nicholas E.	1	2,300
Davis, David E.	2	33,024
Dice, Lee R.	2	12,420
Ginsburg, Benson	1	302,990
Horner, B. Elizabeth	1	2,300
Kavanau, J. Lee	1	48,625
Keener, Helen S.	1	2,300
King, John A.	1	46,277
Klopfer, Peter H.	1	16,214
Little, Clarence C.	1	24,000
Marler, Peter	1	32,845
Rothenbuhler, Walter C.	2	62,647
Shaw, Evelyn	1	21,157
Sheppe, Walter	1	4,025
Simonds, Paul E.	1	12,211
Southwick, Charles H.	1	22,846
Terman, C. Richard	1	12,608
Van der Kloot, William G.	1	1,955
Washburn, Sherwood	2	108,818
Young, William C.	2	501,812
N	24	
Sum		1,353,208
M		56,383

Note. From Program Analysis Section, Division of Extramural Research Programs, National Institute of Mental Health (1964).

As can be seen in Table 3.7, 40 individual comparative psychologists received NSF grants; just 14 of those had also received NIMH awards; 26 received all of their support from the NSF. The top 10 NSF grantees can be seen in Table 3.4. Two individuals, Nissen and Schneirla, placed in the top 10 with both agencies. Nissen was the only grantee in the top 10 to be elected to the NAS; 5 of the NIMH top 10 grant recipients were elected. However, grantees James Gibson, Daniel Lehrman, Curt Richter, and Calvin Stone also were elected. The *Social Sciences Citation Index* for 1956–1965 shows approximately 1,100 citations for the NSF top 10 compared with more than 2,500 for the NIMH top 10.

TABLE 3.7
Individual Comparative Psychologists Who Received Grants From the National Science Foundation

Principal investigator	No. years	Amount ($)
Adler, Helmut E.	3	114,600
Altmann, Margaret	3	41,600
Bernstein, Irwin S.	2	67,100
Bunnell, Bradford N.	2	67,800
Campbell, Byron A.	4	100,300
Carpenter, Clarence R.	1	13,200
Denenberg, Victor H.	1	20,000
Fantz, Robert	1	22,800
Finch, Glen	1	3,600
Finger, Frank W.	1	15,500
Gibson, James	1	12,900
Glickman, Stephen E.	2	24,600
Grosslight, Joseph	2	40,900
Hayward, Sumner C.	1	8,000
Held, Richard	1	24,000
Henderson, Norman D.	1	10,400
Hill, Winifred	1	5,700
Hoffeld, Donald R.	1	5,000
Hurvich, Leo	2	38,600
Jensen, Donald D.	1	9,900
Kellogg, Winthrop N.	3	40,600
Lehrman, Daniel S.	2	34,100
Levine, Seymour	1	47,800
Marx, Melvin	2	15,400
Mason, William A.	1	15,300
McGill, Thomas	1	2,000
Meyer, Donald R.	3	26,100
Montgomery, Kay C.	1	11,400
Nissen, Henry W.	2	160,000
Palmer, Francis H.	2	11,000
Ratner, Stanley C.	1	17,100
Richter, Curt P.	1	61,200
Rumbaugh, Duane	2	43,300
Schneirla, Theodore C.	6	102,600
Stone, Calvin P.	2	16,500
Thompson, William R.	4	87,100
Tobach, Ethel	1	9,100
Tsai, Loh Seng	1	10,600
Walk, Richard D.	3	66,400
Warren, John Michael	1	9,500
No. individuals	40	
No. grants	72	
Total amount		1,433,600

Note. From Program Analysis Section, Division of Extramural Research Programs, National Institute of Mental Health (1964).

Examination of Table 3.5, in which the topics of research supported by the NIMH and the NSF are compared, reveals many striking similarities. In general, the same kinds of research were supported by both agencies. The NSF program, however, was less weighted toward developmental studies and had a greater emphasis on sensation and perception and general studies. The "general" category includes vague titles and numerous studies of the basic behavioral biology of particular species, including such titles as "Studies of Animal Behavior" and "Biological Bases of Behavior in *Neivamyrmex*." These differences with respect to developmental studies and those of the general behavioral biology of species provide the clearest reflections of the different missions of the NIMH and the NSF.

National Science Foundation Support for Other Animal Behaviorists

Whereas just 20% of NIMH support for animal behavior research went to researchers other than comparative psychologists, approximately 60% of NSF support was so allocated (Table 3.1). The typical sizes of NSF grants were similar for comparative psychologists and other animal behaviorists, but the animal behaviorists received more of them (Table 3.1.) As was true for comparative psychologists, the NSF grants were appreciably smaller than those from the NIMH.

The 93 NSF grants were spread over 52 individual animal behaviorists (see Table 3.8). The largest grantees were William Dilger, for his Cornell University program on the behavior of lovebirds, and Peter Marler, for his University of California program on song learning in birds. Dilger was also a coprincipal investigator on another grant. Eight of the 52 grantees were elected to the NAS. Of these 8, 4 (Marler, Arthur Hasler, Donald Griffin, and Charles Michener) were among the top 10 grant recipients; of the remaining 42 grantees, Edward Wilson, Howard Evans, Ernst Mayr, and R. K. Selander also were elected.

It should probably come as no surprise that the NSF, with its mission to support basic science, would be less committed to the work of psychologists than to that of other scientists, whereas the NIMH, with its health-related mandate, should be biased toward the kind of work done by psychologists. However, the psychobiology program started as the psychology program, and thus it is somewhat ironic that psychologists working in the field of animal behavior received less of its support than did other animal behaviorists. Recall that the first grant awarded from the program was to a zoologist, Howard Evans, for a study of the behavior of wasps.

TABLE 3.8
Individual Other Animal Behaviorists Who Received Grants From the National Science Foundation

Principal investigator	No. years	Amount ($)
Altmann, Stuart	1	26,000
Andrew, Richard	2	63,300
Armitage, Kenneth	1	15,000
Bardach, John E.	3	19,700
Barlow, George W.	1	35,700
Bishop, Alison (Jolly)	1	27,400
Brower, Lincoln P.	2	66,200
Cade, T. J.	1	37,600
Caldwell, David	1	3,700
Carpenter, Charles C.	3	58,700
Collias, Nicholas E.	5	68,400
Coppel, H. C.	1	32,600
Dane, Benjamin	1	3,200
Dilger, William C.	3	146,000
Dixon, K. L.	2	31,600
Emlen, John T.	4	76,800
Evans, Howard	3	45,700
Ferguson, D. E.	1	13,200
Fichter, E. H.	1	8,000
Ficken, Robert W.	1	15,700
Fuller, W. A.	1	2,100
Gerhold, H. D.	1	18,500
Graue, L. C.	2	19,200
Griffin, Donald R.	1	111,200
Hasler, Arthur	4	116,800
Howells, W. W.	2	80,000
Johnston, Richard F.	1	1,800
John, K. R.	2	29,400
Kellogg, P. P.	1	50,000
Klopfer, Peter H.	1	15,100
Kramer, Sol	1	13,700
Levine, Louis	1	8,500
Marler, Peter	3	138,500
Marshall, J. T. Jr.	3	42,800
Martof, Bernard S.	2	39,000
Mayr, Ernst	1	11,500
Michener, Charles D.	3	84,800
Moynihan, Martin	3	29,400
Raney, Edward C.	2	33,800
Reese, Ernst	1	24,200
Selander, Robert B.	1	26,500
Selander, R. K.	1	4,200
Shaw, Evelyn	3	113,300
Stokes, Allen. W.	1	18,900
Storer, R. W.	2	38,100
Stuart, A. M.	1	16,800
Test, F. H.	1	5,800

(continued)

TABLE 3.8   *(Continued)*

Principal investigator	No. years	Amount ($)
Walker, Thomas	2	33,400
Wilson, Edward O.	2	49,300
Winn, Howard E.	1	8,300
Wisby, W. J.	2	52,200
N	52	
Sum		2,082,700
M		40,052

Note. From Program Analysis Section, Division of Extramural Research Programs, National Institute of Mental Health (1964).

THE YERKES LABORATORIES OF PRIMATE BIOLOGY (YLPB): A CASE STUDY OF CHANGING PATTERNS OF RESEARCH SUPPORT DURING 1948–1962

The YLPB, of Orange Park, FL, were founded in 1930 by Robert Mearns Yerkes and became the leading center for research on the great apes, with the largest research collection of chimpanzees in the world and a focal facility for research in comparative psychology. They were closed, and the animals were moved to Atlanta as the core of the Yerkes Regional Primate Research Center, in 1965.

The Yerkes Laboratories of Primate Biology and Its Administration

The YLPB provides a locus for considering the changing patterns of funding for research during this period from the perspective of one prominent grantee, rather than the granting agency, as above. The life of the Orange Park facility spans both the time of transition from a dominance of private foundation funding to the age of major federal grants and the period covered in this chapter. They also present a microcosm of changing funding patterns in American science during this important period.

Yerkes received his PhD in comparative psychology from Harvard University in 1902. He then served successively on the Harvard faculty, in the U.S. Army, with the National Research Council, and at Yale University. At Yale, he and President James Rowland Angell secured Rockefeller Foundation funding for the Yale Institute of Psychology in 1924 and for the primate facilities in New Haven, Connecticut, and Orange Park soon after. Yerkes retired as laboratories director in 1941 and died in 1956.

When Harvard's Karl Lashley succeeded Yerkes as director, the YLPB came under the joint aegis of Harvard and Yale. Lashley, in turn, was succeeded from within by member Henry W. Nissen in 1955. By then,

Harvard and Yale had lost interest in the station. Ownership was transferred to Emory University in 1956. The laboratory had an interim director for a year, and then Arthur Riopelle became director in 1959. Geoffrey Bourne, of Emory, assumed the directorship in 1963 and oversaw the transition of the laboratories to Atlanta.

Yerkes began active and persistent lobbying for a research station in 1913. The process would take him 15 years and involved going with his plans from potential benefactor to potential benefactor in an effort to secure funding. All of the potential sources were private, including the Carnegie Institution of Washington, the Carnegie Corporation, E. W. Scripps, and the Rockefeller Foundation.

Eventually Yerkes secured Rockefeller funding for a small primate facility in New Haven with a $10,000 annual budget that began in 1925. His lobbying continued, and in 1929, funds were allocated for a feasibility study of a remote primate station. By March, plans were far enough along for the allocation of an additional $475,000 for the Orange Park facility. This odyssey of Yerkes's repeated contacts with the officers of the major foundations is indicative of the process of securing major funding during this time; the question of federal funding was never a factor.

By 1936 and early 1937, the Rockefeller officials had soured on Yerkes and the YLPB and threatened to terminate funding. There were concerns about the proper use of the funds, the quality of the staff, and Yerkes himself. The foundation was moving toward a more reductionistic model, whereas Yerkes was perceived as a somewhat old-fashioned scientist. The solution that was worked out with the Rockefeller Foundation continued funding at a decreasing rate for an additional 5-year period with Yerkes leaving as director.

Conditions had not changed much when Karl Lashley took over as the second director in 1942. To develop a workable budget, he had to coax and cajole Yale to continue to contribute the equivalent of Yerkes' salary after his retirement, president James Conant of Harvard to release Lashley's time and salary to the YLPB, the Rockefeller and Fels Funds to continue support, and the Carnegie Institution of Washington to initiate funding.

The first federal support for the YLPB came during Lashley's watch. During World War II, Henry Nissen worked on a project to select and train oscilloscope operators that was administered through the laboratories, which thereby secured overhead funding. The first government research grant to the YLPB was the 1948 NIMH support for $5,750 for Lashley's studies of different areas of the cerebral cortex by cutting of their interconnections.

When Arthur J. Riopelle was hired as the new director, following the tenures of Nissen as director and Lelon Peacock as interim director, there was a general feeling that the Orange Park facility needed expansion via improved grantsmanship. Riopelle fully understood the changing funding situation and the fact that one could no longer call up old friends to seek funding. He deliberately brought in new staff members who could be effective in this changed environment. Although the behavioral emphasis continued, there was also an increasing biomedical emphasis.

Funding the Yerkes Laboratories of Primate Biology

The total funding for the YLPB during 1948–1962 is shown in Table 3.9. Note that the numbers for NIMH and NSF support in Table 3.9 and Table 3.10 do not correspond exactly to those in the earlier tables. There are several reasons for this. First, the different agencies used different accounting

TABLE 3.9
Total Funding of the Yerkes Laboratories of Primate Biology for
1948–1962, as Indicated in Annual Reports

Source	Individual sources		Category of sources	
	Total ($)	%	Total ($)	%
All private sources			845,800	33.0
Rockefeller Foundation	$390,000	15.2		
Carnegie Corporation	146,000	5.7		
Ford Foundation	300,000	11.7		
Fels Fund	6,800	0.3		
Wilkie Foundation	1,000	0.0		
Fund for Neurobiology	2,000	0.1		
University funds			149,167	5.8
Yale University	50,000	1.9		
Harvard University	99,167	3.9		
Nonmilitary government			1,302,901	50.8
Atomic Energy Commission	131,455	5.1		
U.S. Public Health Service	104,722	4.1		
NIMH	218,192	8.5		
NIH	182,532	7.1		
National Heart Institute	472,500	18.4		
NSF	193,500	7.5		
Government military sources			168,687	6.6
U.S. Navy	33,000	1.3		
U.S. Army Surgeon General	135,687	5.3		
Other Sources			99,937	3.9
Committee for Research on Problems of Sex	6,200	0.2		
Sale of animals	5,601	0.2		
Rosalia Abreu Memorial Fund	7,286	0.3		
General fund	56,798	2.2		
Miscellaneous	21,772	0.8		
Interest	2,280	0.1		
Total			2,566,492	100.0

Note. NIMH = National Institute of Mental Health; NIH = National Institutes of Health; NSF = National Science Foundation. Data compiled from annual reports (1953–1963) of the Yerkes Laboratories of Primate Biology available at Woodruff Library, Emory University, Atlanta, GA.

TABLE 3.10
Percentage of Funding of the Yerkes Laboratories of Primate Biology by 5-year Block for 1948–1962, as Indicated in Annual Reports

Source	Period		
	1948–1952	1953–1957	1958–1962
All private sources	64.5	41.2	20.1
University funds	25.0	6.1	0.0
Nonmilitary government	1.8	43.7	68.3
Government military sources	7.5	0.0	9.1
Other sources	1.3	9.0	2.5
Total	100.1	100.0	100.0
NIMH	0.0	4.4	12.8
NSF	0.0	12.6	7.6

Note. NIMH = National Institute of Mental Health; NSF = National Science Foundation. Data compiled from annual reports (1953–1963) of the Yerkes Laboratories of Primate Biology available at Woodruff Library, Emory University, Atlanta, GA.

methods and fiscal years, thus producing some variance. Second, the YLPB data include funds from some sources, such as fellowships, not included in the federal research grant data. Third, the YLPB data do not include 1963, for which data are unavailable.

For the period covered, nonmilitary governmental sources provided about half of the support for the YLPB. The private foundations provided about one third of the support. Some support came from the sponsoring universities. After Yerkes' retirement, Yale continued to contribute $10,000 per year, the equivalent of his previous salary; Harvard contributed Lashley's salary. The remaining funding came from the military and assorted other sources. Among these was the Committee for Research on Problems of Sex, a joint operation of the National Research Council of the National Academy of Sciences and the Rockefeller Foundation. The Rosalia Abreu Fund stemmed from a bequest made by Madame Abreu, who maintained private primate colonies in Havana, Cuba, with which Yerkes had worked.

An interesting perspective on these data appears when they are analyzed over time (see Table 3.10). Whereas the private sources provided nearly two thirds of the support for the first 5 years, they provided just 20% during the last 5 years. University funds disappeared among these three periods. It was nonmilitary government support that rose from 2% during 1948–1952 to 68% during 1958–1962. These percentages even underestimate the impact of federal support to some degree because budgets were rising throughout. The total YLPB budget for 1948 was $90,352; by 1962, it had increased over fourfold to $395,613.

An important aspect of the shift from private to federal funding was the locus of control. Most of the private funding was for general support of the laboratory. The director was responsible for the prudent and productive expenditure of funds and had to satisfy the foundations, but he had considerable control over which projects would be conducted. This contrasts with the granting procedures that would be in force at the end of the period, when the bulk of the funds would be for targeted projects. Not all federal funding was for targeted projects; the NSF provided base support of $40,000 per year during 1956–1959.

Although both the Rockefeller and the Carnegie monies had been unrestricted, the Ford Foundation appropriations, which accounted for much of the private funding during 1957–1961 ($300,000), was targeted for Nissen's study of the effects of early experience on the development of behavior in chimpanzees. In his grant proposal, Nissen justified this project in relation to its relevance to problems of mental health.

Rather than knocking on the doors of the officers of private foundations, as Yerkes had, one now submitted written proposals to federal agencies. The research that was proposed and funded depended, in part, on the agencies involved and the priorities they set.

The NIMH support came from nine grants to eight principal investigators. Lashley's first grant was already mentioned. J. M. Warren's grant concerned the functions of association cortex. It should come as no surprise that there was interest in behavioral development. Nissen received a large grant—$231,768—for studies of the development of behavior in chimpanzees. Elaine Kinder received a smaller grant for work on the development of social behavior. Keith Hayes's support was for studies of the effects of experience on mental functions. William Mason secured funds for a study of the effects of social restriction on affective behavior. Mason also was funded for work on social behavior. Finally, Irwin Bernstein's research on the behavior of howling monkeys under natural conditions was supported. Emil Menzel studied perceptual factors in food selection.

Beginning in 1956, Rockefeller funding was reduced from $40,000 per year to $10,000 per year; it was terminated in 1961. As Lashley was approaching retirement, the Rockefeller and Carnegie Foundations informed the YLPB that they would soon be terminating their financial support. Yale had withdrawn support, and Harvard would follow on Lashley's retirement. It became critical that another source of base funding be found. An appeal was made to the NSF. A joint meeting of the Board of Scientific Directors and NSF representatives—including Marston Bates, Frank Beach, Harry Harlow, Louis Levin, W. J. H. Nauta, and John T. Wilson—to evaluate the situation was held on October 8 and 9, 1955 (Lashley & Nissen, 1955). Once it was clear that a smooth transition could be made on Lashley's departure, 3 years of base support at $40,000/year was granted. This was later renewed for a 4th year.

In addition to the base funding, two grants were made to Irwin S. Bernstein for his studies of social organization and activity of primate groups.

Beginning in 1960, base funding was provided by the National Heart Institute at the level of $150,000 per year; this was associated with the developing program of the regional primate research centers. The NSF support had come at a critical time and served as a bridge between private support and the large grants that could be provided by the national institutes. However, it was only when the bigger budgets of the national institutes could be tapped that the facility could make the big move to a larger role and function. The effects of the two agencies on the YLPB were both important, but different.

A couple of other allocations are of interest. In 1952, the Office of Naval Research awarded a $33,000 contract to Lashley for a study of the effects on behavior of different types of partial damage or scar formation of the cerebral cortex. Funding from the Atomic Energy Commission began in 1953, with a contract of $14,380 for work on the effects on chimpanzee behavior of exposure to whole-body irradiation.

As noted above, the changing pattern of patronage for research presented challenges to the administrators of a facility such as the YLPB. They had to remain sensitive to changing patterns and priorities and to adjust their strategies to assure the continuation of the facility. Their struggles and ultimate successes are a microcosm of what was happening throughout the U.S. research community and reveal the shift to near-total support of such research by agencies such as the NIMH and the NSF.

OVERVIEW

It would be difficult to argue that comparative psychology is a focal area in the fight for improved mental health. Nevertheless, a complete understanding of NIMH funding should include its effects on such areas that are somewhat peripheral with respect to the primary mandate of the NIMH. Although its role in the advancement of comparative psychology probably will not be listed in NIMH documents demonstrating its success and importance, the NIMH was nevertheless of critical impact in the developing vibrancy of the field.

As noted above, early on it was decided that research should be supported as long as it

> could be construed as promising a contribution either to a significant mental health problem or to our understanding of behavior, its anteced-ents, corollaries, and consequences, and so long as it was deemed worthy

of support by a panel of the applicant's peers—and so long as funds were available. (Brand & Sapir, 1964, p. 27)

This opened the door for basic research on the comparative psychology of animal behavior.

As compared with the NSF funding patterns, comparative psychologists appear to have done somewhat better, relative to other animal behaviorists, in the competition for NIMH funds than in NSF competitions. These data are difficult to interpret, however, especially because information on the number of submissions and the percentage of submissions funded is lacking. Furthermore, because the average NIMH grant tended to be somewhat larger than the average NSF grant, it is possible that some of the better established investigators emphasized NIMH proposals. This possibility is supported by the greater disparity in apparent eminence, at least as measured here, between the top and second-tier grant recipients at NIMH as compared with the NSF.

Although always a small part of the NIMH endeavor, support for comparative psychology grew rapidly. During the period covered in this chapter, NIMH support for comparative psychology increased by a factor of over 250 (Table 3.2). A recurring issue in studies of federal patronage concerns the emphasis on quality alone versus distribution among states and geographical regions. With the peer review system, the focus tended to be on quality. Nevertheless, grants were widely distributed across 29 states, although just 4 large states received nearly one third of the grants. However, the actual funding did show some concentration, with four large institutions receiving 42% of the monies allocated.

Similarly, support was spread widely among individuals; with 117 grants spread across 78 individuals, the mean number of grants per psychologist was just 1.5. Again, however, it was the principal investigators associated with large programs who received the most support, as typified in the support received by Harry Harlow, Daniel Lehrman, John Paul Scott, and Henry Nissen. All funding agencies face the difficult decision of whether to fund a few major projects or many smaller ones; the NIMH appears to have done some of each. As I have demonstrated herein, psychologists who received the most support were generally of considerable eminence in the field. However, the funding system is a positive feedback system, and it is difficult to determine whether the psychologists received more funding as a result of either their eminence or the traits that led to it or that the grants enabled the work that led to eminence.

The data on the topics of the research that were funded are interesting but difficult to interpret. Was the distribution of funded projects essentially a mirror of the submissions, or were certain topics funded disproportionately? If there was no disproportionate funding, might this have been because it became generally known that certain topics were favored and thus fewer proposals on other topics were submitted? Given the data in Table 3.5, it would appear that the NIMH emphasis on developmental studies and de-emphasis of studies of sensation may have been reflections of its mandate. It would be difficult to demonstrate that the remaining distribution was a function of anything other than the research trends prevalent in the field at the time.

One important implication of the shift from private-foundation to federal funding was an apparently greater emphasis on proposals from individuals or small groups as compared with institutions. This gave researchers some reduced flexibility and may have loosened the control on research that could be exercised by the institutions' leaders. It became more difficult to dictate research topics, as Yerkes tended to do at the YLPB, and fundability became a critical factor. Nevertheless, the data show that some multi-investigator institutions did very well even in the new funding environment.

In many respects as well, the YLPB provides something of a microcosm of funding patterns and their implications for research in the United States. Because the life of the Orange Park facility overlapped so completely with the major shift in funding patterns, one can see the impact those changes had on the quest for survival of the facility and on the kind of research that got conducted there.

What was the effect of this support? The most easily quantified measure of impact is the number of funding credits appearing in published research. The federal government tracked such credits and published them (National Clearinghouse for Mental Health Information, n.d.). Examination of this document reveals that it is seriously flawed, as documentation of funding credits appears much more complete during the early years covered than during the later years. At any rate, the document includes some 751 credits (M = 6.4 credits per grant) from comparative psychologists and 112 (M = 3.7 credits per grant) for other animal behaviorists.

An alternative approach is to simply count the number of funding credits in each article in selected years. I counted the credits in the *Journal of Comparative and Physiological Psychology* (JCPP) for 1949, near the beginning of major federal support for research, and for 1963, near the end of the period under consideration. These data are presented in Table 3.11. The data do not add to 100% because in some articles—indeed, an increasing number over this period—more than one funding source is credited. The major change that is readily apparent is the increase in credits for the federal agencies during this period. This was accompanied by substantial decreases in the number of articles citing no financial support and those crediting local sources, primarily university funding. The data are from all JCPP articles, but the subsample of articles generally fitting the definition of comparative psychology used here is similar. Associated with these changes is a decrease in mean article length over time. It is possible that the federal

TABLE 3.11

Percentage of All Articles in the *Journal of Comparative and Physiological Psychology (JCPP)* for 1949 and 1963 Acknowledging Financial Support From Various Sources

Source	1949 *JCPP*	1963 *JCPP*
None	46.7	17.8
NIMH	0.0	42.8
USPHS/NIH	6.7	21.6
NSF	0.0	14.4
Military	3.3	7.2
Other federal	0.0	0.9
Local	36.7	10.5
Private foundations	0.0	8.6
Other	8.3	4.3
No. articles	60	208
No. credits	61	267
Pages	525	1050
Pages/article	8.75	5.16

Note. Data are for the number of articles in which each source is credited. More than one source can be mentioned per article, but multiple mentions of the same source are counted only once per article. Most "local" sources are from university funds, but there are some grants from states included. References to the National Institute of Mental Health (NIMH) are credited to it only where the NIMH is explicitly mentioned. Some, but not all, credits to the U.S. Public Health Service/National Institutes of Health (USPHS/NIH) should be attributed to the NIMH, as authors were not always meticulous in designating the source. NSF = National Science Foundation.

funding so increased the number of articles that pressures were brought to bear to reduce article size and thus change the nature of the information reported.

Among the greatest changes during this period is the growth of animal research. One indication of this is the increase by a factor of nearly 3.5 in the number of articles in *JCPP* from 1949 to 1963. It is difficult to isolate the effects of federal funding from other factors acting at the same time. It is clear, however, that the increase in federal funding had a major effect on the growth of comparative psychology and related fields.

CONCLUSION

It has often been documented that federal programs, such as the NIMH, had major effects on psychology as a whole and was critical in bringing about the shift in dominance from the basic science approaches to the practice-oriented approaches. The data reported in this chapter suggest that the NIMH also had a major impact, less often acknowledged, on fields not directly involved with mental health. The indirect effect of this, or any, funding on improving the nation's mental health, the primary charge to the program, would be difficult to assess. The field of comparative psychology can provide a broad perspective within which human behavior can be placed. The question of the role of support for basic research in such an agency remains complex, although the stance of the NIMH has been unwavering. Although the portion of its impact that has affected such fields may have been small from the perspective of the agency, from the perspective of the recipients it was huge. As with numerous other fields, it was during this postwar expansion of federal funding that comparative psychology showed substantial growth. The NIMH, together with the NSF, was of critical importance in the developing vibrancy of the field.

REFERENCES

Appel, T. A. (2000). *Shaping biology: The National Science Foundation and American biological research, 1945–1975*. Baltimore: Johns Hopkins University Press.

Brand, J. L., & Sapir, P. (1964). *An historical perspective on the National Institute of Mental Health*. Unpublished manuscript.

Bush, V. (1990). *Science—The endless frontier* (40th anniversary ed.). Washington, DC: National Science Foundation. (Original work published 1945)

Comroe, J. H., Jr., & Dripps, R. D. (1976, April 9). Scientific basis for the support of biomedical science. *Science, 192,* 105–111.

Dewsbury, D. A. (1984). *Comparative psychology in the twentieth century*. Stroudsburg, PA: Hutchinson Ross.

Grob, G. N. (1991). *From asylum to community*. Princeton, NJ: Princeton University Press.

Hicks, L. H. (1969). Current status of federal support for psychology. *American Psychologist, 24,* 691–694.

Institute for Scientific Information. (1989). *Social Sciences Citation Index 1956–1965: 10-year cumulation*. Philadelphia: Author.

Lashley, K. S., & Nissen, H. W. (1955). *Twenty-sixth annual report of the Yerkes Laboratories of Primate Biology, Inc.* Files of the Yerkes Regional Primate Research Center, Woodruff Library, Emory University, Atlanta, GA.

Lomask, M. (1975). *A minor miracle: An informal history of the National Science Foundation*. Washington, DC: National Science Foundation.

Lyons, G. M. (1969). *The uneasy partnership: Social science and the federal government in the twentieth century*. New York: Russell Sage Foundation.

Merton, R. K. (1968, January 5). The Matthew effect in science. *Science, 159,* 56–63.

Morgan, C. L. (1894). *An introduction to comparative psychology*. London: Walter Scott.

National Clearinghouse for Mental Health Information. (n.d.). *Publications resulting from National Institute of Mental Health research grants 1947–1961* (PHS Publication No. 1647). Chevy Chase, MD: U.S. Department of Health, Education, and Welfare.

National Mental Health Act of 1946, Pub. L. No. 79-487.

National Science Foundation Act of 1950, 42 U.S.C. § 1861 *et seq.*

Odbert, H. S., & Cheatham, P. G. (1963, July 10). *Memorandum to Assistant Director for Biological and Medical Sciences.* Unpublished document.

Program Analysis Section, Division of Extramural Research Programs, National Institute of Mental Health. (1964). *Mental health research grant awards: Fiscal years 1948–63.* Chevy Chase, MD: National Institute of Mental Health.

Reingold, N. (1994). Science and government in the United States since 1945. *History of Science, 32,* 361–386.

Rubinstein, E. A., & Coelho, G. V. (1970). Mental health and behavioral sciences: One federal agency's role in the behavioral sciences. *American Psychologist, 25,* 517–523.

Schneider, S. E. (2000). National Institute of Mental Health. In A. E. Kazdin (Ed.), *Encyclopedia of psychology* (Vol. 5, pp. 391–394). Washington, DC: American Psychological Association and New York: Oxford University Press.

Tinbergen, N. (1963). On aims and methods of ethology. *Zeitschrift für Tierpsychologie, 20,* 410–429.

Wang, J. A. (1995). Liberals, the Progressive Left, and the political economy of postwar American science: The National Science Foundation debate revisited. *Historical Studies in the Physical and Biological Sciences, 26,* 139–166.

Wilson, J. T. (1952). Psychology and the National Science Foundation. *American Psychologist, 7,* 497–502.

Wilson, J. T. (1953, May 22). *Memorandum to Assistant Director for Biological and Medical Sciences.* Unpublished document.

Wilson, J. T. (1954, March 24). *Memorandum to Assistant Director for Biological and Medical Sciences.* Unpublished document.

Wolfle, D. (1950). Across the secretary's desk: The National Science Foundation. *American Psychologist, 5,* 206.

4

THE RESEARCH GRANTS PROGRAM OF THE NATIONAL INSTITUTE OF MENTAL HEALTH AND THE GOLDEN AGE OF AMERICAN ACADEMIC PSYCHOLOGY

CHARLES E. RICE

To speak of a *golden age* in an historical account is to make reference to a time of great abundance of resources and great promise. The years following World War II (WWII) may have been such an era for American universities (Freeland, 1992), especially those with aspirations to become centers of research and scholarship. Research activity, particularly in the physical sciences and engineering, but also in the social sciences, requires financial resources; the federal government, continuing a pattern of research funding begun during the war, provided such needed financial support (Geiger, 1993). The growth of American psychology after the war was explosive as it expanded to become a service profession as well as an active and well-funded research discipline. Although it did not require the costly capital investment of the physical sciences and engineering, psychology was fortunate to have several federal research sponsors. One of these was the newly formed National Institute of Mental Health (NIMH). The contributions of American psychologists during the war (Capshew, 1999) had fostered the perception that the discipline was relevant to a number of national priorities, including mental health.

The purpose of this chapter is to examine how American academic psychology was influenced by NIMH research funding during the early years of its grants program, 1948–1963. This is a time period that begins with the start of the NIMH extramural research grants program and concludes with the publication of the sixth and final volume of the influential *Psychology: A Study of a Science*, edited by Sigmund Koch (1963), an attempt to review and evaluate much of the scope of academic psychology during this period. It must be pointed out that it is nearly impossible to precisely isolate NIMH funding as a causative agent for these changes. The mission and scope of American universities changed dramatically in this period, fueled in part by the large infusion of federal funding; NIMH was only one source of such funding.

GOVERNMENT FUNDING OF UNIVERSITY RESEARCH, 1948–1963

Although many universities were wary of accepting federal funding for fear that their activities might be subject to outside control (Geiger, 1993), by academic year 1947–1948, they were receiving over $95 million for research and development; by 1953–1954, this amount had increased to over $280 million (Orlans, 1962), and by fiscal year 1959, it was close to $500 million (Kidd, 1959). By 1953, academic psychologists were receiving $5 million of federal funding for research. More than one third of this amount came from NIMH.

Although the amount of NIMH funding was critically important, of even greater significance to the burgeoning of psychology was the eclectic policy adopted by the agency for the selection of the research to be supported. According to Brand and Sapir (1964), "it was recognized that lacking definite clues to the etiology or best methods of treatment of mental illness, it is wisest to support the best research in any and all fields related to mental illness" (p. 27). Any research proposal pertaining to an understanding of human behavior and its consequences was to be deemed worthy of consideration for funding. Researchers in the life sciences, such as physiology, were recipients of funding, of course, but psychiatrists, many of whom had not pursued research careers, did not receive the share of NIMH dollars that might be expected: In 1964, at the close of the period I am discussing, only 12% of the award recipients came from the field of psychiatry. In contrast, 55% of all the principal investigators funded by the NIMH were psychologists, the vast majority of whom were from universities (Grob, 1991).

TABLE 4.1
NIMH Research Grant Funding, 1948–1963, for American Institutions

Year	No. awards	Total $ amount
1948	37	366,961
1949	45	578,695
1950	57	829,519
1951	99	1,249,024
1952	118	1,626,663
1953	118	1,698,049
1954	166	2,573,457
1955	206	3,609,166
1956	223	3,990,649
1957	439	7,309,406
1958	552	10,439,124
1959	719	14,077,516
1960	908	18,406,509
1961	1,052	23,884,987
1962	1,297	29,422,385
1963	1,425	34,214,314

Note. Data are from *Mental Health Research Grant Awards: Fiscal Years 1948–1963* (PHS Publication No. 1528), by National Institute of Mental Health, 1964, Washington, DC: U.S. Government Printing Office. In the public domain.

The amount of research grant funding climbed steadily during the postwar period, as shown in Table 4.1. Organizations such as the Massachusetts Mental Health Center, the New York State Department of Mental Health, and the Langley Porter Neuropsychiatric Institute received research money, but universities, especially those that had well-developed reputations as research institutions, were the major recipients. That the distribution of NIMH research funds was far from equitable over the American academic landscape is evidenced by the fact that 10 universities received slightly more than 25% of the support during this period; these are listed in Table 4.2. There is little surprise in this, for the list of prestigious scholarly and research universities had remained quite stable since 1925, when an early ranking listed 7 of these schools among its top 10; all 10 of the schools identified in Table 4.2 are listed in a 1957 reputation ranking (Graham & Diamond, 1997). This is a clear illustration of the "Matthew effect" cited by Robert Merton (1968) as characterizing the research economy: "[to] every one that hath shall be given [more]." A large chunk of the history of American academic psychology during this period resides in these universities. Table 4.2 also displays the amount of NIMH funding awarded to principal investigators who were psychologists in each of the schools. Nearly 50% of the total amount for these 10 universities went to psychologists, but this might be an underestimate of the support for psychological research, because some of the award recipients who were not psychologists were pursuing research

TABLE 4.2

Ten Universities Receiving the Most Research Grant Funding From the
National Institute of Mental Health (NIMH), 1948–1963

University	Total NIMH funding ($)	Funding for APA members ($)
Harvard	8,125,630	4,213,588
Michigan	6,494,543	4,003,457
California, Berkeley	5,762,454	1,879,805
Yale	4,512,786	2,487,882
Chicago	4,038,979	2,347,980
Illinois	3,103,667	2,190,528
New York University	3,001,070	1,615,729
Stanford	2,967,621	1,398,181
Columbia	2,751,503	1,369,156
Wisconsin	2,538,135	1,324,833[a]

Note. All table values are in dollars. The State University of New York was omitted from this list because it consisted of a number of different campuses. The data are from Mental Health Research Grant Awards: Fiscal Years 1948–1963 (PHS Publication No. 1528), by National Institute of Mental Health, 1964, Washington, DC: U.S. Government Printing Office. In the public domain. APA = American Psychological Association.
[a]Some data are missing.

that could be called psychological in nature and whose projects involved the efforts of psychologists.

Impact of Federal Funding on Universities: General Considerations

In assessing the effects of such an increase in revenue, it is important to define some indicators of change. First, there were structural changes taking place in the universities during this period. Not only were they growing larger with respect to both the number of students and faculty, but there also were changes in organizational structure that were necessary to accommodate their heightened research mission. Second, it is important to consider the possibility that federal funding may have played a role in altering the content of the research being performed or in somehow affecting the major intellectual themes or issues of a given academic field such as psychology.

Increase in the Number of Students and Faculty in Psychology

Not only was psychological research receiving increased support, but also funds for both research and clinical training helped attract students to the field. One would expect a marked expansion in the size of psychology departments, both in the number of students and in the number of faculty needed to work with them. An increase in the latter would also be expected from the increased research support; faculty members were expected to

TABLE 4.3
Growth of American Psychology During the Years Following World War II

Year	No. psychology doctorates produced	APA membership
1946	84	4,427
1947	122	4,661
1948	179	5,754
1949	275	6,735
1950	356	7,272
1951	490	8,554
1952	586	9,512
1953	656	10,903
1954	665	12,380
1955	733	13,475
1956	627	14,509
1957	723	15,545
1958	780	16,644
1959	809	17,448
1960	762	18,215
1961	870	18,948
1962	871	19,891

Note. Doctoral data are taken from "Production of Psychology Doctorates," by L. R. Harmon, 1964, *American Psychologist*, *19*, pp. 629–633. Copyright 1964 by the American Psychological Association. American Psychological Association (APA) membership data were provided by W. Pickren (personal communication, December 11, 2001).

become active researchers as well as teachers. The data in Table 4.3 illustrate the growth of academic psychology during this period. From 1946 to 1963, there was nearly a tenfold increase in the number of psychology doctorates produced in American universities. During this same period, there was nearly a fivefold increase in the number of American Psychological Association (APA) members, with a declining proportion of members holding academic positions. A clearer indication of what was taking place in universities is given by the data in Table 4.4, which show that the number of APA members listed as affiliated with the 10 largest university recipients of NIMH funding more than tripled from 1945 to 1965. It must be kept in mind that some of the members did not have faculty appointments but were research associates, advanced graduate students, and so on.

Structural Changes in Universities

The organizational structure of universities changed during this time. Before the war, the major academic unit of American universities was the department, the core of an academic field or discipline, the center for production of research and new members of the field and for more popular dissemination of information about the field. The great increase in external funding for research after the war presented the problem of how the expanded research activity could be carried on by faculty already burdened by under-

TABLE 4.4
Growth in the Number of American Psychological Association (APA)
Members in the 10 Universities Receiving the Most Funding From the
National Institute of Mental Health (NIMH), 1945–1965

University	APA members, 1945	APA members, 1965
Harvard	41	102
Michigan	22	194
California, Berkeley	31	141
Yale	33	64
Chicago	30	97
Illinois	22	111
New York University	24	152
Stanford	28	90
Columbia	59	104
Wisconsin	19	108

Note. Membership data were taken from APA directories.

graduate instruction and public service. A major university response to this problem was to use the new flow of funds to purchase more hours of investigational effort, hiring people whose major responsibility was research. Regular faculty thus were allowed more time for research through the mechanism of *released time*, wherein part-time faculty, including graduate student teaching assistants, were hired to carry some of the instructional load, a practice made possible by the research sponsors agreeing to fund a proportion of the faculty's salary (see Appel, 2000, for discussion of this practice in the case of National Science Foundation funding). This opportunity to hire people whose sole purpose was to perform or support research led to the establishment or enlargement of organizational units where research was the major activity. These units were referred to by many names, such as *laboratories, centers, institutes,* or *bureaus.* This development was not a new one for American universities, as a number of such units had been created well before WWII. However, the postwar funding boom led to their proliferation, growth in size, and, in some cases, an increase in their stability.

NIMH FUNDING AND ACADEMIC PSYCHOLOGICAL RESEARCH

Researchers at 10 universities dominated the scene as research grant recipients during the period from 1948 to 1963. An appreciation of the impact of NIMH research grants on psychology can be gained by noting those who are listed as principal investigators in these universities and by considering the impact of their work on American psychology of the time. *Mental Health Research Grant Awards, Fiscal Years 1948–1963* (NIMH, 1964) lists all the principal investigators during the period. One measure of the contribution made by the research of these recipients is constituted by the publications resulting from this research (see NIMH [1966] for data on many of the publications stemming from these grants). Tables 4.6 through 4.15 provide data on the awards received by APA members at each of the top 10 universities; APA membership was established by consulting membership lists and directories. Some of the researchers listed as APA members were not psychologists by training or background, but they are included because their work appears to be clearly psychological.

The content of NIMH-funded academic psychological research during this time is discussed next in a detailed presentation of the research activity at the five universities that received the greatest amount of NIMH funding. In my discussion of the research activity at each school, I briefly describe the nature of the research supported by the NIMH grants program, at least in the case of grants that were either large, too productive, or both, in the sense that many publications resulted from the work. The latter may actually underestimate the productivity of some of the projects because the publications data mostly include items published before 1963.

I then provide a brief survey of the second five largest NIMH recipients, followed by a survey of some of the NIMH-funded projects at other universities.

Table 4.5 lists the largest grants (awards of over $200,000) whose principal investigators could reliably be identified as academic psychologists. Some of the large grant recipients, although not psychologists, involved psychologists in their research. Some of these are mentioned in the discussion of the projects in the major universities.

A Closer Look at the Five Largest Grant Recipients

I turn first to a detailed discussion of NIMH-supported research at the schools that were the largest recipients during this period.

Harvard University

After the war, Harvard, under President Conant's leadership, had been rather reluctant to accept large amounts of federal funding for research, especially for contract and applied research (Freeland, 1992). Funding for medical research appeared to be an exception, however, as seems evident in the fact that the university was the leading recipient of NIMH sponsorship.

By 1946, psychology at Harvard had become more organizationally diffuse (Harvard University, 1954). The older Department of Psychology, having finally gained its independence from the Department of Philosophy in the 1930s, experienced the secession of some of its faculty for the formation

TABLE 4.5
Academic Psychologists Receiving the Largest Funding From the National Institute of Mental Health, 1948–1963: Awards of More Than $200,000

Psychologist	School	Amount ($)	Research project
R. Lippitt	Michigan	699,693	Factors in delinquency
N. Miller	Yale	532,200	Laws of motivation & conflict
H. Harlow	Wisconsin	524,350	Behavioral studies of monkeys
E. A. Haggard	Illinois	458,788	Psychoanalytic therapeutic process
J. W. Whiting	Harvard	414,914	Development of self-control
H. Harlow	Wisconsin	406,308	Social behavior of primates
S. Wapner	Clark	394,509	Perception–personality relations
N. Miller	Yale	356,588	Drug effects on fear and conflict
I. Chein	NYU	307,643	Epidemiological factors in delinquency
S. Sarason	Yale	291,445	Test anxiety in children
H. Murray	Harvard	287,601	Cooperation & competition
H. Witkin	SUNY	268,813	Psychological differentiation
D. Clyde	Miami, Fla.	257,865	Predictors in psychopharmacology
E. Hess	Chicago	257,394	Experimental analysis of imprinting
I. Chein	NYU	246,412	Drug addiction among minors
J. Dollard	Yale	243,086	Quantitative methods in study of therapy
P. Horst	Washington	239,635	Patterns of perceptual data
T. Dembo	Clark	238,616	Mental development in palsy
J. Bruner	Harvard	231,755	Human information processing
R. Cattell	Illinois	219,718	Study of personality dimensions
C. Osgood	Illinois	219,329	Mental health information
E. Bordin	Michigan	218,746	Psychotherapeutic interaction
D. Krech	California	209,725	Brain chemistry and behavior
J. Flanagan	Pittsburgh	205,999	Identification of human abilities
H. Wright	Kansas	204,977	Children's behavior in communities

Note. Data are from *Mental Health Research Grant Awards: Fiscal Years 1948–1963* (PHS Publication No. 1528), by National Institute of Mental Health, 1964, Washington, DC: U.S. Government Printing Office. In the public domain. NYU = New York University; SUNY = State University of New York.

of a new Department of Social Relations. The Department of Psychology, featuring the likes of E. G. Boring, B. F. Skinner, and S. S. Stevens, saw itself as handling what was called the *biotropic* areas of the field—the "hard science" aspects—whereas the new department, which included Gordon Allport, Henry Murray, and Jerome Bruner, was to be concerned with the *sociotropic* areas, such as cognition, personality, and social psychology; the Psychological Clinic was also included (G. W. Allport & Boring, 1946). The Department of Social Relations also included eminent sociologists Talcott Parsons and Pitirim Sorokin as well as anthropologist Clyde Kluckhohn. Psychological research was also conducted at Harvard Medical School and in the Graduate School of Education.

There were several research units at Harvard during this period that involved psychologists. Centers, projects, and laboratories (the last term was a favorite designation at Harvard) were to be found in both the Departments of Psychology and Social Relations and elsewhere in the school. The Laboratory of Human Development, for example, was located in the School of Education. Original funding for the laboratory came from the Rockefeller and Ford Foundations, but NIMH money was not slow in coming. Sears received a grant of over $50,000 for a 1952–1953 study of child rearing and personality development. The Sears research group, which included Eleanor Maccoby, conducted more than 300 interviews with American mothers in an attempt to understand the effect of child-rearing practices on personality development (see, e.g., Sears, Maccoby, & Levin, 1957). In 1954, John Whiting received over $400,000 for a 9-year project on self-control in children. His NIMH-supported projects represented a continuation of Sears's work (e.g., Sears, Whiting, Nowlis, & Sears, 1953) as well as studies of child rearing in other cultures. (See Table 4.6 for a listing of NIMH awards to Harvard faculty who were APA members.)

In the early 1950s, Jerome Bruner received university funds to set up the Cognition Project, beginning research that culminated in the classic *A Study of Thinking* (Bruner, Goodnow, & Austin, 1956), often seen as one of the major works in the emergence of the new cognitive emphasis in academic psychology (Gardner, 1987). The Bruner group studied how people formed concepts, noting especially how they used various strategies for selecting and integrating information, a factor often ignored by traditional behaviorist approaches. The Cognition Project was boosted by Bruner's receipt of NIMH funding of over $150,000 for a 5-year project on cognitive processes (Bruner, 1957).

In 1960, Bruner, working with George Miller, established an interdisciplinary and extradepartmental Center for Cognitive Studies, financed by a grant from the Carnegie Corporation (Bruner, 1983). This was augmented by an NIMH grant of over $200,000 for a 3-year project on cognition. The publications from the center attributed to NIMH funding display a range of approaches to cognition. Perhaps the most interesting new emphasis at the center had to do with the study of language learning and behavior. Linguist Noam Chomsky spent time at the center, some of his work on the theory of transformational grammar was supported by NIMH funding (Chomsky, 1965).

The Harvard Psychological Clinic received generous NIMH funding, including four grants awarded to Murray. The largest award (nearly $300,000) was for a 7-year study of cooperative and competitive social action. It is difficult to discern any central theme to the work supported by this award, but it included Kenneth Kenniston's (1962) well-known work on American youth. Also in the Department of Social Relations, NIMH provided almost $200,000 for Robert Bales's attempt to extend his scheme of interaction analysis to a computerized system for performing content analysis of written text (Stone, Bales, Namenwirth, & Ogilvie, 1962).

TABLE 4.6
National Institute of Mental Health Research Funding to Researchers at Harvard University, 1948–1963

PI	Project title	Total amount ($)	No. year(s) supported	No. publications
Sears, Robert R.	Child rearing and personality development	57,715	2	7
Levinson, Daniel J.	Social structure and adaptation in mental hospitals	118,671	7	9
	Sociopsychological study of hospitalized mentally ill patients	87,137	5	15
	Research conference on patient and the mental hospital	19,375	1	1
Petrie, Asenath	Tolerance for pain and suffering	120,722	5	11
Shapiro, David	Group learning without awareness	56,350	2	11
Kelleher, Roger T.	Effects of drugs on reactions to aversive stimuli	38,406	1	0
Lowell, Edgar L.	Effects of conflict on behavior	6,481	3	0
Murray, Henry A.	Auditory apperception and personality	58,621	5	2
	Interpretation of emotion in others	7,932	1	0
	Competitive and cooperative social interaction	287,601	7	21
	Particularities of expression under stress	1,231	1	2
Whiting, John W.	Child rearing and personality development	8,156	1	1
	Development of self-control in children	414,914	9	19
	Antecedents of adolescent behavior in lower classes	17,265	1	0
Skinner, Burrhus F.	Experimental analysis of psychotic behavior	134,546	5	11
	Analysis of complex behavioral processes	46,000	1	15
Solomon, Richard L.	Autonomic correlates of traumatic avoidance learning	103,350	5	2
Bieri, James	Cognitive factors in behavior	7,948	1	2
Bruner, Jerome S.	Cognitive processes in learning blocks	162,647	5	8
	Factors in efficiency of human information processing	231,755	3	27
Brown, Roger W.	Expressive use of speech intonation	2,252	1	2
	The child's acquisition of grammar	71,349	2	0
Maccoby, Eleanor E.	Measures of strength in children	2,255	1	3
Mednick, Sarnoff A.	Generation in brain damage and schizophrenia	2,270	1	3
Schutz, William C.	Test of interpersonal relations	26,565	1	4
Teitelbaum, Philip	Technique for forced taste discrimination in the rat	2,000	1	1
Mandler, George	Physiological and cognitive interactions in anxiety	12,443	1	6
Kelman, Herbert C.	Social influence and behavior change	106,928	5	6

Principal Investigator	Grant Title	Amount		
Lindsley, Ogden R.	Screening potential stimulants on inactive psychotics	44,649	3	5
McClelland, David C.	Drug sensitive free-operant measures of psychosis	151,932	3	8
Roe, Anne	Diagnostic significance of variations in fantasy	68,675	4	5
	Origin of interests in early family experiences	70,212	3	1
	Changes in scientific activities with age	13,718	1	0
	A center for research in career	49,394	1	0
Mischel, Walter	Delay of gratification in choice situations	16,463	2	3
Orne, Martin T.	Studies in hypnosis	85,726	4	5
Harrison, Robert H.	Experimental induction of repression	56,953	3	0
Bales, Robert F.	Prediction of interpersonal behavior from personality	69,692	4	1
	Prediction of interpersonal behavior	116,188	3	5
Aronson, Elliot	Confirmation and disconfirmation of expectancies	2,300	1	0
Herrnstein, Richard J.	Quantitative studies of reinforcement	21,485	2	4
Gottesman, Irving I.	Twin sample location for behavior genetics research	2,227	1	0
	Behavior genetics of human personality	17,742	2	3
Mann, Richard D.	Authority and intimacy in group discussions	2,300	1	2
Maher, Brendan A.	Telemetric autonomic measure of conflict behavior	22,828	2	2
Giles, Eugene	Microevolution in the New Guinea highlands	10,772	1	0
	Kinship and genetic change in isolated groups	5,470	1	0
Mishler, Elliot G.	Experimental study of families with schizophrenics	16,948	1	0
Huttenlocher, Janellen	Factors affecting inductive reasoning	12,106	1	0
Lindermann, Erich	Relocation and mental health adaption under stress	738,848	6	0
King, Stanley H.	Personality development during college years	404,075	5	4

Note. Total grant funds received: $8,125,630; funds going to psychology: $4,283,280. Number of projects = 52; number of psychologists = 36. PI = principal investigator. Data are taken from *Mental Health Research Grant Awards: Fiscal Years 1948–1963* (PHS Publication No. 1528), by National Institute of Mental Health, 1964, Washington, DC: U.S. Government Printing Office and from *Publications Resulting From National Institute of Mental Health Research Grants, 1948–1961* (PHS Publication No.1647), by National Institute of Mental Health, 1966, Washington, DC: U.S. Government Printing Office. In the public domain.

In the Department of Psychology, an informal research group, led by B. F. Skinner, and including Ogden Lindsley, extended Skinner's work on behavior analysis to the study of how operant techniques could be used with psychotic patients (Lindsley, 1956). Skinner was awarded almost $200,000 in NIMH funding, some of it for the continued study of reinforcement (Skinner, 1958).

Work at the Harvard Medical School Department of Psychiatry and at its affiliated training institutions (e.g., the Massachusetts Mental Health Center) was also funded by NIMH. Psychologist Daniel Levinson received a 7-year award for a project on the social structure of the mental hospital, teaming with psychiatrist Milton Greenblatt. Levinson's research group developed the Custodial Mental Illness Ideology Scale (Gilbert & Levinson 1956) to measure the ideology of psychiatric hospital personnel; this instrument is based in part on scales for assessing the authoritarian personality, a favorite research topic during the postwar era (Gilbert & Levinson, 1956).

University of Michigan

The psychology department at the University of Michigan showed the same rapid growth after World War II as seen in other public universities. The number of faculty increased to 45, which included psychologists holding appointments in one of two well-known research units. The total growth in APA membership during this period, as shown in Table 4.4, was even more noteworthy.

The Institute for Social Research (ISR) began as the Survey Research Center when, in 1946, Rensis Likert joined the psychology faculty. Likert had headed the Division of Program Surveys in the U.S. Department of Agriculture during the war, and he desired a hospitable location to house the further development and application of survey technology (Cannell & Kahn, 1984). In 1948, the Research Center for Group Dynamics, founded by Kurt Lewin shortly before his death, moved to Michigan from its MIT location (Marrow, 1969). This unit, together with the Survey Research Center, became components of the newly created ISR. The ISR was fully self-supporting. All researchers who were not already regular faculty were appointed as research associates; if they wished to teach in an academic department, they could do so, and the university reimbursed the institute for the released time. None of the research associates was given tenure; that is, their appointments depended on soft money. However, the university did provide financial support for the ISR by providing full cost recovery from the indirect costs earned from the research grants.

ISR researchers brought in more than $1,500,000 of NIMH funding during this period. (See Table 4.7 for all NIMH-funded projects at Michigan during this period that had APA members as principal investigators.) Ronald

TABLE 4.7

National Institute of Mental Health Funding to Researchers at the University of Michigan, 1948–1963

PI	Project title	Total amount ($)	Year(s) supported	No. publications
Campbell, Angus	Public concepts of mental illness	14,985	1949	0
Beck, Lloyd H.	Visual functions in the schizophrenic urine	15,231	1961	0
Blocksma, Douglas	Social participation of rejected children	73,651	1955–1957	5
Blum, Gerald S.	Role of defense mechanisms in behavior	13,359	1954	3
Bordin, Edward S.	Analyses of psychotherapeutic interaction	218,746	1952; 1954–1960	12
Butter, Charles M.	Perceptual loss following brain lesions	24,242	1963	0
Coombs, Clyde H.	Risk-taking behavior in decision making	90,798	1961–1963	4
Donahue, Wilma	Social and psychological aspects of aging	36,051	1959; 1963	1
Fox, Stephen S.	Schizophrenic serum and resistance to stress	4,025	1962	1
French, John R., Jr.	Job environment and employee health and performance	27,879	1960	3
Gordon, Jesse	Anxiety and awareness in psychotherapy	2,300	1960	0
Gurin, Gerald	Analysis of a national study of adjustment	72,960	1958–1960	0
Gyr, John W.	Computer simulation of a class of cognitive theories	24,893	1963	0
Isaacson, Robert L.	Electrographic correlates of learning in the hippocampus	2,098	1959	1
Kahn, Robert L.	Conflict and ambiguity in relation to mental health	184,473	1960–1963	7
Kelly, E. Lowell	Heredity of human traits and abilities	43,240	1956–1957	8
Kornblum, Sylvan	Sensory–motor anticipation in choice reaction time	15,163	1963	0
Lippitt, Ronald	Improving the social adjustment of children	59,492	1952–1954	12
Maier, Norman R.	Factors in effective problem solving	139,758	1959–1963	28
Mann, Floyd C.	Shift work and mental health	159,842	1959–1963	1
McConnell, James V.	Learning and regenerative processes	51,663	1959–1963	30
Mednick, Sarnoff A.	Children with schizophrenic parents	42,787	1963	0
Miller, Daniel R.	Origins of defense mechanisms	50,068	1952; 1954–1955	2
Miller, James G.	Behavioral and physiological tests of drugs	119,508	1958–1960	8
Newcomb, Theodore M.	Interim studies of student development	118,521	1960–1963	0
Norman, Warren T.	Taxonomy of personality attributes	44,397	1963	0
Olds, James	Primary drives and intracranial self-stimulation	102,710	1957; 1959–1962	23
Pelz, Donald C.	Participation processes and personal enlargement	79,744	1961–1962	0
Riegel, Klaus F.	Study on the use of association and fluency tests	2,300	1960	1

(continued)

TABLE 4.7   (Continued)

PI	Project title	Total amount ($)	Year(s) supported	No. publications
Seashore, Stanley E.	Determinants of stress in large organizations	42,030	1960–1961	3
Uhr, Leonard M.	Computer simulation of higher mental processes	49,797	1962–1963	9
Veroff, Joseph	Projective measures in a national sample survey	2,300	1958	2
Walker, Edward L.	Stimulus-produced arousal patterns and learning	68,616	1961–1963	13
Wilensky, Harold L.	Labor and leisure—A study of role segregation	130,990	1958–1962	12
Withey, Stephen B.	Analyses of two national studies of adolescents	16,387	1957	6
Zander, Alvin F.	Coordination of community mental health leadership	92,253	1951–1953	6
	Effects of group variables on adaptive behavior	74,098	1954–1956	8
Lippitt, Ronald	Mother's employment and child's adjustment	2,064	1957	1
	Intercenter program on family, youth, and children	176,008	1957–1963	10
	Social and psychological factors in delinquency	699,693	1956–1963	11
Bordin, Edward S.	Free-association project	53,766	1962–1963	2
Blum, Gerald S.	Research program in psychoanalytic behavior theory	41,400	1957–1959	5
Olds, James	Pharmacology of motivational mechanisms	171,018	1959–1963	25
	Mechanisms of reinforcement	118,194	1962–1963	0
Veroff, Joseph	Assessment of motives in children	36,063	1962–1963	0
Mann, Floyd C.	Technological change and mental health	13,570	1960	3
French, John R., Jr.	Job environment and employee health and performance	27,879	1960	3
	Assessment of dependency and hopelessness-helplessness	4,200	1963	0
	A program of research on mental health in industry	151,110	1958–1960	6
	Mental health in industry—Stage II	97,320	1962–1963	0
Pelz, Donald C.	Age, wisdom, and novelty in scientific performance	19,942	1963	0
Uhr, Leonard M.	Experimental tests of computer model for perception	3,277	1961	1

Note. Total grant funds received: $6,494,543; funds going to American Psychological Association (APA) members: $4,003,457. Number of projects = 52; number of principal investigators (PIs) = 36. All investigators were APA members.   Data are taken from *Mental Health Research Grant Awards: Fiscal Years 1948–1963* (PHS Publication No. 1528), by National Institute of Mental Health, 1964, Washington, DC: U.S. Government Printing Office and from *Publications Resulting From National Institute of Mental Health Research Grants, 1948–1961* (PHS Publication No.1647), by National Institute of Mental Health, 1966, Washington, DC: U.S. Government Printing Office. In the public domain.

Lippitt was the most active entrepreneur: He received three awards totaling over $900,000 for projects dealing with the adjustment of children and also juvenile delinquency. Lippitt and his coworkers used measures of group member perceptions to study group social structure and functioning (Lippitt & Gold, 1960). Alvin Zander received NIMH funding for two projects, one of which extended the study of small groups to large social entities, such as the mental health professions (Zander, Cohen, & Stotland, 1957). Robert Kahn was supported by NIMH funds for studies on conflict and ambiguity in relation to mental health, an effort that helped to inaugurate the concept of organizational stress (Kahn, Wolfe, Quinn, Snock, & Rosenthal, 1964). NIMH funds supported John R. P. French for his work on mental health in industry and for research on the effect of organizational environments on mental health (e.g., Cobb, French, & Mann, 1963).

The Mental Health Research Institute (MHRI) was established in 1955 when James G. Miller moved to Michigan from the University of Chicago, bringing several researchers with him. NIMH provided funds, matched by the state, for the construction of a building to house the institute (Mental Health Research Institute, 1957). The institute was administratively a part of the Department of Psychiatry.

The MHRI adopted the institute model of the ISR. Most of the research staff comprised psychologists or psychology graduate students who were given titles of "research assistants" and "research associates" and were supported by soft money. Paul Fitts, Professor of Psychology, was the senior institute representative from his department. The institute, perhaps because of its medical school ties, tended to favor biological research rather than social and behavioral studies, although the latter were not neglected. Director James Miller, trained as a psychiatrist and as a psychologist, had received an NIMH award for studying the behavioral and physiological effects of drugs. Psychologist Leonard Uhr, a research associate, collaborated with Miller on several publications, including an edited book (Uhr & Miller, 1960). Uhr, in fact, later received two awards for computer simulation studies of cognitive processes (Uhr, 1963). James Olds was the major regular faculty member from the Department of Psychology to be affiliated with the MHRI. Olds received three NIMH awards, each greater than $100,000, for his famous work on motivation and intracranial stimulation (e.g., Olds, 1958). He was able to demonstrate that electrical stimulation of various points in the rat brain yielded data suggesting that stimulation of one area constituted positive reinforcement, whereas that provided to another area had punishing effects.

Several well-known members of the Michigan Department of Psychology received substantial NIMH grants and formed effective research groups of younger colleagues and students. Edward Bordin was awarded over $200,000 for his 9-year project on psychotherapeutic interaction, gathering extensive observational data of therapy sessions (Bordin et al., 1954). Norman Maier was awarded more than $100,000 for his work on the problem-solving performance of groups in organizations (e.g., Maier & Hoffman, 1961). Another prominent departmental member was James McConnell, who created something of a stir when he apparently demonstrated that a conditioned response in planarian worms could be transferred to untrained worms by feeding them the minced remains of the trained animals. This work received support from NIMH possibly because of its promise in demonstrating the chemical basis of learning (McConnell, 1964). Finally, experimental psychologist Edward Walker studied the effects of a number of stimulus pattern variables—for example, the effects of their complexity on the motivation and learning of rats (Walker & Walker, 1964).

University of California

The Department of Psychology at the University of California, Berkeley, was an outstanding one well before WWII. Much of its luster was due to the experimental work and behavior theory of Edward Chase Tolman. In addition to Tolman, there were several other major figures on its staff, including Egon Brunswik, Harold E. Jones, and Jean McFarlane (Grold, 1961). Explosive departmental growth occurred during the 15 years after the war, because of the return of students and the influx of federal funding, so that by 1960 there were 30 regular faculty.

Psychologists also held appointments in two research units with close connections to the Department of Psychology. The Institute for Child Welfare was founded in 1927 (Lomax, 1977), with Harold Jones as the first director. Jones and other institute members—Nancy Bayley, Mary Cover Jones, and Erik Erikson—also held research associate appointments in the Department of Psychology; Read Tuttenham and Jean MacFarlane were, in addition, given regular departmental appointments. By the 1960s, the unit's name had changed to the *Institute for Human Development,* a modification reflecting the increasing life span emphasis in developmental psychology.

Three famous longitudinal studies of children were established in the early years of the institute. The Berkeley Growth Study, directed by Bayley, began in 1928 with a cohort of 74 babies, with a follow-up of 54 of these in 1964 (Hilgard, 1987). The Oakland Growth Study, directed by Mary Cover Jones and Herbert Stolz, a physician, was started in 1931 with a sample of 167 fifth- and sixth-grade children selected from local schools who were followed intensively for 8 years; there were five waves of data collection on the sample as adults, the last one in 1980–1981 (Elder, 2002). A third longitudinal database was generated by the Berkeley Guidance Study, directed by MacFarlane, and launched in 1928 with a sample of 248 infants; annual data collection continued until 1946, and there were two adult follow-ups, in 1959 and 1969 (Elder, 2002). NIMH funding began during the 1948–1963 period to provide supplemental support during the postwar years; the funds appear to have been used for both analysis of data from the three studies and for some collection of follow-up data. This funding supported a number of different studies that spawned numerous publications and involved the work of many scholars: for example, Marjorie Honzik, using data from the Oakland Growth Study (e.g., Honzik, 1951); Bayley, using Berkeley Guidance Study data (Bayley, 1951); and Erikson, who studied Berkeley Guidance Study children (Erikson, 1951). John Clausen received an award for his 1962 project that helped to support one of the adult follow-up data collections for the Oakland Growth Study (see, e.g., Haan, 1963, 1964; Stewart, 1962).

The Institute for Personality Assessment and Research was founded in 1949, when Donald MacKinnon and Nevitt Sanford were invited to join the Berkeley psychology faculty. Both had worked under Henry Murray, first at the Harvard Psychological Clinic and then at the Office of Strategic Services assessment centers during the war (University of California, 2001). Much of the research conducted during this period was personality research of the psychometric variety. MacKinnon and Jack Block received an NIMH award for a 3-year study on affective experience (Block, 1957). NIMH supported MacKinnon and William Schutz's research on the fundamental interpersonal relations orientation (Schutz, 1958). Harrison Gough also was the recipient of two NIMH awards; the funds enabled Gough to finish the development of his test, the California Personality Inventory (Gough, 1957), and to generate additional subscales from this instrument for use in other studies (see, e.g., Gough, 1953).

David Krech, Mark Rosenzweig, and biochemist E. L. Bennett garnered an NIMH award of more than $200,000 for a 7-year project on brain chemistry and behavior. This work was notable for its suggestion that brain growth in rats could be stimulated by increasing the complexity of the environment (Krech, Rosenzweig, & Bennett, 1960). Comparative psychologist Frank Beach was supported to the tune of over $100,000 for his work on determinants of species-specific behavior (Beach, 1960). Richard Lazarus, who had received NIMH funding earlier while at Clark University for his work on psychological stress, was awarded almost $200,000 to continue this research (see, e.g., Lazarus, 1964). His work became noted for his concept and study of mechanisms for coping with stress (Lazarus, 1966). (See Table 4.8 for a full listing of NIMH grants to psychologists at Berkeley.)

Yale University

There were 11 active, regular faculty members in the Yale Department of Psychology in 1945; by 1960, this number had swelled to 30. Unlike

TABLE 4.8

National Institute of Mental Health Funding to Researchers at the University of California, Berkeley, 1948–1963

PI	Project title	Total amount ($)	Year(s) supported	No. publications
McFarlane, Jean W.	Personality development from birth to maturity	78,019	1949–1951	49
	Guidance study—Personality, the first 30 years	77,353	1962–1963	0
Gough, Harrison G.	Personality and social adjustment	20,830	1952–1954	12
	Assessment of medical students and practitioners	4,025	1962	2
Sarbin, Theodore R.	Intrapersonal factors in juvenile delinquency	58,469	1953–1957; 1960	4
Jones, Harold E.	Reactions of young children to birth of a sibling	9,920	1954	0
Coffey, Hubert S.	Functions of leader and group in group psychotherapy	64,015	1955–1957	11
	Relation of group tension to interpersonal role	38,241	1955–1957	2
MacKinnon, Donald W.	Research in affective experience	51,027	1956–1958	7
	Tests of a theory of interpersonal relations	17,652	1958–1959	4
Krech, David	Brain chemistry and behavior	209,725	1957–1963	35
Renaud, Harold Robert	Intra- and extratherapeutic interpersonal behavior	1,268	1957	0
Lazarus, Richard S.	Antecedents and consequences of psychological stress	191,779	1958–1963	18
Postman, Leo J.	Effects of verbal reward and punishment on retention	2,300	1959	2
Beach, Frank A.	Psychophysiology of reproductive behavior	19,777	1959–1960	7
	Determinants of species-specific behavior	134,666	1960–1963	9
Mussen, Paul H.	Antecedents and effects of parental identification	44,702	1960–1962	3
	Effects of child training procedures on patterns of adjustment	139,550	1960–1963	0
Ervin, Susan M.	The determinants of word associations	1,219	1960	1
	Development of grammar in child language	70,690	1961–1963	2
Tryon, Robert C.	Pilot computer programing of CC cluster analysis	2,000	1960	0
	Cluster analysis programs in psychosocial studies	121,551	1960–1963	3
Reynolds, Robert W.	Neurophysiology and pharmacology of hunger motivation	9,740	1960	6
DeVos, George A.	Comparative research on delinquency	135,599	1961–1963	4
French, John D.	Conference on computer techniques in EEG analysis	36,779	1960	1
French, Gilbert M.	Role of experience in behavior of frontal monkeys	55,095	1961–1963	2
McConnell, Thomas R.	Student culture and intellectual development	112,884	1961–1963	2
Clausen, John A.	Personality continuity in the Oakland Growth Study	87,026	1962–1963	9
	Attitudes of an adolescent group	3,880	1962	0

Hurst, John G.	Relation between preschool and adult intellect	5,060	1962–1963	0
Sampson, Edward E.	Birth order, personality, sex, and conformity	4,025	1962	0
	Experiments on status congruence	22,100	1963	0
Marler, Peter R.	Sensory control mechanisms in behavior	32,845	1962–1963	0
Landreth, Catherine	Exploring the educational potential of 4-year-olds	4,025	1962	0
Rosenberg, Benjamin G.	Ordinal position, anxiety, and role identification	3,397	1963	0
Block, Jack	Allergen potential index for asthma	4,172	1963	0
Adams, Ernest W.	Assumptions of psychological scale measurements	4,200	1963	0

Note. Total grant funds received: $2,808,774. Funds going to American Psychological Association (APA) members: $1,879,605. Number of projects = 37; number of principal investigators (PIs) = 27. Data are taken from *Mental Health Research Grant Awards: Fiscal Years 1948–1963* (PHS Publication No. 1528), by National Institute of Mental Health, 1964, Washington, DC: U.S. Government Printing Office and from *Publications Resulting From National Institute of Mental Health Research Grants, 1948–1961* (PHS Publication No.1647), by National Institute of Mental Health, 1966, Washington, DC: U.S. Government Printing Office. In the public domain.

some of the other universities surveyed here, a sizable number of psychologists at Yale during this period were housed in the department and performed their research as part of informal groups of faculty and students. However, there were two formal research units involving psychologists, which were established before WWII.

The current Yale Child Study Center evolved from the Juvenile Psycho-Clinic (established in 1930). Psychologists located at the Child Study Center received NIMH funds during this period. William Kessen was supported for a 6-year project on distress and discrimination in infants (Kessen, Williams, & Williams, 1961). Edward Zigler received funding for his work on the rigidity displayed by feebleminded children (Zigler, 1963).

The Institute of Human Relations (IHR, established in 1929) was conceived as a multidisciplinary research unit that was to house nearly all research at Yale concerned with human social and behavioral functioning. In time, anthropology, sociology, and psychology emerged as the intellectual mainstays of the effort (May, 1971).

By 1950, the IHR was encountering difficult days, right at the time when the federal research dollars began to flow. Rockefeller funding was beginning to run out, and organizational problems were weakening the effort (Dollard, 1964). As a result, the unit was allowed to expire. Thus, it can be said that federal funding arrived too late to protect the continuation of the IHR. However, the work begun at the institute gained such visibility in American psychology that Yale researchers had little trouble attracting NIMH funding (see Table 4.9 for a listing of NIMH awards).

Neal Miller received over $900,000 from NIMH for his research efforts. The largest of these supported an 11-year project, begun in 1953, entitled "Behavioral Laws of Motivation and Conflict." This project allowed Miller to continue the development of his theory of social learning. More than 80 publications citing NIMH support stemmed from this work, including Miller's famous chapter on conflict and social learning in the Sigmund Koch-edited *Psychology: A Study of a Science* (N. E. Miller, 1959). However, Miller, working with physiologist Jose Delgado, found that electrical stimulation of the brain could stimulate fear reactions that could motivate learning in rats (Delgado, Roberts, & Miller, 1954). This led him to move from the strictly behavioral realm in the study of motivation and reinforcement to their physiological and biochemical underpinnings (N. E. Miller, 1958, 1961). Miller's second NIMH award supported work on the effects of drugs on fear and conflict, thus extending the earlier work to the realm of psychopharmacology (e.g., Barry & Miller, 1965). John Dollard, a frequent collaborator with Miller, also received an NIMH grant, for a 10-year project of quantitative methods for the study of psychotherapy (e.g., Auld & Murray, 1955).

NIMH supported the Yale Psycho-Educational Clinic, affiliated with the Department of Psychology, which was established under the leadership of Seymour Sarason. Sarason received almost $300,000 for his 10-year project that developed scales for both general and test anxiety, a specific form of anxiety aroused by testing situations in schools (Sarason, Davidson, Lighthall, Waite, & Ruebush, 1960).

Elsewhere in the Department of Psychology there were other groups of faculty and students that received NIMH funding for their work. George Mahl, a member of the Dollard group, received two NIMH grants for his work on the processes of therapeutic intervention (Kasl & Mahl, 1956; Mahl, 1956). Ralph Haber was funded for his studies on the effects of verbal encoding strategies on selective attending to, and memory of, briefly exposed complex stimuli (e.g., Haber, 1964; Harris & Haber, 1963). Frank Beach received NIMH funding that enabled him to launch his ambitious research program on the neural and hormonal control of animal maternal and sexual behavior (Beach, 1958), an effort he continued at the University of California.

Behavioral research in the Yale medical school—notably, the work of Burton Rosner, who received several awards to support his neuropsychological studies (e.g., Rosner, 1964)—also received NIMH funding during this period.

University of Chicago

The University of Chicago, at the close of WWII, had a 7-member psychology department, but by the middle of the 1960s the department had increased to about 20 regular faculty, and there were many other psychologists in the School of Education and the medical school.

There was at Chicago an unusual organizational unit that was the equivalent to a combined graduate school of social sciences and interdisciplinary research center. This was the Committee on Human Development, established in 1940 under the leadership of Ralph Tyler (University of Chicago, 2001a). Faculty typically held joint appointments on the CHD as well as in a traditional disciplinary department. CHD faculty received a number of NIMH grants during this period. Psychologist William Henry, one of a number of persons from the Department of Psychology who was also appointed to the CHD, and who served as director in the 1950s, received a large NIMH award for an 8-year project on successful aging. (See Table 4.10 for a listing of NIMH awards to psychologists at the University of Chicago.) Bernice Neugarten, who had received her doctorate in the CHD and held her sole appointment there (Cohler & Tobin, 2002), was supported for one of the pioneering efforts in the newly developing field of gerontology

TABLE 4.9

National Institute of Mental Health Research Funding to Researchers at Yale University, 1948–1963

PI	Project title	Total amount ($)	Year(s) supported	No. publications
Miller, Neal E.	Behavioral laws of motivation and conflict	532,200	1953–1963	81
	Analysis of drug effects on fear and conflict	356,588	1959–1963	44
Dollard, John	Quantitative methods for the study of psychotherapy	243,086	1954–1960; 1962–1963	17
Sarason, Seymour B.	Measurement of test anxiety in children	291,455	1954–1963	17
Beach, Frank A.	Hormonal–neural control of reproductive behavior	4,374	1954	2
	Psychophysiology of reproductive behavior	59,069	1955–1958	11
Child, Irvin L.	Factors influencing positive social behavior	23,750	1955–1957	2
	Preoccupations, overt behavior, and socialization	6,222	1958	5
	A cross-cultural study of alcohol consumption	28,857	1959–1960	7
Hunt, David E.	Personality patterns in adolescent boys	41,081	1955–1959	4
Rosner, Burton S.	Electrical responses of somesthetic cortex	3,883	1955–1956	0
	Psychophysiology of somesthesia	87,883	1957–1961	13
	Psychophysiology of perception	57,391	1962–1963	2
Mahl, George F.	Patients' language as expressive behavior	77,207	1956–1960	11
	Studies in expressive aspects of speech and gestures	4,025	1963	0
Snyder, Charles R.	Alcohol and higher order problem solving	24,748	1957–1958	1
Laffal, Julius	Language distortions in schizophrenia	19,934	1957–1960	6
	Language in psychopathology and psychotherapy	18,322	1962	0
Prelinger, Ernst	Character structure and selected ego functions	72,033	1957; 1960–1962	2
Buerkle, Jack V.	Factor analysis of the Yale Marital Interaction Scale	2,300	1957	1
Logan, Frank A.	Effect of correlated punishment on performance	2,300	1957	1
	The free responding situation	72,172	1961–1963	1
Kessen, William	Distress and discrimination in infants	85,868	1958–1959; 1961–1963	11
Doob, Leonard W.	Methodological problems in studying acculturation	2,006	1957	5
Trow, Donald B.	A study of changes in group composition	2,300	1958	1
Sarnoff, Irving	Experimental studies of limitless aspiration	6,107	1959	0
Wegener, Jonathan G.	Some integrative functions of the cerebral cortex	3,723	1958	0
Dittes, James E.	Defensive functions of cognitive closure	42,508	1959–1963	3
Flynn, John P.	Effects of alcohol on seizures and learned inhibition	33,411	1959–1961	0
Haber, Ralph N.	Antecedents of perceptual selectivity	54,210	1960–1963	12

Name	Project title	Year(s)	Funds	Pubs
Leventhal, Howard	Cognitive processes and interpersonal impressions	1960	7,070	3
Levine, Jacob	Personality characteristics and humor	1960	2,300	2
Lustman, Seymour L.	Follow-up study of infantile autism	1960–1961	23,440	0
	Normal and pathological personality development	1962–1963	17,100	0
Zigler, Edward F.	Rigidity in performance of the feebleminded	1960–1963	32,232	14
	Motivational factors in the performance of retardates	1963	42,339	0
Carpenter, John A.	Logical induction and alcohol effects	1961–1962	34,703	1
Hershkowitz, Aaron	Intensive observations of chronic neuropsychiatric patient	1961–1962	35,954	1
Abelson, Robert P.	Cognitive mechanisms under belief dilemma	1961–1963	27,406	2
Chandler, Kenneth A.	Psychological study of Alzheimer's disease	1961	2,300	1
Buxton, Claude E.	Development of a measure of academic achievement	1962	4,025	0

Note. Total grant funds received: $4,512,786; funds going to American Psychological Association (APA) members: $2,487,882. Number of projects = 41; number of principal investigators (PIs) = 30. Data are taken from *Mental Health Research Grant Awards: Fiscal Years 1948–1963* (PHS Publication No. 1528), by National Institute of Mental Health, 1964, Washington, DC: U.S. Government Printing Office and from *Publications Resulting From National Institute of Mental Health Research Grants, 1948–1961* (PHS Publication No.1647), by National Institute of Mental Health, 1966, Washington, DC: U.S. Government Printing Office. In the public domain.

TABLE 4.10
National Institute of Mental Health Research Funding to Researchers at the University of Chicago, 1948–1963

PI	Project title	Total amount ($)	Year(s) supported	No. publications
Bettelheim, Bruno	Institutional treatment of disturbed children	46,980	1948–1950	3
	Staff problems in children's institutions	59,076	1952–1956	2
Koch, Helen L.	Effect of age interval on personalities of siblings	20,170	1951–1953	13
	Social adjustment and attitudes of young twins	22,398	1961–1963	0
Hess, Robert D.	Parental influences on the child's personality	37,124	1953–1956	5
	Ego identity, creativity and social role—The actor	40,682	1960–1961	0
	Intrafamily transmission of critical judgment	4,025	1962	0
Seeman, Julius	Play therapy and emotionally disturbed children	11,232	1953	2
Beck, Samuel J.	Psychological study of schizophrenic children	43,416	1953–1955	8
Havighurst, Robert	The mental abilities of older persons	15,120	1953	2
	Cross-national research seminars in human development	15,552	1961–1963	1
Soskin, William F.	Characteristics of interaction of individuals	22,655	1955–1956	3
Stein, Morris I.	Social interaction in a natural setting	15,000	1954	1
Hess, Eckhard H.	Experimental analysis of imprinting	257,394	1955–1963	22
Rogers, Carl R.	The process and facilitation of personality change	118,360	1955–1957	32
Haggard, Ernest A.	Socialization, personality, and mental processes	53,154	1955–1958	3
Henry, William E.	Validation of the TAT	9,411	1956	0
	Psychological and social factors in successful aging	481,009	1955–1960; 1962–1963	26
Bowman, Paul H.	Delinquency and slow learning in school	32,347	1957–1958	4
Chapman, Loren J.	Experimental study of schizophrenic thinking	16,849	1957–1959	11
Wepman, Joseph M.	Psycholinguistic methods for classifying aphasia	106,501	1958–1963	28
Hunt, Howard F.	Effects of drugs on emotional and abnormal behavior	94,181	1957–1959	13
Kluver, Heinrich	Biological mechanisms in behavior	96,328	1958–1963	2
Kamiya, Joe	Behavioral and physiological concomitants of dreaming	64,625	1958–1960	4
Strodtbeck, Fred L.	Juror reactions to legal definitions of insanity	46,222	1958–1960	4
	Studies of family interaction	41,204	1962–1963	0
Stock, Dorothy	The crucial episode in group therapy	57,668	1958–1962	7
	Studies in therapeutic interaction	13,562	1962–1963	3
Weiss, Robert S.	Social role and personality patterns	4,025	1959	0
Wright, Benjamin D.	Grouping methods in multivariate analysis	2,300	1959	0

Cartwright, Desmond S.	An analytic rotation program for UNIVAC	2,300	1959	0
	Psychological assessment of stress corner youth	30,451	1961–1963	0
White, Sheldon H.	Attentional processes in learning	39,833	1960–1963	5
Schaefer, Theodore	Emotionality, stress, and brain amine levels	30,305	1960–1961	1
	Physiological aspects of early handling in the rat	15,084	1962	0
Neugarten, Bernice L.	Age norms and socialization in adulthood	44,434	1961–1963	1
Wagstaff, Alice K.	Effects of expressiveness training for therapists	2,300	1960	0
Butler, John M.	Controlled study of psychotherapy process	88,639	1961–1963	1
Sawyer, Jack	Experiments on resolution of interpersonal conflict	32,924	1962–1963	0
McCleary, Robert A.	Type of behavioral response as an experimental variable	66,370	1962–1963	0
Zald, Mayer N.	Control and change in a private service organization	4,025	1962	0
Harvey, John	CNS lesions and drug action	48,762	1962–1963	0
Gellert, Elizabeth	Developmental aspects of perception of the body image	20,310	1962	0
Fiske, Donald W.	Variation in reactions to psychological tests	28,092	1963	0
Maddi, Salvatore R.	Behavioral correlates of the need for novelty	11,193	1963	0
Kohlberg, Lawrence	Developmental study of sex role concept and attitude	4,004	1962	0
Lieberman, Morton A.	Adaptation and survival under stress in the aged	26,862	1963	0
Wepman, Joseph M.	Change of perceptual organization in deaf children	3,522	1963	0

Note. Total grant funds received: $4,038,979. Funds going to American Psychological Association (APA) members: $2,347,980. Number of projects = 48; number of principal investigators (PIs) = 38. All investigators were APA members. TAT = Thematic Apperception Test; CNS = central nervous system. Data are taken from *Mental Health Research Grant Awards: Fiscal Years 1948–1963* (PHS Publication No. 1528), by National Institute of Mental Health, 1964, Washington, DC: U.S. Government Printing Office and from *Publications Resulting From National Institute of Mental Health Research Grants, 1948–1961* (PHS Publication No.1647), by National Institute of Mental Health, 1966, Washington, DC: U.S. Government Printing Office. In the public domain.

(Neugarten, 1964). Henry had done work with the Thematic Apperception Test, so it seems natural that he, working with Neugarten, would use that instrument to study personality in aging individuals (e.g., Henry & Cumming, 1959; Neugarten & Gutman, 1958). Carl Rogers, a faculty member from 1944 to 1957, held a joint appointment with CHD and the Department of Psychology. He received a grant of over $100,000 for a 3-year project on personality change, an effort that contributed heavily to the development of his client-centered psychotherapy (Rogers, 1957, 1958, 1959).

There was a great deal of other research activity in the Department of Psychology at Chicago during this postwar period, much of it funded by NIMH, the diversity of which is striking, including studies in biological, developmental, and clinical psychology. In the biological realm, Eckhard Hess received a large award (over $200,000) for his experimental studies on imprinting, work that was begun by ethologist Konrad Lorenz and represented a return to the popularity of the concept of instinct (Hilgard, 1987). Hess's studies concentrated on the critical period during which the instinctive following behavior of ducklings first emerged (Hess, 1958). Helen Koch received three small grants for developmental studies, concentrating on the influence of family structure, including birth order, on the development of personality (see, e.g., H. L. Koch, 1956). In the clinical area, Loren Chapman's studies of schizophrenic thinking (e.g., Chapman, 1961) were supported by NIMH.

The medical school at Chicago was also the site of NIMH-supported psychological research. Joseph Wepman, who headed the speech clinic, received a large award for his studies on aphasia, some involving the collaboration of Lyle Jones, a statistically sophisticated junior faculty member who directed the psychology department's psychometric laboratory. In one study, for example, a factor analysis enabled them to identify several dimensions of linguistic structure deficiencies in the performance of aphasic individuals (Jones & Wepman, 1961). Samuel Beck, known for his method of scoring the Rorschach projective technique, and a lecturer in the Department of Psychiatry, was funded for his studies of schizophrenic functioning, some of which involved use of the Rorschach (e.g., Molish & Beck, 1958).

Chicago's School of Education also housed some people receiving NIMH support. Perhaps the best known was Bruno Bettelheim, Director of the Orthogenic School, a treatment center for disturbed, primarily autistic, children. Bettelheim, in fact, was a very early recipient of NIMH funding, receiving support that began in 1948. He produced several books based on this work (e.g., Bettelheim, 1950, 1955) that made him a national figure. Only much later was his reputation damaged by highly critical investigative accounts, such as Richard Pollak's (1996).

A Survey of the Next Top Five Universities

Space limitations preclude as full a discussion of the five remaining universities of the top 10 NIMH recipients. I must add that their research is of no lesser import and quality than those more fully discussed.

University of Illinois

Table 4.11 displays a full listing of the awards to psychologists at the University of Illinois. Psychologist Lee Cronbach received over $100,000 from NIMH for a 6-year project on his work on the measurement of internal consistency test reliability, especially his alpha coefficient (Cronbach & Azuma, 1962), and to begin development of his theory of generalized reliability (Cronbach, Rajaratnum, & Gleser, 1963). Charles Osgood received several NIMH grants during this period, the largest of which, in the amount of $219,000, supported a 5-year project on the communication of information on mental health. The Laboratory for Personality Research and Group Behavior began shortly after Raymond Cattell was appointed Research Professor of Psychology in 1945 (E. P. Cattell & Horn, 2001). Cattell received two NIMH grants. The largest of these was for more than $200,000 for a 6-year project on dimensions of personality, work that featured new forms and applications of factor analysis (R. B. Cattell, 1974). David Shakow, located at the medical school, received an award of over $450,000 for a major project on the process of psychoanalytic therapy. After Shakow moved on, the work was continued by Ernest Haggard (e.g., Sklansky, Isaacs, Levitov, & Haggard, 1965).

New York University

When WWII ended, New York University (NYU) had few psychologists on the faculty at either of the school's two campuses. By 1960, the Graduate Department of Psychology listed 27 tenure-track faculty along with 8 research faculty whose primary responsibility resided in one of several research units (R. A. Katzell, personal communication, March 2001). A listing of NIMH research grants received by APA members at NYU is found in Table 4.12.

In 1950, Stuart Cook was hired by NYU to head the Graduate Department of Psychology and to form the research institute that became the Research Center for Human Relations. Cook brought in over $150,000 for a project on attitude change; the study of attitudes toward segregation and African Americans constituted the focus of Cook's group, and a number of publications appeared later (e.g., Selltiz, Edrich, & Cook, 1965). Isidor Chein also was a major recipient of NIMH funding: He brought in more than $200,000 for a 6-year project dealing with drug addiction among

TABLE 4.11

National Institute of Mental Health Research Funding to Researchers at the University of Illinois, 1948–1963

PI	Project title	Total amount ($)	Year(s) supported	No. publications
Shakow, David	Psychological functioning in schizophrenia	14,652	1949–1950	6
Cattell, Raymond H.	Hereditary and environmental factors in personality	85,204	1949–1954	11
	Determinants and influences of personality dimensions	219,718	1958–1963	31
Kirk, Samuel A.	Preschool training for mentally handicapped children	86,734	1951–1953	3
Mowrer, O. Hobart	Evaluation of two types of psychotherapy	13,228	1952	1
Haggard, Ernest A.	Analysis of psychoanalytic therapy process	458,788	1953	14
McQuitty, Louis L.	Mental health screening techniques	98,267	1954–1959	5
Gage, Nathaniel L.	Studies of social perception in the classroom	67,007	1954–1957	14
Hunt, J. McVicker	Therapeutic-counselor and client relationship	68,181	1957–1960	9
	Experiential roots of intelligence and motivation	12,000	1963	0
Simmel, Marianne	Effects of anterior temporal lobectomy	8,195	1957	0
Erickson, Charles W.	Behavior without awareness	91,485	1957–1963	32
Gilbert, William M.	Diagnosis and predicted outcomes of counseling	7,570	1957	9
Becker, Wesley C.	Reactive inhibition and extraversion-introversion	2,300	1957	2
	Longitudinal study of parent-child relationships	68,042	1961–1963	3
Fiedler, Fred	Interpersonal perception and personality	103,289	1958–1963	14
Cronbach, Lee J.	Integrated studies of psychometric theory	114,924	1958–1963	10
Steiner, Ivan D.	Personality correlates of nonconforming behavior	2,128	1958	2
	Personality and responses to interpersonal conflict	23,894	1961–1963	10
Humphreys, Lloyd G.	Predicting advanced stages of academic learning	30,851	1959–1961	4
Dulany, Don E., Jr.	Reinforcement of verbal behavior	20,889	1960–1961	3
	Verbal hypotheses and intentions	16,666	1963	0
Osgood, Charles E.	Communication of information on mental health	219,329	1954–1959	14
	Semantic measurement in the study of personality	56,221	1960–1962	?
	Survey of psychological research on peace and war	35,176	1962–1963	?
	Studies of comparative psycholinguistics	66,155	1963	0
Triandis, Harry C.	Cultural determinants of social distance	2,242	1960	3
	Replication studies of social distance	3,648	1962–1963	0
London, Perry	Developmental changes in hypnotic suggestibility	2,289	1961	1
	Development of hypnotic suggestibility	30,006	1962–1963	0

O'Kelly, Lawrence I.	Drive intensity factor in thirst motivated behavior	20,166	1962–1963	4
Weir, Morton W.	Predictability and expectancy in children's learning	14,830	1962–1963	0
Jacobs, Harry L.	Psychophysiology and sugar appetite	55,957	1962–1963	10
Becker, Joseph	Personality and blood characteristics of cyclothymics	4,025	1962	1
	Family interaction and type of child disturbance	13,374	1963	0
Ware, Edward E.	Personality differential in person perception inquiry	24,392	1963	0
Wiggins, Jerry S.	Structure of the MMPI	17,597	1963	0
Triandis, Leigh	Fantasy aggression and overt aggression	11,109	1963	0

Note. Total grant funds received: $3,103,667. Funds going to American Psychological Association (APA) members: $2,190,528. Number of projects = 41; number of principal investigators (PIs) = 27. All PIs were APA members. MMPI = Minnesota Multiphasic Personality Inventory. Data are taken from *Mental Health Research Grant Awards: Fiscal Years 1948–1963* (PHS Publication No. 1528), by National Institute of Mental Health, 1964, Washington, DC: U.S. Government Printing Office and from *Publications Resulting From National Institute of Mental Health Research Grants, 1948–1961* (PHS Publication No.1647), by National Institute of Mental Health, 1966, Washington, DC: U.S. Government Printing Office. In the public domain.

TABLE 4.12

National Institute of Mental Health Research Funding to Researchers at New York University, 1948–1963

PI	Project title	Total amount ($)	Year(s) supported	No. publications
Bender, Morris B.	Changes in perceptual functions in functional psychosis	12,500	1950–1952	16
Jahoda, Marie	Mental health in a defense production community	68,163	1952–1954	0
	Psychology of role acceptance in women	10,751	1955	1
Klein, George S.	Perceptual processes below the level of awareness	177,880	1954–1961	26
Cook, Stuart	Experimental approach to attitude change	167,303	1958–1963	1
Damato, Michael	Early experience and adult behavior organization	29,405	1958–1961	14
Roe, Anne	Origins of interests in early family experiences	21,112	1958	1
Katz, Irwin	A study of marital cooperation	29,319	1959–1961	4
Teuber, Hans-Lukas	A program of research in neuropsychology	137,775	1960–1961	48
Axline, Virginia M.	Rehabilitation of disturbed blind children	23,000	1960	0
Holt, Robert R.	Psychomimetic agents and primary process thinking	97,488	1960–1962	9
	Psychoanalytic studies in cognition	129,898	1963	0
Paul, Irving	Study of memory styles	43,218	1961–1963	2
Cohen, Jacob	The power of abnormal–social psychological research	2,171	1961	1
	Statistical power of psychological research	17,439	1962–1963	0
Zimbardo, Phillip	Behavioral assessment of novel emotional experience	4,025	1962	0
Spence, Donald P.	Preconscious thought processes	15,304	1962–1963	1
Neimark, Edith D.	Number of associations in paired-associates learning	4,603	1962–1963	0
Karlin, Lawrence	Use of reaction time in the study of readiness	15,553	1963	0
Chein, Isidor	Factors affecting drug addiction among minors	246,412	1953–1958	6
	Prevention of juvenile delinquency and narcotics use	35,441	1959	0
	Epidemiological vectors of delinquency and its control	307,643	1963	0
Stein, Morris I.	Study of young adult performance in a service program	19,326	1963	0

Note. Total amount received: $3,001,070. Amount received by American Psychological Association (APA) members: $1,615,729. Number of principal investigators (PIs) = 18. Data are taken from *Mental Health Research Grant Awards: Fiscal Years 1948–1963* (PHS Publication No. 1528), by National Institute of Mental Health, 1964, Washington, DC: U.S. Government Printing Office and from *Publications Resulting From National Institute of Mental Health Research Grants, 1948–1961* (PHS Publication No. 1647), by National Institute of Mental Health, 1966, Washington, DC: U.S. Government Printing Office. In the public domain.

children that involved the gathering of data from nearly 3,500 boys in New York City who were narcotics users. The research resulted in a well-known book, *The Road to H* (Chein, Gerard, Lee, & Rosenfeld, 1964).

The Research Center for Mental Health was also established in the 1950s and was greatly aided by NIMH funds. The center, headed by Robert Holt, quickly gained a reputation through its research on emotional factors in perception and cognition and showed a rather distinct psychoanalytic orientation; the work conducted there was instrumental in advancing the "new look" in perception. George Klein had begun this research at the Menninger Foundation prior to his appointment at NYU. Working with Holt, Klein brought in over $150,000 for a project dealing with the increasingly popular topic of subliminal stimulation (Klein & Holt, 1960). Despite a number of studies dealing with subliminal processes conducted by this group (e.g., Klein, Spence, Holt, & Gourevitch, 1958), the concept increasingly came under critical fire by other psychologists.

Stanford University

Stanford was initially reluctant to accept federal funding after the war, but it was fortunate to have a strong advocate for such support in the person of Provost Fred Terman, the son of psychologist Lewis Terman (Lowen, 1997).

In the psychology department, Albert Bandura received four small grant awards, the last two of which supported his famous work on the social learning of aggressive behavior by imitation, the concept that some behavior could be learned from watching a model perform the action without prior reinforcement of that behavior being necessary (e.g., Bandura, 1962; Bandura, Ross, & Ross, 1961). The Bandura group was joined by Walter Mischel, who brought NIMH funding from Harvard to continue his work on the factors determining the ability of children to delay gratification when tempted by preferred rewards (Bandura & Mischel, 1965).

One of the best-known multidisciplinary groups at Stanford was the Institute for Mathematical Studies in the Social Sciences. Faculty from statistics, mathematics, and psychology were affiliated with this research unit. The psychologists were led by William Estes, one of the pioneers of mathematical psychology; younger members included Richard Atkinson and Gordon Bower, a group to which Luce (1992) referred as the "Stanford Mafia." Their mathematical models included signal detection theory (Atkinson, 1963), paired-associate learning (Bower, 1961), and concept identification (Trabasso & Bower, 1964). Both Atkinson and Bower received NIMH funding to support their work.

The Department of Psychiatry in Stanford's medical school was the site of much behavioral research during this period. Neurologist Karl Pribram, an APA member who was eventually appointed Professor of Psychology, was awarded an NIMH grant of over $200,000 for his 5-year project on the neural regulation of behavior. Pribram began to speculate on possible mediators between the processes of perceptual representation and the mechanisms of behavior. He postulated the operation of cognitive processes, also involving intention, that he called *plans* (Pribram, 1963). Some of his ideas were developed in a collaborative work with George Miller and Eugene Galanter, *Plans and the Structure of Behavior,* that became one of the classics of the new cognitive movement in psychology (G. A. Miller, Galanter, & Pribram, 1960). (See Table 4.13 for a list of APA members at Stanford who received such support during this period.)

Columbia University

In addition to the Department of Psychology, psychologists at Columbia were to be found on the faculty of the Teachers College, Barnard, the affiliated Women's College, the medical school, and in the loosely affiliated New York State Psychiatric Institute. (See Table 4.14 for a listing of psychologists at Columbia who received NIMH support.) Joseph Zubin, recipient of nine NIMH grants during this period, was able to be quite liberal in listing his organizational affiliations, including the New York State Psychiatric Institute, the New York State Department of Mental Hygiene, and the Department of Psychology. Already well-known for his biometric studies, Zubin helped to support Kurt Salzinger's research on the effect of chlorpromazine on the verbal behavior of people with schizophrenia. Salzinger, who also held an appointment with the Department of Psychology, received NIMH funding to continue his work with the conditioning of verbal behavior (Salzinger, Portnoy, & Feldman, 1964).

Several research groups receiving NIMH support were located in the Department of Psychology during this period. One of the most active groups consisted of psychologists working in the Skinnerian tradition of the experimental analysis of behavior. Led by Fred Keller, an old friend of Skinner's (McGill, 1997), they also included William Schoenfeld and William Cumming, all of whom received NIMH funding during this period. Stanley Schachter was another member of the department receiving NIMH support. Arriving from Minnesota in 1961, Schachter brought funding to continue the work he had started with Jerome E. Singer, showing that there are social and cognitive determinants of an emotional state as well as physiological ones (Schachter & Singer, 1962). This work received much acclaim because the data suggested that affective experience is interpretive in that it involves a construing of the social situation in which one finds oneself.

University of Wisconsin

When Harry Harlow arrived at Wisconsin in 1930, fresh from his Stanford PhD, he found that the Department of Psychology had no animal

TABLE 4.13

National Institute of Mental Health Research Funding to Researchers at Stanford University, 1948–1963

PI	Project title	Total amount ($)	Year(s) supported	No. publications
Orr, Francis G.	Psychological effects of sibling rivalry	12,500	1950–1953	0
Stolz, Lois M.	Adjustment problems of children born during World War II	44,358	1949–1954	2
Luft, Joseph	Study of adjustment patterns in families	8,542	1952	2
Hilgard, Josephine	Schizophrenia in parents and the age of children	63,908	1954–1958	8
Bandura, Albert	Therapists' anxiety level, self-insight, and competence	1,851	1955	1
	Child-rearing patterns and adolescent disorders	2,265	1956	2
	Family patterns and child behavior disorders	33,280	1957–1959	4
	Transmission of aggression through imitation	2,300	1960	3
	Learning of aggressive behavior through imitation	23,272	1962–1963	13
Little, Kenneth B.	Thematic test of aggression fantasy in children	1,897	1957	3
Lawrence, Douglas H.	Study of discrimination learning	79,412	1958–1963	4
Wiggins, Jerry S.	A social desirability scale for the MMPI	2,300	1958	3
	The structure of the MMPI	20,107	1962	3
Adams, Joe K.	Study of the appropriateness of confidence	13,053	1958	1
Krasner, Leonard	Personality variables related to verbal conditioning	22,506	1959–1960	22
	Effect of verbal conditioning on social behavior	40,547	1962–1963	0
McCord, William	Stanford personality development research project	25,088	1959–1961	13
Winder, C. Leland	Social adjustment in preadolescent boys	23,840	1959–1960	3
Weitzenhoffer, Andre	Investigation of hypnotic time distortion	6,825	1960	1
Sears, Robert R.	Follow-up research of the Terman gifted group	53,887	1960–1962	0
	Identification in 4-year-old children	18,807	1962–1963	1
Pribram, Karl H.	Neural regulation of behavior	222,501	1960–1963	35
Bower, Gordon H.	The learning of observing responses	31,888	1960–1962	16
	Models of human learning	21,459	1963	0
Hilgard, Ernest R.	Development–interactive aspects of hypnosis	88,931	1962–1963	29
Singer, Robert D.	Conditioning and generalization of verbal responses	24,113	1961–1963	2
Deutsch, Jay A.	Control of ingestion and nature of reward	72,841	1961–1963	12
	Fear and intracranial self-stimulation	4,025	1963	0

(continued)

TABLE 4.13 (Continued)

PI	Project title	Total amount ($)	Year(s) supported	No. publications
Atkinson, Richard C.	Mathematical models for discrimination learning	53,452	1962–1963	8
Horowitz, Leonard	Studies in verbal learning	230,239	1962–1963	5
Suppes, Patrick	Computing and programing in mathematical psychology	82,830	1962–1963	0
Mischel, Walter	Delay of gratification in choice situations	13,406	1962–1963	4
Parker, Edwin B.	Cognitive structure and two-person communication	44,146	1962	0
Jackson, Douglas N.	Assessment of personality with judgments of traits	4,025	1963	0
Ekman, Paul	Interpersonal conflict simulation	3,780	1963	0

Note. Total amount received: $2,938,484. Amount received by American Psychological Association (APA) members: $1,398,181. Number of projects = 35. Number of principal investigators (PIs) = 26. MMPI = Minnesota Multiphasic Personality Inventory. Data are taken from *Mental Health Research Grant Awards: Fiscal Years 1948–1963* (PHS Publication No. 1528), by National Institute of Mental Health, 1964, Washington, DC: U.S. Government Printing Office and from *Publications Resulting From National Institute of Mental Health Research Grants, 1948–1961* (PHS Publication No.1647), by National Institute of Mental Health, 1966, Washington, DC: U.S. Government Printing Office. In the public domain.

TABLE 4.14

National Institute of Mental Health Research Funding to Researchers at Columbia University, 1948–1963

PI	Project title	Total amount ($)	Year(s) supported	No. publications
Kallman, Franz	Heredity of health and mental disorder in aging	56,661	1952–1956	5
	Genetic study of mentally defective twins	64,930	1956–1958	8
Pierrel, Rosemary	Instrumental generalization gradients	2,300	1957	1
	Instrumental generalization gradients	35,518	1959–1961	6
Keller, Fred S.	Learning and performance under tranquilizing drugs	52,900	1957–1959	4
	Effect of psychotropic drugs on sensory processes	109,983	1960–1963	14
Bieri, James	Cognitive factors in behavior	41,729	1958–1960	6
	Individual, social, and informational effects on judgment	122,693	1960–1963	6
Hirsch, Jerry	Genetic variables in conditioning	2,300	1958	0
Singer, Jerome I.	Dimensions of fantasy and imagination	88,850	1958–1962	11
	Imagination of cognitively produced cognitive processes	24,840	1963	0
Bush, Robert R.	Theoretical studies of human choice behavior	22,540	1958	6
Hefferline, Ralph F.	Methodology of quantitative study of proprioception	2,300	1958	1
	Electrophysiology of verbal and subverbal processes	82,130	1959–1962	12
Zubin, Joseph	Effect of chlorpromazine on the pupillary reflex	41,662	1959–1960	1
	Immediate effect of chlorpromazine on verbal behavior	69,788	1959–1960	5
Lennard, Henry L.	Communication systems having a mentally ill member	72,942	1959–1961	6
	Microanalysis of communication in psychotherapy	20,945	1962–1963	0
Klausner, Samuel Z.	Individual decision making to undertake psychotherapy	35,535	1959–1960	1
Cumming, William W.	Parametric study of parametrically spaced responding	13,662	1961	1
	Parametric study of parametrically spaced responding	21,020	1963	4
Salzinger, Kurt	Verbal behavior and its conditioning in schizophrenia	77,575	1962–1963	4
Sutton, Samuel	Effect of drugs on the pupillary reflex	74,448	1962	1
	Discrimination learning with and without errors	64,133	1962	0
Schachter, Stanley	Cognitive and physiological determinants of emotion	28,041	1962–1963	6
Terrace, Herbert	Discrimination learning with and without errors	38,924	1962–1963	0
Winograd, Eugene	Effects of punishment on stimulus generalization	23,483	1962–1963	0
Thompson, Robert	Discriminated avoidance behavior in monkeys	34,524	1963	0

(continued)

TABLE 4.14   *(Continued)*

PI	Project title	Total amount ($)	Year(s) supported	No. publications
Dohrenwend, Bruce	Lay appraisal of abnormal behavior	4,025	1963	0
	Psychological disorder—Midtown hypotheses	4,025	1963	0
Tighe, Thomas	Reversal and nonreversal shifts in monkeys	3,696	1963	0
Shoenfeld, William	Reinforcement contingencies and exteroreceptive controls	26,904	1963	0
Youtz, Richard P.	Aphotic digital color sensing	4,150	1963	0

Note. Total amount received: $2,751,503. Amount received by American Psychological Association (APA) members: $1,369,156. Number of projects = 33. Number of principal investigators = 26. Data are taken from *Mental Health Research Grant Awards: Fiscal Years 1948–1963* (PHS Publication No. 1528), by National Institute of Mental Health, 1964, Washington, DC: U.S. Government Printing Office and from *Publications Resulting From National Institute of Mental Health Research Grants, 1948–1961* (PHS Publication No.1647), by National Institute of Mental Health, 1966, Washington, DC: U.S. Government Printing Office. In the public domain.

laboratory. During the next few years, he started a primate colony, eventually restricting it to rhesus monkeys (Dukelow, 1995). Here he carried on his work on discrimination learning and learning sets in monkeys. After returning to the university in 1952, following a stint as chief psychologist for the Army, Harlow further developed the colony as the Wisconsin Primate Laboratory. He received NIMH funding of over $900,000 that supported a great range of work with primates, including many studies of learning and of social behavior.

Harlow's primate research spawned many publications during this period. The NIMH support allowed the continuation of his studies of discrimination learning and learning set (Harlow, Harlow, Rueping, & Mason, 1960), but it was his investigation of the conditions leading to disturbances in the development of the infant monkey's social and affective behavior that received the most notice during this period. For example, Harlow's well-known APA presidential address detailed the series of studies in which baby monkeys were reared by a specially constructed surrogate mother, making it possible to determine that contact comfort seemed to be more important than suckling for the infant's attachment to the mother (Harlow, 1958).

There was departmental activity in social psychology as well at Wisconsin (see Table 4.15 for details). Leonard Berkowitz launched an ambitious program of research on aggression that was funded by NIMH. His intent (see Berkowitz, 1962) was to extend and modify the frustration–aggression theory of Neal Miller and his group at Yale. The effects of aggressive behavior, such as the achievement of catharsis following the expression of hostility, also were studied (Berkowitz, 1964).

When Carl Rogers moved from Chicago to Wisconsin in 1957, as Professor of Psychology and Psychiatry, he was motivated by the desire to extend his thinking about the therapeutic relationship by working with individuals diagnosed with chronic schizophrenia (Rogers, 1967a). In 1960, he received NIMH funding to launch such an effort, assembling a team of psychologists and psychiatrists. The project ran into some difficulties (detailed in Rogers, 1967a), and relatively little was published about the work with schizophrenic individuals until later, when the group assembled a group of papers as a final report (Rogers, 1967b).

Major Research Funded at Other Universities

NIMH, of course, funded psychological research in the 1948–1963 period at a great many colleges and universities other than those discussed above. Space limitations permit only a small additional sample of three. Two of them I selected to point out that some projects were of great

TABLE 4.15
National Institute of Mental Health Research Funding to Researchers at the University of Wisconsin—Madison, 1948–1963

PI	Project title	Total amount ($)	Year(s) supported	No. publications
Harlow, Harry F.	Normal and abnormal social behavior of primates	406,308	1954–1960	49
	Symposium on behavioral and biological sciences	8,910	1955	1
	Comprehensive behavioral studies of monkeys	509,726	1961–1963	34
Leibowitz, Herschel	Analytic studies of visual perception	20,636	1956–1958	19
Wyckoff, L. Benjamin	An experimental study of secondary reinforcement	2,329	1957	2
Berkowitz, Leonard	Expression and reduction of hostility	38,373	1958–1962	19
Rogers, Carl R.	Therapeutic process in schizophrenics and normals		1960–1964	23
	Pilot studies of divergent psychotherapies	3,900	1963	0
Ross, Leonard E.	Methods for the investigation of conditioned fear	2,300	1960	0
Bridgman, Charles S.	Sequential response patterns	2,070	1960	0
Smith, Karl U.	Geometric organization of motion	85,594	1961–1963	15
	Drugs and brain biochemistry in aging and development	81,974	1962–1963	17
Schwartzbaum, Jerome	Role of the limbic system in sensory discrimination	53,671	1961–1963	14
Hetherington, Eileen	Reinforcement delay and learning in retarded children	2,300	1961	0
Borgatta, Edgar F.	Cumulative scaling and error estimation	35,012	1962–1963	2
Banta, Thomas J.	Reinforcement of free social interaction	18,462	1962–1963	0
Hetherington, Eileen M.	Delay of reward and learning in retarded children	28,081	1962–1963	0
Pick, Herbert L.	Adaptation to and recovery from visual distortion	3,829	1962	0
Grant, David A.	Verbal control of behavior in classical conditioning	17,742	1963	0
Porter, John J.	Habit and drive in classical conditioning	3,616	1963	0

Note. Total funding: $2,538,135. Funding received by American Psychological Association members: $1,324,833. Number of projects = 20. Number of principal investigators (PIs) = 16. Data are taken from *Mental Health Research Grant Awards: Fiscal Years 1948–1963* (PHS Publication No. 1528), by National Institute of Mental Health, 1964, Washington, DC: U.S. Government Printing Office and from *Publications Resulting From National Institute of Mental Health Research Grants, 1948–1961* (PHS Publication No.1647), by National Institute of Mental Health, 1966, Washington, DC: U.S. Government Printing Office. In the public domain.

significance for academic psychology even though the principal investigators were not psychologists.

On September 11, 1956, the Symposium on Information, a gathering that some people contend was the founding event for a new field of cognitive science (Gardner, 1987), was held at MIT. Perhaps as an appropriate follow-up to this event, MIT President Jerome Wiesner and Provost Walter Rosenblith joined Dean Henry Zimmerman as principal investigators for one of the largest grants from NIMH during this period. Awarded in 1961, in an amount exceeding $900,000, the funds supported basic research in the communication sciences. A number of different projects were recipients of this financial support and, by 1965, more than 130 publications had been produced, many by a multidisciplinary group of scholars who were among the early leaders of the new cognitive movement. Although only a few psychologists were involved, the work generated by this large group proved to be of great interest to psychology; in fact, some persons from MIT, such as Noam Chomsky, had a great deal of interaction with Bruner and Miller's Center for Cognitive Studies at Harvard, making Cambridge a vital center of the cognitive movement. Chomsky represented the revitalized field of linguistics; some of his work was also supported by NIMH funding of the Harvard Center (Chomsky, 1965). Linguistic philosophers Jerrold Katz and Jerry Fodor were also part of the MIT effort, the latter teaming up with psychologist Thomas Bever to produce research that was published in psychological journals (Bever, Fodor, & Weksel, 1965; Fodor & Bever, 1965).

Roger Sperry at the California Institute of Technology headed another NIMH-funded research program. Sperry received over $400,000 in 1959 to fund an ambitious research effort on neural mechanisms in behavior. Technically, Sperry was a zoologist and not a psychologist, although he had earned a master's degree in psychology and had served a postdoctoral stint under Lashley at Harvard (Puente, 1995). Sperry's research team included several psychologists, including Michael Gazzaniga. Although a diversity of projects were funded by the grant, the most famous was Sperry's investigation of split-brain phenomena, occasioned by his having access to patients whose cerebral commissures had been surgically severed. By devising techniques for the separate testing of the functioning of the two cerebral hemispheres, Sperry and Gazzaniga established that the left hemisphere appeared to specialize in verbal tasks while the right hemisphere was dominant in spatial and fine discrimination tasks (Gazzaniga, Bogen, & Sperry, 1962, 1965; Sperry, 1964). Thus was born the famous left brain–right brain distinction that has become almost mythical; Sperry's continuing work on the problem showed that the extent of the divided functioning depends on a number of factors. Sperry was awarded a share of the Nobel Prize for medicine in 1981 as a result of this work.

Finally, it is of interest to note that Donald Hebb and Peter Milner at McGill University in Canada received NIMH funding of over $100,000 for their studies of perception, motivation, and learning. Hebb's significant book, published early in this time period (Hebb, 1949), was one of the major stimuli for the increased emphasis on neuropsychology. His speculative but highly influential theory of cell assemblies and phase sequences (dynamic structures formed in the brain as a result of the organism's experience) were developed well before he received the NIMH grant in 1959. The award appeared to provide support for the neuropsychological studies of his students and younger colleagues, although he did further develop his theory (Hebb, 1959).

IMPACT OF NIMH RESEARCH FUNDING

What can be said, by way of a summary, about the role that NIMH's research funding program played in American academic psychology during the postwar period of 1948 to 1963? It is difficult to precisely isolate the effect of NIMH research grants on academic psychology, as psychologists also received support from other sources. There was, for example, additional NIMH funding for supporting the training of researchers and clinicians. Support also came from other governmental agencies, such as the Office of Naval Research and the National Science Foundation. Private foundations continued to support academic psychological research. However, one can say that NIMH was the major financial supporter of this research by the end of this period. Although further research may lead to a more precise evaluation of its impact, one can say, with some degree of confidence, that the effect of the grants program was considerable even when the total revenue stream is considered.

It seems clear that one effect of this research support on the structure and organization of academic psychology during this period was to make psychology a more visible presence on campuses, especially in the major universities. Not only the number of tenure-track faculty in psychology departments but also the total number of psychologists on campus grew during this period, as shown in Table 4.5. Many of the additional psychologists were not tenure-track members of any department, although they may have had courtesy appointments. Some were members of research units, such as the ISR at Michigan; the Research Center for Human Relations at NYU; and, in the case of Columbia University, the New York State Psychiatric Institute. There were also part-time teaching faculty added to perform the classroom duties of tenured faculty released from teaching duties because of their research grants.

The NIMH grants program was directed at individual researchers and was not directly aimed at the creation of large institutional activities, involving costly capital investment, that were an important feature of what has been called *Big Science*, a term loosely applied to projects funded to support the development and acquisition of facilities such as telescopes and cyclotrons (Appel, 2000; Price, 1963). It was not until 1961 that NIMH established a large-scale program of project grants to set up clinical research centers (Brand & Sapir, 1964), although individual grants were awarded to psychologists who were clearly involved in these Big Science organizations, such as Harry Harlow at the Wisconsin Regional Primate Center and those at Michigan's ISR and MHRI.

The grants listed in Table 4.4, as well as a great many others in the six-figure range, helped to support what might be called *medium science*, a term I do not use in a derogatory manner. These awards made possible the enlarged and quickened pace of psychological research at American universities, enabling small and local but promising projects to blossom and become nationally known. These grants, in addition to supporting the salaries of faculty and nonfaculty researchers (including students hired as research assistants), funds for travel, publication costs, laboratory animals, and so on, enabled researchers to gain access to developing technological resources that increased the sophistication of psychological research. One thinks immediately of computers, the large digital mainframe machines that enabled researchers to analyze large batches of data using statistical methods that could not be used before, such as factor analysis and other multivariate methods. These grants supported not the purchase of computers but the purchase of computer time at either a university computer center or some outside commercial firm; desktop microprocessor machines were not widely available during this period. Then, of course, there were technological developments involving laboratory equipment and associated methodology, some of which are mentioned in the following paragraphs.

I turn finally to the content of the research performed during this period. It seems clear that, with one possible exception, there was no marked change in direction, no new field of investigation that was directly initiated by the NIMH grants program. Rather, trends that had begun prior to or during the war received augmented support that aided in their development. The one new direction that may be mentioned was the emphasis on the etiology, diagnosis, and treatment of mental illness and, even here, it cannot be said that this trend was started *de novo* during this period.

As one surveys the many psychological studies supported by NIMH in the postwar era, the variety of this work seems confusing. I structure this discussion in terms of several conceptual trends that can be noted during this time, some of which were discussed by S. Koch (1959) in his review of the changes in American psychological thought during the period 1930–1959. In each case, I review examples of NIMH-supported projects that helped to further these trends. Studies in each category that exemplify the mental health emphasis also are noted. NIMH, of course, awarded much grant money for this type of research, but it cannot be forgotten that it also supported much "pure" psychological research during the postwar period.

I start with the observation, also noted by S. Koch (1959), that the era of the grand behavior theories, such as those of Hull and Tolman, was ending. The efforts of individuals such as Neal Miller at Yale, Harry Harlow at Wisconsin, and B. F. Skinner at Harvard show that the behavioral tradition was still very much alive, although in an increasingly altered form. One of the changes in this tradition featured the abandonment of the grand theory mission and an emphasis on more modest theoretical ventures or models. One form of this was the increased use of mathematical formalization to build models of more circumscribed processes, such as concept identification and signal detection, an effort inspired by Estes and furthered by the work at Columbia and especially at Stanford. Another form of simplification of behavior theory was begun with Skinner in the 1930s; this experimental analysis of behavior movement continued not only at Harvard under Skinner but also at other universities. Skinner, incidentally, as I have mentioned, was funded by NIMH to study psychotic behavior, a clear mental health application, and Keller, too, was supported for work related to mental health. Another change in behavior theory was its increasing concern with central processes—not just the classic intervening variables of Tolman and Hull but processes associated with brain functioning. The work of James Olds at Michigan, suggesting the neural basis of reinforcement, is one of the clearest examples.

There is another change in behavior theory that must be mentioned: the cognitive movement, although it may be seen by some as an entirely new development in American psychology. However, Herbert Simon, one of the best-known proponents of cognitivism, saw it as a continuation of behavior theory (Simon, 1969). Like the changing behavioral approach, the cognitive movement focused on the modeling of discrete processes, much of it by the use of computer simulation, such as in the work of Leonard Uhr at Michigan. There is, however, a change in lexicon from the use of terms such as *learning* and *conditioning* to a vocabulary sprinkled with terms and concepts not only from the world of computers and information processing but also from linguistics and mathematical biology, as found in the work at MIT. The cognitive approach found its way into a number of different areas of psychological thought and research. Perhaps inspired by the thinking of Piaget, one finds it appearing in developmental psychology, as exemplified by some of Bruner's work at Harvard and in Stanley Schachter's work on emotional experience. Also, in the form of Gestalt and Lewinian concepts, it can be found in much of the social psychological work of the day, including that of Leonard Berkowitz at Wisconsin. It also appears in some of the clinical research of the time, such as Joseph Wepman's work at Chicago on aphasia.

I turn next to another change in American psychology, also mentioned by S. Koch (1959): the alterations occurring in the concept of perception. Perhaps the most important of these is found in the study of what Floyd Allport (1955) called the *directive-state approach* to perception, the notion that central emotional and cognitive processes influence what is perceived. Some of this work found inspiration from the thinking of Freud that exerted some influence in American psychology at this time. Such was certainly the case for George Klein, Robert Holt, and their colleagues at NYU. Their work on cognitive and perceptual styles not only represented an experimental approach to the study of psychoanalytic concepts but also, as expected, found application to the study of psychopathology.

As noted, research in developmental psychology was handsomely supported by the NIMH grants program in this time period. Much of the work had relevance for mental health because it focused on the possible influence of early childhood experience on the adequacy of later functioning. The work of John Whiting and Robert Sears of Harvard, Helen Koch at Chicago, and much of the research funded at Berkeley represent outstanding examples of this. However, there was a trend in this field that had really started before the war. What was called *genetic psychology* or *child psychology* much earlier was becoming a study of human development that spanned the entire life cycle. The role of external funding from foundations enabled researchers to mount longitudinal studies that followed children well into maturity. After the war, NIMH funding enabled such longitudinal work to continue. There was also another emphasis, one that capped the study of the life cycle: the increased research on aging. There were a number of large projects in this area, including the one at Chicago headed by William Henry, as well as a variety of smaller projects. It is obvious that these longitudinal efforts could not be mounted or maintained without external funding.

The study of the human brain and nervous system had been, from the beginning of American psychology, a permanent feature of the field, but any study of their role in experience and behavior had to await the development of a technology suitable for such research. The prewar work of Karl Lashley inspired the efforts of an entire generation of younger researchers eager to pursue the study of brain–behavior relationships. Many whom I have mentioned as supported by NIMH funding—such as David Krech, Donald Hebb, and Frank Beach—had worked with Lashley (Dewsbury, 2002). However, there were a great many other projects, some of them quite large. The research programs of James Olds at Michigan and Burton Rosner at Yale come readily to mind. Even though the sophisticated imaging techniques of today were not in use during this postwar period, there was nonetheless a new level of technology introduced to make possible such methods as the electrical recording of neural activity, precise electrical stimulation of the brain, and techniques for studying brain biochemistry. Although there had long been an area of physiological psychology that had included study of the brain and nervous system, because of this increased research activity this term appears to have been superseded by a field called *neuropsychology*.

The vastly increased capability that psychologists acquired in collecting and processing data was also of critical importance for the development of psychology. Two fields in particular benefited from this technological advance: personality psychology and social psychology. The field of personality study was greatly enhanced by the ability to collect and process data, especially psychometric data, on people. The work of Raymond Cattell at Illinois provides a good example. Cattell was able to define the domain of personality structure by using the techniques of factor analysis and inventing some new versions. The ability to purchase computer time was essential for this work, as it was for handling the large amounts of data collected in social psychological studies like those mounted at Michigan's ISR.

Space does not allow the analysis of the many studies, some already mentioned, that were specifically aimed at psychopathology and therapy. They were important during this period because they enabled psychology departments to produce clinicians and also remain scientific. Clinical psychology students could participate in studies that could qualify as "good science." The academic psychology programs had justification for claiming that they were trying to produce scientist–practitioners.

It is rather obvious that America's involvement in two world wars has had a marked impact on the discipline of psychology. Psychologists' contribution of testing and measurement to the earlier war effort resulted in a markedly increased public visibility during the 1920s and there was some notable foundational funding for university research. After a much broader and more solid contribution during WWII, much of it in the mental health field, the popularity of and respect for psychology were consolidated. There seems to be little doubt that the substantial government funding of academic psychology, much of it stemming from the research grants program of NIMH, contributed to making psychology a secure and major discipline in American colleges and universities.

REFERENCES

Allport, F. H. (1955). *Theories of perception and the concept of structure*. New York: Wiley.

Allport, G. W., & Boring, E. G. (1946). Psychology and social relations at Harvard University. *American Psychologist, 1,* 119–122.

Appel, T. A. (2000). *Shaping biology: The National Science Foundation and American biological research, 1945–1975.* Baltimore: Johns Hopkins University Press.

Atkinson, R. C. (1963). A variable sensitivity theory of signal detection. *Psychological Review, 70,* 91–106.

Auld, F., & Murray, E. J. (1955). Content analysis studies of psychotherapy. *Psychological Bulletin, 52,* 377–395.

Bandura, A. (1962). Social learning through imitation. In M. R. Jones (Ed.), *Nebraska Symposium on Motivation: Vol. 10* (pp. 211–269). Lincoln: University of Nebraska Press.

Bandura, A., & Mischel, W. (1965). Modifications of self-imposed delay of reward through exposure to live and symbolic models. *Journal of Personality and Social Psychology, 2,* 698–705.

Bandura, A., Ross, D., & Ross, S. A. (1961). Transmission of aggression through imitation of aggressive models. *Journal of Abnormal and Social Psychology, 63,* 575–582.

Barry, H., III, & Miller, N. E. (1965). Comparison of drug effects on approach, avoidance, and escape motivation. *Journal of Comparative and Physiological Psychology, 59,* 18–24.

Bayley, N. (1951). Some psychological correlates of somatic androgeny. *Child Development, 22,* 47–60.

Beach, F. A. (1958). Neural and chemical regulation of behavior. In H. F. Harlow & C. N. Woolsey (Eds.), *Biological and biochemical bases of behavior* (pp. 263–285). Madison: University of Wisconsin Press.

Beach, F. A. (1960). Experimental investigations of species-specific behavior. *American Psychologist, 15,* 1–18.

Berkowitz, L. (1962). *Aggression: A social psychological analysis.* New York: McGraw-Hill.

Berkowitz, L. (1964). Aggressive cues in aggressive behavior and hostility catharsis. *Psychological Review, 71,* 104–122.

Bettelheim, B. (1950). *Love is not enough.* Glencoe, IL: Free Press.

Bettelheim, B. (1955). *Truants from life.* Glencoe, IL: Free Press.

Bever, T. G., Fodor, J. A., & Weksel, W. (1965). Theoretical notes on the acquisition of syntax: A critique of "contextual generalization." *Psychological Review, 72,* 467–482.

Block, J. (1957). A study of affective responsiveness in a lie-detector situation. *Journal of Abnormal and Social Psychology, 55,* 11–15.

Bordin, E. S., Cutler, R. L., Dittman, A. T., Harway, N. I., Raush, & Rigler, D. (1954). Measurement problems in process research on psychotherapy. *Journal of Consulting Psychology, 18,* 79–82.

Bower, G. H. (1961). Application of a model to paired-associate learning. *Psychometrika, 26,* 255–280.

Brand, J., & Sapir, P. (1964). An historical perspective on the National Institute of Mental Health. In D. E. Woolridge (Ed.), *Biomedical science and its administration* (pp. 1–84). Unpublished report.

Bruner, J. (1957). On perceptual readiness. *Psychological Review, 64*, 123–152.

Bruner, J. (1983). *In search of mind: Essays in autobiography*. New York: Harper & Row.

Bruner, J., Goodnow, J., & Austin, G. (1956). *A study of thinking*. New York: Wiley.

Cannell, C. F., & Kahn, R. L. (1984). *Some factors in the origins and development of the Institute for Social Research, the University of Michigan*. Ann Arbor: Institute for Social Research, University of Michigan.

Capshew, J. H. (1999). *Psychologists on the march: Science, practice, and professional identity in America, 1929–1969*. Cambridge, England: Cambridge University Press.

Cattell, E. P., & Horn, J. (2001). *A short biography: Raymond Bernard Cattell*. Retrieved December 11, 2001, from http://www.stanford.edu/~cattell/rbcbio.htm

Cattell, R. B. (1974). Travels in psychological hyperspace. In T. S. Krawiec (Ed.), *The psychologists* (Vol. 2, pp. 85–134). New York: Oxford University Press.

Chapman, L. J. (1961). A reinterpretation of some pathological disturbances in conceptual breadth. *Journal of Abnormal and Social Psychology, 62*, 514–519.

Chein, I., Gerard, D. L., Lee, R. S., & Rosenfeld, E. (1964). *The road to H: Narcotics, delinquency, and social policy*. New York: Basic Books.

Chomsky, N. (1965). *Aspects of the theory of syntax*. Cambridge, MA: MIT Press.

Cobb, S., French, J. R. P., & Mann, F. C. (1963). An environmental approach to mental health. *Annals of the New York Academy of Sciences, 107*, 596–606.

Cohler, B. J., & Tobin, S. S. (2002). Bernice Levin Neugarten (1916–2001). *American Psychologist, 57*, 288.

Cronbach, L. J., & Azuma, H. (1962). Internal-consistency reliability formulas applied to randomly sampled single-factor tests: An empirical comparison. *Educational and Psychological Measurement, 22*, 645–665.

Cronbach, L. J., Rajaratnum, N., & Gleser, G. (1963). Theory of generalizability: A liberalization of reliability theory. *British Journal of Statistical Psychology, 16*, 137–163.

Delgado, J. M., Roberts, W. W., & Miller, N. E. (1954). Learning motivated by electrical stimulation of the brain. *American Journal of Physiology, 179*, 587–593.

Dewsbury, D. A. (2002). The Chicago Five: A family group of integrative psychobiologists. *History of Psychology, 5*, 16–37.

Dollard, J. (1964, Winter). Yale's Institute of Human Relations: What was it? *Ventures*, 32–40.

Dukelow, W. R. (1995). *The alpha males: An early history of the regional primate research centers*. Lanham, MD: University Press of America.

Elder, G. (2002). *The Oakland Growth and Berkeley Guidance Studies of the Institute for Human Development, University of California, Berkeley*. Retrieved March 2, 2002, from http://www.cpc.unc.edu/lifecourse/berkoak.html

Erikson, E. H. (1951). Sex differences in the play configurations of pre-adolescents. *American Journal of Orthopsychiatry, 21,* 667–692.

Fodor, J. A., & Bever, T. G. (1965). The psychological reality of linguistic segments. *Journal of Verbal Learning and Verbal Behavior, 4,* 414–420.

Freeland, R. M. (1992). *Academia's golden age: Universities in Massachusetts 1945–1970*. New York: Oxford University Press.

Gardner, H. (1987). *The mind's new science*. New York: Basic Books.

Gazzaniga, M. S., Bogen, J. E., & Sperry, R. W. (1962). Some functional effects of sectioning the cerebral commissures in man. *Proceedings of the National Academy of Sciences, 48,* 1765–1769.

Gazzaniga, M. S., Bogen, J. E., & Sperry, R. W. (1965). Observations on visual perception after disconnexion of the cerebral hemispheres in man. *Brain, 88,* 221–236.

Geiger, R. L. (1993). *Research and relevant knowledge: American research universities since World War II*. New York: Oxford University Press.

Gilbert, D. C., & Levinson, D. J. (1956). Ideology, personality, and institutional policy in the mental hospital. *Journal of Social and Abnormal Psychology, 53,* 263–271.

Gough, H. G. (1953). The construction of a personality scale to predict scholastic achievement. *Journal of Applied Psychology, 37,* 361–366.

Gough, H. G. (1957). *Manual for the California Psychological Inventory*. Palo Alto, CA: Consulting Psychologists Press.

Graham, H. D., & Diamond, N. (1997). *American research universities: Elites and challengers in the postwar era*. Baltimore: Johns Hopkins University Press.

Grob, G. N. (1991). *From asylum to community*. Princeton, NJ: Princeton University Press.

Grold, J. D. (1961). *A history of the University of California psychology department at Berkeley*. Unpublished manuscript, University of California, Berkeley.

Haan, N. (1964). The relationship of ego functioning and intelligence to social status and social mobility. *Journal of Abnormal and Social Psychology, 69,* 594–605.

Haber, R. N. (1964). Effects of coding strategy on perceptual memory. *Journal of Experimental Psychology, 68,* 357–362.

Harlow, H. F. (1958). The nature of love. *American Psychologist, 13,* 673–685.

Harlow, H. F., Harlow, M. K., Rueping, R. R., & Mason, W. A. (1960). Performance of infant rhesus monkeys on discrimination learning, delayed response, and discrimination learning set. *Journal of Comparative and Physiological Psychology, 53,* 113–121.

Harmon, L. R. (1964). Production of psychology doctorates. *American Psychologist, 19,* 629–633.

Harris, C. S., & Haber, R. N. (1963). Selective attention and coding in visual perception. *Journal of Experimental Psychology, 65,* 328–333.

Harvard University. (1954). *The behavioral sciences at Harvard: Report by a faculty committee.* Unpublished manuscript.

Hebb, D. O. (1949). *The organization of behavior.* New York: Wiley.

Hebb, D. O. (1959). Intelligence, brain function, and the theory of mind. *Brain, 82,* 260–275.

Henry, W. E., & Cumming, E. (1959). Personality development in adulthood and old age. *Journal of Projective Techniques, 23,* 383–390.

Hess, E. (1958). "Imprinting" in animals. *Scientific American, 198,* 81–90.

Hilgard, E. R. (1987). *Psychology in America: A historical survey.* New York: Harcourt Brace.

Honzik, M. P. (1951). Sex differences in the occurrence of materials in the play construction of pre-adolescents. *Child Development, 22,* 15–36.

Jones, L. V., & Wepman, J. (1961). Dimensions of language performance in aphasia. *Journal of Speech and Hearing Research, 4,* 220–232.

Kahn, R. L., Wolfe, D. M., Quinn, R. P., Snock, J. D., & Rosenthal, R. A. (1964). *Organizational stress: Studies in role conflict and ambiguity.* New York: Wiley.

Kasl, S. V., & Mahl, G. F. (1956). A simple device for obtaining certain verbal activity measures during interviews. *Journal of Abnormal and Social Psychology, 53,* 388–390.

Kenniston, K. (1962). Social change and youth in America. *Daedalus, 91,* 145–171.

Kessen, W., Williams, E. J., & Williams, J. P. (1961). Selection and test of response measures in the study of the human newborn. *Child Development, 32,* 7–24.

Kidd, C. V. (1959). *American universities and federal research.* Cambridge, MA: Belknap Press.

Klein, G. S., & Holt, R. R. (1960). Problems and issues in current studies of subliminal stimulation. In G. J. Peatman & E. L. Harley (Eds.), *Festschrift for Gardner Murphy* (pp. 76–93). New York: Harper & Brothers.

Klein, G. S., Spence, D. P., Holt, R. R., & Gourevitch, S. (1958). Cognition without awareness: Subliminal influences upon conscious thought. *Journal of Abnormal and Social Psychology, 57,* 255–266.

Koch, H. L. (1956). Attitudes of young children toward their peers as related to certain characteristics of their siblings. *Psychological Monographs, 70*(Whole No. 426).

Koch, S. (1959). Some trends of Study I (Vols. 1–3) epilogue. In S. Koch (Ed.), *Psychology: A study of a science. Vol. 3: Formulations of the person and the social context* (pp. 729–788). New York: McGraw-Hill.

Koch, S. (Ed.). (1963). *Psychology: A study of a science. Vol. 6: Investigations of man as socius: Their place in psychology and the social sciences.* New York: McGraw-Hill.

Krech, D., Rosenzweig, M. R., & Bennett, E. L. (1960). Effects of environmental complexity and training on brain chemistry. *Journal of Comparative and Physiological Psychology, 53,* 505–519.

Lazarus, R. S. (1964). A laboratory approach to the dynamics of psychological stress. *American Psychologist, 19*, 400–411.

Lazarus, R. S. (1966). *Psychological stress and the coping process*. New York: McGraw-Hill.

Lindsley, O. R. (1956). Operant conditioning methods applied to research in chronic schizophrenia. *Psychiatric Research Reports, 5*, 118–139.

Lippitt, R., & Gold, M. (1960). Classroom social structure as a mental health problem. *Journal of Social Issues, 15*, 40–49.

Lomax, E. M. R. (1977). The Laura Spelman Rockefeller Memorial: Some of its contributions to early research in child development. *Journal of the History of the Behavioral Sciences, 13*, 283–293.

Lowen, R. S. (1997). *Creating the Cold War university: The transformation of Stanford*. Berkeley: University of California Press.

Luce, R. D. (1992). Mathematical modeling of perceptual, learning, and cognitive processes. In S. Koch & D. E. Leary (Eds.), *A century of psychology as science* (pp. 654–677). Washington, DC: American Psychological Association.

Mahl, G. F. (1956). Disturbances and silences in the patient's speech in psychotherapy. *Journal of Abnormal and Social Psychology, 53*, 1–15.

Maier, N. R. F., & Hoffman, R. L. (1961). Organization and creative problem solving. *Journal of Applied Psychology, 45*, 277–280.

Marrow, A. J. (1969). *The practical theorist: The life and work of Kurt Lewin*. New York: Harper & Row.

May, M. A. (1971). A retroflective view of the Institute of Human Relations at Yale. *Behavior Science Notes, 6*, 141–173.

McConnell, J. V. (1964). Cannibalism and memory in flatworms. *New Scientist, 21*, 465–468.

McGill, W. J. (1997). Fred Simmons Keller (1899–1996). *American Psychologist, 51*, 743–744.

Mental Health Research Institute. (1957). *First annual report*. Ann Arbor: University of Michigan Press.

Merton, R. K. (1968, January, 5). The Matthew effect in science. *Science, 159*, 56–63.

Miller, G. A., Galanter, E., & Pribram, K. H. (1960). *Plans and the structure of behavior*. New York: Holt.

Miller, N. E. (1958). Central stimulation and other new approaches to motivation and reward. *American Psychologist, 13*, 100–108.

Miller, N. E. (1959). Liberalization of basic S–R concepts: Extensions to conflict behavior and social learning. In S. Koch (Ed.), *Psychology: A study of a science* (Vol. 2, pp. 196–292). New York: McGraw-Hill.

Miller, N. E. (1961). Analytical studies of drive and reward. *American Psychologist, 16*, 739–754.

Molish, H. B., & Beck, S. J. (1958). Psychoanalytic concepts and principles discernible in projective personality tests: III. Mechanisms of defense in schizophrenic reaction types as evaluated by the Rorschach test. *American Journal of Orthopsychiatry, 28*, 47–60.

National Institute of Mental Health. (1964). *Mental health research grant awards: Fiscal years 1948–1963* (PHS Publication No. 1528). Washington, DC: U.S. Government Printing Office.

National Institute of Mental Health. (1966). *Publications resulting from National Institute of Mental Health research grants, 1948–1961* (PHS Publication No. 1647). Washington, DC: U.S. Government Printing Office.

Neugarten, B. L. (1964). *Personality in middle and late life: A set of empirical studies.* New York: Atherton Press.

Neugarten, B. L., & Gutman, D. L. (1958). Age–sex roles and personality in middle age: A thematic apperception study. *Psychological Monographs, 75*(17), 1–33.

Olds, J. (1958). Satiation effects in self-stimulation of the brain. *Journal of Comparative and Physiological Psychology, 51*, 675–678.

Orlans, H. (1962). *The effects of federal programs on higher education: A study of 36 universities and colleges.* Washington, DC: Brookings Institution Press.

Pollak, R. (1996). *The creation of Dr. B.* New York: Simon & Schuster.

Pribram, K. H. (1963). The new neurology: Memory, novelty, thought and choice. In G. H. Glaser (Ed.), *Encephalography and behavior* (pp. 149–173). New York: Basic Books.

Price, D. J. (1963). *Little science, big science.* New York: Columbia University Press.

Puente, A. E. (1995). Roger Walcott Sperry (1913–1994). *American Psychologist, 50*, 940–941.

Rogers, C. R. (1957). The necessary and sufficient conditions of therapeutic personality change. *Journal of Consulting Psychology, 21*, 95–103.

Rogers, C. R. (1958). A process conception of psychotherapy. *American Psychologist, 13*, 142–149.

Rogers, C. R. (1959). A theory of therapy, personality, and interpersonal relationships, as developed in the client-centered framework. In S. Koch (Ed.), *Psychology: A study of a science* (Vol. 3, pp. 184–256). New York: McGraw-Hill.

Rogers, C. R. (1967a). Carl Rogers. In E. G. Boring & G. Lindzey (Eds.), *A history of psychology in autobiography* (Vol. 5, pp. 341–384). New York: Appleton-Century-Crofts.

Rogers, C. R. (Ed.). (1967b). *The therapeutic relationship and its impact: A study of psychotherapy with schizophrenics.* Madison: University of Wisconsin Press.

Rosner, B. (1964). Temporal interaction between electrocutaneous stimuli. *Journal of Experimental Psychology, 67*, 191–192.

Salzinger, K., Portnoy, S., & Feldman, R. S. (1964). Experimental manipulation of continuous speech in schizophrenic patients. *Journal of Abnormal and Social Psychology, 68*, 508–516.

Sarason, S. B., Davidson, K. S., Lighthall, F. F., Waite, R. R., & Ruebush, B. K. (1960). *Anxiety in elementary school children*. New York: Wiley.

Schachter, S., & Singer, J. (1962). Cognitive, social, and physiological determinants of emotional state. *Psychological Review, 69,* 379–399.

Schutz, W. C. (1958). *FIRO: A three-dimensional theory of interpersonal behavior*. New York: Rinehart.

Sears, R. R., Maccoby, E., & Levin, H. (1957). *Patterns of child rearing*. Evanston, IL: Row, Peterson.

Sears, R. R., Whiting, J. W. M, Nowlis, V., & Sears, P. S. (1953). Some child-rearing antecedents of aggression and dependency in young children. *Genetic Psychology Monographs, 47,* 135–236.

Selltiz, C., Edrich, H., & Cook, S. W. (1965). Ratings of favorableness of statements about a social group as an indicator of attitude toward the group. *Journal of Personality and Social Psychology, 2,* 408–415.

Simon, H. (1969). *The sciences of the artificial*. Cambridge, MA: MIT Press.

Skinner, B. F. (1958). Reinforcement today. *American Psychologist, 13,* 94–99.

Sklansky, M. A., Isaacs, K. S., Levitov, E. S., & Haggard, E. A. (1965). Verbal interaction and levels of meaning in psychotherapy. *Archives of General Psychiatry, 14,* 158–170.

Sperry, R. W. (1964). The great cerebral commissure. *Scientific American, 201,* 42–52.

Stewart, L. H. (1962). Social and emotional adjustment during adolescence as related to the development of psychosomatic illness in adulthood. *Genetic Psychology Monographs, 65,* 175–215.

Stone, P. J., Bales, R. F., Namenwirth, J. Z., & Ogilvie, D. M. (1962). The general inquirer: A computer system for content analysis and retrieval based on the sentence as a unit of information. *Behavioral Science, 7,* 484–498.

Trabasso, T., & Bower, G. H. (1964). Presolution reversal and dimensional shifts in concept identification. *Journal of Experimental Psychology, 67,* 398–399.

Uhr, L. (1963). The development of perception and language. In S. Tompkins & S. Messick (Eds.), *Simulation of personality processes* (pp. 231–266). New York: Wiley.

Uhr, L., & Miller, J. G. (Eds.). (1960). *Drugs and behavior*. New York: Wiley.

University of California. (2001). *IPSR: A brief history*. Retrieved October 23, 2001, from http://www.1s.berkeley.edu/dept/ipsr/history.html

University of Chicago. (2001). *Committee on Human Development*. Retrieved December 4, 2001, from http://www.humdev.uchicago.edu

Walker, E. L., & Walker, B. E. (1964). Response to stimulus complexity in the rat. *Psychological Record, 14,* 489–497.

Zander, A., Cohen, A. R., & Stotland, E. (1957). *Role relations in the mental health professions*. Ann Arbor, MI: Institute for Social Research.

Zigler, E. (1963). Social reinforcement, environmental conditions, and the child. *American Journal of Orthopsychiatry, 33,* 614–623.

5

PSYCHOTHERAPY RESEARCH AND THE NATIONAL INSTITUTE OF MENTAL HEALTH, 1948–1980

RACHAEL I. ROSNER

To speak of psychotherapy research and the National Institute of Mental Health (NIMH), particularly since the mid-1960s, is to speak primarily of a set of extramural administrative bodies that has solicited research from the field, overseen NIMH-funded research, appointed members to review committees, and negotiated with the director of the NIMH and Congress over policies. It may be helpful to think of the history of psychotherapy at NIMH as a partnership between psychotherapists in the field and agents of the government and to conceptualize this partnership as existing in a kind of virtual realm demarcated by the space between the institute and the researchers—in other words, by the give and take of their relationship. In

I thank Morris Parloff for clarifying and correcting many points in a draft of this chapter; Morris Parloff, Barry Wolfe, Robert Cohen, Hussein Tuma, and Leo Madow for participating in personal interviews; Irene Elkin for reading the chapter carefully and correcting a number of historical errors; and Wade Pickren, Barry Wolfe, Tena Rosner, Debbie Fleetham, Debbie Weinstein, and the research group at the Danielsen Institute for comments on drafts. Some of this material was presented to members of the Department of Psychology at the University of New Hampshire. Research for this chapter was conducted with the support of a National Science Foundation Post-Doctoral Fellowship.

this chapter I explore the history of the relationship between these two communities and the influence of this relationship on the development of objective knowledge about the processes and outcome of psychotherapy. I hope to show that in the last 50 years, researchers (scientists) and agents of the federal government in Congress and NIMH (politicians and administrators) both have sought "objective" answers about how, why, and whether psychotherapy works, and with whom, and that the interdependence of Congress, NIMH, and psychotherapy researchers in the pursuit of these answers has ensured that political as well as scientific motives have contributed to the very language psychologists use to describe data in their science.

The field of psychotherapy research over the last 50 years consistently has been defined by a quest to make psychotherapy an objective, legitimate science and by an epistemological divide among researchers between those who privilege clinical inference (relying on the subjective wisdom of the therapist) and those who privilege statistical designs (relying on numerical data).[1] The difficulty in making psychotherapy objective, due in part to these epistemological disagreements, appeared, in the mid-1950s, almost insurmountable. One NIMH psychiatrist in 1956 concluded:

> The evaluation of psychotherapy is a very controversial and unsettled field, about which all would agree it is very important to study, quantify and assess—but everyone is at a loss as to the best way to proceed. No acceptable criteria for evaluation by objective means yet exist, and efforts are proceeding in the attempt to determine and set up these criteria . . . Both methods of analysis and criteria need to be established on much firmer scientific footing before assessment of individual or group psychotherapy becomes a reasonably "scientific" procedure. ("Unsigned memorandum," 1956, p. 5)

Although scientific progress has been made since 1956, the epistemological debate has remained remarkably constant. In the 1950s, the two basic positions were known as *naturalism* and *experimentalism*. Later, as techniques for evaluating psychotherapy improved, psychologists formulated the epistemological difference in terms of process research versus outcome research or as those interested in basic research versus those interested in applied research. The pendulum of general scientific opinion has swung from one side to the other over the last 50 years, and many therapists in response have tried to find a middle ground that integrates the methods of clinical and statistical predictions (Holt, 1958). However, rarely have scientists agreed about the greater power of one over the other to capture fully and accurately what is going on in psychotherapy. This tension within the

---

[1] This discussion of the interplay of subjectivity and objectivity is inspired by Peter Galison's (1998) insights into subjectivity and objectivity in the history of physics.

community of psychotherapy researchers has been manifest as a competition of sorts between different epistemologies for government dollars.

The contribution of NIMH to this partnership is most evident in the numbers. Between 1949 and 1977, the federal government spent over $55 million on approximately 530 psychotherapy research grants ("Memorandum from Chief," 1980). In 1977 it was estimated that federal money supported 75% to 85% of all large-scale psychotherapy outcome studies in the United States and 55% to 65% of all psychosocial treatment assessment research worldwide ("Memorandum from Chief," 1977). Federal money virtually built the field. The financial interests of the federal government have been as central to the evolution of psychotherapy research as the scientific interests of the individuals conducting the research. The changing priorities of the government in its allocation of mental health research dollars have influenced the direction of cash flow toward or away from these competing epistemologies. Consequently, government interests have played a key role in the shift over the last 50 years between the nodes of subjective and objective epistemologies in psychotherapy research.

To argue that NIMH has been a scientific partner in the quest for objective data about psychotherapy, rather than merely a shareholder, is to state explicitly what a number of historians of psychotherapy have argued implicitly. Karla Moras's (2002) recent contribution to the *Encyclopedia of Psychotherapy* pays consistent attention to the impact of NIMH funding policies on researchers. Moras (2002) virtually wrote an organizational history of psychotherapy at NIMH in accounting for shifts from process to outcome research and, in recent years, to *Diagnostic and Statistical Manual of Mental Disorders* (3rd ed., DSM–III; American Psychiatric Association, 1980) categories. Russell and Orlinsky (1996), too, made reference to NIMH.

THREE EPISODES

In this chapter I present three episodes illustrating specific moments in the history of American psychotherapy when the pervasive influence of NIMH in shaping the terms of these epistemological debates has been particularly clear. These episodes serve a number of additional functions. First, they identify three different (although not exhaustive) locations in which psychotherapy researchers and NIMH administration have interacted through the person of the psychotherapist–administrator: (a) the laboratory, (b) the research community, and (c) policy making. Second, they tell a chronological story of the evolutions of psychotherapy research and the NIMH both independently and in relation to each other. They show the pendulum of scientific consensus swinging from the case study to the randomized controlled trial (RCT) and back to some middle ground and of the concurrent descendance of psychoanalysis and ascendance of behavioral and cognitive–behavioral therapies. They also document the transformation of federal policies from the support of basic research to the support of applied research and from a spirit of methodological permissiveness to a consumerist emphasis on quantitative, market-based results.

The first episode zooms the lens very closely onto the mechanics of a single psychoanalytic project that received unusual attention from NIMH in the formative years of the institute, David Shakow's psychoanalytic film study. The episode narrates a kind of natural history of Shakow's project, which was the first effort to film an entire course of psychoanalysis for research purposes. Shakow was director of the Intramural Psychology Laboratory at NIMH from 1954 to 1966, and he was considered a luminary in the field of clinical psychology throughout the postwar period. Shakow's film project first received extramural funding from NIMH in 1953 when he was at the University of Illinois at Chicago, and he continued to receive NIMH funding for the project from 1954 to 1966 after he moved to NIMH's Intramural Laboratory of Psychology. The film project illustrates how the federal government's emphasis on pioneering basic research in the postwar period found expression in the idea that filmed psychoanalytic sessions could provide a common language for psychoanalysts seeking objective data as well as an opportunity for the mechanics of democracy to infiltrate the authoritarianism of orthodox psychoanalysis.

The second episode turns the lens from the intramural to the extramural research program and widens the view from the study of an individual scientist to the study of community. The episode begins, chronologically, with a return to the mid-1950s to examine a burgeoning consciousness of community among psychotherapy researchers, embodied in three national NIMH-funded invitation-only work conferences (1958–1966). The pivotal point of the episode is a reorganization of the NIMH extramural research program in 1966 to give greater administrative support to psychotherapy research and to give the federal government greater authority in directing mental health research toward practical applications. The episode then follows the development of a new administrative role for psychotherapists after 1966, what I call the *psychotherapist–administrator*,[2] who embodied the needs of both Congress and psychotherapy researchers in shaping federal research funding policies.

The third episode picks up the story in 1976 and narrows the lens again, looking at the political climate that gave birth to the first multisite

---

[2] The term "psychotherapist–administrator" was not used at the time. Rather, it conveys my sense of the nature of a new type of administrative position that emerged at NIMH in the 1960s. See audiotape of an interview with A. H. Tuma (Pickren, 2000), who emphasizes the dual role of new federal health science administrators as both scientists and managers.

"manualized treatment protocol"—a randomized controlled design that became the benchmark for good objective psychotherapy outcome research designs after 1980. The episode begins with an examination of the policy negotiations between Congress and a few NIMH scientists in response to the Carter Administration's push for national health insurance. Congress, in the effort to establish criteria for reimbursement of medical treatments, pointed the finger directly at the failure of psychotherapy researchers to produce experimental data documenting the relative safety and efficacy of specific therapeutic techniques. Congress had an ally in Gerald Klerman, director of the Alcohol, Drug and Mental Health Administration (ADAMHA), the parent institute of NIMH in the 1970s, who set policies for psychotherapy research encouraging the use of RCTs. These political imperatives provided the medium in which the Treatment of Depression Collaborative Research Project (TDCRP), the first multisite, collaborative RCT of psychotherapy, was born.

When taken together, these three episodes offer not a comprehensive picture of NIMH-funded psychotherapy research, or of the many branches and sections within the NIMH that sponsored psychotherapy research, but rather a dynamic illustration of how persistently and consistently psychotherapy researchers from both epistemological positions have responded to Congressional needs in their shared quest to establish norms of objectivity. They offer a kind of "macro" perspective on the ways in which NIMH funding policies for psychotherapy research have been the result of compromises between different groups with different understandings of "objectivity"— but with a unified goal of building a new and viable science. From this perspective, objectivity has been a concept as plastic and mutable as subjectivity in the history of psychotherapy research, and the pursuit of objectivity has been a task particularly susceptible to the winds of political change.

EPISODE 1: PSYCHOANALYTIC NATURALISM AND THE SOUND–MOVIE CAMERA

David Shakow's film project was conceived at the height of U.S. optimism about the clinical and cultural power of psychoanalysis in the years immediately following World War II. Many psychiatrists believed that new psychoanalytic psychotherapies, some born directly on the frontlines of the war itself, could treat successfully not only the normally neurotic individual, or the traumatized soldier, but even the most entrenched psychotic disorders, including schizophrenia (Fromm-Reichmann, 1959; Hale, 1995; Herman, 1995). These emergent psychoanalytic systems emphasized the interaction of the person with the environment, the psychosocial model, as a presumed etiology of mental illness. Many modifications of psychoanalytic theory in the postwar period, from Erik Erikson's to David Rapaport's, emphasized the "meaning" of symptoms as products of conflicts between the person and the environment. Furthermore, the introduction of increasingly large numbers of clinical psychologists to the practice of psychotherapy through broad-based federal funding of scientist–practitioner training programs in clinical psychology further solidified the influence of social sciences in psychotherapy.

A "Utopia of Scientific Investigation"

A small group of practitioners of these new approaches, many of whom were clinical psychologists rather than psychiatrists, developed an interest in establishing rigorous objective methods for measuring psychoanalytic processes. Those psychoanalysts in search of objectivity—David Rapaport, Lawrence Kubie, Margaret Brenman, Merton Gill, David Shakow, and Sybille Escalona, among others—reflected a more general trend among social scientists in the postwar years of gaining political, scientific, and cultural advantage by linking specific scientific practices with the virtues of a free democratic society. David Hollinger has analyzed similar rhetorical strategies of postwar philosophers, historians, and social scientists in their efforts to combat religious intolerance at home and the threats of fascism and communism abroad. Hollinger (1995) illustrates how

> a secular, increasingly Jewish, decidedly left-of-center intelligentsia based largely but not exclusively in the disciplinary communities of philosophy and the social sciences . . . selected from the available inventory . . . those (images of science) serving to connect the adjective scientific with public rather than private knowledge, with open rather than closed discourses, with universal rather than local standards of warrant, with democratic rather than aristocratic models of authority. (p. 444)

He continues:

> To these intellectuals it mattered enormously to be "objective," to look upon factual realities "without prejudice," to "actually test with experience" one's opinions, and to report "honestly" the results of one's inquiries. These men and women saw a world filled with "prejudice" and with efforts to "impose certain opinions by force." Against these evils one must affirm "free inquiry" and "open-mindedness" in order that our society might be organized realistically on the basis of the conditions life actually presents. If this was what scientists did, then the idea of imitating scientists, of following a "scientific approach," was a capital idea. (p. 444)

Scientific objectivity understood in this way presented a unique set of challenges to these psychoanalysts. Subjectivity was too intrinsic to psychoanalytic thinking to yield itself willingly to the campaign for this kind of objectivity. Kubie, Brenman, Gill, Shakow, and others, such as Else Frenkel-Brunswik, understood that they could not excise those subjective features of the psychoanalytic encounter without altering the very subject they were trying to study; they also recognized that reliance on the case study method inadvertently rendered psychoanalytic scientists virtually invulnerable to serious independent research challenge, a cornerstone of objective science.

The idea of using film to resolve this dilemma crystallized in a series of roundtable discussions at the American Orthopsychiatric Association meetings between 1946 and 1948 (Brenman et al., 1947, 1948; Bronner et al., 1949). Kubie, Brenman, Gill, Carl Rogers, Margaret Mead, Paul Bergman, David Shakow, and others entertained different ways that film might allow researchers to approach objectivity through the subjective rather than to the exclusion of it. Shakow, who joined the conversation at the American Orthopsychiatry Association meeting in 1948, suggested that film offered researchers the opportunity to catch, suspend, and inscribe objectivity.[3] Once inscribed, he argued, the material would be less susceptible to the inevitably biased interpretations of therapist–researchers. To further enhance objectivity, Shakow suggested, the clinician being filmed and the clinician analyzing the film should not be the same person.[4] He also introduced the technique of the therapist dictating into a sound-recorder his thoughts about the session immediately on its completion to capture the subjective experiences of maneuvering through a therapeutic encounter. This situation would allow both the filmed therapists and the researchers to express their intrinsically subjective viewpoints without fearing that they were straying from the pursuit of objectivity.

Finally, Shakow was particularly keen to use film analyses as a vehicle through which more democratic processes might infiltrate the authoritarian culture of traditional psychoanalytic science. He urged the readers of *Psychoanalytic Quarterly*, for instance, that "we cannot continue to depend upon the gimlet eyes of the psychologist–genius or the sensitive strokes of the psychologist–artist to provide us with the relevant data. They must be made

---

[3] Shakow first encountered sound films at Worcester State Hospital (Carmichael, 1956), where, between 1935 and 1937, he built a film room "to permit the study of social situations which are too complex for adequate recording by other means, e.g., having a group of four or more patients in the room at once with opportunity for various group activities" ("Undated proposal entitled 'A project for the study of psychosis by means of sound cinema and sound records for instruction and experimental purposes.' David Shakow Papers, Box M1552, ff: Sound Movie Room—Worcester State Hospital—Teaching, Archives of the History of American Psychology). During these same years, he completed a course of psychoanalytic treatment (Shakow, 1940). By 1947, Shakow had planned to study psychoanalytic processes with film (transcript of interview with David Shakow, Bethesda, MD, July 30, 1975, p. 31).
[4] Margaret Mead was the first to propose the idea of separating the researcher from the clinician (Brenman et al., 1947, p. 227).

available to the ordinary scientific investigator" (Shakow, 1960, p. 96). To do so called for

> an unusual willingness to put one's basic tenets and practices under the searching and challenging gaze of colleagues who wear different-colored and different-powered spectacles. It calls, further, for a readiness to work together on the part of persons representing different points of view, points of view which have not in the past been notorious for bed-fellowship or even market-fellowship. (Bronner et al., 1949, p. 479)

Objectivity would then emerge as a kind of common denominator of the subjective experiences of members of the research community:

> The film and the accessory material made available by the therapist are studied independently by each of the investigators. Each makes an independent judgment according to a schema previously worked out jointly by the group, a schema which includes the important aspects presumably involved in the therapeutic procedure ... A group study session follows these independent study sessions. During this meeting, the film is run off again and group discussion, built up around the schema and the previous individual evaluation, takes place. The aim of these meetings is to achieve pooled judgments about the various aspects covered in the therapeutic session. (Bronner et al., 1949, p. 477)

For Shakow, a psychoanalytic film project conceived in this way was nothing short of a kind of scientific utopia:

> This day-by-day, persistent and detailed discussion, based on the examination of concrete data, by a group of persons having common goals but different backgrounds, should be one of the most effective methods for the development of a common rigorous language and the discovery of fundamental principles, as well as for the determination of effective techniques of therapy. In some ways it provides a kind of Utopia of psychological investigation. (Bronner et al., 1949, p. 477)

Pilot Studies at the University of Illinois at Chicago and at NIMH

The film project was an exercise in creating a) a specific set of environmental conditions most likely to produce a film unbiased by the influence of the film technology on the subjects (and presumably, therefore, an objective inscription) and b) a sociological framework for generating an "objective" evaluation of the film that played on the researchers' strengths in subjective interpretation. Every step in this process became an effort to establish new or rectify existing conditions as a way to calibrate the multi-faceted subjective instrument to the specific frequency out of which objectivity would emerge.[5]

---

[5] Shakow's memoranda underscore the impression that this project was an exercise in calibrating both human and machine. He wrote in 1954, for example, that

When left to its own devices, however, the psychoanalytic environment both inside and outside of the filming room was an unpredictable creature. Shakow struggled unsuccessfully to keep all of the technical and sociological conditions in proper balance, and he was constantly caught short by unanticipated consequences. The film study ultimately became a kind of Rorschach test on the grandest scale, encouraging into expression the most personal frameworks of meaning but burdened with the expectation that somehow these idiosyncratic frameworks could be inscribed, pooled, debated, quantified, and formulated into grand, objective statements about what happens in the course of psychoanalytic treatment.

The first set of pilot studies, conducted at the University of Illinois at Chicago between 1947 and 1955,[6] looked at the intrusion of the camera on the experience of patients and therapists (Sternberg, Chapman, & Shakow, 1958). Shakow built a room that approximated the comfort and aesthetics of a consulting room but also accommodated and concealed the sound and film machines (see Figure 5.1). He acquired décor from Marshall Fields ("equipped like a living room, rather than like an office, the furniture making it appropriate for individual interviews, group interviews, group therapy or group conferences"; Carmichael, 1956, p. 591) and high-quality cameras, film, lighting, sound equipment, and sound-proofing.[7] The ceiling of the room was made of "opaque plexiglass [sic] . . . covering fluorescent bulbs" necessary for proper lighting (Haggard, Hiken, & Isaacs, 1965, p. 173). One wall of the room contained "a floor-to-ceiling decorative panel that has parts which can be removed to provide a camera aperture, and there (were) two one-way-vision screens between the treatment room and the adjoining camera room for use in direct interviewing" (Carmichael, 1956, p. 591; see Figure 5.2). Three microphones were placed around the room, in sight of the therapist and patient. A "16 mm. camera . . . was modified to accommodate a

---

the requirements of the data-gathering aspects of this research are very stringent: . . . Lighting must be adequate for either color or black-and-white photography and yet not introduce unnatural conditions and special strain on persons being photographed . . . Background noise level must be so low that when subjects do not talk directly into microphone their conversation may still be recorded with high enough signal-to-noise level that listening may be carried on easily and without fatigue to investigators . . . Ambient temperature of the room must not be allowed to rise in spite of the heat coming from the necessary great amount of lighting. ("Memorandum from Chief," 1954)

[6]NIMH funded the project, entitled "Analysis of the Process of Psychoanalytic Psychotherapy," from 1953 to 1966. Members of the original research team included Shakow, Rae Shifrin Sternberg, Hugh T. Carmichael, Morris Sklansky, Leon Bernstein, Joel S. Handler, Reuben H. Segel, and Jean P. Chapman (Carmichael, 1956).

[7]David Shakow Papers, Box M1648.2: ff: Psychotherapy Project. Archives of the History of American Psychology. Purchase order no. 75561 from the University of Illinois, Psychiatry Room 7 South to Marshall Field Company, June 23, 1952. See also Letter from R. W. Barbour, Marshall Field Company to S. M. Stein, University of Illinois, January 11, 1952. Both documents in Box M1648.2: ff: Psychotherapy Project.

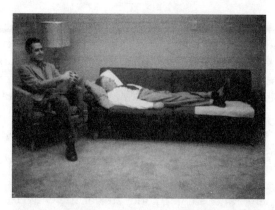

Figure 5.1 View of the inside of the psychotherapy film room, with David Shakow on the couch and unidentified researcher in the chair, circa 1952. Text on the back of the photograph reads: "Friday November 28. Polaroid #2 stop. Distance = 12–15 ft. Photo from inside of room at wall close to bottom opening." Archives of the History of American Psychology, University of Akron.

single 50-minute film run of 2,000 feet" (Carmichael, 1956, p. 591) in the adjoining viewing room.

After 8 years of pilot work (1948–1954), however, Shakow (1954) reported "many, many frustrations, delays and errors." For instance, because Shakow's group had difficulty finding volunteers to serve as therapists, two researchers had to serve as filmed therapists (Carmichael, 1956).[8] This condition compromised the requirement that the therapist and the re-searcher be different people. The filming situation also intruded unpleasantly on the therapists. One therapist commented "the patient actually was much less anxious than I was" (Sternberg et al., 1958, p. 198). Yet another, whose experience was reported in two publications, "began to dread the seemingly never-ending exposure of himself and his technique" (Sternberg et al., 1958, pp. 197–198) "when he thought of the effort he would have to exert to maintain (an attitude of equanimity without undue strain or anxiety) throughout an indefinite series of recordings" (Carmichael, 1956, p. 592).

In 1954, in the midst of this work, Shakow left Illinois to head the new Intramural Laboratory of Psychology at NIMH, where a spirit of method-ological permissiveness and pioneering experimentation was prominent. Seymour S. Kety, associate director of intramural research in 1951, promised that his philosophy as director (and as Shakow's boss) "(would) be to avoid directed research, allowing the program to develop as freely as possible, at the same time developing methods for stimulating research, particularly of

---

[8] Carmichael, president of the Chicago Psychoanalytic Institute (1953–1954), treated one of the patients. Carmichael and Sternberg used Carmichael's process notes as data (Carmichael, 1956). (See also "Untitled notes," 1956).

Figure 5.2 Photograph of the viewing wall from inside of the psychotherapy film room, University of Illinois, circa 1952. Archives of the History of American Psychology, University of Akron.

an interdisciplinary nature" ("Minutes, meeting of September 21–22," 1951). In fact, Shakow was drawn to NIMH because of

> that most essential quality—the compound of freedom, long-term goals, and pioneering spirit. One certainly felt that he was a participant in a group endeavor which was breaking new ground rather than in an enterprise that was directed merely at solving immediate practical problems. (Shakow, 1968, p. 88)

In this new, exciting, and pioneering environment, Shakow continued the film project,[9] eventually constructing a filming room identical to the one at Illinois ("Memorandum from Chief," 1954).[10] Shakow organized a new group in Bethesda that included Allen Dittmann, a clinical psychologist from the University of Michigan; Robert Cohen, Director of Clinical Research in the intramural program; Mabel Blake Cohen of Chestnut Lodge; and Morris Parloff. Shakow's new Bethesda group analyzed the Illinois films themselves as well as a film by Carl Rogers[11] while waiting for the completion of the construction of the film room (1954–1957). Their independent analysis of the Illinois films rectified the "contamination which (had been) involved in (the) acquaintance" (Shakow, 1954) of the researchers and therapists of the Illinois group. Also, as Shakow had predicted, their "objective" responses were quite idiosyncratic. One researcher noticed "how Carmichael pulled for transference reactions, increasing the anxiety, while Rogers pulled for empathy, decreasing anxiety" ("Undated and unsigned note," 1956). Dittmann was drawn to the linguistic aspects of the data (Dittmann & Wynne, 1961).[12] Mabel Blake Cohen and Robert Cohen noticed their "counter-transferential" reactions to the therapist and his interventions, confessing that "it took us months to achieve a modest degree of objectivity" (Cohen & Cohen, 1961, p. 49). Parloff and Dittmann consulted with psychoanalysts and anthropologists such as Else Frenkel-Brunswik, Lawrence Kubie ("Untitled and unsigned memorandum," 1956), and Ray Birdwhistell (Parloff, 1959) about films, naturalistic observation, linguistics, and kinesics.

Despite their differences, however, they agreed that creating a set of conditions where objectivity would emerge was difficult. Anonymous judges tended to identify with the patients and to be critical of the therapists. They also agreed that the filming situation did not approximate very closely the conditions of a typical analysis. Parloff reported in 1959 that

> The investigators' sights were repeatedly lowered until finally it was agreed that the treatment situation could be viewed as providing an opportunity for investigating the development of a fairly prolonged, intense, and intimate relationship between two persons. No assumption would be made that this therapy was typical of the psychoanalytic process nor could conclusions be generalized beyond the two partici-

---

[9] The film project at Illinois continued for 2 more years with Shakow as consultant. In 1956, Ernest Haggard and Kenneth Isaacs took over the Illinois project. They continued studying the verbal content of therapy sessions through films until the completion of the grant in 1966 (Haggard et al., 1965).

[10] The cost of the room construction was estimated at between $15,000 and $20,000.

[11] The film may have been "Psychotherapy in Process: The Case of Miss Mun" from State College Psychological Cinema.

[12] Dittmann and Lyman Wynne concluded that linguistics was not useful for psychotherapy research (Parloff, June 1959).

pants. During this period considerable time was devoted to considering recurrent arguments regarding the difficulties if not impossibility of conducting research in this area. (Parloff, 1959, p. 2)

"Shakow's Folly" at NIMH

In 1957, as construction of the film room neared completion, Shakow selected Paul Bergman, a psychoanalyst formerly of the Menninger Clinic, to serve as the analyst to be filmed.[13] Bergman chose Edith Weigert of Chestnut Lodge (Bergman, 1957) as his supervisory analyst. The treatment would be a "traditional" psychoanalysis, with "four or five sessions per week, the patient lying on the couch, and the therapist seated out of the patient's view" (Haggard et al., 1965, p. 174). The therapist would dictate his "subjective ideas about the material and possibly some subjective reactions to the situation and to the events of the therapy" immediately after each session (Bergman, 1957). Mabel Blake Cohen selected as the patient a woman of middle age, named Anna, who was experiencing marital difficulties and anxieties. Anna underwent an intake interview with both Bergman and Mabel Blake Cohen, completed a battery of psychological tests, and had a physical examination (Cohen & Cohen, 1961). Anna's filmed psychoanalysis began sometime in late 1958 or early 1959.

As the first few hours of film came in, Shakow encouraged his researchers to conduct independent unstructured, global analyses of the film, expecting that these initial reactions would provide fodder for later discussions (NIMH, 1957, p. 51).[14] When the group reconvened, however, the scientists had difficulty integrating their individual analyses sufficiently to complete an instrument for objective evaluation of the content of the films. Dittmann suggested building an index to help research assistants document for later use what transpired in each session.[15] Items would have a "low level of inference so that a technician with no special experience in psychotherapy could find them in typescripts"[16] (Dittmann, 1959; Dittmann, Stein, & Shakow, 1966). However, the initial items were not sufficiently operationalized to permit consistent coding, so they developed what became an

---

[13] Bergman had participated with Shakow in the 1948 American Orthopsychiatry Association panel on psychotherapy research. Bergman's specific contribution to the panel was an articulation of those characteristics he believed to be most necessary for a good therapist under filmed conditions (Bronner et al., 1949).
[14] Merton Gill and Timothy Leary's detailed system for evaluating the content of psychotherapy sessions inspired this protocol.
[15] The source for this is a revised transcript of an interview with Morris Parloff by Ingrid Farreras, National Institutes of Health History Office, April 18, 2002.
[16] By 1960, Dittmann had completed indexes for the 60 hr of film. See M. B. Parloff, "Dynamic Analysis: Session TB15R1A". Undated document, Box M1373, Folder: Dynamic Analysis and Psychotherapy. Archives of the History of American Psychology.

unsuccessful supplemental coding system known as *Dynamic Analysis*. Interest turned briefly to a "microscopic" analysis of the dynamics of the relationship,[17] but they had no adequate list of defenses with which to standardize their observations. They tried unsuccessfully to generate their own list of defenses. By 1959, however, Parloff noted that

> not a single instrument of the many undertaken was actually completed. Not a single group research has been completed. Not a single group publication has been prepared. In fact, not a single film of psychoanalytic sessions which is to be the subject of our research has been viewed by the group. (Parloff, 1959, p. 6)

Shakow continued to hope a coding scheme would emerge out of the give-and-take of the group process. In 1959, he asked each of the researchers to become specialists in one aspect of the material. His specific area would be "defining the process of shift of material from peripheral to focal attention, how the ucs/pcs becomes conscious" by experimenting with "active and passive analytical approaches to the data" (Shakow, 1959). Robert Cohen and Mabel Blake Cohen conducted a naturalistic study of 10 hours of film (Cohen & Cohen, 1961; see also Cohen, 1959). Dittmann continued to index and to study the relationship between facial and body language (Dittmann, 1962; Dittmann, Parloff, & Boomer, 1965). Parloff, growing frustrated with the efforts to "prove" psychoanalytic theory, developed hypotheses about the relationship between kinesthetic, facial, and vocal cues and emotional experience.[18]

The project encountered even more problems over the next several years. The sheer number of films was becoming burdensome. In 1959, it had taken them over 4 months to analyze only a fragment of the first hour. By May 1961, the group had collected films from approximately 500 psychoanalytic psychotherapy sessions,[19] and when Anna finally ended treatment in 1963, they had collected more than 600 sessions. Furthermore, observers continued to identify with the characters in the film, making it difficult to "give objective reports of the events recorded in the film" (Shakow, 1964, p. 130). In 1963, Dittmann traveled to the Agostino Gemelli Institute of the Experimental Study of the Social Problems of Visual Information in Milan to develop methods "which can reduce the identifications so

---

[17] This work resulted in "The Form, Motivation, Implications for Relationship" sheets (Dittmann, 1959).

[18] He recalls that his interest in the relationship between these cues and emotional experiences began when he noticed that analyst–consultants, hired to review some of the filmed sessions, would look at the screen and then bow their heads. When asked what was wrong, they would reply, "In analysis I never look at the patient, so who needs a film? I listen." Analysts did not seek visual cues, Parloff suggests, because they sat behind the patient during analysis (M. Parloff, personal communication, September 15, 2002).

[19] See Parloff's "Summary Report: Therapist's Contribution (A)," p. 257 (Parloff, 1962).

that transference, resistance, interpretation, and the like, which depend on global judgment by experienced psychotherapists, can be studied" (Shakow, 1964, pp. 130–131).

The pressure of being the lone therapist also exacted a toll on Bergman. Parloff believes that Bergman began modifying his technique to produce a successful treatment. Although Bergman believed he had stayed close to the psychoanalytic model (Bergman, 1966, pp. 45–46), the researchers came to the "shocking and depressing" conclusion that Bergman was not actually doing psychoanalysis at all:

> This study, like all such studies of that day, was premised on the belief that psychoanalysis worked with appropriately selected patients when performed by well-trained analysts. When it became apparent to Paul that his lone patient was not showing the nature and quality of therapeutic benefits expected from well-conducted psychoanalyses, he became rather desperate. As time began to run out, he felt he needed quickly to effect the necessary personality changes. He resorted to using some anomalous interventions that were either no longer accepted as *echt* psychoanalytic or had never been considered characteristic of psychoanalysis. (M. Parloff, personal communication, July 4, 2002)

Bergman's modifications, according to Parloff, thwarted their hopes that they could convince psychoanalysts that the presence of the camera did not interfere with the analytic process. They also called into question whether psychoanalytic treatment as analysts described it publicly was actually commensurate with what happened in the privacy of the therapy room.

Anna, too, introduced an unexpected obstacle to the completion of the study. She ended treatment prematurely, some time in 1963, "after four years, three months, and 632 filmed interviews" (Bergman, 1966, p. 47). As a condition of participation she had been given authority over any publications that might come out of the research. In 1961, Cohen and Cohen published a fragment of an analysis of the first 10 hours (Cohen & Cohen, 1961), and in 1964, Bergman hoped that reports of her treatment would be forthcoming (Bergman, 1966). However, when Anna ended treatment she refused to authorize publication of any further articles about her case. Robert Cohen believed that "the detailed report of even a less-than-perfect psychoanalysis would have had merit . . . (but) we could not get out of the box into which we put ourselves" (R. A. Cohen, personal communication, July 10, 2002).

By the end of Anna's treatment in 1964, the project had "drifted, necessarily . . . in the direction of studies on communication" (Dittmann et al., 1966; Shakow, 1966). Other film projects inspired in part by this study used fragments of Anna's analysis, but they were less ambitious in scope (Haggard et al., 1965; Luborsky, 1964). Some researchers consulted about the technicalities of recording psychotherapy (Dittmann et al., 1966).

In the meantime, the films were put into storage at NIMH and, in the absence of any archive willing to accept them, eventually destroyed. In 1975, Shakow concluded as follows:

> This was a failure, very expensive failure. But it illuminated some things about the problem and it is a very difficult problem and you have to start it early in life and just continue it and I was too old . . . the one thing I got out of it was the complexity of the process, that little nuances may make the difference between one and a thousand.[20]

"Shakow's folly," as it was known euphemistically among his colleagues, was a project uniquely suited to its time. It reflected the unparalleled generosity of Congress in supporting creative basic research and the unparalleled optimism of some psychoanalysts that subjectivity, objectivity, and democracy could work hand in hand in the creation of a new, "objective," psychotherapeutic science. Not all NIMH scientists were equally aware of the political obligations to which their unlimited scientific freedoms had been pinned, but Shakow, for his part, was explicit in his political convictions:

> I see a solution, in a way, to what Freud recognized as the battle between the self and the culture . . . Here is one opportunity for the culture (Government) to show that it is a community which recognizes the importance of individuality, and, at least in this area, is ready to give individuality an avenue for expression. Unless some such view is included in our aspirations for Government, it is difficult to see how Government activities will avoid being doomed to mediocrity, when excellence should be its goal. (Shakow, 1968, pp. 90–91)

The naturalistic, individualistic, and psychosocial approach to objectivity at the heart of the psychoanalytic film project was a celebration of these same virtues, and, at least in the 1950s, found a receptive and sympathetic audience in Congress.

EPISODE 2: ECUMENICISM, EXPERIMENTALISM, AND THE NIMH PSYCHOTHERAPIST–ADMINISTRATOR

During the years that Shakow was working on the film project at NIMH, new controversies about the most appropriate scientific method with which to study psychotherapy objectively emerged, centered on the question of whether the subjective judgment of the clinician (otherwise known as *clinical inference*) had greater predictive power than statistically controlled designs. Hans Eysenck galvanized researchers in 1952 when he

---

[20]The source for this is a transcript of an interview with David Shakow, Bethesda, Maryland, July 30, 1975.

took a hard line against subjectively based case study and naturalistic methods and challenged them to produce quantitative evidence that psychotherapy was more effective than no treatment at all (Eysenck, 1952). By the late 1950s, the terms of an epistemological debate had been set: clinical versus statistical prediction, also known as *naturalism* versus *experimentalism* (Holt, 1958; Meehl, 1954). Naturalists preferred to study psychotherapy processes; experimentalists preferred to study psychotherapy outcomes. Thus the debate also hinged on arguments for the relative merits of basic research versus applied research.

Three NIMH-Funded National Conferences on Psychotherapy Research

The role of NIMH in these epistemological debates within the emergent science of psychotherapy research, at least at first, was as neutral moderator and as midwife to the birth of a consciousness of community. In 1956, as Shakow's group prepared for filming in Bethesda, Morris Parloff and Eli Rubinstein, of the NIMH training division, proposed bringing together for the first time leading psychotherapy researchers for a national conference on the "Objective Evaluation of Psychotherapy." Parloff and Rubinstein were also members of the research committee of Division 12 of the American Psychological Association (Clinical Psychology) and through this organization applied for and received NIMH extramural funding for a 3-day invitation-only research conference in 1958. The implicit hope was to find one "simple, reassuring, authoritative principle that clearly supports one approach and demonstrates the invalidity of others" (Parloff & Rubinstein, 1959, p. 292). Parloff and Rubinstein moderated the conference. Two more invitation-only NIMH-funded conferences followed (in 1961 and 1966).

These three national psychotherapy conferences were the product of the same spirit of creative freedom within NIMH that had fertilized Shakow's film project. The emphasis of the extramural program (known in the early years as the *Research Grants and Fellowship Branch*) in the 1950s was "basic research"—"research into the 'process' and 'mechanisms' of action, whether psychological, social or biological, as the quickest path to an understanding of etiology and thence to the development of therapeutic and preventive measures" (Brand & Sapir, 1964, p. 29). Congress was both generous and permissive in its allocation of resources, entrusting study sections composed of leading scientists and the National Advisory Mental Health Council with the power to judge the worthiness of the methodology and content of grant proposals. James A. Shannon, director of the National Institutes of Health, fostered an environment of creative freedom: "There must be room in American science for more environments which foster creativity by extending a protective cloak over the few with real imagination, some of whom, hopefully, will become creative."[21] As early as 1951, the National Advisory Mental Health Council was concerned in particular about stimulating work on methodology in fields of "special public concern" (Brand & Sapir, 1964, p. 30). The National Advisory Mental Health Council sponsored working conferences on interdisciplinary research[22] ("Report of Subcommittee on Methodology in Mental Health Research," 1951). The American Psychiatric Association held a 3-day working conference in 1953 on methods in psychiatric research (Wilson, 1993). The American Psychological Association-sponsored psychotherapy conferences followed in this tradition.

The first conference, in 1958, was designed as a meeting place at which adherents to different traditions might seek common ground. Participants in the first conference agreed that the basic data of psychotherapy were observations made of the therapeutic process. They continued to disagree over the epistemological criteria that should be used in making meaning out of those data. They divided naturally into experimentalist and naturalist camps, loosely demarcated by those who were and were not psychoanalytically inclined. The naturalists invoked the "Heisenberg principle of indeterminacy . . . in support of the notion that by the very act of measurement one distorts the data one is seeking to measure" (Rubinstein & Parloff, 1959, p. 284). Other participants, in contrast, "took sharp issue with the seemingly popular practice of assuming that the Heisenberg principle as formulated regarding quantum theory is appropriate for describing the approximate character of psychological knowledge" (Rubinstein & Parloff, 1959, p. 284). Ultimately, the participants concluded, "each investigator must fall back on his own values and tastes" (Parloff & Rubinstein 1959, p. 292).

Despite their apparent failure to reach common scientific ground, however, conference participants almost uniformly welcomed the opportunity to discuss their ideas with other researchers. Robert Wallerstein, for instance, recalled that

> one of the fruits of the first Conference, at least as manifest in its spirit, seemed to be a breaking down of the barriers of isolation between the various workers. People at least became aware in a much fuller and more precise way of the kind of work done by others and found

---

[21] This is an excerpt from an address given at Harvard University, July 21, 1959, quoted in a revised transcript of an interview of Morris Parloff by Ingrid Farreras, April 18, 2002, p. 16.
[22] The conferences were held in conjunction with the American Psychological Association, the American Sociological Society, the American Anthropological Association, the American Orthopsychiatric Association, the American Psychiatric Association, and the American Neurological Association. See also discussion of "APA Committee on Therapy" in "Mental Health Study Section Minutes, January, 1952". National Archives and Research Administration, RG511, MHSS Committee Reports, 1947–57, Box 4, ff: Study Section Meeting, January 11–12, 1952.

themselves with what seemed to be a new respect for the appropriateness of the problems that others were tackling and the ways they seemed to be going about it. Whether anybody was inclined to alter very much what he himself was doing on the basis of this wider knowledge of what was going on in the entire field, seemed more problematic. (Wallerstein, 1961 p. 1)

Parloff and Rubinstein (1959) similarly observed that although

considerable interest was expressed in determining how individuals of intelligence, experience and integrity arrived at and maintained their contrary views . . . Investigators were able to listen to each other and to experience to a surprising degree the development of mutual respect. Under conditions of such respect communication was remarkably enhanced. (p. 293)

This new spirit of cooperation between groups of different persuasions was so welcome that

many participants expressed the hope that it might be possible to meet again, to exchange ideas, to follow up research projects which were then getting under way, and to encourage critical examination of the major theoretical, methodological, and practical issues facing the investigator in this difficult field. (Strupp & Luborsky, 1962, p. v)

Consequently, a second NIMH-funded conference, larger than the first in numbers of invited participants but narrower and less ambitious in scope, took place in Chapel Hill, North Carolina, in May 1961. The second conference organizers, Hans Strupp and Lester Luborsky, organized the conference around methodological problems associated with studying the subjective objectively, or of "bridging the gap between dynamic events observed in the clinical situation and their assessment and measurement by objective means").[23] The results of this conference were similar to those of the first: While "everyone at [the second] conference seemed to be going his own way," Luborsky and Strupp observed, they did not go "so blithely as was the case three years [before] . . . One response at the conference was that we should congratulate ourselves on our diversity" (Luborsky & Strupp, 1962, pp. 308–309).

By the third conference, in 1966, the field had witnessed a "massive proliferation of therapy forms, techniques, applications, part-theories, research efforts, duplication of published ideas, and increased research design sophistication" (Wolfe, 1974, p. 8). Conference organizers had to comb through grant files in the NIMH office merely to be able to "represent

---

[23] This is from an undated, unsigned announcement of the Second Conference on Research in Psychotherapy.

the field in its current diversity" (Wolfe, 1974, p. 8). Psychoanalysis and naturalistic approaches, they discovered, were receiving fewer grants, while "behavior therapy," "therapist–patient interactions" and "psychopharmacology in relation to psychotherapy" (notably LSD) were receiving proportionately more ("Proposal for 'Third Research in Psychotherapy Conference', n.d."; Shlien, 1968). Consequently, the aim of the third working conference was to introduce these new approaches to the community.

With the financial strain of the Vietnam war, the federal government withdrew support for working conferences (Shlien, 1966), ending the tradition of American Psychological Association-initiated, NIMH-funded psychotherapy research conferences. Still, these conferences helped to create a climate of "productive tension" similar to what Peter Galison has described within the field of physics research. In physics, Galison (1998) suggests, "different traditions of theorizing, experimenting, instrument making, and engineering meet—even transform one another—but for all that, they do not lose their separate identities and practices" (p. 782). After 1966, researchers from the broader community emulated the NIMH working conference model by organizing open meetings prior to annual conventions of the American Psychological Association. In 1970, a group of them established the Society for Psychotherapy Research (Strupp & Howard, 1992), the first national organization to serve the entire field of psychotherapy researchers.

Experimentalism, Behavior Therapy, and the NIMH Psychotherapist–Administrator

In 1961, the House Government Operations Committee, known as the *Fountain Committee*, began scrutinizing the administration of congressionally funded biomedical research programs. "By the late 1960s", Harry Marks (1997) observed, "both laboratory and investigator-initiated research—the centerpiece of NIH research policy in the postwar era—were under increasing congressional attack . . . (with) demands to see more practical applications from NIH" (pp. 191–192). NIMH withdrew much of its administrative support for the intramural research program, and by 1972, psychotherapy research within it had essentially disappeared.

At the same time, the extramural research program was growing rapidly, and a new role for psychotherapists within it, what I call the *psychotherapist–administrator*, was established. In 1966, the extramural research program was reorganized to give greater administrative support to clinical outcome research. The new Clinical Research Branch was formed, with a section for psychotherapy research. The psychotherapist–administrator emerged as a new profession with the twin aims of guiding researchers toward quantitative methods consistent with Congressional interest in "practical applications" on the one hand, and of advocating for the growing numbers of researchers in their efforts to secure NIMH funds, on the other. These psychotherapist–administrators were clinical psychologists and psychiatrists with laboratory experience. A. Hussein (Sein) Tuma, a clinical psychologist, became the first acting chief of the new psychotherapy section. Tuma's job was not to do research but to keep his finger on the pulse of the field and to stimulate research

Tuma attended the third psychotherapy conference in 1966 as the first official NIMH observer, and in this position he encouraged researchers Allen Bergin and Hans Strupp to consider developing an NIMH-funded, collaborative, multisite RCT of psychotherapy outcomes. This project would create a unifying set of variables with which outcome data from different schools of psychotherapy might be compared. Bergin and Strupp argued that it would first be necessary to determine if members of the research community would be willing to support a multisite RCT. Between 1966 and 1972, Bergin and Strupp, with a grant from NIMH, conducted the most extensive survey of the psychotherapy research literature to date, followed by the most extensive series of site visits and interviews with leading researchers. They found that although the spirit of community continued to be strong, the desire for collaboration was not, and they recommended that the time was not ripe for such an undertaking (Bergin & Strupp, 1972).

In these same years, Tuma and his staff convened workshops with leading researchers to lay out the problems inherent in using the tools of experimental science to study the effectiveness of psychotherapy (Fiske et al., 1970, p. 727). The proceedings of a 1969 NIMH workshop on experimental methods in psychotherapy research were published simultaneously in the journals *American Psychologist* and *Archives of General Psychiatry* (to reach audiences of both psychologists and psychiatrists; Fiske et al., 1970). In 1970, Irene Waskow (Elkin), a postdoctoral Fellow in Shakow's laboratory who had moved to the extramural program, initiated the collaborative "Outcome Measures Project" to respond to the "need for a standard battery of instruments to be used in psychotherapy outcome research" that had been "voiced by researchers in the field for a number of years" (Waskow & Parloff, 1975, p. 3). Elkin invited Parloff, who joined the extramural program in 1972 and had been a participant in the "Core Battery Selection Conference," to coedit *Psychotherapy Change Measures* (I. Elkin, personal communication, April 4, 2003). In 1971, Tuma convened a workshop on the current and future status of behavior modification therapy.

Psychotherapy process researchers were concerned that these winds of change at NIMH were not in their favor. Back in 1965, Edward Bordin, a psychotherapy–researcher at the University of Michigan, confided to

Shakow that the tide was turning away from psychoanalytic research at NIMH because of a new "climate insisting on practical applications"[24] (Bordin, 1965). Leo Madow, a psychoanalytic psychiatrist at Temple University, remembered that

> we couldn't develop grants that satisfied the . . . psychologists and social workers who were running grant departments at NIMH. I went down to Washington (and) I got nowhere because we couldn't formulate psychoanalytic research in a way that was "one, two, three, four, five." Psychoanalysis is not that way. (L. Madow, personal communication, June 13, 1996)

In contrast, behavior therapy, a relative newcomer in the field of psychotherapy systems, was much better suited to this increasingly applied and quantitative climate at NIMH. Behavior therapy emerged in the mid-1960s as a loose collection of Skinnerian conditioning and behavior modification principles, Eysenck's work with learning theory, and Joseph Wolpe's reciprocal inhibition (Fishman & Franks, 1992). Behavior therapy was predicated on the idea that only observable behavior had clinical and scientific value. Extramural review committees increasingly funded applications from behavior therapists over those from other schools. Between 1957 and 1961, behavior therapies accounted for 8% of all NIMH psychotherapy research support (a total of 5 grants). By 1971, behavior therapy accounted for 43% of all psychotherapy research funding (58 grants), for almost $8 million. Only a year later, behavior therapy projects accounted for 55% of the total budget, and by 1984, 75% of the budget was allocated to behavior therapy projects. NIMH-funded psychoanalytic projects, in contrast, declined precipitously. Between 1957 and 1961, psychoanalytic studies accounted for 11% (7 grants) of all research funds; by 1971, psychoanalysis had dropped to 6% of all research funds (10 grants), for $1.1 million (Wolfe, 1974).

Nonetheless, these new extramural psychotherapist–administrators—Marty Katz (chief of the Clinical Research Branch), Sein Tuma (assistant chief of the Clinical Research Branch), Morris Parloff (chief of the Psychotherapy and Behavioral Interventions Section [PBIS]), Irene Waskow (research psychologist in the PBIS), and Barry Wolfe (psychologist in the PBIS)—played a delicate balancing game. They gently guided both naturalist and experimentalist researchers in search of funding toward methodological and epistemological compromise. As an example, Parloff, who became chief of the section on psychotherapy in 1972, decided to rename it the *Psychotherapy and Behavioral Interventions* Section. Parloff's decision to rename the

---

[24] Irene Elkin notes that Bordin as well as researchers from a variety of orientations later participated in the "Core Battery Selection Conference" that was part of the NIMH-sponsored Outcome Measures Project (I. Elkin, personal communication, April 4, 2003).

section was in response to the "growing numbers of behavior therapists who were genuinely and bitterly offended at having had their scientifically based Behavior Therapy hidden beneath the fanciful locution, Psychotherapy" (personal communication from M. Parloff to K. Moras, March 20, 2001). This "unhyphenated Germanic solution," as Parloff would later call it, was a cumbersome yet practical solution through which these two epistemologies were able to coexist within the administrative structure of NIMH. Psychoanalytic and process researchers such as Bordin responded to these changes with mixed reviews. Some struggled to adjust their research methods and models (and their theories) to the increasingly quantitative bent of the institute, whereas others chose to adhere strictly to the subjectivist principles of their original naturalist approach.

EPISODE 3: NATIONAL HEALTH INSURANCE, CONSUMERISM, AND THE RANDOMIZED CONTROLLED TRIAL

President Carter, in his drive to create a National Health Insurance program, almost singlehandedly completed the transformation of government mental health policy from the pursuit of basic science to the pursuit of applied science. Under the new economic conditions of a proposed National Health Insurance program, Congress began to hold psychotherapy researchers accountable for their failure to answer, to its satisfaction, practical and quantifiable questions of whether psychotherapy worked and with whom. Parloff, chief of the PBIS during the Carter years, alerted readers of *American Psychologist* that

> From time to time, psychotherapy researchers have complained that their findings have not impacted sufficiently on the practitioner or on the policymaker. We have carped that our voices have not been heard in high councils and that our wisdom has gone unrecognized and unrequited by government decision makers. I regret to inform you that those idyllic days are now gone. We can no longer be confident that our papers will be read only by fellow researchers. Policymakers are reading our reports, and the clinicians are listening. (Parloff, 1979, p. 296)

Gerald Klerman, director of ADAMHA, the parent body of NIMH in the 1970s, warned that psychotherapy was one of a number of health care fields where "the pace by which the invisible hand of the scientific marketplace generates progress has not been sufficient to meet public health needs" (Asher, 1980a). Psychotherapy researchers hoping to win NIMH funding would need to abandon the old worldview of the pioneer and adopt the new worldview of the marketplace.

Two significant shifts in biomedical research between the mid-1960s and 1980 provided the terms with which Congress and psychotherapist-administrators at NIMH negotiated a scientific response to the new consumerist demands: a growing consensus that the randomized controlled (or clinical) trial (RCT) was most appropriate for studying the efficacy and safety of medical treatments and the third revision of *DSM*, which resulted in *DSM–III*. The decision of the Food and Drug Administration in 1962 to use RCTs to determine the efficacy and safety of drugs led to a general consensus in the biomedical world that the RCT was the most appropriate method for a new health care marketplace. A number of biomedical fields experienced epistemological convulsions similar to those experienced in psychotherapy research as a result of governmental pressure to adopt the RCT. David Jones has shown how cardiac surgeons heatedly debated in the 1970s the relative utility of the subjective power of visual technology or the statistical power of RCTs in understanding the behavior of coronary artery disease. Surgeons eager to adopt the RCT used the rhetoric that "since researchers and regulators, particularly the Food and Drug Administration, demanded RCTs of medical therapy, they should also require them of surgical therapy" (Jones, 2000, p. 520). By the late 1970s, researchers from a broad spectrum of fields— including cardiology, oncology, and diabetes—conceded to the dominance of the RCT in a new consumerist and regulatory climate (Marks, 1997).

Psychotherapy research followed suit in the late 1970s, largely through the combined efforts of Congress, Klerman at ADAMHA, and extramural psychotherapist–administrators at NIMH. New and reorganized Congressional oversight bodies, such as the National Center for Health Care Technology and the Office of Technology Assessment, scrutinized psychotherapy research for evidence of proper experimental methodologies in an attempt to evaluate the efficacy and cost-effectiveness of mental health treatments. In 1980, the Office of Technology Assessment produced a cost-effectiveness analysis of psychotherapy specifically (U.S. Office of Technology Assessment, 1980). In addition, in 1980, Sens. Spark M. Matsunaga and Daniel K. Inouye introduced Bill S-3209, otherwise known as the *efficacy bill*, to give increasing emphasis on the efficacy of mental health treatments and reimbursement issues (DeLeon, VandenBos, & Cummings, 1983).[25] All of these initiatives made clear that the RCT was the preferred standard of objective measurement.

Forces converging in psychiatry between 1975 and 1979 during the revision of *DSM–II* (American Psychiatric Association, 1968) underscored Klerman's recommendation of the use of RCTs for psychotherapy research. The *DSM–III* task force, with funding from NIMH, used the third revision as an opportunity to assert the emergent biomedical model in place of the

---

[25] See Kiesler, Cummings, and VandenBos (1979) for a summary of the National Health Insurance initiative and the efficacy bill.

old psychosocial model in psychiatric research, including in psychotherapy research. The new *DSM–III* jettisoned the language of psychoanalysis, the emphasis on etiology and the environment, and the epistemology of clinical inference entirely, replacing them with descriptive categories emphasizing easily observable symptoms. These categories were designed to work in tandem with RCT protocols, providing the basis for homogeneous research samples (Wilson, 1993). A small but vocal minority of psychiatrists and psychologists refused to endorse the *DSM–III*; but those who championed it permanently established the RCT as the methodological norm for psychiatric research, making *DSM–III* a landmark in the transformation of psychiatry into a competitive biomedical research field (Moras, 2002; Wilson, 1993). Gerald Klerman quickly offered Congress a new set of NIMH funding policies that endorsed both of these complementary methodological solutions to the problem of efficacy and outcome research in psychotherapy. Indeed, Klerman was well-positioned to do so: He was an expert both in the psychopharmacology of depression (Klerman & Cole, 1967) and in the field of psychotherapy research, having developed a new school of psychotherapy for depression called *interpersonal therapy* (Klerman et al., 1974). He also was a consultant to the *DSM–III* task force (American Psychiatric Association, 1980).

These new policies at NIMH involved integrating the methodologies of psychopharmacology research and psychotherapy research under the more general category of "treatments." In 1977, Klerman made treatment assessment research (TAR) a high priority for ADAMHA (and NIMH). The objective of TAR was "the study of the efficacy, safety, and efficiency (cost-effectiveness) of individual techniques or combinations of techniques drawn from within or across treatment modalities"[26] ("Minutes, 119th meeting," 1979). Klerman unified psychotherapy and psychopharmacology research under the epistemology of the RCT and anchored them to new *DSM–III* diagnostic categories. NIMH site review committees soon were urging psychotherapy researchers not only to use RCTs but also to orient their research toward specific *DSM–III* categories. Barry Wolfe (personal communication, March 22, 2001) remembers that

> it soon became virtually impossible to get a grant in the area of psychotherapy, particularly outcome, unless it was focused on *DSM*. We actually had to tell certain grantees who weren't working on specific categories that they were going to have to shift their research . . . Marsha Linehan originally started her research of a 12-week behavior therapy which she called parasuicidal women. And these were folks who were rather frequently attempting in a mild way or at least making suicidal

---

[26] James Isbister, the director of ADAMHA in 1975, initiated TAR originally as a topic for a working group across the three institutes. Klerman expanded the scope of TAR after he became director in 1976.

gestures. She was trained behaviorally, had no interest in diagnostic categories. We went out there, this was again around 1980 or so, and said "Look, these folks look a lot like Borderline and so you'd probably be better off if you start calling them Borderlines."

These two changes—Congressional pressure for quantifiable measures of the efficacy of psychotherapy and the revision of the *DSM*—as well as Klerman's response to them left much less room than before for adherents of the subjectivist epistemology within psychotherapy research to compete for research funding from NIMH.

Initiating the Treatment of Depression Collaborative Research Program

Parloff, as chief of the PBIS, faced the challenge of implementing Klerman's new TAR initiative while continuing to represent psychotherapy researchers of both epistemological positions. Parloff's most immediate problem, however, was to secure sufficient institutional funding and administrative support to begin projects that would provide Klerman and Congress with some answers to their questions of efficacy and safety. First, Parloff requested that the NIMH provide greater institutional and financial support for TAR-based psychotherapy research ("Memorandum from Chief," 1979). Klerman agreed, and in 1980 the NIMH established the Psychosocial Treatments Research Branch, giving psychotherapy research a status equal to that of the newly renamed Psychopharmacology Treatments Research Branch (Asher, 1980b) and endowing it with a budget of $5.1 million (DeLeon et al., 1983). The elevation of the PBIS to the status of a branch was a boon for psychotherapy research, the only time in the history of the NIMH when psychotherapy research was recognized at branch level. Parloff also convinced Klerman to provide the PBIS an additional $1.3 million out of the administrator's budget (rather than from competing grant funds) for a PBIS-sponsored multisite, collaborative randomized study of the relative efficacies of two new forms of psychotherapy (cognitive–behavioral therapy and interpersonal therapy), a standard reference condition (imipramine plus clinical management), and a control condition, in the treatment of depression (Elkin, Parloff, Hadley, & Autry, 1985; Parloff & Elkin, 1992). This project became known as the Treatment of Depression Collaborative Research Program (TDCRP).[27]

The TDCRP revisited in a different political and scientific climate the proposal at the heart of Bergin and Strupp's work in the 1960s—that, among other things, a multisite, collaborative RCT might allow outcome results from different schools of psychotherapy to be compared quantitatively.

---

[27] For summaries of the history of the TDCRP, see Parloff and Elkin (1992) and Elkin (1994).

The TDCRP group hoped that such research would build a methodological bridge between different schools of therapy to facilitate studies on the efficacy of specific interventions in specific treatment modalities. The TDCRP research group also hoped their study would make it "possible to address, within the framework of such a large study, a number of the methodological and substantive problems facing the field of psychotherapy research" (Elkin et al., 1985, p. 306), including the question of whether the effects of therapy are due to nonspecific factors, such as the strength of the relationship, or to specific interventions within specific therapeutic systems. Between 1977 and 1980, Parloff and Irene Elkin, whom Parloff appointed in 1978 as TDCRP coordinator, began selecting the schools of psychotherapy to be investigated and choosing neutral sites in which to conduct treatments. They appointed an advisory group of researchers and developed a "standard protocol and an agreed-on set of standardized measures for describing and assessing the problem being treated, the characteristics of the treatment interventions and the nature, rapidity and durability of patient change" (Elkin et al., 1985, p. 305).

Each of the four selected treatments were packaged into treatment manuals "describing the theoretical underpinnings of the approach, the general strategies involved, the major techniques that could be used, and suggestions for dealing with specific problems" (Elkin et al., 1989, p. 972; "Memorandum from Chief," 1979, p. 5). These manuals created a standardized regimen for each treatment in the study "so that conclusions could be drawn regarding their specific effects" (Elkin et al., 1989, p. 972). All treatment conditions were designed to be 16 weeks long, all psychotherapy sessions were 50 minutes long, and all of the treatments were both videotaped and audiotaped (Elkin et al., 1985, p. 311). The manuals were published to assist other researchers and clinicians (Beck, Rush, Shaw, & Emery, 1979; Epstein & Fawcett, 1982; Fawcett & Epstein, 1980; Fawcett, Epstein, Fiesterr, Elkin, & Autry, 1987; Klerman, Weissman, Rounsaville, & Chevron, 1984). In addition, "the originators of each of the treatments," Irene Elkins remembers, "were instrumental in developing the treatment protocols and therapist training programs and in choosing instruments to reflect specific effects of their treatments" (I. Elkin, personal communication, April 4, 2003). Pilot studies commenced in 1980, and the outcome study began in 1982 (Elkin et al., 1985). The pilot/training phase and the outcome study received NIMH funding from 1980 to 1986, and the last follow-up evaluations were completed in 1986.[28]

---

[28] Parloff retired from NIMH in 1983 but continued as "special consultant" and member of the TDCRP advisory group until about 1988. Irene Elkin, as TDCRP coordinator, helped to establish and maintain therapist training programs at each of the training sites, oversaw quality control at each of the three research sites, collated all the TDCRP data (which were analyzed at the Veterans Affairs. Cooperative Studies Program, Perry Point, MD), and collaborated on TDCRP-related

Because the TDCRP design, or what was known as the *manualized treatment protocol*, was an RCT, it was also built on an instrumentalist understanding of the process of studying psychotherapy. For the standardization aspect of the design to work, researchers and therapists had to become instruments of a larger truth-determining machine represented by the statistical aggregate. It may be useful to compare Shakow's film project and the TDCRP as a way of illustrating how psychotherapeutic activities inscribed on film could be placed in the service of objectivist projects with two different epistemological foundations. The TDCRP researchers videotaped and audiotaped almost every therapy session in the study for analysis, just as Shakow's group had filmed every session. Furthermore, the TDCRP group and Shakow both invested the sound–movie recordings with the capacity to generate objective data records accurately and reliably. However, there were differences in their attribution of agency in making meaning out of the films. Shakow relied on his researchers to bring their own subjective opinions as psychotherapeutic experts to bear on the filmed material. The unique but subjective ability of the researchers to "discover" the meaning of that reality was the primary instrument of the research design. The TDCRP group, in contrast, used the videotapes in part as agents of quality control for the standardized component of their study. Trainers of the therapists periodically viewed the videotapes "to maintain 'quality control' and to prevent 'drifting' " (Elkin et al., 1985, p. 310). Whereas the goal of the therapist was to adhere as closely as possible to the manuals, the goal of the monitor was to "ensure that therapists continue(d) to carry out the treatments as defined in the manuals and training programs" (Elkin et al., 1985, p. 310).[29]

Adjusting the Field to the Manualized Treatment Protocol

During the design phase of the TDCRP (1977–1980), Parloff remained cautious, however, about the greater value of RCTs over other designs for psychotherapy research. In 1979, Parloff urged the director of NIMH not to restrict the kinds of questions that could be asked of psychotherapy under

---

publications with authors from collaborating research sites (M. Parloff, personal communication, February 27, 2003). Although the original NIMH-funded TDCRP research ended in 1986, researchers from a variety of orientations continue to analyze TDCRP data available on public use data tapes and on transcripts of sessions (I. Elkin, personal communication, April 23, 2002). For an updated list of publications based on TDCRP data, see "Publications Based on the NIMH Treatment of Depression Collaborative Research Program (TDCRP)—1983 to 2003" (May, 2003; personal collection, Dr. Irene Elkin).

[29]The researchers also used audiotapes to determine therapist adherence as well as to differentiate one approach from another. Hollon et al. (1984) developed the Collaborative Study Psychotherapy Rating Scale for this purpose, and it was applied to outcome study audiotapes by Hill (see Elkin et al., 1989, p. 973, for a discussion and citation of the Hollon et al. rating scale; I. Elkin, personal communication, April 4, 2003).

TAR ("Memorandum from Chief," 1979). He reminded the director that psychotherapy did not behave in the same way as pharmacotherapy and that TAR was not as suitable for questions about the processes and outcomes of psychotherapy as it was for pharmacotherapy. Parloff criticized the TAR model for downplaying the potential of nonspecific factors to influence the outcome of therapy:

> Each therapy appears to owe its potency to nonspecific components common to all psychotherapy approaches: instilling confidence and hope in the patient, offering a rational explanation for the bases of the disorder, outlining a plan, plausible to the patient, for its amelioration or cure, providing some success experiences, and developing a sense of mastery and competence. ("Minutes, 122nd meeting," 1980)

Parloff also argued that the results of RCTs could never generalize to psychotherapy as it existed in the real world: "There is little basis for believing that the general practice of 'psychotherapy' is consistent even within a group of practitioners claiming adherence to a particular school of therapy" ("Minutes, 119th meeting," 1979).[30] TAR required the voluntary cooperation of psychotherapy researchers, restricting the number of researchers (and therapeutic systems) willing to subject themselves and their systems to critical evaluation. The RCT protocol, although ostensibly objective, would result in so skewed a research sample, he concluded, that there would be nothing objective or generalizable at all about the results.

Finally, Parloff rejected the consumerist impulse driving policymakers. He argued against affixing "monetary weights" to "competing sets of humanistic values" and against being compelled to rank on a scale of effectiveness equally viable forms of treatment:

> Concerns with cost are typically of more direct interest to the policy maker than to the basic researcher. Indeed, the kinds of skills required in order to make wise decisions regarding the cost-effectiveness of treatment forms generally are different from those possessed by the psychotherapy researcher. Training may be required in economics and perhaps political science. Among the qualifications required for making what appear to be Solomon-like decisions is the capacity and willingness to confidently affix differential monetary weights to competing sets of humanistic values. The decisions are made all the more difficult by the fact that one is asked to differentiate among degrees of "good" rather than simply "good versus evil." ("Memorandum from Chief," 1979, p. 5)

---

[30] Klerman was sympathetic to Parloff's position, noting that "much of [Parloff's] own research has centered around the evaluation of therapies, both pharmacological and psychotherapeutic (and that) he is aware of the complexities and challenges of this area" ("Minutes, 122nd meeting," 1980; p. 13).

Parloff concluded that

> The NIMH should attempt to provide as sound a body of research evidence as it can muster regarding treatment efficacy; however, for the NIMH to undertake to offer direct advice to policy makers about which patient categories, problems, therapists, professions, or techniques should be judged eligible for third-party reimbursements and which should be excluded from such benefits seems to far exceed its research function. ("Memorandum from Chief," 1979, p. 15)

The TDCRP was designed to "model an application of a rigorous research methodology in the field of psychotherapy outcome research" (I. Elkin, personal communication, April 4, 2003) in the service of demonstrating that a collaborative, multisite RCT was possible for psychotherapy research. By the early to mid-1980s, however, the manualized treatment protocol became the benchmark for all NIMH psychotherapy research funding independent of whether the projects were collaborative, multisite, or both. According to Parloff (personal communication, March 21, 2001):

> The (TDCRP) study set the tone for the review committees because if a new grant came in and it didn't have a manual, the hell with it. If nobody was monitoring whether you really were delivering the therapy you said you were delivering . . . It became impossible. And it was an unintended consequence.

In 1984, Lester Luborsky and Robert DeRubeis documented a "small revolution in psychotherapy research style" with manualized treatment protocols (Moras, 2002, p. 536).

Barry Wolfe and Irene Elkin of the Psychosocial Treatments Research Branch began offering workshops for outcome researchers to help them develop manualized treatment protocols to win NIMH funding. As an example, Wolfe convened a 2-day workshop in 1982 specifically for psychoanalytically oriented researchers on "The Feasibility of Clinical Trials Research on Psychoanalytically Oriented Psychotherapy." The branch selected 10 researchers to "discuss the feasibility of designing a randomized clinical trial that would evaluate the efficacy of dynamic therapy in comparison with another, nondynamic form of therapy applied to a specific class of nonpsychotic disorders" ("Summary of Coolfont Conference," 1982, p. 2). Participants recognized that

> The randomized clinical trial is considered by many as the elite in research designs, that is, it is the only design which will allow a determination of the relative and differential effectiveness of two or more treatment modalities. While to many the randomized clinical trial is the ultimate design of verification, to others, primarily those who are identified with the psychodynamic framework, it is a premature or

perhaps inappropriate design for evaluating dynamic therapy. ("Summary of Coolfont Conference," 1982, p. 2).

By 1987, the workshop had facilitated the creation of two psychodynamic manualized protocols: (a) Hans Strupp's time-limited dynamic therapy and (b) Lester Luborsky's supportive–expressive therapy, both of which were piloted for the treatment of *DSM–III* major depressive disorders (Wolfe, 1988).

Psychotherapy outcome and psychoanalytic researchers who were not able or willing to adopt *DSM–III* categories and RCTs in their research had little chance of winning NIMH funding. Karla Moras (2002) remembers that "it became evident rather quickly to researchers that the NIMH grant review committees were, in essence, requiring grant applications for psychotherapy outcome studies to be focused on a specific disorder" (p. 530). The challenge for both outcome and process researchers seeking grants became even more complicated with a subsequent NIMH reorganization. In 1985, the Psychosocial Research Branch was "eliminated and psychotherapy research grants were redistributed among a number of (new) diagnosis-focused and developmentally-oriented branches," including the Affective and Anxiety Disorders Branch, the Schizophrenia Research Branch, the Child and Adolescent Disorders Branch, and the Mental Disorders of the Aging Branch (B. E. Wolfe, personal communication, September 29, 2002; see also Parloff, 1985, for a contemporary critique of the new reorganization). These new branch names inscribed even more deeply into the NIMH administration the authority of *DSM–III* categories and RCTs in psychiatric and psychotherapy research.

CONCLUSION

By the mid-1980s, it appeared that both scientific and political opinion had endorsed experimentalism to the exclusion of naturalism as the epistemological basis for psychotherapy research. However, NIMH funding policies and scientific opinion never swung fully away from naturalism. Even with the explosion in popularity of the manualized treatment protocol, both experimentalists and naturalists recognized the need for some kind of epistemological balance. This attempt at balance can be seen in the TDCRP design itself. The first report, in 1985, detailed a much broader latitude for researchers in the use of the psychotherapy films than strict adherence to RCT standards. Parloff and Elkin built into the TDCRP opportunities for both process and outcome researchers from a variety of traditions to analyze their data by making available videotapes of sessions (Elkin et al., 1985, pp. 313–314). They welcomed the opportunity to share questions, dilemmas, and resolutions with other researchers (Elkin et al., 1985, p. 315). From this standpoint, the TDCRP maintained a commitment to both subjective and statistical interpretations of objectivity.

NIMH administrators and psychotherapy researchers after 1980 also continued to endorse process research based on naturalistic designs (Russell & Orlinsky, 1996, p. 711). For instance, Wolfe and Elkin sponsored workshops and developed funding initiatives for psychologists who were interested in process research (Wolfe & Goldfried, 1988).[31] The emergence of the psychotherapy integration movement in the late 1980s reasserted the preference of many for encouraging a multiplicity of viewpoints (Goldfried & Newman, 1992); new constructivist approaches swung the pendulum even farther in the opposite direction by rejecting objectivity in favor of the subjective capacities of the therapist and client to cocreate therapeutic knowledge (Neimeyer & Mahoney, 1995).

Ruth E. Malone (1999) observed that "if health policy is regarded as having an implicitly moral dimension, policymakers must be regarded as agents who are involved in making or shaping moral choices on behalf of the larger society" (p. 19). In this chapter I have argued that leading NIMH administrators and psychotherapy researchers, working as allies in their independent quests for "objectivity," were instrumental in setting the agenda with which the larger community of psychotherapists determined the conceptual, linguistic—and, indeed, even moral—structures from which psychologists continue to ask questions about why psychotherapy works and with whom. It has examined how Congress and NIMH administrators needed psychotherapy researchers to fulfill a changing set of sociocultural missions over the last 50 years, and, as new political realities emerged, so did new mandates for asking "fundable" questions about psychotherapy. Psychotherapy researchers, in contrast, needed funds from NIMH to build a foundation, and later to provide further justification, for their field as a viable experimental science. The terms with which NIMH and psychotherapy researchers from both epistemological positions negotiated the funding of this emergent science became conceptual guideposts on the rather winding path toward objectivity.

REFERENCES

American Psychiatric Association. (1968). *Diagnostic and statistical manual of mental disorders* (2nd ed.). Washington, DC: Author.

---

[31] See, for example, Irene Elkin's summary of the NIMH-sponsored "Criteria for Evaluating Psychotherapy Process Research" workshop, June 1986; Agenda from the "State of the Art in Family Therapy Efficacy Research" conference, January 25–27, 1984; and Summary of "NIMH Workshop on Experiential Psychotherapy Research," June 2, 1984 (personal collection of Barry E. Wolfe).

American Psychiatric Association. (1980). *Diagnostic and statistical manual of mental disorders* (3rd ed.). Washington, DC: Author.

Asher, J. (1980a, April 4). Professions back psychotherapy panels. *ADAMHA News*, 1–5.

Asher, J. (1980b, June 13). DERP reorganization reflects treatment research priorities. *ADAMHA News*, 2.

Beck, A. T., Rush, A. J., Shaw, B. F., & Emery, G. (1979). *Cognitive therapy of depression*. New York: Guilford Press.

Bergin, A. E., & Strupp, H. H. (1972). *Changing frontiers in the science of psychotherapy*. Chicago: Aldine Atherton.

Bergman, P. (1957, November 4). Notes on meeting of Oct. 31, 1957. David Shakow Papers, Box ff. Psychotherapy project conferences. Archives of the History of American Psychology, University of Akron, Akron, OH.

Bergman, P. (1966). An experiment in filmed psychotherapy. In L. A. Gottschalk & A. H. Auerbach (Eds.), *Methods of research in psychotherapy* (pp. 35–49). New York: Appleton-Century-Crofts.

Bordin, E. (1965, April 1). Letter to D. Shakow. David Shakow Papers, M1329, Archives of the History of American Psychology, University of Akron, Akron, OH.

Brand, J. L., & Sapir, P. (1964). *An historical perspective on the National Institute of Mental Health*. Unpublished document.

Brenman, M., Kubie, L. S., Murray, H. A., Kris, E., Gill, M., Goldstein, K., et al. (1947). Problems in clinical research round table, 1946. *American Journal of Orthopsychiatry, 16*, 196.

Brenman, M., Kubie, L. S., Rogers, C. R., Gill, M., Anderson, H. H., Olson, W., et al. (1948). Research in psychotherapy round table, 1947. *American Journal of Orthopsychiatry, 18*, 92.

Bronner, A. F., Kubie, L. S., Hendrick, I., Shakow, D., Bergman, P., Brosin, H. W., & Bibring, E. (1949). The objective evaluation of psychotherapy round table, 1948. *American Journal of Orthopsychiatry, 19*, 463–491.

Carmichael, H. T. (1956). Sound film recording of psychoanalytic therapy: A therapist's experiences and reactions. *Journal of the Iowa State Medical Society, 46*, 590–595.

Cohen, R. A. (1959). Psychotherapy Research Project. David Shakow Papers, M1373, ff. Psychoanalytic Papers—Miscellaneous Archives of the History of American Psychology, University of Akron, Akron, OH.

Cohen, R. A., & Cohen, M. B. (1961). Research in psychotherapy: A preliminary report. *Psychiatry, 24*([Suppl. 2]), 46–61.

DeLeon, P. H., VandenBos, G. R., & Cummings, N. A. (1983). Psychotherapy— Is it safe, effective, and appropriate? *American Psychologist, 38*, 907–911.

Dittmann, A. (1959). Project history, Dittmann version. David Shakow Papers, M1373, Archives of the History of American Psychology, University of Akron, Akron, OH.

Dittmann, A. T. (1962). The relationship between body movements and moods in interviews. *Journal of Consulting Psychology, 26,* 480.

Dittmann, A. T., Parloff, M. B., & Boomer, D. S. (1965). Facial and body expression: A study of receptivity of emotional cues. *Psychiatry, 28,* 239–244.

Dittmann, A. T., Stein, S. N., & Shakow, D. (1966). Sound motion picture facilities for research in communication. In L. A. Gottschalk & A. Auerbach (Eds.), *Methods of research in psychotherapy* (pp. 25–33). New York: Appleton-Century-Crofts.

Dittmann, A. T., & Wynne, L. C. (1961). Linguistic techniques and the analysis of emotionality in interviews. *Journal of Abnormal and Social Psychology, 63,* 201–204.

Elkin, I. (1994). The NIMH Treatment of Depression Collaborative Research Program: Where we began and where we are. In A. E. Bergin & S. L. Garfield (Eds.), *Handbook of psychotherapy and behavior change* (4th ed., pp. 114–139). New York: Wiley.

Elkin, I., Parloff, M. B., Hadley, W. S., & Autry, J. H. (1985). NIMH Treatment of Depression Collaborative Research Program: Background and research plan. *Archives of General Psychiatry, 42,* 305–316.

Elkin, I., Shea, T., Watkins, J. T., Imber, S. D., Sotsky, S. M., Collins, J. F., et al. (1989). National Institute of Mental Health Treatment of Depression Collaborative Research Program: General effectiveness of treatments. *Archives of General Psychiatry, 46,* 971–983.

Epstein, P., & Fawcett, J. (1982). *Addendum to clinical-management-imipramine-placebo administration manual: NIMH Treatment of Depression Collaborative Research Program.* Chicago: Rush Presbyterian–St. Luke's Medical Center.

Eysenck, H. J. (1952). The effects of psychotherapy. *Journal of Consulting Psychology, 16,* 319–324.

Fawcett, J., & Epstein, P. (1980). *Clinical management-imipramine-placebo administration manual: NIMH Psychotherapy of Depression Collaborative Research Program.* Chicago: Rush Presbyterian–St. Luke's Medical Center.

Fawcett, J., Epstein, P., Fiesterr, S. J., Elkin, I., & Autry, J. H. (1987). Clinical management-imipramine/placebo administration manual: NIMH Treatment of Depression Collaborative Research Program. *Psychopharmacology Bulletin, 23,* 309–324.

Fishman, D. B., & Franks, C. M. (1992). Evolution and differentiation within behavior therapy: A theoretical and epistemological review. In D. K. Freedheim (Ed.), *History of psychotherapy: A century of change* (pp. 159–196). Washington, DC: American Psychological Association.

Fiske, D. W., Hunt, H. F., Luborsky, L., Orne, M. T., Parloff, M. B., Reiser, M. F., & Tuma, A. H. (1970). Planning of research on effectiveness of psychotherapy. *American Psychologist, 25,* 727–737.

Fromm-Reichmann, F. (1959). *Psychoanalysis and psychotherapy.* Chicago: University of Chicago Press.

Galison, P. (1998). Judgment against objectivity. In C. A. Jones & P. Galison (Eds.), *Picturing science, producing art* (pp. 327–359). New York: Routledge.

Goldfried, M. R., & Newman, C. F. (1992). A history of psychotherapy integration. In J. C. Norcross & M. R. Goldfried (Eds.), *Handbook of psychotherapy integration* (pp. 46–93). New York: Basic Books.

Haggard, E. A., Hiken, J. R., & Isaacs, K. S. (1965). Some effects of recording and filming on the psychotherapeutic process. *Psychiatry, 28,* 169–191.

Hale, N. (1995). *The rise and crisis of psychoanalysis in the United States.* Oxford, England: Oxford University Press.

Herman, E. (1995). *The romance of American psychology.* Berkeley: University of California Press.

Hollinger, D. A. (1995). Science as a weapon in *kulturkampfe* in the United States during and after World War II. *Isis, 86,* 440–454.

Hollon, S. D., Waskow, I. E., Evans, M., & Lowery, H. A. (1984, May 9). *System for rating therapies for depression.* Paper presented at the annual meeting of the American Psychiatric Association, Los Angeles.

Holt, R. R. (1958). Clinical and statistical prediction: A reformulation and some new data. *Journal of Abnormal and Social Psychology, 56–57,* 1–12.

Jones, D. S. (2000). Visions of a cure: Visualization, clinical trials, and controversies in cardiac therapeutics, 1968–1998. *Isis, 91,* 504–541.

Kiesler, C. A., Cummings, N. A., & VandenBos, G. R. (1979). *Psychology and national health insurance: A sourcebook.* Washington, DC: American Psychological Association.

Klerman, G. L., & Cole, J. O. (1967). Clinical pharmacology of imipramine and related antidepressant compounds. *American Journal of Psychiatry, 3,* 267–309.

Klerman, G. L., DiMascio, A., Weissman, M. M., Prusoff, B., & Paykel, E. S. (1974). Treatment of depression by drugs and psychotherapy. *American Journal of Psychiatry, 131,* 186–191.

Klerman, G. L., Weissman, M. M., Rounsaville, B., & Chevron, E. S. (1984). *Interpersonal psychotherapy of depression.* New York: Basic Books.

Luborsky, L. (1964, April 29). Letter to D. Shakow. David Shakow Papers, M1324, Archives of the History of American Psychology, University of Akron, Akron, OH.

Luborsky, L., & Strupp, H. H. (1962). Research problems in psychotherapy: A three year follow-up. In H. H. Strupp & L. Luborsky (Eds.), *Research in psychotherapy: Volume II* (pp. 308–329). Washington, DC: American Psychological Association.

Malone, R. E. (1999). Policy as product: Morality and metaphor in health policy discourse. *Hastings Center Report, 29*(3), 16–22.

Marks, H. (1997). *The progress of experiment: Science and therapeutic reform in the United States, 1900–1990.* Cambridge, England: Cambridge University Press.

Meehl, P. (1954). *Clinical versus statistical prediction.* Minneapolis: University of Minnesota Press.

Memorandum from Chief, Laboratory of Psychology, National Institute of Mental Health, to Associate Director, National Institutes of Health. (1954, December 9). National Archives and Research Administration, RG511 Central Subject Files, 1954–1957, Box 42.

Memorandum from Chief, Psychotherapy and Behavioral Interventions Section, to Chief, Clinical Research Branch. (1977, March 4). Personal collection of Barry E. Wolfe.

Memorandum from Chief, Psychotherapy and Behavioral Interventions Section of the Clinical Research Branch, to Director, National Institute of Mental Health. (1979, June 18). Personal collection of Barry E. Wolfe.

Memorandum from Chief, Psychotherapy and Behavioral Interventions Section of the Clinical Research Branch, to Director, National Institute of Mental Health. (1980, July 15). Personal collection of Barry E. Wolfe.

Minutes, meeting of September 21 and 22, 1951, Mental Health Study Section. (1951). National Archives and Research Administration, RG511, Box: MHSS Committee Reports 1947–57, ff: Research Study Section September 21 and 22, 1951.

Minutes, 119th meeting of the National Advisory Mental Health Council (p. 13). (1979, December 6–7). Department of Health, Education and Welfare, Public Health Service, ADAMHA, NIMH.

Minutes, 122nd meeting of the National Mental Health Advisory Council. (1980, September 16–17). Department of Health, Education and Welfare, Public Health Service, ADAMHA, NIMH.

Moras, K. (2002). Research in psychotherapy. In M. Hersen & W. Sledge (Eds.), *Encyclopedia of psychotherapy* (Vol. 2, pp. 525–545). New York: Academic Press.

National Institute of Mental Health. (1957). *Annual report of program activities.* Bethesda, MD: National Institutes of Health, U.S. Department of Health, Education and Welfare.

Neimeyer, R. A., & Mahoney, M. J. (Eds.). (1995). *Constructivism in psychotherapy.* Washington, DC: American Psychological Association.

Parloff, M. B. (1959, June). Review of Psychotherapy Research Project. David Shakow Papers, M1373, Archives of the History of American Psychology, University of Akron, Akron, OH.

Parloff, M. B. (1962). Summary report: Therapists contribution (A). In H. H. Strupp & L. L. Luborsky (Eds.), *Research in psychotherapy II.* Washington, DC: American Psychological Association.

Parloff, M. B. (1979). Can psychotherapy research guide the policymaker? *American Psychologist, 34,* 296–306.

Parloff, M. B. (1985). Treatment research and the NIMH re-reorganization. *Hospital and Community Psychiatry, 1,* 1259.

Parloff, M. B., & Elkin, I. (1992). The NIMH Treatment of Depression Collaborative Research Program. In D. K. Freedheim (Ed.), *History of psychotherapy* (pp. 442–449). Washington, DC: American Psychological Association.

Parloff, M. B., & Rubinstein, E. A. (1959). Research problems in psychotherapy. In E. A. Rubinstein & M. B. Parloff (Eds.), *Research in psychotherapy* (pp. 276–293). Washington, DC: American Psychological Association.

Pickren, W. E. (2000). Interview with A. H. Tuma, July 14. APA archives.

Proposal for "Third Research in Psychotherapy Conference." (n.d.). American Psychological Association Collection, Library of Congress, Box 109.

Report of Subcommittee on Methodology in Mental Health Research. (1951). National Institute of Mental Health M. Health SS Meeting, April 19–21, 1951, pp. 1–3. National Archives and Research Administration, RG511 NN1-90-91-002, Mental Health Study Section Committee Reports, 1947–1957, Box 4.

Rubinstein, E. A. (1968). The federal health scientist–administrator: An opportunity for role integration. *American Psychologist, 23,* 558–564.

Rubinstein, E. A., & Parloff, M. B. (Eds.). (1959). *Research in psychotherapy.* Washington, DC: American Psychological Association.

Russell, R. L., & Orlinsky, D. D. (1996). Psychotherapy research in historical perspective: Implications for mental health care policy. *Archives of General Psychiatry, 53,* 708–715.

Shakow, D. (1940). One psychologist as analysand. *Journal of Abnormal and Social Psychology, 35,* 198–211.

Shakow, D. (1954, December 29). Letter to P. Sapir. David Shakow Papers, M1373, Archives of the History of American Psychology, University of Akron, Akron, OH.

Shakow, D. (1959, June). Psychotherapy Project Review: Shakow. David Shakow Papers, M1373, Archives of the History of American Psychology, University of Akron, Akron, OH.

Shakow, D. (1960). The recorded psychoanalytic interview as an objective approach to research in psychoanalysis. *Psychoanalytic Quarterly, 29,* 82–97.

Shakow, D. (1964). Annual Report of the Laboratory of Psychology, January 1, 1963–June 30, 1964. In *Annual Report* (p. 130), Department of Health, Education and Welfare, Public Health Service, National Institutes of Health.

Shakow, D. (1966, February 4). Letter to Hans Strupp. David Shakow Papers, M1522, Archives of the History of American Psychology, University of Akron, Akron, OH.

Shakow, D. (1968). On the rewards (and, alas, frustrations) of public service. *American Psychologist, 23,* 87–96.

Shlien, J. M. (1966, January 14). Letter to F. Halpern. American Psychological Association Collection, Library of Congress, Division 12 Papers.

Shlien, J. M. (Ed.). (1968). *Research in psychotherapy III.* Washington, DC: American Psychological Association.

Sternberg, R. S., Chapman, J., & Shakow, D. (1958). Psychotherapy research and the problem of intrusions on privacy. *Psychiatry, 21,* 195–203.

Strupp, H. H., & Howard, K. I. (1992). A brief history of psychotherapy research. In D. K. Freedheim (Ed.), *History of psychotherapy* (pp. 309–334). Washington, DC: American Psychological Association.

Strupp, H. H., & Luborsky, L. (Eds.). (1962). *Research in psychotherapy II*. Washington, DC: American Psychological Association.

Summary of Coolfont Conference entitled "Workshop on the feasibility of clinical trials research on psychoanalytically oriented psychotherapy." (1982, October 19–20). Personal collection, Barry E. Wolfe.

Undated and unsigned note. (1956, March 15). David Shakow Papers, M1646, Archives of the History of American Psychology, University of Akron, Akron, OH.

Unsigned memorandum from the Adult Psychiatry Branch to Director of Clinical Investigations, NIMH. (1956, May 15). National Archives and Research Administration, RG511 Central Subject Files, 1954–57, Box 42.

Untitled and unsigned memorandum. (1956, April 9). David Shakow Papers, M1646, Archives of the History of American Psychology, University of Akron, Akron, OH.

Untitled notes. (1956, March 15). David Shakow Papers, M1646, Archives of the History of American Psychology, University of Akron, Akron, OH.

U.S. Office of Technology Assessment. (1980). *The implications of cost-effectiveness analysis of medical technology: The efficacy and cost-effectiveness of psychotherapy* (Background Paper No. 3). Washington, DC: Office of Technology Assessment.

Wallerstein, R. S. (1961). Reflections on the Second Conference on Research in Psychotherapy to be held in Chapel Hill, North Carolina, May 18–20, 1961. David Shakow Papers, 1501, Archives of the History of American Psychology, University of Akron, Akron, OH.

Waskow, I. E., & Parloff, M. B. (Eds.). (1975). *Psychotherapy change measures*. Washington, DC: National Institute of Mental Health.

Wilson, M. (1993). DSM–III and the transformation of American psychiatry: A history. *American Journal of Psychiatry, 150*, 399–410.

Wolfe, B. E. (1974). *NIMH research support for psychotherapy and behavior therapy, 1947–1973*. Unpublished report.

Wolfe, B. E. (1988). Report on the May 27, 1988, meeting of the Psychodynamic Therapy Research Planning Group, June 30, 1988. Personal collection of Barry E. Wolfe.

Wolfe, B. E., & Goldfried, M. R. (1988). Research on psychotherapy integration: Recommendations and conclusions from an NIMH workshop. *Journal of Consulting and Clinical Psychology, 56*, 448–451.

III

TRAINING PSYCHOLOGISTS FOR SCIENCE AND PRACTICE

6

THE HISTORICAL CONTEXT FOR NATIONAL INSTITUTE OF MENTAL HEALTH SUPPORT OF AMERICAN PSYCHOLOGICAL ASSOCIATION TRAINING AND ACCREDITATION EFFORTS

INGRID G. FARRERAS

The earliest relationship between the field of psychology and the National Institute of Mental Health (NIMH) centered on the development and expansion of formal graduate training in clinical psychology following World War II (WWII). Because the NIMH did not obtain funding and was not formally established as one of the National Institutes of Health until April 1, 1949, psychologists first dealt with the NIMH's predecessor, the Mental Hygiene Division of the U.S. Public Health Service (PHS). Thanks to a $31,000 PHS grant, the American Psychological Association (APA) was able to organize the now-renowned Conference on Graduate Education in Clinical Psychology, held in August 1949 in Boulder, Colorado (see chap. 7, this volume). It is often claimed that professionalized clinical psychology emerged from this conference. From this conference, too, derives the dominant model of training in clinical psychology known as the *scientist–practitioner*, or *Boulder*, model of training, whereby clinicians are trained as both research scientists and service providers. The Boulder model, however, was not the first model proposed for training in clinical psychology.

The context for these developments was the rapid growth in the number of applied psychologists between the world wars. Many of these applied psychologists were women and Jews, and many of them worked with a master's degree, rather than a doctorate, in psychology (Finch & Odoroff, 1939, 1941; Pickren & Dewsbury, 2002). Since the beginning of the 20th century, various individual psychologists and professional psychological organizations had attempted to set guidelines for the training and education of clinical psychologists.[1] In this chapter, I focus on the development of training models in the 1930s and 1940s and assess their impact on the development of the Boulder model.

THE AMERICAN ASSOCIATION FOR APPLIED PSYCHOLOGISTS (1937–1945)

The American Association of Applied Psychologists (AAAP) was formally established on August 31, 1937.[2] It emerged from the Association of Consulting Psychologists, formed in New York in 1930. A National Committee for Affiliation and Association of Applied and Professional Psychology, chaired by Douglas Fryer (New York University), was established at the 1936 APA convention to plan such an association, and it was decided that a single national organization would be preferable to a federation of regional and state organizations (Napoli, 1981). It is ironic that although the committee eventually consisted of 29 members, it did not truly represent the field of applied psychology. Two thirds of the committee members were male APA members, that is, occupationally secure academicians who were involved in teaching and research (Napoli, 1981). It did not represent the young, master's-level, female-dominated field of applied psychology of the 1930s.

The AAAP consisted of four semi-autonomous sections: (a) Clinical, (b) Consulting, (c) Educational, and (d) Business and Industrial Psychology. On September 1, 1937, the members of the APA Clinical section voted to disband as a section and joined the AAAP ("News Notes," 1937). The first chair of the Clinical section of the AAAP was Francis N. Maxfield, who

---

[1] For further information on individual and organizational clinical training guideline proposals from 1896 to 1949, see Farreras (2001).
[2] The American Association of Applied Psychologists would be incorporated as the American Association for Applied Psychology in 1938.

had also been chair of the APA's Clinical section during its first 3 years (Routh, 1994). On September 2, 1937, a day after the APA Clinical section had disbanded, the Association of Consulting Psychologists also voted to disband in favor of the AAAP (Napoli, 1981).

The AAAP became the home for many clinical practitioners. Its main goal was to guarantee professional competence and to control professional standards in clinical psychology as well as other applied fields of psychology (Nawas, 1972). To achieve this goal, the AAAP imposed rigid membership requirements. Despite the high standards required, membership in the AAAP grew very quickly, surpassing 400 by September 1938 (Napoli, 1981). The 1940 APA yearbook revealed that over half of the AAAP membership consisted of Members or Associates of the APA: 169 (30%) of 551 AAAP Fellows were APA members, and 148 (27%) of 551 AAAP Associates were also APA Associates (English, 1940). The fact that 166 AAAP fellows met criteria only for the lower Associate rank of APA membership (when AAAP membership standards were similar to or higher than those of the APA) and that 16 other AAAP fellows did not belong to the APA at all seemed to indicate that APA continued not to recognize the professional needs, interests, and qualifications of psychology's practitioners (English, 1940).

The AAAP was uncertain about the importance of the doctoral degree. In theory, requiring some fieldwork as part of the doctoral program would provide some necessary clinical experience, but the increasing and dominant numbers of students seeking training for applied careers made this solution untenable on a large scale, and thus alternatives had to be pursued. Albert T. Poffenberger, professor of psychology at Columbia University, suggested three such alternatives in the *Journal of Consulting Psychology*: (a) "liberalize" the traditional PhD program in the direction of professional training, (b) create a PsyD (Doctor in Psychology) professional degree for applied psychologists,[3] or (c) create a professional clinical training program that would lead to a certificate or diploma (Poffenberger, 1938b).

Poffenberger attempted to implement the third alternative at Columbia. He proposed a course of graduate training in clinical psychology that would be completed over the course of 3 years (Poffenberger, n.d.). The first 2 years consisted of coursework, and during the 3rd and last year students would be assigned to a full-year internship to acquire "experience in institutional work" (Poffenberger, n.d.). Because Poffenberger suggested doing an internship in place of the usual dissertation, he proposed awarding a professional certificate, rather than the doctoral degree, at the end of the 3 years (Poffenberger, 1938b). As Poffenberger admitted in a letter dated

---

[3] For the original proposal to create a PsyD professional degree, see Hollingworth (1918).

January 19, 1937, "the program is intended not so much to conform to current standards of training as to provide some eventual basis for setting up proper and adequate standards" (Poffenberger, 1937). Poffenberger's proposed plan was intended to "provide the training which will qualify students for recommendation for state, city, and other clinical positions" (Poffenberger, n.d.).

In January 1937, Poffenberger sent copies of his proposed program to David Shakow, chief psychologist at Worcester State Hospital, and 11 other "well-known and successful clinical psychologists, all attached to prominent institutions" (Poffenberger, 1938b, p. 2). Poffenberger received a variety of responses. These included suggestions that students should arrive already well trained in "Biology, Anthropology, Sociology, General Physiology, Anatomy, Philosophy of Education, Psycho-analysis, Educational, Experimental and Animal Psychology, the Theory of Measurement and the Psychology of Learning" (Poffenberger, 1938b, p. 3). Other recommendations included "a breadth of philosophical outlook," "a depth of insight into human nature," and a heavier emphasis on normal over abnormal psychology. Several respondents felt that statistics was overemphasized, and there was also some concern that internship directors and state associations would not accept students who only had a professional certificate, as opposed to a doctorate.

In February 1938, Poffenberger informed Shakow that the proposed plan had been tentatively adopted by his department: "The program of clinical training began this academic year with three students. We are merely trying out what would be the second year of the program, and we will continue it at least one more year" (Poffenberger, 1938a). It is unfortunate that it did not continue for very long; Poffenberger's program was vetoed by the Graduate Committee on Instruction of the Faculty of Philosophy at Columbia (Capshew, 1999; Morrow, 1946).

In the meantime, the AAAP attempted to address members' concerns about competition from quacks and charlatans. It appointed committees to address the varied professional problems of applied psychologists. Specifically, the AAAP was interested in pursuing four different areas: (a) training, (b) internal activities of the profession, (c) applied techniques, and (d) public and professional relations ("Organization Reports," 1938). Three committees were appointed in the training area; the most important one was the Committee on Graduate Instruction in Applied Psychology, chaired by F. N. Freeman (who was also a member of the two other committees). The other members were Walter V. Bingham, H. E. Burtt, Douglas Fryer, Albert T. Poffenberger, E. K. Strong, and Frederic L. Wells ("Organization Reports," 1938). Its purpose was to "survey and establish standards of graduate instruction in applied psychology" ("Organization Reports," 1938, p. 47).

The Association of Consulting Psychologists (1932) and the APA Clinical section's Committee (1935) on Standards of Training for Clinical Psychologists had published reports on the training and duties of clinical psychologists, but no follow-up of the issues had ensued. The expansion of the field, however, now made these issues even more pressing.

The First Conference on Graduate Training in Clinical Psychology

The first conference on graduate training in clinical psychology was held on May 3, 1941, in response to a request from Donald B. Lindsley. Lindsley, director of the Psychological and Neurophysiological Laboratories at the Emma Pendleton Bradley Home in East Providence, Rhode Island, approached Chauncey M. Louttit, then executive secretary of AAAP, about attending "a small, informal conference [at the New York State Psychiatric Institute] . . . for the discussion of clinical psychology: its problems, methods and training for people entering the field" (Lindsley, 1941a). Lindsley invited 16 individuals (including Louttit) for the day-long conference (see Table 6.1).

Louttit applauded Lindsley's conference idea and suggested that the "discussion . . . stick to problems of training, which . . . I see . . . of greatest importance at the present time" (Louttit, 1941a). He noted, however, that only 11 of the 17 individuals suggested by Lindsley to attend the conference (including Lindsley) were members of the AAAP, when this clearly involved an applied issue. In a letter to Louttit dated April 10, 1941, Lindsley explained his choice of individuals by claiming that he had "no intention . . . to be exclusive nor to be all-inclusive, but simply to bring together a few people representing different points of view on the subject with the hope that a good discussion could be aroused" (Lindsley, 1941b).

As it turned out, Louttit and six of the other invited psychologists were unable to attend the conference, although they were otherwise actively involved in the discussion. Louttit was keenly interested in what had transpired, however, and Lindsley sent him a copy of his six-page summary of the conference discussion (Lindsley, 1941c; Louttit, 1941b). Poffenberger, as chair and coordinator of the conference, presented six issues for discussion, including questions about training (Lindsley, n.d.). Participants distinguished clinical psychology from industrial, vocational, and consulting psychology and from psychometrics, psychotherapy, and psychopathology. Carl Rogers offered a definition of clinical psychology that the group accepted with little modification: "the technology and art of applying psychological principles to problems of the individual person for purposes of bringing about a more satisfactory adjustment" (Lindsley, n.d.). They agreed that the position and standing of psychologists, although usually under the

TABLE 6.1
Psychologists Invited to the 1941 Lindsley Conference

Individual	Institutional affiliation(s)	Professional affiliation(s)
Edgar E. Doll	Vineland Training School	APA Member and AAAP President and Fellow
W. C. Halstead	Psychiatry Department, University of Chicago	APA Member
Florien Heiser*	Norwich State Hospital and University of Connecticut	APA Associate
J. Q. Holsopple*	New Jersey State Hospital and Princeton University	APA Member and AAAP Fellow
Carlyle Jacobsen	Washington University Medical School and Barnes and St. Louis Children's Hospital	APA Member and AAAP Fellow
Elaine Kinder*	Letchworth Village and Columbia University	APA Member and AAAP Clinical Section Secretary and Fellow
Carney Landis*	New York State Psychiatric Institute and Columbia University	APA Member and AAAP Fellow
H. S. Liddell	Cornell University	APA Member
Donald B. Lindsley*	Emma Pendleton Bradley Home and Brown University	APA Member
C. M. Louttit	Indiana University	APA Member and AAAP Executive Secretary and Fellow
Donald Marquis*	Yale University	APA Member
Henry Murray*	Harvard University	APA Member
Albert Poffenberger*	Columbia University	APA Member and AAAP Fellow
Carl Rogers*	Ohio State University	APA Member and AAAP Fellow
David Shakow*	Worcester State Hospital	APA Member and AAAP Fellow
Robert M. Yerkes	Yale University	APA Member and AAAP Fellow
Joseph Zubin*	New York State Psychiatric Institute	APA Member and AAAP Fellow

Note. Sources: Lindsley (1941a, 1941b, n.d.). Individuals who attended the conference are marked with an asterisk. APA = American Psychological Association; AAAP = American Association of Applied Psychology.

supervision of psychiatrists, were improving and that establishing higher standards for the training and experience of psychologists could only increase the services provided and improve their recognition in relation to psychiatry. Participants listed the functions they performed in their daily work. Most of the functions converged around four tasks: (a) diagnosis (psychometric testing), (b) research (mainly on developing new diagnostic tools and methods and in therapeutic efficacy), (c) therapy (mostly confined to psychosocial retraining and re-education of people with disabilities and problem behavior), and (d) teaching (clinical courses to university students or elementary psychology to nurses and attendants). Of these four, research and teaching were the most commonly listed functions (Lindsley, n.d.).

In terms of the qualifications needed to undertake these functions, the conference group agreed that a "suitable personality" and "high intellectual abilities" were the most essential criteria in the selection of students. Following the selection of students by personality and abilities, the group agreed that the most appropriate model of training to follow was the medical one, where a fixed program of courses would culminate in more clinical experience and an internship.

There was some variation in the specific courses suggested, however. With the exception of Rogers, who already had a course of training outlined for his psychology majors at Ohio State University, most members at the conference preferred a strong liberal arts education for undergraduates, with little exposure to psychology. Students could subsequently obtain their psychological training during the graduate years, with a heavy medico–physiological background during the first year, followed by more psychological courses in later years, with multiple opportunities for practical experience in between (Lindsley, n.d.).

There was general agreement that the training for such students should be provided primarily by university psychology departments with allowances made for qualified outside professionals to be invited to teach appropriate courses in the university. Hospitals, clinics, and other professional institutions located near the universities were viewed as advantageous to the exchange of ideas and experiences and to the possibility of openings for internships. The timing of the internship year was not yet a fixed concept, although all saw it as an essential element. Some thought it should take place during the course of study, others after the master's degree, and still others following the doctoral degree. The conference group hoped that if APA and the AAAP sponsored suitable standards, then funding for internships could be obtained, if not through university fellowships (during the course of study) then through foundation support or the support of institutions where the internships were held (Lindsley, n.d.).

The specific degree with which to identify qualified psychologists was not discussed in depth, but it was generally agreed that training that led to a PhD degree was most desirable. Although a PsyD degree for those devoted entirely to clinical work was suggested, Lindsley concluded that "this was believed to be undesirable" (Lindsley, n.d.). However, a certificate that would identify individuals who had undergone a period of training similar to that of the internship but for which no academic credit was received was considered useful.

At the conference's conclusion, Lindsley hoped that a proposal for action specifically outlining a course of academic and professional training for clinical psychologists could be formulated in time for the APA and AAAP's annual meeting in September of that year (Lindsley, 1941c). When Lindsley expressed hope that the APA would "set up and sponsor" the proposed training criteria, however, Louttit strongly disagreed, writing to Lindsley:

> This whole problem is one within the . . . AAAP . . . Because the whole plan must be worked out in connection with academic centers I beieve [sic] in a joint Committee [with the APA], but the AAAP should invite the joint Committee (Louttit, 1941c).

There clearly was deep disagreement over which organization should oversee the licensing and education of clinical psychologists.

David Shakow's Proposal for Clinical Training

In addition to his own conference summary, Lindsley also sent Louttit a copy of the 24-page proposal submitted by Shakow regarding a course of training for clinical psychologists. Because psychology was, at the time, concerned with establishing itself professionally, the overall goal of the proposal was that the training course should prepare clinical psychologists to be competent in diagnosis, therapy, and research (as opposed to becoming a technician). The proposed training program covered undergraduate through postgraduate years of training and was as rigorous as the traditional PhD requirements (with the addition of the internship year; Shakow, n.d.).[4] Shakow outlined an undergraduate program intended to provide a flexible and general scientific background consisting of a major in the biological and physical sciences with a minor in the social sciences; some work in mathematics, philosophy, and comparative literature; three or four introductory psychology courses, languages (French and German), and statistics (Shakow, n.d.).

Shakow proposed a 4-year professional graduate program, including the 1-year internship, modeled on the medical school program. The 1st year would consist of two courses each of systematic general psychology,

---

[4]For the published version, see also Shakow (1942).

systematic dynamic psychology, and developmental psychology, and four courses in medical science, to provide a foundation of knowledge of psychology and an acquaintance with medical science. The 2nd year would provide the student with a background in experimental, psychometric, and therapeutic approaches to clinical psychology by requiring two courses each of experimental dynamic psychology, intelligence testing, and projective testing, as well as a course each of therapeutic theory and methods, educational theory and practice, and introductory clinical medicine, with all courses emphasizing as much clinical contact as possible. Shakow suggested that the 3rd year be devoted to the internship, during which students could be exposed to clinical experience through psychometrics, research, courses and conferences, and therapeutics.[5] Finally, the 4th year of graduate study would be spent finishing the dissertation and taking cross-disciplinary seminars and seminars on professional problems (Shakow, n.d.).

Shakow's proposal for training differed in several ways from the proposal Poffenberger circulated among Shakow and other key psychologists. Shakow was proposing a 4-year plan of study, in contrast to Poffenberger's 3-year plan. Both Shakow and Poffenberger envisioned the first 2 years of graduate study as consisting of coursework and the third year as devoted to obtaining clinical experience through a year-long internship, but Shakow's first 2 years of study relied more heavily on medical courses, and Poffenberger's emphasized coursework in educational or remedial psychology. Shakow also required a fourth year to complete a doctoral dissertation that would lead to the PhD degree, whereas Poffenberger advocated the internship instead of the research dissertation and, thus, also a professional certificate in lieu of the PhD degree.

Not everyone agreed with Shakow's proposal for the training of clinical psychologists, however. Louttit wrote to Lindsley and the remaining conference members, agreeing with the general principles but disapproving of Shakow's reliance on the medical model and the medical background required, and expressed a preference for students obtaining a background more strongly grounded in the liberal arts and psychology. He also believed Shakow should expand the internship experience. He wrote on June 30, 1941:

> Requiring a major in biological and medical sciences introduces a hurdle to acceptance ... I think that the social sciences are neglected ... what about education ... The whole paper shows the ... psychiatric hospital influence. There are many problems in crime, delinquency, school adjustment, industrial adjustments, college personnel, etc., which are very definitely clinical, but not psychopathological ... I would argue that internships in prisons, in public schools, in social case work agencies

---

[5]This internship plan had already been outlined by Shakow (1938).

are as valuable as those in psychiatric or feebleminded institutions. (Louttit, 1941c)

Edgar E. Doll, from the Vineland Training Institute in New Jersey and, at the time, president of the AAAP, also disagreed with the heavy psychiatric outlook. He encouraged a broader view of clinical psychology, a background in liberal arts, a broader selection of internship sites, and an acknowledgement of the progress and accomplishments that applied psychology had achieved in the previous 40 years (Doll, 1941).

Shakow had also recommended awarding a doctoral degree, preferably the PhD (but he acknowledged the need to consider the PsyD as an alternative). Anyone receiving a PhD degree would automatically qualify for Associateship in the AAAP and, depending on the number of years of experience following the degree, for Fellowship. In addition, Shakow suggested the establishment of a specialty board, an "American Board of Clinical Psychology," consisting of AAAP leaders, who would certify individuals who passed a specialty examination in clinical psychology and had a certain number of years of clinical experience. Such certification could then be seen as evidence of achievement in the field of clinical psychology.

Toward the end of his proposal for clinical training, Shakow also recommended that APA and the AAAP appoint a joint "Professional Training for Clinical Psychology" committee to consider a proposal such as the one he had presented. The committee would also supervise a pilot program of a small number of students in the full training program so that the committee could subsequently educate universities as to how to establish such training programs (Shakow, n.d.).

Former APA president Robert Yerkes agreed with Shakow's inclusion of APA in this plan. In a letter to Lindsley, Marquis, and Shakow dated July 7, 1941, Yerkes wrote the following:

> Although this whole matter is primarily the concern of the AAAP, it would not seem to me wise that the APA be ignored. As our oldest national organization in psychology it should be vitally interested in the professionalizing of the subject and in every step which can be taken to increase the adequacy of training. I therefore am heartily in favor of the suggestion that a joint Committee of the two societies be proposed to make a careful study of the general problem of professionalization. (Yerkes, 1941)

Elaine Kinder believed this issue concerned the AAAP more than it did APA but nonetheless believed that endorsement from APA would help provide much of the support such a program required. In a letter dated August 1, 1941, she wrote to Lindsley:

> The suggestion of a joint Committee of the A.A.A.P. and the APA seems to afford the soundest possible basis for professional action along

the lines suggested by the May 3rd conference. I would agree with Dr. Louttit that the Committee should be recognized as primarily a Committee of the A.A.A.P., since that is the association which represents the professional interests of psychologists in applied fields. We should recognize, I think, that the endorsement of the APA, which is a long established and recognized organization, may be of particular value in the securing of the Foundation support which is essential to the project. (Kinder, 1941)

In the same letter, Kinder also advocated for what would come to be the standardization of guidelines for training adopted by universities only a few years later:

I would like to suggest that the joint Committee, in addition to undertaking the task of securing aid for the project, be instructed to call upon representatives of (a) a selected group of universities, and (b) a selected group of clinical centers which have already demonstrated an interest in providing opportunities for training, to formulate a proposed program which could then be submitted for endorsement to the proper authorities of both the universities and the clinic centers, with a view to establishing the program for a trial period. The Committee might set up specifications to be met by the universities and institutions or clinics cooperating in such a program, participation to be determined by the willingness of the respective authorities to accept and comply with these conditions. (Kinder, 1941)

Although he wholeheartedly agreed with Kinder's assessment as regards the APA endorsement, Louttit believed that the interests of academic and institutional psychologists were already too well represented among the conference attendees, to the exclusion of other, more applied psychologists, and in a letter to Kinder dated August 3, 1941, he wrote:

I can't help but feel that the group as now organized is a little too heavily weighted with people from institutions and with academic people whose interests revolve around factors largely in common with the institution workers. I am afraid that the interes [sic] of school systems and community mental hygiene clinics, as only two examples, are not too well represented. (Louttit, 1941d)

Louttit clearly saw the Lindsley conference as too heavily dominated and influenced by the academicians. Although he was fully cognizant of the need for, and was agreeable to, the further discussion of training models, he nonetheless felt that more members of the AAAP should be involved to give a more representative assessment of what applied training should be. Although Louttit passed on Shakow's training proposal for approval by APA, he especially looked forward to the establishment of the AAAP Committee for Training to study this issue.

Louttit's recommendation was passed. Lindsley's summary report of the May 3, 1941, conference, as well as Shakow's training proposal, were submitted to the AAAP secretary with the recommendation that the AAAP appoint a committee

> to draw up a program for the Professional Training of Clinical Psychologists that would address academic training, . . . field training (interships) [sic], . . . [and the] selection of academic and field training centers for [the] experimental trial of the formulated program. (Louttit, 1942, p. 24)

THE COMMITTEE ON PROFESSIONAL TRAINING IN CLINICAL (APPLIED) PSYCHOLOGY

In September 1941, the AAAP board established the Committee on Professional Training in Clinical (Applied) Psychology (CPTCAP), with subcommittees that represented all of the sections of the AAAP: Educational Institutions, Business and Industry, and Health and Welfare Institutions. The last group represented clinical interests. It was chaired by Donald Lindsley, and its members included Edgar Doll, G. I. Giardini, Albert Poffenberger, and David Shakow (Louttit, 1942). The CPTCAP met at Pennsylvania State College in June 1942 and generated a "Proposed Program of Professional Training in Clinical Psychology" that was accepted at the annual AAAP meeting in September 1942 and published in the January–February issue of the *Journal of Consulting Psychology* (CPTCAP, 1943). In contrast to Shakow's proposal (which had been published in the previous issue of the *Journal of Consulting Psychology*), this training program emphasized a more general liberal arts undergraduate education and a less medicalized graduate education in favor of coursework more relevant to the particular area of interest in applied psychology (as broadly suggested by the AAAP section divisions; see Exhibit 6.1).

The proposed graduate program consisted of three areas: (a) basic psychology courses, (b) courses in related fields, and (c) courses on specific techniques. Also listed were seven areas related to clinical practice, from which the student had to choose at least three, depending on the area of applied psychology chosen. For students choosing clinical as their applied area, the committee recommended choosing Medical Science, Sociology, and Professional Relationships. Finally, all students were also required to take four courses on specific techniques: (a) Psychological Tests and Measurements, (b) Methods of Case Study and Analysis, (c) Psychological Counseling and Therapy, and (d) Survey of Educational and Vocational Guidance Techniques. In addition to the academic courses required in those

EXHIBIT 6.1

The Training Proposals of David Shakow and of the Committee on Professional Training in Clinical (Applied) Psychology (CPTCAP)

Shakow's Proposal (11/1942)	CPTCAP's Proposal (1/1943)
Undergraduate Level	Undergraduate Level
Major in biological (and physical) sciences	20 hr of psychology
Minor in social sciences	6 hr of biology
4–5 introductory psychology courses	6 hr of physics and/or chemistry
"Work" in mathematics, philosophy, and comparative literature	6 hr of mathematics
French and German	3–6 hr of sociology
Statistics	3–6 hr of anthropology
	3–6 hr of economics and/or political science
Graduate Level	3–6 hr of the foundations of education
Year 1	3 hr of introduction to education
6 hr of general psychology	Practical field experience (when possible)
6 hr of dynamic psychology	
6 hr of developmental psychology	Graduate Level
12 hr of medical science	6 basic psychology courses:
Year 2	Systematic
6 hr of experimental dynamic psychology	Developmental
6 hr of the theory and practice of intelligence tests	Dynamic
6 hr of the theory and practice of projective tests	Experimental methods
3 hr therapeutic theory and methods	Quantitative methods
3 hr of educational theory and practice	Psychology of the deviate
3 hr of clinical medicine	3 courses in related fields:
Optional didactic analysis	Medical science
Year 3	Sociology
Internship	Professional relationships
Year 4	4 courses on specific techniques:
Dissertation and related coursework	Tests and measurements
	Case study and analysis methods
	Counseling and therapy
	Educational and vocational guidance techniques
	1-year supervised internship

Note. Sources: CTPCAP (1943), Shakow (1942).

three areas, a 1-year internship was required. Such internships had to provide exposure to clinical psychometrics and interviewing, conferences and seminars, therapy, and research (Louttit, 1942).

After the publication, in 1943, of the proposed curriculum for training in professional psychology, CPTCAP was enlarged to seven subcommittees of two members each (under the new name "Committee on Professional Training in Applied Psychology"), and suggestions for the revision of the proposed training program to encompass *all* areas of applied psychology were solicited (Bryan, 1944b; Louttit, 1943).

Around this time, in May 1943, the Intersociety Constitutional Convention, headed by Yerkes and under the auspices of the National Research Council, met to discuss planning an organization that would unite academic and applied organizations in one common front for national service (Capshew & Hilgard, 1992). The reorganized APA's mission was expanded, and two classes of membership were proposed—Fellow (formerly Member) and Member (formerly Associate)—as well as divisions, to have a minimum of 50 members (Poffenberger & Bryan, 1944). Despite a minor skirmish involving some applied psychologists who believed that their voice would once again be silenced and unrepresented under the APA umbrella, the reorganized APA was successfully and formally inaugurated on September 6, 1945, shortly after the end of WWII (Bryan, 1944a; Capshew & Hilgard, 1992; O'Shea & Rich, n.d.; Poffenberger & Bryan, 1944). Most important, the reorganized APA would now embrace a dual mission, one that pursued the advancement of psychology as both a science as well as an applied profession that would serve society by promoting human welfare.[6]

World War II expanded the duties expected of psychologists. The number of psychological casualties in WWII was overwhelming. Psychiatrists who until then had relied on psychologists exclusively for assistance in assessment and diagnosis were now faced with having also to request that they aid in the treatment of casualties (Abt, 1992; Capshew, 1999; Frank, 1984, 1986; Herman, 1995; Pottharst, 1976; Strickland, 1988). Suddenly, psychologists were finding themselves engaging in a variety of activities in addition to mental testing: psychological evaluations; pilot selection; training techniques; and adult psychotherapy, both individual and group (Abt, 1992; Capshew, 1999; Herman, 1995; Hoffman, 1992; Strickland, 1988).

The sudden demand for psychological services for treatment of war casualties highlighted the paucity of trained mental health providers. Because psychiatric training was so time consuming and trained so few psychiatrists at any one time, the government initiated training grants for other mental health providers, particularly clinical psychologists. Although individual psychologists and professional psychological organizations had made sporadic attempts to establish training criteria in the past, it was WWII that provided the broader and more urgent impetus for psychologists to establish and standardize training in clinical work (Frank, 1986).

Talk of such training had already been initiated within APA. Robert Sears, at the Iowa Child Welfare Research Station, had read Shakow's

---

[6] For further information on the events leading to the APA reorganization, see Capshew and Hilgard (1992) and Capshew (1999).

training proposal (the one that resulted from the Lindsley conference of May 1941) suggesting that the psychological associations "take the lead in officializing some [training] program" (Sears, 1943). In response, Sears wrote to APA President John E. Anderson in January 1943 urging the creation of APA's own committee on clinical training, separate from the joint AAAP–APA one:

> I feel that this is a rather important matter to be undertaken by the APA because it represents the more scientifically minded and academically oriented group of psychologists. The AAAP has, of course, developed a very strong program, and their Committees are apparently headed in the right direction. The APA, however, still retains an academic prestige position, and an influence in psychology, particularly on the training side, that no other organization can develop in a short time. Furthermore, in order that any academic training programs be developed and set in motion, it seems to me that it will be necessary to have the official support of the APA. (Sears, 1943)

Both Sears and Anderson felt Shakow overemphasized applied psychologists working in psychiatric institutions such as hospitals or asylums for the insane or feebleminded (as opposed to all of those involved in the school systems) and were dissatisfied with the narrow, basic training he had proposed (Anderson, 1943).

THE APA COMMITTEE ON THE GRADUATE AND PROFESSIONAL TRAINING OF PSYCHOLOGISTS

In September 1943, APA Executive Secretary Willard Olson invited Sears, Bruce Moore, Donald Marquis, and some other psychologists to serve under Edwin Guthrie on the Committee on the Graduate and Professional Training of Psychologists (CGPTP). Sears created a questionnaire to survey the existence of facilities and programs for professional training in psychology at the leading U.S. universities so as to be able to "recommend a standard curriculum and facilities that would be the minimum necessary for effective training in clinical psychology" (Sears, 1944). He mailed the questionnaire out to 101 institutions of higher education on September 5, 1945 (Morgan, 1946; Sears, 1945).[7] Fifty-nine institutions (58%) responded, 32 of which reported offering clinical training at the doctoral level (Sears, 1946a).

With the close of WWII, such institutions needed to adjust to hundreds of men returning from war to pursue or continue their graduate work in

---

[7] Sears (1946a) mentioned having sent it out to 102 institutions, but Morgan's letter to Sears mentions that 106 universities were contacted but that 5 did not offer graduate programs, thus leaving a total of 101, not 102, to which the questionnaires would have been mailed.

psychology as well as to new professional demands and enrollees. The most pressing request came from the Veterans Administration (VA), which after the war employed the greatest number of psychologists. There had been a significant number of psychiatric casualties during the war and an equally significant shortage of personnel in all fields of mental health to treat them during and after the war (Brand, 1964). The VA approached the APA board of directors in December 1945 with a request for help in identifying universities that could provide adequate doctoral training in clinical psychology.

THE PROBLEM OF ACCREDITATION

By February 1946, Daniel Blain, neuropsychiatry director of the VA, had sent psychology departments the VA's proposed training program for clinical psychologists, a proposal that resembled Shakow's 1942 proposal on internship training except that 50% of the intern's time had to be spent working with VA patients.[8] Students were to be accepted first into the psychology departments, and when their names were forwarded to the VA for approval, they would be assigned to one of four ranks and respective salaries and have all tuition expenses and other perks paid by the VA. The program was set to begin in September 1946.

As Blain was circulating the VA training proposal to graduate schools, Sears wrote to APA executive secretary Dael Wolfle with a list of 27 doctoral institutions he could mail to the VA, broken down into two categories according to the quality and number of clinical facilities and staff available. Sears published this list in the journal *American Psychologist* in May 1946 under his own name and with a list of 32 schools listed only in alphabetical order (the original 27 plus 5 more that offered doctoral-level training but lacked either specialized clinical staff, practicum facilities, or specialized clinical and basic psychology courses). The report consisted of information on both general and clinical training. It listed which institutions offered the MA and PhD degrees in two broad areas of psychology—"teaching and research" or "professional"—as well as information on admission require-

---

[8]The joint AAAP–APA Subcommittee on Graduate Internship Training, headed by Shakow, published a report (1945) in the *Journal of Consulting Psychology* based on Shakow's (1942) training proposal. The changes the subcommittee made to Shakow's 1942 proposal were primarily in the first 2 years of graduate training. Whereas Shakow (1942) had originally recommended four courses in medical–physical sciences during the first year, the subcommittee (1945) now recommended only two, with the remaining two courses being in theory and practice of psychological tests and measurements and in advanced statistics and quantitative methods. Similarly, during the 2nd year, Shakow (1942) had recommended two courses in projective techniques, one in educational theory and practice, and one in therapeutic theory and methods. The subcommittee (1945) changed those recommendations to one course in projective techniques, one in case study and analysis, one in educational and vocational guidance techniques, and two in therapeutic theory and methods. The 3rd-year internship remained similar to that proposed by Shakow (1938).

ments, tuition, and stipends/assistantships. With respect to clinical training, it evaluated the resources of departments that offered clinical training according to the clinical staff and practicum facilities they had (Sears, 1946a). Sears did not send the VA a list of all of the departments offering doctoral-level training, however, "only those whose facilities were most comprehensive" (Sears, 1946b, 1946c).

The publication of alphabetized institutions, however, led to disputes; the VA funding helped only the institutions that already had the best and largest programs, and institutions not included on the list were clamoring to get on it. In their efforts to meet the minimum clinical criteria to obtain VA funding, many of them neglected and weakened their general doctoral programs. Sears thus wrote to the CGPTP chair at the time, Sidney Pressey, in May 1946, asking for a larger subcommittee on evaluation; he felt uncomfortable that evaluations had until then rested on the CGPTP alone (indeed, on Sears alone) without overall APA approval. At the September 1946 APA convention, the CGPTP was reconstituted, and Sears was named its chair.

Reluctant to add small institutions to the list that barely met the required clinical criteria but offered weak general doctoral programs, Sears anticipated needing additional criteria for accrediting clinical training (Sears, 1946b, 1946c). Now more than ever, academic psychologists emphasized the necessity of an academic background in general and experimental psychology as the foundation for training in clinical psychology and disagreed with training in applied, clinical psychology alone. The way for them to court governmental funding for training without compromising their hegemony in the department was by requiring this traditional, academic background of all doctoral-level psychologists, independent of specialization.

The reconstituted CGPTP continued to collaborate with the VA in the training of future clinical psychologists and began working closely with the PHS. The PHS provided funding for accredited institutions but was also willing to offer financial aid to those with minor deficiencies.

The U.S. Public Health Service's Division of Mental Hygiene

By 1947, the VA had 200 students enrolled in 22 APA-approved institutions. The VA funding had dramatically changed the resources available to train clinical students. Sears mailed out more questionnaires to psychology departments in December 1946 to collect new data on what doctoral work was being offered. The 40 institutions that had replied by January were judged according to 13 criteria, and 29 met almost all of them; the list of these 29 institutions was passed on to the VA.

Robert Felix, director of the PHS Division of Mental Hygiene, began requesting similar lists of qualified institutions in March 1947. In addition to these lists, however, he also wanted APA to provide the PHS with lists of institutions that did not meet the criteria for accreditation but would be able to if only they had enough funding to make up for certain deficiencies. On April 10, 1947, Sears sent the VA and the PHS another list of 27 institutions and the PHS an additional list of 9 institutions that needed some improvement. Two years into the VA program, 464 graduate trainees were studying at 36 APA-accredited institutions.

The APA Committee on Training in Clinical Psychology

The increased focus on, interest in, and funding of clinical training by the VA and the PHS empowered APA to appoint a Committee on Training in Clinical Psychology (CTCP) under Shakow to take over Sears's CGPTP. The critical difference between the two training committees was that the CTCP was now to assess training facilities by personally visiting and evaluating institutions rather than relying on self-report questionnaires from departmental chairs.

The CTCP's first report was published in *American Psychologist* in December 1947 and focused explicitly on 4-year doctoral programs (CTCP, 1947). The report was based on the joint AAAP–APA Subcommittee on Graduate Internship Training report published in 1945. In contrast to the 1945 report, however, the CTCP's report had no year-by-year breakdown but instead recommended six broad areas of study, to avoid undue influence that might result from VA funding.

Some universities were unhappy with this "ideal" model published by the CTCP.[9] Some did not feel they had been fairly evaluated, possibly because the CTCP was implementing more rigorous standards that included personal visits, and institutions that had been accredited by Sears's CGPTP did not now meet the new committee's standards. Some universities also believed that the CTCP's ideal model was not illustrative of clinical training and would take longer than the prescribed 4 years to complete. Nonetheless, departments felt coerced into adopting it so as to be considered adequate for accreditation purposes. There was also strong disagreement over publishing the list of accredited institutions. The disagreement proved acrimonious enough that the APA decided not to publish the differentiated lists in the CTCP's August 1949 *American Psychologist* report but instead listed the institutions, in a footnote, in alphabetical order.

Overall, although the CTCP believed that many schools were doing a very good job of clinical training, it nonetheless highlighted several factors of concern. Many programs seemed to be emphasizing clinical techniques

---

[9]For further detail, see Farreras (2001).

over psychological theory and research methodology. There also did not seem to be a concerted enough effort to seek field training at institutions beyond the predominant (medically dominated) psychiatric hospitals and clinics of the time, such as at guidance centers, schools, or prisons (Shakow, 1978). Given the lack of reliable knowledge in the field of clinical psychology, there was also concern about the students' motivations for seeking training—that is, scientific versus economic versus human welfare—and about whether students would be entering private practice, which was considered inappropriate (APA Committee on Training in Clinical Psychology, 1949).[10]

Despite these concerns, APA and the PHS seemed to be satisfied with the CTCP's work. The APA applied for and was granted $31,096 from the PHS for the 1948–1949 year to fund a "Conference on Graduate Education in Clinical Psychology" (what would come to be known as the *Boulder conference*) scheduled for August 1949 (Hilgard, 1948). It had appropriated $2,500 toward the CTCP's second year of evaluation of doctoral programs, and the Surgeon General, on the recommendation of the National Advisory Mental Health Council, had also approved a $10,000 grant to continue support for the CTCP's activities for the following year (1949–1950; American Psychological Association, Committee on Training in Clinical Psychology, 1949; Felix, 1949; see chap. 7, this volume).

DISCUSSION

Despite their controversial status at the time, the reorganized APA's CTCP 1947 and 1949 reports are considered the foundation of the scientist–practitioner model of graduate training in clinical psychology. The CTCP's proposed 4-year doctoral program, which included a 1-year internship, set the stage for the model of training and represented APA's first attempts at accreditation of institutions for doctoral training in clinical psychology (Maher, 1991; Nawas, 1972).

The scientist–practitioner, or Boulder model, derives its name from the fact that APA, sponsored by the PHS's Division of Mental Hygiene, held a conference in Boulder, Colorado, between August 19 and September 3, 1949. The directors of clinical training of the 43 universities listed in the 1948 Shakow report were invited to the conference, which was organized and administered by the CTCP (Wolfle, 1948a, 1948b). The CTCP decided that the conference program would best serve the needs of the university departments if it were designed by a new committee that represented all

---

[10] Some departments would not even accept students who indicated an intention to enter private practice.

interested parties. The executive committee that resulted included E. Lowell Kelly as chair, Ann Magaret, William Hunt, James Miller, Wayne Dennis, and John Eberhart. Kelly and Magaret were elected by the CTCP, Hunt and Miller were elected by a vote by all of the clinical directors, Dennis was nominated by the Committee of Department Chairmen, and Eberhart represented the PHS (Kelly, 1949; Shakow, 1948; Wolfle, 1948a, 1948b). According to Shakow, the CTCP expected not that new proposals would result from the conference but rather that the conference would allow for this group of key participants to discuss the CTCP's 1947 report (Shakow, 1975).

The consequences of the scientist–practitioner model that was established at the Boulder conference were both positive and negative for the field of psychology. On the one hand, it bridged the academic-versus-practitioner rift by terming both *psychologists,* independent of their place of work (Frank, 1984). Earlier, psychologists had been described on the basis of the content of what they studied: traditionally, experimental topics such as perception, learning, memory, and so on. Clinicians had been expected to ground their theory in basic research on such topics, but that research was not readily applicable to social problems, and thus clinicians ended up using tests and psychotherapeutic techniques that were not derived from traditional, experimental psychology. The scientist–practitioner model now provided a way for academics and practitioners to find common ground through a shared methodology (Frank, 1984). Since APA's 1945 reorganization, with its consequent expansion in mission from the advancement of psychology as a science to include its advancement as a way to promote human welfare, practitioners were now expected, in return, to be psychologists first and clinicians second, thus allowing for all PhD students to be trained in research.

Research played a unique role for clinical psychologists after WWII. In addition to being qualified to assist psychiatrists in the treatment of war neuroses, another important issue was at stake for psychologists: their status within the mental health arena. Psychologists certainly wanted to help in the war effort, but they also wanted to establish an identity within the mental health field that was independent of the authority of psychiatrists. Toward this goal, psychologists codified and strengthened the sketchy model of training that had been available previously and included research as a significant component of the new training model (Frank, 1984). As Wolfle confirmed in a letter: "The average practicing physician or psychiatrist has neither the research interest nor the research skill [training in statistics and experimental design] that we attempt to develop in the student receiving his Ph.D. in clinical psychology" (Wolfle, 1949). Requiring that aspiring clinical psychologists now conduct research toward their PhD would provide them "with a professional identity that made [them] unique in the mental health world . . . and differentiate[d] the clinical psychologist from the rest of the pack" (Sanderson & Barlow, 1991, p. 37). As a result, the focus on research would not only enable clinical psychologists to shed the reputation of being "mere technicians," but would also lead to their being the only mental health providers able to advance knowledge through research at a time when there was widespread ignorance about mental health (Ellis, 1992; Rosenzweig, 1950; Strupp, 1982; Tryon, 1963).

A negative consequence of the scientist–practitioner model, however, was that academic psychologists were now faced with having to train doctoral students not only for careers in teaching and research but also for professional practice. This created problems on a variety of levels. The most pragmatic one was that there was a shortage of qualified faculty who could do this (Rosenzweig, 1950). In addition, this upset a long-standing tradition of academic dominance in the field. Before WWII, academic psychologists had historically been the dominating faction, seeing themselves as "basic" and "pure" scientists who conducted research that had legitimized psychology as a science. To many of the academic psychologists, applied psychology had been viewed as a lower and baser calling, ordinarily relegated to women or Jews, who were not as welcome in the ivory tower (Finison, 1978; Harris, 2004; Tryon, 1963).

The increasing professionalization of clinical psychologists threatened the traditionalists' stronghold. The reorganized APA of 1945 had already made some attempts at establishing and accrediting formal PhD training in clinical psychology, but external factors, such as governmental agencies and outside funding, markedly accelerated their professionalization in academic departments. Suddenly, these departments were being evaluated by outside committees that not only evaluated the departments that the academics held dearly but also forced an imbalance in favor of the clinical faculty by granting or withdrawing funding from students, facilities, and fellowships, depending on whether they met the necessary criteria for clinical training (Tryon, 1963). This created tension with the academic psychologists, who were concerned not only that external forces might come to control their programs and determine their curricula but also about what that meant for the future of their traditional experimental programs (Baker & Benjamin, 2000).

A larger negative consequence of the scientist–practitioner model was its uncritical acceptance of the medical model. The CTCP's 1947 report is viewed as the backbone of the model, and that report primarily reflected Shakow's 20 years of experience in the field and of work at Worcester State Hospital. According to former APA president George Albee, such an uncritical and ignorant acceptance of the medical model and the psychiatric worldview led to psychology being an ancillary profession in relation to psychiatry (Albee, 2000).

The individual and organizational training models proposed during the first half of the 20th century, as well as the struggles over membership requirements to national organizations, the establishment of codes of ethics, and the certification and accreditation issues, are all examples of attempts to define the field of clinical psychology and what standards and training it should pursue at a time when it was struggling to legitimize itself. The Boulder conference should not be seen as merely the beginning of the scientist–practitioner model of clinical psychology today but as the product of a number of complex historical factors. The early individual and professional attempts to develop training models sought to professionalize and create an image of scientific status. This, in turn, set clinical psychologists apart from other, similarly trained individuals working in similar occupations. The demands and effects that World Wars I and II had on the budding profession of psychology were also important factors. The need to address boundary and professionalization issues vis-à-vis other mental health practitioners and the conflicting missions of the various clinical organizations and APA all helped shape the emergence of the scientist–practitioner model.

REFERENCES

Abt, L. E. (1992). Clinical psychology and the emergency of psychotherapy. *Professional Psychology: Research and Practice, 23,* 176–178.

Albee, G. (2000). The Boulder Model's fatal flaw. *American Psychologist, 55,* 247–248.

American Association for Applied Psychology, Committee on (Professional) Training in Clinical (Applied) Psychology. (1943). Proposed program of professional training in clinical psychology. *Journal of Consulting Psychology, 7,* 23–26.

American Psychological Association and American Association for Applied Psychology, Committee on Graduate and Professional Training (David Shakow, Chairman). (1945). Subcommittee report: Graduate internship training in psychology. *Journal of Consulting Psychology, 9,* 243–266.

American Psychological Association, Clinical Section Committee. (1935). The definition of clinical psychology and standards of training for clinical psychologists. *Psychological Clinic, 23*(1–2), 1–8.

American Psychological Association, Committee on Training in Clinical Psychology. (1947). Recommended graduate training program in clinical psychology. *American Psychologist, 2,* 539–558.

American Psychological Association, Committee on Training in Clinical Psychology. (1949). Doctoral training programs in clinical psychology: 1949. *American Psychologist, 4,* 331–341.

Anderson, J. E. (1943, March 16). Letter to R. R. Sears. Robert R. Sears Papers, Special Collections and University Archives Department of the Stanford University Green Library, Stanford, CA.

Association of Consulting Psychologists. (1932). Training and standards for the clinical psychologist. *Psychological Exchange, 1*(5), 10–11.

Baker, D. B., & Benjamin, Jr., L. T. (2000). The affirmation of the scientist–practitioner: A look back at Boulder. *American Psychologist, 55,* 241–247.

Brand, J. L. (1964, February). Antecedents of the NIMH in the Public Health Service. In J. L. Brand & P. Sapir (Eds.), *An historical perspective on the National Institute of Mental Health* [Mimeograph]. (Prepared as section 1 of the NIMH Report to the Woolridge Committee of the President's Scientific Advisory.)

Bryan, A. I. (1944a). Letter to Presidents, Secretaries and Representatives to the Board of Affiliates of Affiliated Societies. American Association for Applied Psychology, Affiliates, 1943–1945, Box 689, American Psychological Association Papers, Library of Congress, Washington, DC.

Bryan, A. I. (1944b). Seventh annual meeting of the summarized proceedings and reports of the American Association for Applied Psychology. *Journal of Consulting Psychology, 8,* 8–15.

Capshew, J. H. (1999). *Psychologists on the march: Science, practice, and professional identity in America, 1929–1969.* Cambridge, England: Cambridge University Press.

Capshew, J. H., & Hilgard, E. R. (1992). The power of service: World War II and professional reform in the American Psychological Association. In R. B. Evans, V. S. Sexton, & T. C. Cadwallader (Eds.), *The American Psychological Association: A historical perspective* (pp. 149–175). Washington, DC: American Psychological Association.

Committee on Professional Training in Clinical (Applied) Psychology. (1943). Proposed program of professional training in clinical psychology. *Journal of Consulting Psychology, 7,* 23–26.

Committee on Training in Clinical Psychology. (1947). Recommended graduate training program in clinical psychology. *American Psychologist, 2,* 539–558.

Doll, E. E. (1941, July 7). Letter to D. B. Lindsley. Box 12, Folder 223, Chauncey McKinley Louttit Papers, Yale University Sterling Memorial Library, New Haven, CT.

Ellis, H. C. (1992). Graduate education in psychology: Past, present, and future. *American Psychologist, 4,* 570–576.

English, H. B. (1940). Forum: Notes on membership standards. *Journal of Consulting Psychology, 4,* 79.

Farreras, I. G. (2001). Before Boulder: Professionalizing clinical psychology, 1896–1949. *Dissertation Abstracts International, 62*(2-B), 1076. (UMI No. 2001-95016-365)

Felix, R. H. (1949, July 7). Letter to D. Wolfle. Committee on Training in Clinical Psychology, Correspondence, General, May–July 1949, Box 515, American Psychological Association Papers, Library of Congress, Washington, DC.

Finch, F. H., & Odoroff, M. E. (1939). Employment trends in applied psychology. *Journal of Consulting Psychology, 3*, 118–122.

Finch, F. H., & Odoroff, M. E. (1941). Employment trends in applied psychology, II. *Journal of Consulting Psychology, 5*, 275–278.

Finison, L. J. (1978). Unemployment, politics, and the history of organized psychology, II: The Psychologists' League, the WPA, and the national health program. *American Psychologist, 33*, 471–477.

Frank, G. (1984). The Boulder model: History, rationale, and critique. *Professional Psychology: Research and Practice, 15*, 417–435.

Frank, G. (1986). The Boulder model revisited. *Psychology Reports, 59*, 409–413.

Harris, B. (2004). *Boundary skirmishes in applied psychology, 1932–1939: The Psychological Exchange and the Psychologists' League*. Manuscript in preparation.

Herman, E. (1995). *The romance of American psychology: Political culture in the age of experts*. Berkeley: University of California Press.

Hilgard, E. R. (1948, January 19). Application for training grant under National Mental Health Act. Committee on Training in Clinical Psychology, Miscellany, 1949–1951, Box 514, American Psychological Association Papers, Library of Congress, Washington, D.C.

Hoffman, L. E. (1992). American psychologists and wartime research on Germany, 1941–1945. *American Psychologist, 47*, 264–273.

Hollingworth, L. S. (1918). Further communications regarding "A Plan for the Technical Training of Consulting Psychologists." *Journal of Applied Psychology, 2*, 280–285.

Kelly, E. L. (1949, February 23). Letter to Executive Committee members. Committee on Training in Clinical Psychology, Correspondence, December 1948–1949, Box 513, American Psychological Association Papers, Library of Congress, Washington, DC.

Kinder, E. F. (1941, August 1). Letter to D. B. Lindsley. Box 12, Folder 223, Chauncey McKinley Louttit Papers, Manuscripts and Archives Division of the Yale University Sterling Memorial Library, New Haven, CT.

Lindsley, D. B. (1941a, March 26). Letter to C. M. Louttit. Box 12, Folder 223, Chauncey McKinley Louttit Papers, Manuscripts and Archives Division of the Yale University Sterling Memorial Library, New Haven, CT.

Lindsley, D. B. (1941b, April 10). Letter to C. M. Louttit. Box 12, Folder 223, Chauncey McKinley Louttit Papers, Manuscripts and Archives Division of the Yale University Sterling Memorial Library, New Haven, CT.

Lindsley, D. B. (1941c, June 27). Letter to May 3rd, 1941 conference members. Box 12, Folder 223, Chauncey McKinley Louttit Papers, Manuscripts and Archives Division of the Yale University Sterling Memorial Library, New Haven, CT.

Lindsley, D. B. (n.d.). Lindsley's summary of the May 3rd, 1941 Conference on the Training of Clinical Psychologists. American Association for Applied Psychology Professional Training in Clinical Psychology, 1939–1941, Box 691,

American Psychological Association Papers, Library of Congress, Washington, DC.

Louttit, C. M. (1941a, March 29). Letter to D. B. Lindsley. Box 12, Folder 223, Chauncey McKinley Louttit Papers, Manuscripts and Archives Division of the Yale University Sterling Memorial Library, New Haven, CT.

Louttit, C. M. (1941b, May 6). Letter to D. B. Lindsley. Box 12, Folder 223, Chauncey McKinley Louttit Papers, Manuscripts and Archives Division of the Yale University Sterling Memorial Library, New Haven, CT.

Louttit, C. M. (1941c, June 30). Letter to D. B. Lindsley. Box 12, Folder 223, Chauncey McKinley Louttit Papers, Manuscripts and Archives Division of the Yale University Sterling Memorial Library, New Haven, CT.

Louttit, C. M. (1941d, August 3). Letter to E. F. Kinder. Box 12, Folder 223, Chauncey McKinley Louttit Papers, Manuscripts and Archives Division of the Yale University Sterling Memorial Library, New Haven, CT.

Louttit, C. M. (1942). Summarized proceedings and reports of the fifth annual meeting of the American Association for Applied Psychology. *Journal of Consulting Psychology, 6,* 19–49.

Louttit, C. M. (1943). Summarized proceedings and reports of the sixth annual meeting of the American Association for Applied Psychology. *Journal of Consulting Psychology, 7,* 1–22.

Maher, B. A. (1991). A personal history of clinical psychology. In M. Hersen, A. E. Kazdin, & A. S. Bellack (Eds.), *The clinical psychology handbook* (2nd ed., pp. 3–25). New York: Plenum Press.

Morgan, J. (1946, January 5). Letter to R. R. Sears. APA Standing Boards and Continuing Committees, Continuing Committees, Committee on Graduate and Professional Training, Correspondence, 1945–July 1946, Box 470, American Psychological Association Papers, Library of Congress, Washington, DC.

Morrow, W. R. (1946). The development of psychological internship training. *Journal of Consulting Psychology, 10,* 165–183.

Napoli, D. S. (1981). *The architects of adjustment: The practice and professionalization of American psychology, 1920–1945.* Port Washington, NY: Kennikat Press.

Nawas, M. M. (1972). Landmarks in the history of clinical psychology from its early beginnings through 1971. *Journal of Psychology, 82,* 91–110.

News notes. (1937). *Journal of Consulting Psychology, 1,* 106–107.

Organization reports. (1938). *Journal of Consulting Psychology, 2,* 47–54.

O'Shea, H., & Rich, G. (n.d.). Letter to Presidents, Secretaries and Representatives to the Board of Affiliates of Affiliated Societies. American Association for Applied Psychology, Affiliates, 1943–1945, Box 689, American Psychological Association Papers, Library of Congress, Washington, DC.

Pickren, W. E., & Dewsbury, D. A. (2002). Psychology between the world wars. In W. E. Pickren & D. A. Dewsbury (Eds.), *Evolving perspectives on the history of psychology* (pp. 349–352). Washington, DC: American Psychological Association.

Poffenberger, A. T. (n.d.). Confidential and tentative outline: A training program for clinical psychologists. David Shakow Papers, M1389, Poffenberger, A. T., Archives of the History of American Psychology, University of Akron, Akron, OH.

Poffenberger, A. T. (1937, January 19). Letter to D. Shakow. David Shakow Papers, M1389, Poffenberger, A.T., Archives of the History of American Psychology, University of Akron, Akron, OH.

Poffenberger, A. T. (1938a, February 25). Letter to D. Shakow. David Shakow Papers, M1389, Poffenberger, A. T., Archives of the History of American Psychology, University of Akron, Akron, OH.

Poffenberger, A. T. (1938b). The training of a clinical psychologist. *Journal of Consulting Psychology, 2*, 1–6.

Poffenberger, A. T., & Bryan, A. I. (1944). Toward unification in psychology. *Journal of Consulting Psychology, 8*, 253–257.

Pottharst, K. E. (1976). A brief history of the professional model of training. In M. Korman (Ed.), *Levels and patterns of professional training in psychology: Conference proceedings, Vail, Colorado, July 25–30, 1973* (pp. 33–40). Washington, DC: American Psychological Association.

Rosenzweig, S. (1950). Bifurcation in clinical psychology. *Journal of Psychology, 29*, 157–164.

Routh, D. K. (1994). *Clinical psychology since 1917: Science, practice, and organization.* New York: Plenum Press.

Sanderson, W. C., & Barlow, D. H. (1991). Research strategies in clinical psychology. In C. E. Walker (Ed.), *Clinical psychology: Historical and research foundations* (pp. 37–49). New York: Plenum Press.

Sears, R. R. (1943, January 29). Letter to J. E. Anderson. Robert R. Sears Papers, Special Collections and University Archives Department of the Stanford University Green Library, Stanford, CA.

Sears, R. R. (1944, June 1). Letter to D. G. Marquis. Robert R. Sears Papers, Special Collections and University Archives Department of the Stanford University Green Library, Stanford, CA.

Sears, R. R. (1945, January 29). Letter to E. Guthrie. Robert R. Sears Papers, Special Collections and University Archives Department of the Stanford University Green Library, Stanford, CA.

Sears, R. R. (1946a). Graduate training facilities—I. General information, II. Clinical psychology. *American Psychologist, 1*, 135–150.

Sears, R. R. (1946b, March 6). Letter to D. Wolfle. Robert R. Sears Papers, Special Collections and University Archives Department of the Stanford University Green Library, Stanford, CA.

Sears, R. R. (1946c, March 6). Letter to S. L. Pressey. Robert R. Sears Papers, Special Collections and University Archives Department of the Stanford University Green Library, Stanford, CA.

Shakow, D. (1938). An internship year for psychologists (with special reference to psychiatric hospitals). *Journal of Consulting Psychology, 2,* 73–76.

Shakow, D. (1942). The training of the clinical psychologist. *Journal of Consulting Psychology 6,* 277–288.

Shakow, D. (1948, December 16). Letter to Committee on Training in Clinical Psychology members. Board of Directors representatives and United States Public Health Service representatives, Committee on Training in Clinical Psychology, Correspondence, December 1948–1949, Box 513, American Psychological Association Papers, Library of Congress, Washington, DC.

Shakow, D. (1975). Oral history. NIMH Oral History Project, Robert Felix Folder, Box 1, Accession Number 1999–039, History of Medicine Division, National Library of Medicine, National Institutes of Health, Bethesda, MD.

Shakow, D. (1978). Clinical psychology seen some 50 years later. *American Psychologist, 33,* 148–158.

Shakow, D. (n.d.). The training of the clinical psychologist. American Association for Applied Psychology Professional Training in Clinical Psychology, 1939–1941, Box 691, American Psychological Association Papers, Library of Congress, Washington, DC.

Strickland, B. R. (1988). Clinical psychology comes of age. *American Psychologist, 43,* 104–107.

Strupp, H. H. (1982). Some observations on clinical psychology. *Clinical Psychologist, 36,* 6–7.

Tryon, R. C. (1963). Psychology in flux: The academic–professional bipolarity. *American Psychologist, 18,* 134–143.

Wolfle, D. (1948a, December 16). Letter to chairmen. Committee on Training in Clinical Psychology, Correspondence, December 1948–1949, Box 513, American Psychological Association Papers, Library of Congress, Washington, DC.

Wolfle, D. (1948b, December 16). Letter to R. R. Sears. Committee on Training in Clinical Psychology, Correspondence, December 1948–1949, Box 513, American Psychological Association Papers, Library of Congress, Washington, DC.

Wolfle, D. (1949, May 18). Letter to D. C. Goldberg. Robert R. Sears Papers, Special Collections and University Archives Department of the Stanford University Green Library, Stanford, CA.

Yerkes, R. M. (1941, July 7). Letter to D. B. Lindsley. David Shakow Papers, M1506, Conference on the Training of Clinical Psychologists, Archives of the History of American Psychology, University of Akron, Akron, OH.

7

CREATING A PROFESSION: THE NATIONAL INSTITUTE OF MENTAL HEALTH AND THE TRAINING OF PSYCHOLOGISTS, 1946–1954

DAVID B. BAKER AND LUDY T. BENJAMIN JR.

There was a time when mental health mattered in America. On July 3, 1946, passage of the National Mental Health Act set into motion an aggressive set of initiatives aimed squarely at creating a mentally healthy nation. The Depression-era embrace of federal aid, the advance of medical knowledge in conquering disease, and alarm over increasing incidences of psychiatric impairment among World War II veterans and in the general population helped to move a national program of mental health into Congress and across the desk of President Harry S. Truman (Grob, 1991).

Mental health was a distant goal; in reality, postwar America was poorly equipped and grossly understaffed to understand and treat mental illness. To carry out the goals of the National Mental Health Act of 1946, a cadre of specialists was needed, a group that was in short supply and heavy demand. The creation of a talent pool—the engineering of a mental health workforce—was an important feature of the act, a feature that was to forever change psychology in America.

DEFINING THE NEED

The recognition of the acute shortage of mental health professionals was in direct proportion to the recognition of mental illness in America. During WWII, concerns about psychopathology rose. Data indicated that approximately 17% of recruits were ineligible for service because of psychiatric disturbance (Deutsch, 1949). Such numbers were of concern. It is obvious that there were mental health issues in the population at large, yet there was almost no mechanism to identify and treat them. Likewise, the psychological casualties of war meant that large numbers of veterans would be released into civilian life while still in need of mental health services. Indeed, it seemed as if the numbers kept rising. The majority of discharges from service were for psychiatric reasons, and more than half of all beds in Veterans Administration (VA) hospitals were occupied by psychiatric casualties (Grob, 1991; VandenBos, Cummings, & DeLeon, 1992).

Identifying whom to treat was easy; finding solutions proved more troublesome. The available supply of trained personnel to deal with these numbers was a fraction of the need. With fewer than 3,000 trained psychiatrists and estimated shortages of psychologists at 92% (Brand & Sapir, 1964), it was apparent that what was needed was an immediate and explosive growth in the ranks of trained mental health professionals.

The Beginning of the Training Committee

The framers of the National Mental Health Act of 1946 knew the numbers and had planned accordingly. The Training and Standards Section, known as the *Committee on Training*, was responsible for this portion of the act. Robert Felix described the members of the committee as "Special Consultants most qualified by knowledge and skill to furnish advice as to scope of activities and policy determinations" ("Agenda, Committee on Training," 1947, p. 1). Felix called the group to Washington for the first time on January 22, 1947, appointing psychiatrist Edward Strecker as chair ("Agenda, Committee on Training," 1947). The committee was divided into four groups: (a) psychiatry, (b) psychiatric nursing, (c) psychiatric social work, and (d) psychology (for a list of the groups and members, see Table 7.1). Felix believed these were the groups that could have greatest impact on training mental health workers. In the brief history of treatment of mental illness in America, these four groups had a proven record of service, having been involved in earlier U.S. Public Health Service (PHS) projects

TABLE 7.1
Members of the Committee on Training, January 1947

Psychiatry	Psychology	Psychiatric social work	Psychiatric nursing
Edward A. Strecker	David Shakow	Elizabeth Ross	Margaret Arnstein
William Malamud	Elaine Kinder	Charlotte Towle	
Spafford Ackerly	J. M. Bobbitt	Marion Kenworthy	
Franz Alexander	Dael Wolfle	Daniel O'Keefe	
Frederick Allen			
Karl Bowman			
Franklin Ebaugh			
Alan Gregg			
Donald Wilson Hasting			
Paul Lemkau			
Karl A. Menninger			
William C. Menninger			
Hugh Morgan			
John M. Murray			
Thomas A. C. Rennie			
Howard Rome			

Note. These names are compiled from Meeting of the Committee on Training National Advisory Mental Health Council, January 22–23, 1947,"David Shakow Pape rs, M1360, Archives of the History of American Psychology, University of Akron, Akron, OH.

and the mental hygiene movement (Brand & Sapir, 1964; Pols, 2001; Rubinstein, 1975).

The primacy of psychiatry was obvious. Of the 25 members of the training committee, 16 were psychiatrists, 4 were psychologists, 4 represented psychiatric social work, and 1 represented psychiatric nursing. Members of each area met to decide on the allocation of training funds, submitting their recommendations to the entire training committee, which in turn made final recommendations to the National Advisory Mental Health Council, the governing authority. Ultimate decision making rested with this group, which was dominated by psychiatrists. Not at all afraid of protecting the interests of psychiatry, the council's funding formula provided psychiatry 40% of available funds, with the remaining three areas each receiving 20% (Rubinstein, 1975).

To accomplish its mission of creating a well-trained and ample supply of mental health workers, the Committee on Training was to provide grants and stipends to deserving institutions and individuals. Training grants were to be used for hiring faculty, whereas stipends would support students in training. Of particular importance to the psychiatry-dominant council was the expansion and improvement of instruction in psychiatry. It was reasoned that good teachers of psychiatry would positively influence medical students toward careers in psychiatry, both as practitioners and teachers ("Summary of Present Policies and Practices," 1952). In addition to funding for grants and stipends, awards were made for special projects. Among the most important and historically significant of these was the money given to sponsor training conferences in professional psychology. Clinical psychology had the Boulder conference, counseling psychology had the Ann Arbor conference, and school psychology had the Thayer conference. We discuss the impact of these later.

The meeting of January 1947 lasted only 2 days, but it provided rudimentary guidelines for allocating funds and stipulated an agreement to allocate 150 training stipends to support students in each of the four areas. Goodwill seemed to prevail, and the participants, believing their mission an important one, could not anticipate the ways in which it would grow in complexity.

The group met again in April and October of 1947, facing a full agenda, including a rapidly growing list of requests for funding (Felix, 1947). There were some changes in the members of the individual groups, but psychiatrists still maintained a clear majority, something that may have been an issue with the other areas. At the October meeting, consideration was given to integrating the four fields of study. A subcommittee on integrative policy was formed that included a representative from each area. Members of the subcommittee themselves appeared unsure of their mission, noting that they had been "charged rather vaguely with the responsibility of considering policies and methods of integrating the training in the four fields" (Subcommittee on Integrative Policy, 1947, p. 1). The subcommittee acknowledged the central role and responsibility of psychiatry for mental health and urged that opportunities for integrative collaboration and training take place whenever possible (Subcommittee on Integrative Policy, 1947). The recommendations did not imply any urgency, and they appear to have had little impact.

By 1948, the Committee on Training was in full swing. In the brief span of a year, applications were pouring in, and committee members were busy clarifying standards. Facing 132 training grant applications and 1,040 requests for training stipends, the committee was forced to pick and choose as the requests far exceeded the $1 million in available funds.

The procedures for the Committee on Training were straightforward. Each area's members met in separate sessions, reporting the results back to the entire training committee. Of prime concern to all areas was agreement on establishing standards to evaluate institutions applying for funds. It is obvious that there was ambiguity in awarding grants and stipends to programs that were not yet developed.

For the psychiatry subcommittee this was less of a problem: There were already-established programs of psychiatry, many of which were familiar to the psychiatrists on the committee. Familiarity, although not a substitute for formal criteria, did serve as an initial level of screening. From there, it was a matter of formulating criteria and conducting site visits. The psychiatry subcommittee ranked highest those institutions that had a program in place, possessed adequate faculty and facilities for training, and had an administration that was supportive of the training in accordance with the National Mental Health Act of 1946 (Psychiatry Sub-Committee Report, 1947).

Like psychiatry, psychiatric nursing and psychiatric social work had programs of study, although neither had enough programs that offered substantive training in mental health issues. The psychiatric social work subcommittee members recognized that they would be working from the ground up, especially in the provision and supervision of field placement. The group quickly allocated funds to the American Association of Schools of Social Work for assistance in developing standards of training for psychiatric social work, identifying programs worthy of support, and monitoring quality control in field placements (Sub-Committee on Psychiatric Social Work, 1947).

Psychiatric nursing, long recognized for its complementary relationship to psychiatry, established three criteria for evaluating funding requests: (a) quality of psychiatric department and teaching, (b) quality of the clinical and community facilities, and (c) quality of the instruction in nursing and nursing education (Sub-Committee on Psychiatric Nursing Report, 1947). Each program applying for funds was evaluated on each criterion with a 4-point scale. To increase the number of psychiatric nurses, the nursing committee decided to "give priority to programs that prepare head nurses, supervisors, administrators and consultants for both institutions in which nurses are employed and for public health nursing activities and other community agencies where nurses are employed" (Sub-Committee on Psychiatric Nursing Report, 1947, p. 47).

The Place of Clinical Psychology

Clinical psychology was fortunate to be included as one of the training areas recognized by the PHS in 1947. Others who did not make the cut—including groups representing forensic psychiatry, occupational therapy, school social work, school psychology, experimental psychology, psychological counseling, and psychiatric aides—would lobby for federal recognition and federal dollars (Committee on Review, 1953).

The prominent and immediate position given clinical psychology can be attributed to two factors. First, clinical psychologists were recognized service providers in medical settings, familiar to psychiatrists, who found their diagnostic skills useful and their deference to the authority of the physician essential. This type of clinical psychology was exemplified in the work of David Shakow (1901–1981). Shakow, the prototype of the new professional psychologist, was hospital trained right down to his ability to understand the milieu of authority in the psychiatric setting. He moved easily between the world of the psychiatrist and the psychologist and had the respect for and ear of both. It was not surprising that Shakow was appointed to the Committee on Training and elected as chair of the clinical psychology subcommittee. A ubiquitous figure, Shakow had, for nearly a decade, been in major positions of responsibility and influence in defining standards of training for clinical psychologists.

During the 1940s, every major program, conference, meeting, and committee that had anything to say about clinical psychology training had David Shakow as a member, if not chair. He was indefatigable in attending meetings, writing reports, and in general leading the charge to create a national model for doctoral training in clinical psychology. Before his appointment to the Committee on Training, he had crafted a rather complete document on the training of doctoral students in clinical psychology (American Psychological Association [APA], Committee on Training in Clinical Psychology, 1947). It eventually became the working document for the Boulder conference of 1949 (for a more complete discussion, see Baker & Benjamin, 2000).

The subcommittee on clinical psychology of the Committee on Training included many of Shakow's old friends in the training struggle, such as Elaine Kinder, E. Lowell Kelly, and Ernest Hilgard. Also included were psychologists representing the PHS, including John Eberhart and Jerry Carter. In what might appear as a conflict of interest, Shakow chaired the clinical psychology section of the training committee at the PHS while simultaneously chairing APA's Committee on Training in Clinical Psychology (CTCP). In actuality, there was little in this that could be construed as a conflict of interest. If anything, the appointment represented Shakow's desire to serve and APA's ability to mobilize its members and resources to help support and promote the potential largesse resulting from the provisions of the National Mental Health Act of 1946.

The CTCP was appointed by APA President Carl Rogers. Its members included Ernest Hilgard, E. Lowell Kelly, Bertha Luckey, Nevitt Sanford, and Laurance Shaffer. The agenda was considerable and included developing a plan for training clinical psychologists; formulating standards for doctoral training in clinical psychology; conducting on-site visits and evaluating training programs; and maintaining relations with other interest groups, such as the National Committee for Mental Hygiene (APA, Committee on Training in Clinical Psychology, 1947).

The PHS and the VA had exerted significant pressure on APA to come up with training standards, a job they had been unable and unwilling to do themselves (see chap. 6, this volume). With Shakow as chair, the VA, the PHS, and the CTCP held a joint meeting in Washington, DC, on September 5, 1948 ("Agenda for VA–USPHS Conference," 1948). The meeting made clear the federal agencies' desire to have more trained psychologists available in the workforce and their willingness to stay out of the way of university departments and APA in the development of training standards for professional psychologists.

By 1949, Shakow and his committees at both the PHS and APA were moving forward in the development of training programs. Forty-three doctoral training programs had been accredited, and 175 students had successfully completed doctoral training in clinical psychology (APA, Committee on Training in Clinical Psychology, 1949). In reviewing this progress, the CTCP pointed to a number of concerns. It was noted that clinical techniques were taking precedence over instruction in theory and research methodology, that the focus on the severely mentally ill was overly restrictive, and that students were not provided enough clinical supervision throughout the training years (Baker & Benjamin, 2000). These and other issues would receive considerable attention at the PHS-sponsored Conference on Graduate Education in Clinical Psychology in Boulder in 1949.

Training Grants and Stipends

Training grant money made available to clinical psychology could be used in a variety of ways; it could be used to purchase equipment, books and media and, most important (and widely used), to support salaries for faculty members. This allowed departments to hire clinical faculty, an obvious necessity if departments were to offer doctoral degrees in clinical psychology. It also led to some creative proposals. In 1950, when Marshall Jones, Director of Clinical Training in Psychology at the University of Nebraska, was preparing his clinical training grant for the PHS, he was concerned because there were only nine faculty members in the Nebraska department. He felt that the clinical doctoral students needed exposure to a broader array of psychological ideas than the small faculty could offer. So, he added a small amount to his training grant budget to bring guest faculty members on campus. A total of six visited in the 1951–1952 academic year, including Roger Barker, Bruno Bettelheim, Leon Festinger, Robert Sears, and Muzafer Sherif. Although the guest faculty presentations were a success, there was concern about better integrating them if the colloquia were repeated. A decision was made to invite speakers for the next year for a series of presentations on the theme of motivation. Thus was born the Nebraska Symposium on Motivation, which was funded annually by the PHS as part of Nebraska's clinical training grant through 1962. In 1962, NIMH began funding the Nebraska clinical program and agreed as well to fund the Nebraska Symposium, an arrangement that lasted until 1976. Speaking at a meeting at Stanford University in the early 1960s, National Institute of Mental Health (NIMH) director Robert Felix said that he considered the funds that NIMH spent on the Nebraska Symposium the most productive money in the whole agency (Benjamin & Jones, 1978).

Training stipends were awarded to individual graduate students within approved training programs. In most cases, departments that sought training grants also requested training stipends. The awards made in clinical psychology for the year 1948 are presented in Table 7.2. Most schools were located in the northern half of the United States; many of these in 1948 were not closely identified with clinical psychology. Whereas the psychologists on the training committee in Washington were clearly identified with clinical psychology, the recipients of their generosity were not necessarily so. The grumbling of individuals in the academy who were opposed to the creation of the new psychologist, and generally in favor of maintaining psychology as a laboratory science, probably could never have estimated the impact that the government surge in spending in support of clinical psychology would have on American psychology.

DEFINING PROFESSIONAL PSYCHOLOGY

The training grants program in clinical psychology was complemented by the ambitious and omnipresent efforts of the VA. The VA began its clinical psychology training program in 1946 with 200 trainees, compared

TABLE 7.2

Training Grants and Stipends in Clinical Psychology, July 1948–June 1949

Institution	Address	Department head	Training grant ($)	Stipends	
				No.	Amount ($)
University of California, Berkeley	Psychology Department Berkeley, CA	Robert C. Tryon	4,580	4	5,200
University of California Medical School	Psychiatry Department Berkeley, CA	Karl M. Bowman			
Columbia University Teachers College	Department of Guidance	Laurance F. Shaffer			
Duke University	Psychology Department Durham, NC	Donald K. Adams	13,500	2	2,400
University of Illinois	Psychology Department Urbana, IL	Herbert Woodrow	7,398	3	4,000
University of Illinois College of Medicine	Psychology Department Chicago, IL	David Shakow	8,640	3	6,400
State University of Iowa	Psychology Department Iowa City, IA	Kenneth W. Spence	15,066	2	4,000
University of Michigan	Psychology Department Ann Arbor, MI	Donald G. Marquis	2,074	3	4,800
University of Minnesota	Psychology Department Minneapolis, MN	Richard M. Elliott	6,998	2	2,800
New York State Psychological Intern Training Program	Rockland State Hospital Orangeburg, NY	Elaine F. Kinder			

(continued)

TABLE 7.2   (Continued)

Institution	Address	Department head	Training grant ($)	Stipends	
				No.	Amount ($)
Northwestern University	Psychology Department Evanston, IL	Robert H. Seashore	1,944	4	7,200
Ohio State University	Psychology Department Columbus, OH	Harold E. Burtt	6,480	4	6,000
University of Pennsylvania	Psychology Department Philadelphia, PA	Robert A. Brotemarkle		4	6,400
Princeton University	Psychology Department Princeton, NJ	Carroll C. Pratt	10,260	1	1,600
University of Rochester	Psychology Department Rochester, NY	G. R. Wendt	8,076	1	1,200
Stanford University			13,392	2	3,200
Western Reserve University			5,832	2	2,400
Western State Psychiatric Institute				1	1,200
Worcester State Hospital			4,860	3	5,200

Note. These data are from a National Institute of Mental Health memo dated August 9, 1948, David Shakow Papers, M1360, Archives of the History of American Psychology, University of Akron, Akron, OH.

with the initial offering of 40 traineeships by the PHS. The ratio remained relatively constant throughout the early years of both programs (Clark, 1957; Miller, 1946). Likewise, the building of faculty in clinical psychology that was accomplished by the PHS was matched by the VA's generosity in providing funds that paid faculty members to supervise VA trainees and in cases, where necessary, to hire additional faculty.

Operating under different mandates, the PHS and the VA sought the same ends in the 1940s: the establishment of a substantial force of specialists to meet the mental health needs of the civilian and military populations. Although there were numerous differences in the ways each organization went about these activities, there was common agreement on financial support for training in clinical psychology. A clear expression of this was demonstrated in the PHS's sponsorship of the Boulder conference.

Clinical Psychology

The PHS and the VA each had a vested interest in seeing that America's universities had a uniform system of training, and the Boulder conference was an attempt to bring interested parties together to discuss the issues. The 73 participants who gathered that August in Boulder carved out a niche for clinical psychology. Through their efforts, clinical psychology would stake its claim to an identity within the burgeoning postwar mental health field, an identity complete with standards of training, guidelines for student selection, accreditation of university programs, and recommendations for licensure and certification (Raimy, 1950).

The meeting carried the imprimatur of the PHS, with invitations extended to all representatives of the allied mental health professions that the PHS championed (for a list of participants, see Exhibit 7.1). There is no doubt that the support of the PHS brought with it a mandate, implicit or not, that all those gathered—chairs of academic departments, trainers of clinical psychologists and related professionals, and assorted government representatives—would address how all could cooperate to bring the greatest good to the greatest number of people. In terms of the actions of clinical psychology, the PHS, now operating under the moniker of the National Institute of Mental Health, allowed clinical psychology significant latitude in determining priorities and how to address them.

Robert Felix, NIMH's first director, offered the opening address at Boulder. As was customary for his frequent appearances at such gatherings, he exhorted the participants to join in the national struggle to understand and prevent mental illness and, in the process, promote mental health. He noted the following:

> the first need is to understand what should go into the training of
> psychologists who are to work in this broad field and how this training

EXHIBIT 7.1
Participants in the Conference on Graduate Education in Clinical Psychology, Boulder, Colorado, August–September, 1949

Donald K. Adams, Duke University
Thelma G. Alper, Clark University
Eston J. Asher, Purdue University
Delton C. Beier, Indiana University
Chester C. Bennett, Boston University
Arthur L. Benton, University of Iowa
Robert G. Bernreuter, Pennsylvania State College
Robert Blake, University of Texas
Joseph M. Bobbitt, National Institute of Mental Health
Edward S. Bordin, University of Michigan
Joseph E. Brewer, Wichita (KS) Guidance Center
Robert A. Brotemarkle, University of Pennsylvania
Marion E. Bunch, Washington University
Jerry W. Carter, Jr., National Institute of Mental Health
Robert C. Challman, Menninger Foundation, Topeka, KS
Rex M. Collier, University of Illinois
Wayne Dennis, University of Pittsburgh
Graham B. Dimmick, University of Kentucky
John C. Eberhart, National Institute of Mental Health
Robert H. Felix, National Institute of Mental Health
Charles S. Gersoni, U.S. Army
Virginia T. Graham, University of Cincinnati
William R. Grove, Phoenix (AZ) Elementary Schools
Robert E. Harris, University of California Medical School
Starke R. Hathaway, University of Minnesota
Karl F. Heiser, American Psychological Association
Harold M. Hildreth, Veterans Administration, Washington, DC
Jane Hildreth, American Psychological Association Staff (Guest)
Nicholas Hobbs, Columbia University
Howard F. Hunt, University of Chicago
William A. Hunt, Northwestern University
Paul E. Huston, University of Iowa
Max L. Hutt, University of Michigan
Carlyle Jacobsen, University of Iowa
Marshall R. Jones, University of Nebraska
Bert Kaplan, Harvard University
E. Lowell Kelly, University of Michigan
Isabelle V. Kendig, St. Elizabeth's Hospital, Washington, DC
David B. Klein, University of Southern California
James W. Layman, University of North Carolina
Lyle H. Lanier, University of Illinois
George F. J. Lehner, University of California, Los Angeles
George E. Levinrew, American Association of Psychiatric Social Workers
Howard P. Longstaff, University of Minnesota
Bertha M. Luckey, Cleveland (OH) Public Schools
Jean W. McFarlane, University of California, Berkeley
Cecil W. Mann, Tulane University
Dorothea A. McCarthy, Fordham University
Dwight W. Miles, Western Reserve University
James G. Miller, University of Chicago

(continued)

EXHIBIT 7.1 *(Continued)*

O. Hobart Mowrer, University of Illinois
Paul Henry Mussen, University of Wisconsin
C. Roger Myers, University of Toronto
T. Ernest Newland, University of Tennessee
John Gray Peatman, City College of New York
Albert I. Rabin, Michigan State College
Victor C. Raimy, University of Colorado
Dorothy Randall, University of Colorado (Conference Assistant)
Eliot H. Rodnick, Worcester (MA) State Hospital
Julian B. Rotter, Ohio State University
Seymour B. Sarason, Yale University
Martin Scheerer, University of Kansas
Mary Schmitt, National League of Nursing Education
Laurance F. Shaffer, Columbia University
David Shakow, University of Illinois Medical School, Chicago
John W. Stafford, Catholic University
Charles R. Strother, University of Washington
Earl E. Swarzlander, Veterans Administration Hospital, Long Island, NY
Ruth S. Tolman, Veterans Administration Hospital, Los Angeles, CA
Brian E. Tomlinson, New York University
George Richard Wendt, University of Rochester
Carroll A. Whitmer, University of Pittsburgh
Clarence L. Winder, Stanford University
Dael Wolfle, American Psychological Association
Helen M. Wolfle, American Psychological Association

can be given in a reasonable time. At the same time it must never be forgotten that the individual whom we call the clinical psychologist, although desperately needed, is only one type of psychologist who must make a contribution to the total effort. (Felix, quoted in Raimy, 1950, p. xv)

Felix, a psychiatrist, was warm to the idea of multidisciplinary collaboration in seeking to cultivate a national program that would emphasize mental health; community approaches to prevention; and, in the end, a high-functioning, well-adjusted public. A broadband thinker, he nonetheless kept psychiatry at the top of the mental health pyramid. Conquering mental illness, he noted, "involves the treatment of psychological disorders and the promotion of the mental health of the individual or the group by the utilization of appropriate and established psychological techniques and principles of therapy under psychiatric direction" (Felix, quoted in Raimy, 1950, p. xvii).

The impact of the Boulder conference was immediate and was incorporated into the rapid development of training programs and accreditation that so dominated clinical psychology during the postwar years. A lasting legacy of the Boulder conference has been the endorsement of the scientist–practitioner model of training, a compromise solution that attempted to bridge the gulf between those who held fast to the traditional laboratory-based psychology and those seeking a place for the application of psychology to the treatment of psychological problems of people of all ages and with all levels of discomfort and disturbance (Baker & Benjamin, 2000; see also chap. 7, this volume). As a compromise, it allowed both sides to save face, but it held the seeds of conflict between traditional psychological scientists and professional psychologists that within a decade began blossoming.

In addition to sanctifying the psychologist as both researcher and clinician, the conferees, in the span of 15 days, addressed almost every conceivable issue in the creation of clinical psychology and the clinical psychologist (see Raimy, 1950, for the complete proceedings). The role of the clinical psychologist received considerable attention. Earlier complaints about the overly medicalized and hospital-based psychology advocated by Shakow were overruled in favor of a more normative one that would be of service to "normal" people in the context of their everyday lives and that was offered in cooperation with allied fields and professions. The endorsement of prevention and coordinated community-based service certainly was part of the vision of Felix and the NIMH.

Conferees affirmed the doctoral degree as the credential of the clinical psychologist and were in general accord with the program of study offered by the CTCP's report of 1947. The recommended core curriculum along with the recommended training in research ensured that faculty in departments with clinical training programs could continue to teach and conduct research without interruption. On these grounds, there was not much that was threatening about the new clinical discipline. However, the insertion of significant federal dollars and the federal oversight they brought with them was another matter. Participants at the Boulder conference voiced concern about federal control of departments and worried that accreditation standards for clinical programs would result in blanket endorsements of entire departments and the imposition of a uniform curriculum. Resolutions and reassurance sought to assuage these concerns and, in the end, seemed convincing enough for the participants to move forward.

In the time since the Boulder conference, clinical psychology has claimed the meeting as its own, a watershed event that is part of the origin myth of the development of clinical psychology. The historical record indicates that although the term *clinical psychology* was carried throughout much of the deliberations that comprised the Boulder conference, it was envisioned as a meeting of the minds that was intended for the consumption of all mental health professionals. The NIMH was not concerned with issues of turf, with the exception perhaps of the fact that psychiatry was in charge of the whole affair. Psychiatry, psychiatric social work, psychiatric nursing, school psychology, and counseling psychology were all represented at Boulder but did not receive the attention perhaps they or the NIMH would have envisioned or preferred.

Counseling Psychology

Counseling psychology, with a history as long as that of clinical psychology, wanted its place at the table of professional psychology. Clinical psychology, however, had a leg up, getting to the training table first, largely because of its association and proximity to the medical profession and hospital-based work. The reorganization of APA in 1945 produced separate divisions representing clinical and counseling interests. Debates about distinctions seemed blurred from the beginning, but distinctions were nonetheless made, and each sought its own path toward recognition and funding from the federal government.

The success of counseling psychology in gaining the endorsement of the NIMH appears related in part to its appeal to a community-minded approach to mental health. A large and important branch of the evolutionary tree of this group was based in education and, by extension, in service to children through guidance. *Guidance,* a rather generic term, referred to a variety of activities aimed at improving the lives of youth (Baker, 2002). Guidance was ubiquitous by the 1940s and could claim success as a means of reaching large groups of school-age children, college students, and young adults seeking vocational counseling. Furthermore, vocational guidance and rehabilitation counseling had received federal support for decades before 1940, largely in connection with services to veterans of World War I and to civilians during the Depression (Blocher, 2000). The reorganization of APA in 1945 brought all these interests together with the formation of APA Division 17 (Counseling and Guidance). Like their clinical colleagues, the counseling group collaborated with the NIMH in its efforts to professionalize.

A relatively unknown fact is that the PHS funded a meeting on the training of counselors at the University of Michigan on July 27 and 28, 1949, and again on January 6 and 7, 1950. A joint project of the NIMH, APA's Division of Counseling and Guidance (now known as the Society of Counseling Psychology), and the University of Michigan, its chief engineer was Michigan faculty member and counseling center director Edward S. Bordin. A major figure in the evolution of counseling psychology, Bordin was close to developments in professional training. Meeting for the first time just a month before Boulder, the Ann Arbor conference had 12 participants (see Exhibit 7.2 for a list of the participants) who were carefully selected to represent "the range of attitudes toward counseling represented within the Division of Counseling and Guidance of the APA," (Bordin, 1950, p. 4).

EXHIBIT 7.2
Participants at the Ann Arbor Conference

Joseph M. Bobbitt, Chief Psychologist, Office of Professional Services, National Institute of Mental Health, U.S. Public Health Service, Washington, DC

Edward S. Bordin, Chair and Editor of the Counseling Division of the Bureau of Psychological Services, Associate Professor of Psychology and Educational Psychology, University of Michigan

John A. Bromer, Assistant Personnel Director, Counseling Center, Prudential Insurance Co. of America

John M. Butler, Assistant Professor of Psychology, University of Chicago

Mitchell Dreese, Professor of Educational Psychology, Dean of the Summer Sessions, George Washington University

Clifford P. Froehlich, Specialist for Training Guidance Personnel, Occupational Information and Guidance Service; Office of Education, Federal Security Agency; Associate Professor of Education, Johns Hopkins University

Milton E. Hahn, Professor of Psychology, Dean of Students, University of California, Los Angeles

Nicholas Hobbs, Chair, Department of Psychology, Louisiana State University

Max L. Hutt, Associate Professor of Psychology, University of Michigan

E. Lowell Kelly, Director, Bureau of Psychological Services, Professor of Psychology, University of Michigan

Victor C. Raimy, Director of Clinical Training Program, Department of Psychology, University of Colorado

C. Gilbert Wrenn, Professor of Educational Psychology, University of Minnesota

Note. From *Training of Psychological Counselors: Report of a Conference Held at Ann Arbor, Michigan, July 27 and 28, 1949, and January 6 and 7, 1950* (p. 2), by E. Bordin, 1950, Ann Arbor: University of Michigan Press. Copyright 1950 by the University of Michigan Press. Reprinted with permission.

For the casual or uninterested observer, the host of training proposals generated in the decade from 1945 to 1955 all seem rather similar. The differences, however, were there, and foretold things to come. The deliberations at the Ann Arbor conference illustrated the divergence in counseling and clinical approaches to training and teaching of professional psychology. Psychological counselors and counseling were differentiated from clinical psychologists and psychotherapy. The attendees attempted to highlight commonalities but could not disguise some true differences. A psychological counselor was likely to be found in an educational setting, working with essentially normal individuals seeking information that would aid in adjustment to everyday life. This was in contrast to a clinical psychologist, who was most likely to be working in a hospital setting with more seriously mentally ill populations, with personality reorganization as the goal of psychotherapy. The roads began to diverge more fully when subdoctoral training was discussed. The Boulder conference held firm to the conviction that the degree of the clinical psychologist was the PhD. Psychological counselors held out much more promise for professionals at the master's level of training, and the Ann Arbor group gave considerable time to discussions of the proper program of training for master's-level psychological counselors (Bordin, 1950).

The long association of guidance and counseling with education meant that many educators found a professional identification and home in the broad and burgeoning field of counseling and guidance. For many in this group, the master's degree was the terminal degree. For the traditional laboratory-trained psychologists who had migrated into the applied psychology of measurement and selection and the like, the doctorate in psychology was the requisite degree. The duality in the identity of the newly organized division of guidance and counseling of the APA soon came under scrutiny, both from within and without.

The national need for mental health professionals, and the resulting government funds made available to establish this working core, pushed and pulled counseling and guidance professionals into liaisons with federal agencies such as the VA and the NIMH in support of programs of rehabilitation, education, clinical work, and community counseling. The final document of the Ann Arbor meeting was brought forward to Division 17 for careful consideration and deliberation on the campus of Northwestern University just prior to the annual APA convention in Chicago in 1951.

The *Northwestern conference*, as it has come to be known, adopted an approved statement on doctoral training of counseling psychologists that was published in the journal *American Psychologist* in 1952 (APA, Division of Counseling and Guidance, Committee on Counselor Training, 1952). Like Boulder, the conferees recommended training in the scientist–practitioner model. In asserting the independence of counseling psychology, the report offered statements on the identity and location of the counseling psychologist. A counseling psychologist was defined as someone who worked with essentially normal individuals, promoted optimal personal development, and emphasized the "positive and preventative" (APA, Division of Counseling and Guidance, Committee on Counselor Training, 1952, p. 175). Most often, this occurred in the context of an educational setting, although the document made frequent reference to the value of a broad range of training experiences. In essence, counseling psychology defined itself as the opposite of clinical psychology. Terms such as *positive, broad,* and *normal* were intended to set counseling psychology apart from clinical psychology, which was perceived as a hospital-based activity that focused on pathology. In a further attempt to establish this new declared identity, a decision was made to change the name of the division from *Counseling and Guidance* to *Counseling Psychology* (APA, Division of Counseling and Guidance, Committee on Counselor Training, 1952).

The adoption of recommended training standards at the doctoral level also met with approval from the VA, which shortly thereafter created two new positions for counseling psychologists in the VA Central Office. Psychologist Robert Waldrop was appointed chief of the VA's Vocational Counseling Services, and it was his job to encourage and enlist universities to provide doctoral programs in counseling psychology (many of which would be located in colleges of education). Like his clinical counterparts, Waldrop found many in the academy concerned about the federal government injecting itself into local departmental affairs. The advent of APA accreditation for counseling psychology programs in 1951 helped to bring greater interest and participation (R. Waldrop, personal communication, May 2001).

School Psychology

The final professional area of psychology to be included under the auspices of the training branch program was school psychology. The Division of School Psychologists (APA Division 16, now called School Psychology), like its cousins in counseling and clinical psychology, appeared as part of the reorganization of APA in 1945. As mentioned earlier, the pleas for inclusion of public school personnel were constant throughout the early implementation of the National Mental Health Act of 1946. An amalgam of interests argued for inclusion of services to children and families through school-based initiatives. This might be in the form of a public health specialist, a social worker, or a psychologist. At the urging of the National Association of School Social Workers, the training branch appointed a subcommittee in Mental Hygiene Personnel in School Programs, which in November 1949 released a report ("Meeting of Subcommittee on Mental Hygiene Personnel in School Programs," 1949). It offered limited hope to school social workers and allied professionals. The subcommittee stated that it would not support any other mental health group other than those already recognized by NIMH. It did offer limited support for exploratory projects.

Again, the strength and protection offered the four chosen groups (psychiatry, psychology, social work, and nursing) determined that these would be the ones to create the new mental health specialists in America. None of the other specialties would or could make school personnel training a priority.

There were enough psychologists with experience in mental testing, child development, social service, vocational guidance, and psychological clinics that school psychology could easily be seen as a member of the nuclear family of the nascent professional psychology movement. It would be these common interests and areas of overlap that propelled school psychologists into the domain of professional expansion, an activity in which NIMH would invest, even if only as an exploratory activity. The investment was small in terms of dollars and time, but it proved to be a defining moment in the development of school psychology.

In 1953, school psychologists realized something that counseling and clinical psychologists had already known and acted on. The supply-and-demand equation showed the imbalance: plenty of schoolchildren and far too few school psychologists to serve them. There were not only dramatic shortages of trained personnel but also corresponding deficits in recognized training programs and curricula (Cutts, 1955). As the brief history of the NIMH had shown, when these issues were identified it was possible to secure funding for a conference to address them.

As with the Boulder and the Ann Arbor conferences, NIMH funds for a training conference in school psychology were secured through applications made by APA. A familiar figure in training, E. Lowell Kelly, in his capacity as chair of APA's Education and Training Board, and in consultation with Division 16, appointed a steering committee of 10 that included Edward S. Bordin (University of Michigan), Dale B. Harris (Institute of Child Welfare, University of Minnesota), Nicholas Hobbs (George Peabody College), Noble H. Kelley (Southern Illinois University), Samuel A. Kirk (University of Illinois), Beatrice Lantz (Los Angeles County Public Schools), Bertha Luckey (Cleveland Pubic Schools), Bruce V. Moore (Education & Training Board), Frances Mullen (Chicago Public Schools), and T. Ernest Newland (University of Illinois). The committee was successful in securing NIMH funding and set about planning for 48 participants to convene at the Hotel Thayer in West Point, New York, from August 22 to August 31, 1954, just prior to the annual APA convention in New York City (for a list of participants, see Exhibit 7.3).

Using the Boulder conference as a model, the participants discussed the needed architecture for the proper creation of the newest member of the professional psychology trilogy, the school psychologist. The document produced by the Thayer conference, *School Psychologists at Mid-Century: A Report of the Thayer Conference on the Functions, Qualifications and Training of School Psychologists* (Cutts, 1955), outlined the shape and substance of school psychology, offering a guide to training that was quickly adopted by the membership.

NIMH director Felix, writing in the introduction of the report, echoed a familiar refrain: the need for all quarters in the community to take part in the movement toward the prevention of mental illness. Felix stated that the roles of schools

> have long been recognized as an influence second only to the home in
> determining the degree to which our citizens achieve that adult goal
> which the layman calls adequacy or happiness or self sufficiency and

EXHIBIT 7.3
Participants at the Thayer Conference

S. Spafford Ackerly, MD, Chair of the Department of Psychiatry and Mental Hygiene, and Director of Louisville Child Guidance Clinic, University of Louisville School of Medicine

Harry V. Bice, Consultant on Psychological Problems, New Jersey State Crippled Children's Commission, Trenton

Jack W. Birch, Director of Special Education, Board of Public Education, Pittsburgh, PA

Joseph M. Bobbitt (Guest), Chief, Professional Services Branch, National Institute of Mental Health, U.S. Public Health Service, Bethesda, MD

Edward S. Bordin, Associate Professor of Psychology, University of Michigan

Opal Boston, Supervisor, School Social Workers, Indianapolis (IN) Public Schools; President, National Association of School Social Workers

Esallee Burdette, Washington (GA) High School, representing the National Education Association Department of Classroom Teachers

Jerry W. Carter, Jr. (Guest), Chief Clinical Psychologist, Community Services Branch, National Institute of Mental Health, U.S. Public Health Service, Bethesda, MD

Walter W. Cook, Dean, College of Education, University of Minnesota

Ethel L. Cornell, Associate in Educational Research, State Education Department, Albany, NY

Norma E. Cutts, Professor of Psychology and Education, New Haven (CT) State Teachers College; Lecturer in Educational Psychology, Department of Education, Yale University

Gertrude P. Driscoll, Professor of Education, Teachers College, Columbia University

James M. Dunlap, School Psychologist, University City (MO) Public Schools

Merle H. Elliott, Director of Research, Oakland (CA) Public Schools

Mary D. Fite, Psychologist, Gilbert School, Multonomah County, OR

Robert Gates, Consultant, Education for Exceptional Children, State Department of Education, Tallahassee, FL

May Seagoe Gowan, Professor of Education, University of California, Los Angeles

Susan W. Gray, Associate Professor of Psychology, George Peabody College

Dale B. Harris, Professor and Director, Institute of Child Welfare, University of Minnesota

Nicholas Hobbs, Chair, Division of Human Development & Guidance, George Peabody College

Noble H. Kelley, Chair, Department of Psychology, Director Psychological Services, Southern Illinois University

Samuel A. Kirk, Professor of Education and Director, Institute for Research on Exceptional Children, University of Illinois

Morris Krugman, Assistant Superintendent of Schools and Guidance, Board of Education, New York City

M. C. Langhorne, Chair, Department of Psychology, Emory University

Beatrice Lantz, Consultant, Division of Research and Guidance, Los Angeles County Schools

Max M. Levin (Guest), Psychologist, Training and Standards Branch, National Institute of Mental Health, U.S. Public Health Service, Bethesda, MD

Bertha M. Luckey, Supervisor, Psychological Service, Cleveland (OH) Board of Education

Boyd R. McCandless, Professor and Director, Iowa Child Welfare Research Station, State University of Iowa

(continued)

EXHIBIT 7.3 *(Continued)*

Guy N. Magness, MD, Director, School Health Service of University City (MO) Public Schools

W. Mason Mathews, Chair, Laboratory Services (School Services), Merrill–Palmer School, Detroit, MI

Bruce V. Moore, Education and Training Board, American Psychological Association

Frances A. Mullen, Assistant Superintendent of Schools in Charge of Special Education, Chicago Public Schools

C. Roger Myers, Professor of Psychology, University of Toronto, Department of Health

T. Ernest Newland, Professor of Education, University of Illinois

Ralph H. Ojeman, Professor of Psychology and Parent Education, Child Welfare Research Station, State University of Iowa

Willard C. Olson, Professor of Education and Psychology, and Dean, School of Education, University of Michigan

Harriet E. O'Shea, Associate Professor of Psychology, Purdue University

Victor C. Raimy, Chair and Professor, Department of Psychology, University of Colorado

S. Oliver Roberts, Professor of Psychology and Education, Chair, Department of Psychology, Fisk University

Francis P. Robinson, Professor of Psychology, Ohio State University

Eliot H. Rodnick, Chair, Department of Psychology, Director of Clinical Training, Duke University

Milton A. Saffir, Director, Chicago Psychological Guidance Center; Principal of Marshall Elementary School, Chicago

Marie Skodak, Director, Division of Psychological Services, Dearborn (MI) Public Schools

Charles R. Strother, Professor of Psychology, Professor of Clinical Psychology in Medicine, University of Washington

Simon H. Tulchin, Consulting Psychologist, New York City

William D. Wall, Department of Education, UNESCO, Paris

Emalyn R. Weiss, Supervisor of Special Education, Berks County Schools, Reading, PA

Albert T. Young Jr., School Psychologist, Falls Church (VA) Public Schools

Visitors at the conference:

Jack R. Ewalt, MD, Commissioner, Massachusetts Department of Mental Health, Professor of Psychiatry, Harvard Medical School

Palmer L. Ewing, Superintendent of Schools, Buffalo, NY

E. Lowell Kelly, Professor of Psychology, University of Michigan, President-Elect, American Psychological Association

Fillmore H. Sanford, Executive Secretary, American Psychological Association

Note. From *School Psychologists at Mid-Century: A Report on the Thayer Conference on the Functions, Qualifications, and Training of School Psychologists* (pp. 207–209), by N. E. Cutts, 1950, Washington, DC: American Psychological Association. Copyright 1950 by the American Psychological Association.

which the psychiatrist calls maturity. The schools have long shown that they are sensitive to this responsibility, as indicated by their increasing utilization of specialized personnel such as counselors, school social workers, guidance personnel, and school psychologists. (Cutts, 1955, p. viii).

The recommendations for training school psychologists bore resemblance to those offered by clinical and counseling psychologists. A major difference was in the open endorsement of training of master's-level practitioners. At Boulder, the topic of subdoctoral training was broached but largely ignored—more to the point, it was shunned. Counseling psychologists at Ann Arbor had been open to consideration of training and certification at the master's level, going so far as to offer a recommended curriculum. However, in the formal statement of training of counseling psychologists released after the Northwestern conference, only the doctoral degree was considered in the standards. Attendees at the Thayer conference reserved the title *school psychologist* for individuals with doctoral training; the title of *psychological examiner* was acceptable for those with 2 years of graduate training. Although there was much debate about the proper title for individuals with training at the master's level, a curriculum was offered in the report, the general content of which was approved by the attendees.

Like its predecessors, the Thayer conference set forth an allegiance to APA. By defining the doctoral standard as necessary for calling oneself a school psychologist, Division 16 helped to ensure recognition and accreditation of school psychology as a professional area by APA. Publication of doctoral training guidelines appeared in *American Psychologist* in 1963, with the first program certification awarded to the University of Texas in 1971 (Fagan, 1996).

SUMMARY

The passage of the National Mental Health Act of 1946 carried with it a blueprint for change, a change in the ways in which mental health and mental illness were treated in America. The training branch program was launched within the PHS and the NIMH in an effort to quickly infuse American culture with a competent corps of mental health professionals. The Committee on Training, dominated by psychiatrists, accomplished its goals through awarding grants to universities and institutions to improve teaching and to individual students in support of graduate training. Grants to institutions were the predominant method of giving. Psychiatry received the greatest amount of aid, and the remaining support was equally divided among psychiatric nursing, social work, and psychology.

The first review of the training program took place in 1953. Little was offered to change the program's design and implementation. There was a feeling of satisfaction with the ways in which the allied disciplines were funded and the results they were producing (Committee on Review, 1953). It appeared that the ideals of providing more teachers and more training opportunities were having the desired effect of producing more mental health professionals. By 1953, however, the program was still in its infancy. The broader success of the NIMH in winning government support and approval was evident in substantial funding increases that began in 1956. In fact, the funds awarded from 1948 through 1955 were only one fourth of those that would be awarded in the period from 1956 through 1961 (NIMH, 1962), yet the early years proved to be of major significance for the emergence of professional psychology in America.

The grants and stipends offered through the training branch program allowed universities to hire clinical faculty to teach graduate students, whose education and training were often supported by those stipends. In doing so, more attention was given to clinical teaching, and more professionals were trained. These activities represented over 95% of program funding for psychology during the years 1948 to 1954. Less than 5% was given to the special projects that have clearly been the lasting image of impact of the training branch program in psychology (NIMH, 1962).

Special project funds were used to subsidize the Boulder, Ann Arbor, and Thayer conferences. In a sense, all of these conferences were about the same thing and produced a similar result. Each provided a forum for a specialty in professional psychology to show its willingness and ability to draw together academic departments of psychology, the largest national association of psychologists (APA), and major federal agencies such as NIMH and the VA. All this was done in a directed effort to create the professional psychologist, be it the clinical, counseling, or school variety. Boulder cleared the way by defining the doctoral standard, offering a recommended curriculum, and endorsing the fusion of science and practice in the newly minted professional. Counseling psychologists, meeting at Ann Arbor and at Northwestern, adopted a similar model, adding the caveats particular to the field's emphasis on normal functioning and guidance. School psychologists at Thayer did likewise, making provisions that signified an emphasis on the mental health of children and, while holding to the doctoral standard, made room for expansion by recommending subdoctoral certification.

In the end, all professional specialties achieved identities that served their members; served their various publics; attracted students and faculty; and ensured survival by maintaining the mechanisms necessary for professional accreditation and, later, for certification and licensure. Yet the gains were not without cost. The dependence of the training program and applied researchers on NIMH funds meant a profession initially in service to psychiatry and the adoption of a medical model of the etiology and treatment of psychological disorders, especially in clinical psychology. Still, there is no denying that the weight of the NIMH, both by force of federal authority and its pocketbook, was critical in bringing about the rapid development of psychological professions after World War II.

In postwar America, professional psychology became synonymous with psychotherapy, an activity that transcended professional monikers such as *psychologist, psychiatrist, social worker*, and the like. As the public became more familiar, although not necessarily more comfortable, with the therapeutic hour, psychotherapy was quickly incorporated into popular culture. The relationship between psychotherapy and popular culture, a *folie á deux* of sorts, has provided a seemingly inexhaustive admixture of humor, drama, and general pathos.

In the free market economy, many people trained for public service have found greener pastures in private practice. The rise of health insurance and associated benefits in the 1960s freed psychotherapy from public service. As third-party payments for psychotherapy became a reality, so too did the fight for those dollars. Psychiatry tried and failed to block certification and licensure of psychologists (Buchanan, 2003). By the 1970s, the mental heath family that the NIMH had created in the 1950s was coming apart. The success of psychology in gaining reimbursement parity with psychiatry was soon followed by similar demands from social workers, psychiatric nurses, and other allied disciplines whose cause was aided by the introduction of managed health care. Such practitioners are well represented in the for-profit mental health care system (VandenBos et al., 1992).

Still, the professional psychologist engineered at mid-century has endured. The training conference format inaugurated by the NIMH in 1949 has continued unabated for 5 decades, planned and supported largely through the auspices of APA. Many of the same issues remain. The uneasy marriage of science and practice continues to be debated and alternatives to the Boulder model offered. The rise of free-standing professional schools of psychology provides an obvious example (Stricker & Cummings, 1992). The confrontation between psychology and psychiatry also continues as psychologists move closer to obtaining prescription privileges (Daw, 2002).

Not recognizing the priority established by the National Mental Health Act of 1946, a recent headline in the March 2002 *APA Monitor* announced "Psychology Training Gets Major Recognition: For the First Time Ever, Congress Has Established a Program Exclusively for Psychology Training" (Murray, 2002, p. 22). The article went on to describe APA's success obtaining federal approval for the funding of graduate psychology education through the offices of the Bureau of Health. The program is intended to "support programs that train health service psychologists to work with underserved populations, such as older persons, children, rural communities, victims of terror and abuse, and people with disabilities or chronic illness" (Murray, 2002, p. 22). Through a process of competitive grants, funds "will go to APA-accredited doctoral, internship or postdoctoral residencies, to use for trainee stipends, faculty and curriculum development, demonstration programs and technical assistance" (Murray, 2002, p. 22).

In the end, we are reminded that history does indeed have a way of repeating itself. Perhaps now is still a time when mental health matters in America.

REFERENCES

Agenda, Committee on Training. (1947). David Shakow Papers, M1360, Archives of the History of American Psychology, University of Akron, Akron, OH.

Agenda for VA–USPHS Conference on Training in Clinical Psychology. (1948, September 5). David Shakow Papers, M1389, Archives of the History of American Psychology, University of Akron, Akron, OH.

American Psychological Association, Committee on Training in Clinical Psychology. (1947). Recommended graduate training program in clinical psychology. *American Psychologist, 2*, 539–558.

American Psychological Association, Committee on Training in Clinical Psychology. (1949). Doctoral training programs in clinical psychology: 1949. *American Psychologist, 4*, 331–341.

American Psychological Association, Division of Counseling and Guidance, Committee on Counselor Training. (1952). Recommended standards for training counselors at the doctoral level. *American Psychologist, 7*, 175–181.

Baker, D. B. (2002). Child saving and the emergence of vocational counseling. *Journal of Vocational Behavior, 60*, 374–381.

Baker, D. B. (2003). Counseling psychology. In D. Freedheim (Ed.), *History of psychology*. Volume 1 in I. B. Weiner (Editor-in-Chief), *Handbook of psychology* (pp. 357–364). New York: Wiley.

Baker, D. B., & Benjamin, L. T., Jr. (2000). The affirmation of the scientist–practitioner: A look back at Boulder. *American Psychologist, 55*, 241–247.

Benjamin, L. T., Jr., & Jones, M. R. (1978). From motivational theory to social-development: Twenty-five years of the Nebraska Symposium on Motivation. In H. Howe & R. Dienstbier (Eds.), *Human emotion: Nebraska Symposium on Motivation, 1978. Vol. 26.* (pp. ix–xix). Lincoln: University of Nebraska Press.

Blocher, D. H. (2000). *The evolution of counseling psychology*. New York: Springer.

Bordin, E. (1950). *Training of psychological counselors: Report of a conference held at Ann Arbor, Michigan, July 27 and 28, 1949, and January 6 and 7, 1950.* Ann Arbor: University of Michigan Press.

Brand, J., & Sapir, P. (1964). An historical perspective on the National Institute of Mental Health. In D. E. Woolridge (Ed.), *Biomedical science and its administration* (pp. 1–84). Unpublished manuscript.

Buchanan, R. (2003). Legislative warriors: American psychiatrists, psychologists, and competing claims over psychotherapy in the 1950s. *Journal of the History of the Behavioral Sciences, 39*, 225–249.

Clark, K. E. (1957). *America's psychologists: A survey of a growing profession*. Washington, DC: American Psychological Association.

Committee on Review. (1953, January 12–16). Report of committee on review of training policies. David Shakow Papers, M1360, Archives of the History of American Psychology, University of Akron. Akron, OH.

Cutts, N. E. (1955). *School psychologists at mid-century: A report on the Thayer conference on the functions, qualifications, and training of school psychologists*. Washington, DC: American Psychological Association.

Daw, J. (2002, March). Steady and strong progress in the push for Rx privileges. *APA Monitor*, 56–58.

Deutsch, A. (1949). *The mentally ill in America* (2nd ed.). New York: Columbia University Press.

Fagan, T. K. (1996). A history of Division 16 (School Psychology): Running twice as fast. In D. Dewsbury (Ed.), *Unification through division: Histories of the divisions of the American Psychological Association* (Vol. 1, pp. 101–135). Washington, DC: American Psychological Association.

Felix, R. H. (1947, December 12). Memo to National Advisory Health Council. David Shakow Papers, M1375, Archives of the History of American Psychology, University of Akron, Akron, OH.

Grob, G. N. (1991). *From asylum to community: Mental health policy in modern America*. Princeton, NJ: Princeton University Press.

Meeting of Subcommittee on Mental Hygiene Personnel in School Programs. (1949, November 5–6). David Shakow Papers, M1360, Archives of the History of American Psychology, University of Akron, Akron, OH.

Miller, J. G. (1946). Clinical psychology in the Veterans Administration. *American Psychologist, 1*, 181–189.

Murray, B. (2002, March). Psychology training gets major recognition. *APA Monitor, 33*, 22–23.

National Institute of Mental Health. (1962). *Training grant program: Fiscal years 1948–1961* (PHS Publication No. 966). Washington, DC: U.S. Government Printing Office.

National Mental Health Act of 1946, Pub. L. No. 79-487.

Pols, H. (2001). Divergences in American psychiatry during the Depression: Somatic psychiatry, community mental hygiene, and social reconstruction. *Journal of the History of the Behavioral Sciences, 37*, 369–388.

Psychiatry Sub-Committee Report. (1947). David Shakow Papers, M1360, Archives of the History of American Psychology, University of Akron, Akron, OH.

Raimy, V. C. (Ed.). (1950). *Training in clinical psychology.* Englewood Cliffs, NJ: Prentice Hall.

Rubenstein, E. A. (1975). Unpublished interview with Robert Felix. Available from the Archives of the American Psychological Association.

Stricker, G., & Cummings, N. A. (1992). The professional school movement. In D. K. Freedheim (Ed.), *History of psychotherapy: A century of change* (pp. 801–828). Washington, DC: American Psychological Association.

Subcommittee on Integrative Policy. (1947). Report of the Subcommittee on Integrative Policy to the Committee on Training, Division of Mental Hygiene, U.S. Public Health Service. David Shakow Papers, M1360, Archives of the History of American Psychology, University of Akron, Akron, OH.

Sub-Committee on Psychiatric Nursing Report. (1947). David Shakow Papers, M1360, Archives of the History of American Psychology, University of Akron, Akron, OH.

Sub-Committee on Psychiatric Social Work. (1947). David Shakow Papers, M1360, Archives of the History of American Psychology, University of Akron, Akron, OH.

Summary of Present Policies and Practices (1952, December 12). David Shakow Papers, M1375, Archives of the History of American Psychology, University of Akron, Akron, OH.

VandenBos, G. R., Cummings, N. A., & DeLeon, P. H. (1992). A century of psychotherapy: Economic and environmental influences. In D. K. Freedheim (Ed.), *History of psychotherapy: A century of change* (pp. 65–102). Washington, DC: American Psychological Association.

IV

PSYCHOLOGISTS ON SITE: PRACTICE AND COMMUNITY

8

SERVICES AT THE NATIONAL INSTITUTE OF MENTAL HEALTH'S MENTAL HEALTH STUDY CENTER OF PRINCE GEORGE'S COUNTY, MARYLAND

MILTON F. SHORE AND F. VINCENT MANNINO

After World War II, the role of the U.S. Public Health Service (PHS), especially the National Institutes of Health, expanded rapidly. As part of a larger effort to address the nation's health needs, Congress passed the National Mental Health Act of 1946, which established the National Institute of Mental Health (NIMH) as one of the National Institutes of Health and gave it a broad mandate to develop research, training, and services in mental health. This contributed to the recognition of mental health as a distinct field, separate from other sections of the PHS, and it established the association of mental health with public health as a national issue. Two international associations that stressed mental health as a specialty were

We express our sincere thanks to Ruth I. Knee, MSW, for her generosity and invaluable assistance, particularly in the area of gathering historical data and materials regarding the early years of the National Institute of Mental Health.

concurrently established: (a) the World Health Organization of the United Nations and (b) the World Federation for Mental Health, a nongovernmental autonomous organization. (See Table 8.1 for legislation affecting mental health service delivery in the United States.)

With extraordinary foresight and creativity, Robert Felix, the first director of NIMH, developed a twofold strategy for the national improvement of mental health services. The fostering of a public health approach by giving grants-in-aid to the states and encouraging the improvement and expansion of community-based services was his first strategy. His second strategy was to establish demonstration clinics in local communities staffed by federal personnel to test and study new approaches to mental health service delivery. The focus of this chapter is the development of one of these demonstration clinics and its role in the development of mental health services.

THE MENTAL HEALTH STUDY CENTER OF PRINCE GEORGE'S COUNTY

The NIMH demonstration clinics had a dual mandate. First, they used principles that had effectively reduced the incidence of other kinds of illnesses in the population to find and develop means for an attack on mental health problems. Second, they generated information on how mental health services could best be delivered in a community. (Community mental health was a new field with a limited knowledge base.) In 1948 and 1949, three mental health demonstration clinics staffed by federal employees were established. One was in Phoenix, Arizona, which closed within a year of opening; the second was a mental health clinic in the Juvenile Court of Washington, DC. The third demonstration clinic, located in Prince George's County, Maryland, continued until 1983.

Prince George's County, Maryland, is a rural–suburban county adjacent to the county housing the central offices of the National Institutes of Health. Its demonstration clinic was originally housed in space provided by the University of Maryland in College Park. In 1954, the name was changed from the Prince George's Mental Health Center to the Mental Health Study Center (MHSC), reflecting the completion of the demonstration stage and a new focus on conducting studies in community mental health services. At that time, the MHSC was also moved from the University of Maryland to a shopping center in a nearby, rapidly growing community.

Although many communities fought strongly for the MHSC, Prince George's County was most successful, and the MHSC was established through a cooperative agreement between the NIMH, the Maryland State Department of Health, and the Prince George's County Health Department.

TABLE 8.1
Legislative Statutes and Amendments Regarding Service Delivery

Date	Act	Purpose
1946	National Mental Health Act (P.L. 79-487)	Enabled establishment of the National Institute of Mental Health (NIMH) in 1949; provided for training, research, and services; Surgeon General was authorized to study causes and treatment of psychiatric disorders
1955	Mental Health Study Act (P.L. 84-182)	Established Joint Commission on Mental Illness and Health to study the status of mental health in the United States
1956	Health Amendments Act (P.L. 84-911)	Established Title V, mental health project grants, and technical assistance projects to develop a wide range of community-based innovations in service delivery
1956	Alaska Mental Health Act (P.L. 84-830)	Provided for territorial treatment facilities for mentally ill individuals in Alaska
1963	Mental Retardation Facilities and Community Mental Health Centers Construction Act (P.L. 88-164)	Authorized staffing grants for services to be provided by community mental health centers nationwide
1965	Community Mental Health Center Staffing Amendments (P.L. 89-105)	Authorized staffing grants for services to be provided by community mental health centers
1965	Social Security Amendments Act (P.L. 89-97)	Provided funds to study mental health in children and to establish the Joint Commission on Mental Health for Children
1966	Narcotic Addiction Rehabilitation Act (P.L. 89-793)	NIMH to provide total treatment and aftercare with renewed emphasis on community care
1966	Comprehensive Health Planning and Public Health Service Amendments (P.L. 89-749)	Authorized grants to support comprehensive state planning for health services, manpower, and facilities, including mental health; superseded grants-in-aid in the National Mental Health Act
1967	Mental Health Amendments (P.L. 90-31)	Extended the provisions of the Community Mental Health Centers Act to 1970; NIMH separated from the National Institutes of Health and was raised to bureau status
1968	The Alcoholic and Narcotic Rehabilitation Amendments (P.L. 90-574)	Authorized funds for the construction and staffing of new facilities for the addict, prevention of alcoholism, and the treatment and rehabilitation of alcoholics
1970	Community Mental Health Centers Amendments (P.L. 91-211)	Authorized construction and staffing of centers for 3 more years, with priority on areas of poverty plus support for services to children

(continued)

TABLE 8.1 *(Continued)*

Date	Act	Purpose
1970	Comprehensive Drug Abuse Prevention and Control Act (P.L. 91-515)	Broadened addiction programs to include drug abuse and drug dependence programs
1970	Centers Act Amendment	Added a new subsection dealing with maintenance of effort for staffing grants
1970	Comprehensive Alcohol Abuse and Alcoholism Prevention, Treatment and Rehabilitation Act (P.L. 91-616)	Transferred the training and research programs related to alcohol abuse and alcoholism into the new National Institute of Alcohol Abuse and Alcoholism within NIMH
1972	Drug Abuse Office and Treatment Act (P.L. 92-255)	Transferred the training and research programs related to drug abuse to the new National Institute on Drug Abuse within NIMH
1973	Health Programs Extension Act (P.L. 93-45)	Authorized funds to extend federal health programs, including the community mental health center program
1974	Comprehensive Alcohol, Drug Abuse and Mental Health Act (P.L. 93-282)	Authorized the establishment of the Alcohol, Drug Abuse and Mental Health Administration
1975	Community Mental Health Centers Amendment Act (P.L. 94-63)	Extended and revised the original Community Mental Health Centers Act for 2 years
1977	Centers Act Extension (P.L. 95-83)	The Centers Act was extended for 2 more years, through September 30, 1978
1978	Centers Act Extension (P.L. 95-622)	The Centers Act was extended for 2 more years, with modifications
1979	Technical Amendment (P.L. 96-32)	Clarified or corrected items related to health and mental health legislation; also made the grant-accounting procedures of the Centers Act Extension of 1978 applicable to fiscal year 1978 grantees
1979	Department of Education Organization Act (P.L. 96-88)	Created the Department of Education and renamed the Department of Health, Education and Welfare the *Department of Health and Human Services*
1980	Mental Health Systems Act (P.L. 96-398)	Renewed emphasis on case management services, comprehensive treatment planning, and interagency cooperation
1981	Omnibus Budget Reconciliation Act (P.L. 97-35)	Consolidated funding for mental health, alcoholism, and alcohol and drug abuse services into a block grant; repealed the Community Mental Health Centers Act and the grant programs authorized under the Mental Health Systems Act

The initial purpose of the MHSC was to function as a mental health clinic, testing the applicability of public health principles of prevention, research, and service as they relate to mental health in the community. It was in the mid-to-late 1950s that professionals at the MHSC intensified their efforts in evaluation (a relatively new field), social research, and program planning while continuing to offer outpatient services (later, many of an innovative kind, e.g., multiple group therapy, couples therapy, and home visiting by psychiatrists to county residents). It also offered extensive consultation and education services to the school system, the courts, and local community agencies and professionals.

The Mental Health Study Center was interdisciplinary, with representatives over the years from the fields of child, adolescent, and adult psychiatry; pediatrics; cultural anthropology; demography; public health; sociology; nursing; and social work. The psychology staff reflected a broad range of psychological specialties, including clinical psychologists, developmental psychologists, social psychologists, and psychologists from the new field of community psychology (see Exhibit 8.1 for a list of the psychologists who were on the staff over the years; one of the authors of this chapter, F. Vincent Mannino, was licensed in both psychology and social work). Thus, professionals at the MHSC could conduct research from a variety of clinical and service system perspectives and frameworks. MHSC research focused on the development and functioning of individuals and families within the broad social and community context (an excellent presentation of this framework can be found in O'Connor & Lubin's [1984] book).

Eight principles guided the Mental Health Study Center in its organization, development, and delivery of community mental health services (Greenspan, 1980). These principles serve as headings for the organization of the rest of this chapter.

EXHIBIT 8.1
Staff Psychologists at the Mental Health Study Center, 1948–1983

Charles A Ullmann	Susan Ott	Alicia F. Lieberman
Margaret Royce	Charlotte Malasky	Julie R. Schamp
Joseph P. Margolin	Julie Kisielewski	Gail Bleach
James G. Kelly	Brian Flynn	Mary Blehar
Robert Newbrough	Beryce W. MacLennan	Joan Houghton
Howard J. Ehrlich	Sheila C. Feld	Malcolm F. Gordon
F. Vincent Mannino	Lucy Olson	Thomas E. Anderson
Derek V. Roemer	Barbara J. Silver	Ben Dean
Milton F. Shore	Suzanne B. Sobel	JoAnne Carpenter
Robert S. Shellow	Dee N. Lloyd	Mary Pharis

Community Origin and Base

A major principle of community-based mental health services is sensitivity and responsivity to community needs. The Mental Health Study Center's Community Advisory Board was the basic resource for the determination of community needs. It consisted of 12 representatives of local groups, PTAs, school systems, clergy, medical societies, courts, business and industry, fraternal organizations, service clubs, social agencies, and the health department. The advisory board acted as a liaison between the MHSC and the community, advised the MHSC on matters pertaining to community relationships, and provided an opportunity for people in the community to learn about the activities and problems in the field of mental health.

The community fought very hard to see that the MHSC be situated within Prince George's county. The MHSC, in return, was eager to help define the community's needs. A demographer studied the geographical distribution and population trends of the county. The MHSC, with limited staff, particularly in its early years, defined what it was and was not able to do. Because it was responsible to the federal government, it could not assume responsibility for the county's services. Staff members became involved through contacts with community agencies—schools, courts, hospitals, and so forth. Psychologists and other staff members joined boards of various community groups (e.g., a local day-care center for mentally retarded children) to understand what was taking place in the community. Professional staff members often gave public talks to both lay and professional organizations and offered data to county officials so they could plan adequately, especially in the area of services. For example, because of the large numbers of people requesting clinic services, the MHSC presented its "waiting list" problem to the advisory board, which accepted it as a problem on which they would act. A project committee was formed to study several approaches that the community itself might undertake. At the same time, the MHSC began using new approaches. One such approach was the "traveling clinic," which made services available to people in distant parts of the county. MHSC staff also provided consultative services to the schools in connection with problems presented by children in cases where direct clinic care either was not feasible or where the school desired assistance in planning an adjustment class within the school setting.

Even the research activities of the MHSC involved the establishment and maintenance of relationships with the community. MHSC research was conducted in collaboration with the community, thus involving the constant sharing of information with the community. The community, through its participants, provided the MHSC with cooperation and information, which in turn necessitated that MHSC staff work closely with community members, cooperating and informing them of the MHSC's work. It was essential that the community members understand that their county was viewed as an integral participant in the research and not as a "guinea pig" to be criticized or have its secrets exposed. There were a number of projects in which the role of community as collaborator was carried to completion, or end result, by having selected project members both from the community and the Mental Health Study Center serve as coauthors of publications. The following publications included community members—denoted by asterisks— as coauthors: Boone and Tighe* (1962); Brown, Esquibel,* Grant,* and Pickford* (1962); Mannino and Conant* (1969); Mannino, Trickett,* Shore, Kidder,* and Levin (1986); and Spencer* and Mackey (1964). Each community member who served as a coauthor was a professional in his or her field but not part of the MHSC's staff.

One of the MHSC's earliest research efforts began in 1949, when school officials expressed concern over maladjusted schoolchildren and the large number of youth who were dropping out of school. Psychologist Charles A. Ullmann worked with the schools for several years to identify and screen a cohort of schoolchildren to determine from data in the school records and other sources whether a child would drop out of school. This project, called the "Reading Study," included extensive reviews of the existing literature, analysis of school records, and the collection of data on more than 3,000 students; multiple analyses were done on the data. The psychologists who were interested in intervention in the school system made suggestions for early identification and ways to improve reading skills and help develop competencies (Miller, Margolin, & Yolles, 1957; Ullmann, 1952).

Another involvement of particular interest was with the county police, who expressed great concern that an annual meeting of Hell's Angels at a county racetrack might result in a riot that would spill over into the local community and lead to vandalism and injury. As a result of consultation with MHSC psychologist Robert Shellow, the Hell's Angels meeting took place with police presence and involvement and without confrontation or rioting of any kind. Known as "The Riot That Didn't Happen," it was reported in a number of professional journals (Shellow & Roemer, 1966).

In 1963, the County courts were deeply distressed over the number of youth who were running away from home. Psychologist Robert Shellow and his colleagues at the MHSC undertook one of the first major studies of teenage runaways and their families. In-depth interviews with the teenagers and their families revealed two types of runaways: (a) those with acute dissatisfaction at home, who were signaling distress to their families by running away, and (b) those who had severe personal, family, school, and community problems of a chronic nature. The MHSC research team concluded that the latter group needed more comprehensive intervention by the court and community agencies (Shellow, Schamp, Liebow, & Unger, 1967). The MHSC staff consulted with agencies in the community to bring about changes to help these youth. The results also formed the basis for a national service program to help runaways under P.L. 107-146, Title 42, the Runaway and Homeless Youth Grant Program of the federal Juvenile Justice and Delinquency Prevention Act in 1975 (called *the Runaway Act*). The Runaway Act funded settings such as runaway houses as well as counseling services, coordinated services with schools, and social services.

Long-Range Perspective

Because the Mental Health Study Center remained in the community for many years, it had a unique opportunity to study community problems over an extended period of time. Psychologists used this opportunity to conduct a 12-year follow-up study of a sample of 14 youth from Shellow et al.'s (1967) runaway study. The runaways were compared with their siblings. The research documented that the act of running away from home should be taken seriously and required intervention. Major problems were found in the runaways as compared with their siblings, unless there was significant intervention to resolve the issues that led to running away (Olson, Liebow, Mannino, & Shore, 1980).

A longitudinal study involved the retesting of 29 boys, ages 8 through 10, first tested 6 years earlier with regard to certain achievement characteristics of the boys and the attitudes of their mothers toward independent accomplishment. The findings showed achievement consistency over the 6-year period, which encompassed childhood and adolescence, thus providing support for the assumption of the achievement motive as a stable personality characteristic (Feld, 1967).

A follow-up study of adolescents who had been adjudicated as delinquents, been put on probation, and had dropped out of school, was another MHSC research project that demonstrated the advantages of long-term community involvement. The adolescents were in an innovative community-based, comprehensive, vocationally oriented psychotherapy program that was independent of school or traditional agencies. A 15-year follow-up evaluation revealed that, compared with an untreated group, the teens who had participated in the program showed significant changes in overt behavior (legal involvement), achievement, and personality structure (Shore & Massimo, 1979). This study received national recognition and was a forerunner of the National Job Corps and Neighborhood Youth Corps programs.

Interdisciplinary Focus

The breadth of interests and training of the interdisciplinary staff contributed to an exchange and broadening of ideas in regard to providing mental health services to a diverse community. The weaving together of the various disciplines contributed to the understanding of the County from a number of different perspectives, as each discipline brought its unique way of viewing service delivery and its specialized data collecting techniques.

Cultural anthropologists worked together with psychologists to study various groups (Olson et al., 1980). In addition, staff anthropologist Elliott Liebow (1967) received a number of awards for his work on urban African American males, which was completed at the MHSC.

Service and Research Integration

From the beginning, the Mental Health Study Center was grounded in the development, organization, and delivery of mental health services in the community. Many of the psychologists had been clinically trained and continued to see clients. All services were free. The purpose of the MHSC, however, was to integrate mental health services within a broader framework of theory and research so that it could contribute to the national program. The staff were deeply involved in research and evaluation activities. In addition, students from a number of universities spent time at the MHSC working on staff projects and on their own projects related to the MHSC's purposes. Often, students as well as staff collected data for their own theses and dissertations, many of which were published. All of the studies related theory and research to clinical practice and decisions regarding the delivery of mental health services. (See Table 8.2.)

TABLE 8.2
Examples of Work With Students

Study	Topic
Nover et al. (1984)	Relationship of maternal perception and mental behavior
Scrofani et al. (1973)	Effect of training on the intelligence scores of Black and White children of different socioeconomic classes
Goebes and Shore (1978)	Effects of bi- and monolingual school climates on children's personality development
Roemer (1968)	Peer group formation in African American adolescents
Kirsch et al. (1976)	Adolescent identity and attitudes toward sex role egalitarianism
Goebes and Shore (1975)	Behavioral expectations of students as related to the sex of the teacher
Holman and Shore (1978)	Community adjustment following a stay in a psychiatric halfway house

TABLE 8.3
Reference Guide and Reviews

Study	Topic
Silver et al. (1979)	Review of clinically relevant infant research
Mannino and Delgado (1969)	Review of the literature on trichotillomania
Mannino et al. (1975)	Reference guide to mental health consultation
Baldwin et al. (1962)	Reference guide to community mental health
MacLennan and Levy (1967, 1968, 1969, 1970, 1971)	Reviews of the group psychotherapy literature
Mannino et al. (1977)	Annotated bibliography of community residential facilities for formerly hospitalized mental patients
Shore and Mannino (1976)	Mental health services for children and youth, 1776–1996

The efforts at integrating service delivery within a research framework led to a number of working guides and reviews of the community mental health literature and related areas (see Table 8.3). Such guides not only economized the efforts of researchers in reviewing the diversity of research strategies but also provided mental health programmers and administrators ready access to policy-relevant materials for improving services.

Multiple Research Methodologies

At the time, the provision of mental health services from a community-based mental health center was a new approach that required the development of a knowledge base through multiple research methodologies. That was particularly true of research that was based on a model of collaboration with the community (e.g., Kelly & Newbrough, 1963). The mandate of the MHSC was to contribute knowledge on a practical level through various programs, activities, and demonstrations. One such study, for example, was the employment of adolescents to collect information from other adolescents in a study of what was called the "effective community of the lower class adolescent" (Roemer, 1968). By collecting diaries of activities, it was possible to understand the way African American youth interacted in their communities and perceived their roles so appropriate community activities and services could be planned.

Information was exchanged and shared with the NIMH central office, regional offices, and others in the field through meetings, presentations, publications, and informal contacts. In a political sense, the County saw the MHSC as giving it visibility in that the County became a microcosm of issues that needed to be addressed nationally. Because these issues were

TABLE 8.4
Examples of the Multiple Research Methodologies Used at the
Mental Health Study Center

Methodology	Sample study
Epidemiological studies	Miller et al. (1957)
Case studies	Nover et al. (1977)
Evaluation studies	Mannino and Wylie (1965)
Surveys	Mannino and Shore (1976)
Participant observation	Liebow (1967)
Exploratory studies	Roemer (1968)
Action research	Shellow (1965)
Demonstration projects	Mannino and Shore (1974)
Experimental studies with control groups	Massimo and Shore (1963)
Program evaluation	Shore et al. (1971)
Cohort studies	Mannino (1966)
Development of assessment tools	Greenspan and Lieberman (1980)
Correlational studies	Nover et al. (1984)

multidimensional and were expected to be grounded in reliable and valid knowledge, they required a variety of approaches and methodologies (see Table 8.4).

Relevance

Major social changes that could not be ignored were occurring during the years the MHSC was in operation. A delicate balance between community forces and national demands existed. One of these concerned school desegregation. Psychologists from the MHSC served as consultants to local agencies responsible for implementing national policy in a county situated in a state below the Mason–Dixon line (MacLennan, 1970; Shellow, 1965). The involvement of a federal agency in local affairs of high political significance required careful understanding of the role mental health people can play in such highly charged situations. Although the federal law on school desegregation had to be implemented, federal employees needed to be cautious in maintaining a neutral stance and be sensitive to the cultural and community forces that were operating (MacLennan, 1970).

There was also an important shift in the delivery of pediatric care. Local parents, aware of the research on the importance of emotional attachments in early life, were requesting major changes in the pediatric environment so that they could stay with their young children when the children were in the hospital. Many health professionals, especially those in the hospitals, were opposed to the idea despite evidence that when young children returned home they would often show psychological symptoms that lasted for some time. Hospital personnel were fearful that parents would interfere with medical care, would bring in bacteria from the outside, or both. One of the authors of this chapter (Milton F. Shore) organized a workshop at the national meeting of the American Orthopsychiatric Association in 1965. At the meeting, internationally known experts in psychoanalysis, child psychiatry, pediatrics, nursing, anthropology, and architecture presented recent mental health research on how necessary changes in pediatric care could be implemented. The proceedings were published as *Red Is the Color of Hurting: Planning for Children in the Hospital* (Shore, 1967). It was the first government publication in the area of mental health aspects of pediatric care. The volume became very popular and contributed to a change in hospital practices in regard to children so that those practices would be more in line with mental health understanding. The Minneapolis Children's Hospital, for example, used the book to construct a new children's hospital with large playrooms and provisions for parents of young children to stay overnight. The book also was selected to be placed into a time capsule of the city of Minneapolis, to be opened in the year 2076.

The awareness of the mental health aspects of pediatric care, especially for children, has led to major changes in hospital settings, including the origin of a new profession in hospitals: that of the child life specialist, who establishes playrooms and works with the families of sick children. Now pediatric hospitals have unlimited visiting hours, play activities, and close family ties. Indeed, family-centered medical care has become a major area of interest. In addition, the increased focus on the mental health aspects of pediatric care has led to the rise of pediatric psychology as a specialty, resulting in a recently formed division in the American Psychological Association (Division 54, Society of Pediatric Psychology).

Anticipation of Areas of National Priority

The 1960s in particular saw the growth of interest in community mental health. Two major professional issues arose, both of which were addressed by psychologists at the Mental Health Study Center. The first was the effort to conceptualize community-based research. In a series of articles, psychologists James Kelly and Robert Newbrough elaborated on how communities can become an integral part of research strategies (Kelly, 1964; Kelly & Newbrough, 1963; Newbrough, 1965). New directions in training psychologists were outlined by Newbrough (1965). After leaving the MHSC, and as community psychology developed as a new area of specialization within the American Psychological Association, both Kelly and Newbrough continued to develop these ideas and their implications for the training of psychologists (see chap. 9, this volume; Newbrough, 1965).

As community-based programs expanded, a number of new ethical issues emerged. The expansion necessitated changes in roles and professional involvement for psychologists and other mental health professionals. Milton F. Shore led a national workshop on the emerging ethical issues of community research, record keeping, and confidentiality, among other issues. The proceedings were published as *Emerging Ethical Issues in Mental Health* (Shore & Golann, 1973). Other psychologists were prompted to explore the ethical issues specifically related to mental health consultation (Snow & Gersick, 1986).

Psychologists at the MHSC actively participated in major new programmatic directions. One was related to manpower development and the training of people in nontraditional ways. In association with the Adult Psychiatry Branch of NIMH, a psychologist and a psychiatrist from the MHSC were involved in the training of sensitive, mature women who had no formal training as mental health counselors to do selective treatment and counseling (Rioch et al., 1962). Through careful supervision and training, these individuals were able to contribute to the development of community programs. Indeed, one of them became the chief of the emergency mental health service in the County's health department (developed under contract to the MHSC). The training of indigenous workers was another significant thrust. MHSC psychologist Beryce MacLennan was instrumental in fostering programs in lower-class areas where there were many members of ethnic–minority groups. This activity, called "New Careers," was one of the early attempts to enlist members of ethnic–minority groups in mental health work (MacLennan, 1969). The program's aim was to train indigenous youth to work in mental health and encourage them to pursue a career in mental health.

In addition to local and national directions, MHSC staff were involved in international studies to determine their relevance to the developing national program. Psychologist Milton F. Shore was particularly interested in alternative services for youth and became a consultant to the World Health Organization of the United Nations, which employed him to study the delivery of services to youth through agencies out of the traditional health system (e.g., hotlines, drop-in centers, "rap" centers, etc.) in six European countries—the Netherlands, Poland, Great Britain, Czechoslovakia, Denmark, and Sweden. The principles governing these programs and their effectiveness were described and integrated into the national U.S. program (Shore, 1976). For example, staff members at the MHSC created a training guide for a youth-operated hotline in Prince George's County (Robinson & Yeager, 1974).

In line with the prevention thrust of the national program, and consistent with the changes brought about by such programs as parents being able to stay with their young hospitalized child, the MHSC, working with psychologist Ed Trickett from the University of Maryland, published a comprehensive review of and reference guide to primary prevention programs (Buckner, Trickett, & Corse, 1985).

Consultation and education were also areas of research, and although they had gone on for a number of years (with the NIMH regional offices playing a major role), they had not been systematically investigated. The area was pursued through a literature review, research, and a major publication with contributions from experts in the area (Mannino et al., 1986). Still another area was research dealing with assessment, clinical intervention, and evaluation of high-risk infants and their families in an effort to prevent conditions that could lead to developmental disorders (Greenspan, 1981). Another study involved intervening with unmarried, pregnant teenagers who were resistant to mental health services. Through contacts with the county hospital, these young women were identified, approached when they were pregnant, and involved in a comprehensive program that was evaluated and found to be effective (O'Leary, Shore, & Wieder, 1984).

Federal, State, and Local Partnerships of Private and Public Resources

Because of its status in the community, the Mental Health Study Center was able to play a significant role in developing partnerships with the local government. Because the center was a federal agency, it was clear to local authorities that it could not take responsibility for the services of the County. MHSC staff were aware of those limits and acted as catalysts for developing local services. One major example involved a study conducted under contract to the local family agency with the assistance of a faculty member in the School of Social Work at the University of Maryland. The study's purpose was to determine the needs of patients who had been discharged from the state hospital to help prevent them from being reinstitutionalized. A significant finding was that housing was the top priority. This study led to the development of cooperative apartments that offered many support services. Because of the program's success, a conference on different models of cooperative apartments, the proceedings of which were published by the Department of Health, Education, and Welfare (Goldmeier, Mannino, & Shore, 1978), was held. Of even greater significance was that the state and county governments took over the funding of the program, which became a model program. Thus, what began as a federal demonstration project at the local level became an integral part of the state mental health system.

Although the role of the Mental Health Study Center was clear to those in the county, the role it played with regard to the NIMH Central Office varied. The Central Office often posed questions that could not be answered by a unit such as the Mental Health Study Center. For example, although the MHSC research findings were useful in national planning, one had to be cautious about generalizing from a suburban/rural community to urban communities in other geographical areas with different cultural and ethnic populations.

The MHSC employed a number of professionals who went on to high-level academic careers in community mental health. Others became high officials at federal and state levels. Two such professionals were Stanley Yolles and Bertram Brown; both later served terms as NIMH director.

At times, efforts were made to change the direction of the MHSC to conform to changing emphases and political pressures. Thus, at one point it was believed the MHSC could become a model comprehensive community mental health center. Some people also believed that it could become an academic center doing traditional behavioral research. A third approach was to try to convert it into a biologically oriented research unit similar to that of the intramural research unit at the NIMH Clinical Center. In the 1970s, attempts were made to close the MHSC. At that time, the community came to its defense. None of the three changes took place, and the Mental Health Study Center was able to continue as a community laboratory exploring issues of community mental health and related areas until its demise in 1983. In 1983, with the gradual elimination of the regional offices, the use of federal block grants to the states, and the reduction of the federal role in the provision of mental health services, the Mental Health Study Center was closed.

CONCLUSION

It has been more than 50 years since the establishment of NIMH. NIMH was intended to be the prime mover in developing a national program aimed at improving the mental health of the entire population. In regard to service, its purpose was to encourage, facilitate, foster, and originate a national program of comprehensive community-based services. However, two historical forces have hindered the full implementation of the program: (a) the ambivalent relationship between the federal government and state governments and (b) conflicting professional views among individuals in the mental health field.

The Reagan Administration's decision to make federal block grants to states for mental health services has led to a patchwork of isolated programs throughout the country with different levels of quality and mixed success. The deinstitutionalization of severely mentally ill people, which arose from the concept of community-based care and was meant to be accompanied by aftercare in the community, has instead led to increased homelessness and vagrancy for individuals discharged from hospitals. In many states, adequate services were never developed, and aftercare needs were ignored. The result has been large numbers of people with severe mental disorders returning to jails or prisons, a situation similar to that found by Dorothea Dix in the 1800s (Applebaum, 2003; Grob, 1995).

The second hindrance to the success of a national mental health program has been the internal conflicts in the mental health field itself. It is unfortunate that, as resources and funding have decreased, the opposing sides have become polarized and vocal, leading to the rise of politically active advocates on both sides. A variety of ideological and philosophical conflicts have plagued the field. Among the most important are questions of whether the emphasis should be on mental illness, with a concomitant focus on illness and medicine, or whether the emphasis should be on mental health. Questions of resource allocation have also been raised; that is, should the majority of resources be used for the rehabilitation and treatment of individuals with severe and persistent mental illness, or should priority be given to individuals at high risk for mental disorders? Primary prevention versus early diagnosis and treatment, support for mental health promotion, biological versus psychosocial etiology, and questions of professional alignment (medical settings vs. educational/social welfare settings) have also become part of the ideological and professional battlefield.

Readers should keep in mind that the growth of NIMH and the resources it was able to muster paralleled the growth of psychology as a profession, from its minimal involvement in services to the birth of community psychology as a field in the 1950s and 1960s (see chap. 9, this volume). As with the other mental health professions, in the early years few psychologists were trained to deliver clinical services in the community—indeed, most clinical psychologists had been trained in hospital settings. Challenged by the new directions the field was taking, psychologists became active in new roles, conceptualizing the new approaches by sharing information; developing competencies in technical assistance; discovering new evaluative methodologies; planning new service structures while improving those in operation; and demonstrating how community-based programs could be implemented, evaluated, and disseminated. Many psychologists at NIMH were participating as members of interdisciplinary teams in regional offices and in the Central Office. Others were developing their own projects in local communities.

Psychologists have increasingly begun to view mental health within an ecological framework (Kelly, 1968; Mannino & Shore, 1984). As a result, the boundaries with other fields have become more fluid and the issues to be addressed more complex. New specialties, such as community psychology and pediatric psychology, have emerged in part from the activities and direction provided by psychologists at the MHSC. Despite strong efforts to limit federal involvement only to standard settings and evaluation, and despite significant attempts to medicalize the field of mental health, recent events have suggested a return to the public health model, with greater national involvement in areas of social concern. In the delivery of services, this return has been necessitated by HMOs' restrictions on mental health care and the lack of parity for the treatment of mental illness as opposed to physical illness in medical insurance plans. The recent Surgeon General's reports on mental health, youth suicide, and violence have aroused renewed interest in involving the federal government in the prevention and treatment of mental health problems ("Mental Health: A Report of the Surgeon General," 1999; "Report of the Surgeon General: Conference on Children's Mental Health, A National Action Agenda," 2001). Preventing terrorism, eliminating bullying in schools, family planning, reform of systems of care, the effects of the media on emotional development, high-quality child care, and aging are all national interests that require psychological expertise and support. Psychologists at NIMH contributed significantly to the increased visibility of mental health as a national issue and were highly active and involved in creating services that could improve the lives of all U.S. residents.

REFERENCES

Applebaum, P. S. (2003). The "quiet" crisis in mental health services. *Health Affairs*, 22(5), 110–116.

Baldwin, J. A., Gelfand, S., Kelly, J. G., Lange, H., Newbrough, J. R., & Simmons, A. J. (1962). *Community mental health and social psychiatry: A reference guide*. Cambridge, MA: Harvard University Press.

Boone, D., & Tighe, H. (1962). Public mental health approach to alcoholism: "The Prince George's Story." In *Interagency development and coordination of services for alcoholics and their families: Proceedings of a conference held in Dauphin Island, Alabama* (pp. 26–41). Bethesda, MD: National Institute of Mental Health.

Brown, B. S., Esquibel, A., Grant, M., & Pickford, E. M. (1962). Health Department alcoholism program in Prince George's County, Maryland. *Public Health Reports, 77,* 480–484.

Buckner, J. C., Trickett, E. J., & Corse, S. J. (1985). *Primary prevention in mental health: An annotated bibliography*. Washington, DC: U.S. Government Printing Office.

Feld, S. C. (1967). Longitudinal study of the origins of achievement strivings. *Journal of Personality and Social Psychology, 7,* 408–414.

Goebes, D. D., & Shore, M. F. (1975). Behavioral expectations of students as related to the sex of the teacher. *Psychology in the Schools, 12,* 222–224.

Goebes, D. D., & Shore, M. F. (1978). Some effects of bicultural and monocultural school environments on personality development. *American Journal of Ortho-psychiatry, 48,* 398–407.

Goldmeier, J., Mannino, F. V., & Shore, M. F. (1978). *New directions in mental health care: Cooperative apartments.* Washington, DC: U.S. Government Printing Office.

Greenspan, S. I. (1980). Introduction. In R. F. Clarke (Ed.), *Building community mental health through research: A bibliography of Mental Health Study Center staff publications, 1948–1979* (pp. v–viii). Washington, DC: U.S. Department of Health and Human Services.

Greenspan, S. I. (1981). *Psychopathology and adaptation in infancy and early childhood.* New York: International Universities Press.

Greenspan, S. I., & Lieberman, A. F. (1980). Infants, mothers, and their interaction: A quantitative clinical approach to developmental assessment. In S. I. Greenspan & G. H. Pollock (Eds.), *The course of life: Psychoanalytic contributions toward understanding personality development: Vol. 1. Infancy and early childhood* (DHEW Publication No. ADM-80-786, pp. 271–313). Washington, DC: Department of Health, Education and Welfare.

Grob, G. N. (1995). Government and mental health policy: A structural analysis. In P. J. Boyle & D. Callahan (Eds.), *What price mental health: The ethics and politics of setting priorities.* Washington, DC: Georgetown University Press.

Holman, T., & Shore, M. F. (1978). Halfway house and family involvement as related to community adjustment for ex-residents of a psychiatric halfway house. *Journal of Community Psychology, 6,* 123–129.

Juvenile Justice and Delinquency Prevention Act, 42 U.S.C. § 5632 (1975).

Kelly, J. G. (1964). The mental health agent in the urban community. In Group for the Advancement of Psychiatry (Eds.), *Urban America and the planning of mental health services* (pp. 474–494). New York: Group for the Advancement of Psychiatry.

Kelly, J. G. (1968). Toward an ecological conception of preventive intervention. In J. W. Carter (Ed.). *Research contributions from psychology to community mental health* (pp. 75–99). New York: Behavioral Publications.

Kelly, J. G., & Newbrough, J. R. (1963). Community mental health research symposium. *Public Health Reports, 78,* 57–64.

Kirsch, P., Shore, M. F., & Kyle, D. (1976). Personality and ideology: Aspects of identity formation in adolescents with strong attitudes toward sex role equalitarianism. *Journal of Youth and Adolescence, 5,* 387–401.

Liebow, E. (1967). *Tally's corner: A study of Negro streetcorner men.* Boston: Little, Brown.

MacLennan, B. W. (1969). New careers: Program development and the process of institutional change. In M. F. Shore & F. V. Mannino (Eds.), *Mental health and the community: Problems, programs, and strategies* (pp. 179–190). New York: Behavioral Publications.

MacLennan, B. W. (1970). Mental health and school desegregation: An attempt to prevent community conflict. In *Proceedings of the 78th Annual Convention, Part 2* (pp. 801–802). Washington, DC: American Psychological Association.

MacLennan, B. W., & Levy, N. (1967). The group psychotherapy literature: 1966. *International Journal of Group Psychotherapy, 17,* 378–398.

MacLennan, B. W., & Levy, N. (1968). The group psychotherapy literature: 1967. *International Journal of Group Psychotherapy, 18,* 375–401.

MacLennan, B. W., & Levy, N. (1969). The group psychotherapy literature: 1968. *International Journal of Group Psychotherapy, 19,* 382–408.

MacLennan, B. W., & Levy, N. (1970). The group psychotherapy literature: 1969. *International Journal of Group Psychotherapy, 20,* 380–411.

MacLennan, B. W., & Levy, N. (1971). The group psychotherapy literature: 1970. *International Journal of Group Psychotherapy, 21,* 345–380.

Mannino, F. V. (1966). A cohort study of school withdrawals with implications for mental health. *Community Mental Health Journal, 2,* 146–151.

Mannino, F. V., & Conant, M. M. (1969). Dropouts from parent education groups. *Family Coordinator, 18,* 54–59.

Mannino, F. V., & Delgado, R. A. (1969). Trichotillomania in children: A review. *American Journal of Psychiatry, 126,* 505–511.

Mannino, F. V., MacLennan, B. W., & Shore, M. F. (1975). *The practice of mental health consultation: A reference guide to the consultation literature.* New York: Gardner Press.

Mannino, F. V., Ott, S., & Shore, M. F. (1977). Community residential facilities for former mental patients: An annotated bibliography. *Psychosocial Rehabilitation Journal, 1,* 43.

Mannino, F. V., & Shore, M. F. (1974). Demonstrating effectiveness in an aftercare program. *Social Work, 19,* 351–354.

Mannino, F. V., & Shore, M. F. (1976). Perceptions of social supports by Spanish-speaking youth with implications for program development. *Journal of School Health, 46,* 471–474.

Mannino, F. V., & Shore, M. F. (1984). An ecological perspective on family intervention. In W. A. O'Connor & B. Luben (Eds.), *Ecological approaches to clinical and community psychology* (pp. 75–93). New York: Wiley.

Mannino, F. V., Trickett, E. J., Shore, M. F., Kidder, M. G., & Levin, G. (Eds.). (1986). *Handbook of mental health consultation.* Washington, DC: U.S. Government Printing Office.

Mannino, F. V., & Wylie, H. W. (1965). Evaluation of the physical examination as a part of psychiatric intake practice. *American Journal of Psychiatry, 122,* 175–179.

Massimo, J. L., & Shore, M. F. (1963). The effectiveness of a vocationally oriented psychotherapy program for adolescent delinquent boys. *American Journal of Orthopsychiatry, 33*, 634–643.

Miller, A. D., Margolin, J. P., & Yolles, S. F. (1957). Epidemiology of reading disabilities: Some methodologic considerations and early findings. *American Journal of Public Health, 45*, 1250–1256.

National Mental Health Act of 1946, Pub. L. No. 79-487.

Newbrough, J. R. (1965). Community mental health: A movement in search of a theory. In *Community mental health: Individual adjustment of social planning*. A symposium presented at the 9th InterAmerican Congress of Psychology, Miami, Florida, Dec. 18, 1964 (pp. 1–17). Bethesda, MD: National Institute of Mental Health.

Nover, R. A., Greenspan, S. I., Lourie, R. S., Silver, B. J., & Taylor, P. (1977). High risk pregnant women and families: A case study. In *Proceedings of the Conference on Child Abuse: Where Do We Go From Here?, Feb. 18–20* (pp. 71–75). Washington, DC: Children's Hospital Medical Center.

Nover, A., Shore, M. F., Timberlake, E., & Greenspan, S. I. (1984). The relationship of maternal perception and maternal behavior: A study of normal mothers and their infants. *American Journal of Orthopsychiatry, 54*, 210–223.

O'Connor, W. A., & Lubin, B. (1984). *Ecological approaches to clinical and community psychology*. New York: Wiley.

O'Leary, K., Shore, M. F., & Wieder, S. (1984). Reaching pregnant adolescents: Are we missing important cues? *Social Casework, 65*, 297–307.

Olson, L., Liebow, E., Mannino, F. V., & Shore, M. F. (1980). Runaways twelve years later: A follow-up. *Journal of Family Issues, 1*, 165–188.

Rioch, M. J., Elkes, C., Flint, A., Newman, P., Shellow, R., Usdansky, B., et al. (1962). *Pilot project in training mental health counselors: Summary 1960–1962*. Bethesda, MD: National Institute of Mental Health.

Robinson, S. E., & Yeager, J. A. (1974). *What it's all about: A training guide for a youth-operated hotline*. Rockville, MD: National Institute of Mental Health.

Roemer, D. V. (1968). *Adolescent peer group formation in two Negro neighborhoods*. Unpublished doctoral dissertation, Harvard University.

Scrofani, P. J., Suziedelis, A., & Shore, M. F. (1973). Conceptual ability in Black and White children of different social classes: An experimental test of Jensen's hypothesis. *American Journal of Orthopsychiatry, 43*, 541–553.

Shellow, R. (1965). The training of police officers to control civil rights demonstrations. In A. M. Rose & C. B. Rose (Eds.), *Minority problems: A textbook of readings in intergroup relations* (pp. 425–430). New York: Harper & Row.

Shellow, R., & Roemer, D. V. (1966). The riot that didn't happen. *Social Problems, 14*, 221–233.

Shellow, R., Schamp, J. R., Liebow, E., & Unger, E. (1967). Suburban runaways of the 1960s. *Monographs of the Society for Research in Child Development, 32*, 1–51.

Shore, M. F. (Ed.). (1967). *Red is the color of hurting: Planning for children in the hospital*. Bethesda, MD: National Institute of Mental Health.

Shore, M. F. (1976). Mental health services for youth: What we can learn from the Europeans. *Journal of Clinical Child Psychology, 5*, 10–13.

Shore, M. F., & Golann, S. E. (Eds.). (1973). *Current ethical issues in mental health*. Washington, DC: U.S. Government Printing Office.

Shore, M. F., & Mannino, F. V. (1976). Mental health services for children and youth: 1776–1976. *Journal of Clinical Child Psychology, 5*, 21–25.

Shore, M. F., & Massimo, J. L. (1979). Fifteen years after treatment: A follow-up study of comprehensive vocationally oriented psychotherapy. *American Journal of Orthopsychiatry, 49*, 240–245.

Shore, M. F., Milgram, N. A., & Malasky, C. (1971). The effectiveness of an enrichment program for disadvantaged young children. *American Journal of Orthopsychiatry, 41*, 442–449.

Silver, B. J., Greenspan, S. I., Lourie, R. S., & Nover, R. A. (1979). Review of clinically relevant infant research. In *Clinical infant research programs: Selected overview and discussion* (DHEW Publication No. ADM-79-748). Washington, DC: U.S. Government Printing Office.

Snow, D. L., & Gersick, K. E. (1986). Ethical and professional issues in mental health consultation. In F. V. Mannino, E. J. Trickett, M. F. Shore, M. G. Kidder, & G. Levin (Eds.), *Handbook of mental health consultation* (pp. 393–433). Washington, DC: U.S. Government Printing Office.

Spencer, C. S., & Mackey, R. A. (1964). Home visiting in pupil personnel work. *International Journal of Pupil Personnel Work, 8*, 26–32.

Ullmann, C. A. (1952). *Identification of maladjusted school children* (Public Health Monograph No. 7). Washington, DC: U.S. Government Printing Office.

U.S. Department of Health and Human Services. (1999). *Mental health: A report of the Surgeon General*. Washington, DC: Government Printing Office.

U.S. Department of Health and Human Services. (2001). *Report of the Surgeon General: A conference on children's mental health: A national action agenda*. Washington, DC: Government Printing Office.

9

THE NATIONAL INSTITUTE OF MENTAL HEALTH AND THE FOUNDING OF THE FIELD OF COMMUNITY PSYCHOLOGY

JAMES G. KELLY

The field of community psychology would not have been established without the multiple and sustained contributions of the staff of the National Institute of Mental Health (NIMH) and the financial resources that NIMH made available to fund community-oriented psychologists and other mental health professionals. Although the field of community psychology was founded at the Swampscott Conference, May 4–8, 1965, the roots can be found in the establishment of the NIMH on July 3, 1946, as Public Law 79-487 of the 79th Congress (Bennett et al., 1966; Brand & Sapir, 1964).

The mission and policies of the NIMH advocated for a public health–community approach to the treatment and prevention of mental illness

This chapter was enhanced and enlarged in specific details by the committed interests and background information provided by former National Institute of Mental Health staff. My debt of gratitude is expressed especially to Leonard J. Duhl, J. Wilbert Edgerton, Stephen E. Goldston, Ruth Knee, and Alan Miller. Others have provided invaluable insights and commentary. I particularly thank Bruce Bobbitt, Ingrid Farreras, John C. Glidewell, Dorothy Gruich, Gerald Grob, Erin Hayes, Carmi Schooler, Stephen P. Stelzner, and Bianca Wilson.

during the 20 years after World War II (WWII). The first director of NIMH, public health-trained psychiatrist Robert H. Felix (1904–1990), articulated this policy. The NIMH was the primary federal resource that created opportunities for psychologists to obtain grants to test community approaches. This policy continued with the next two directors, also public health-trained psychiatrists, Stanley F. Yolles (1964–1970) and Bertram S. Brown (1970–1978). Without such funding, and the opportunities and incentives that the funds created, it is unlikely that the notion of communities as resources in the treatment and prevention of mental health would have evolved within the profession of psychology. However, it was not only the funds that made a difference. The NIMH, under Robert Felix's leadership, became a source of conceptual and strategic support to implement new ways of conceiving how mental health services could be delivered.

It is important to emphasize that having a public health approach meant focusing on populations, in contrast to individuals, and designing prevention programs, in contrast to treatment of already-disabled individuals. A public health approach also meant a comprehensive and coordinated series of community-based services with equal concern for mental health and mental illness (Leavell & Clark, 1953; Rosen, 1993; Starr, 1982). The public health approach, in contrast to conventional psychiatric care, represented a paradigm shift in how mental health services were conceived and delivered.

The NIMH's public health philosophy provided an alternative point of view to the treatment of already-sick individuals in hospitals and clinics and served as a stimulus for psychologists to move beyond individual treatment approaches. By virtue of its location within the structure of the National Institutes of Health (NIH), NIMH also benefited from favorable congressional support for scientific research in the 1950s, the Sputnik era (Dickson, 2001; Strickland, 1972). Through its many funding and grant programs, the NIMH was a social force that altered the focus for mental health care and created new options for the prevention of mental illness and the promotion of mental health with the participation of the mental health professions and behavioral scientists (Parascandola, 1993).

PREHISTORY

Before NIMH was established, there were several legislative acts and federal policies that helped establish precedents for federal investment in the health and welfare of communities. One example is the Maternity and Infancy Welfare and Hygiene (Sheppard–Towner) Act (1921), which provided funds directly to states and local communities through the U.S. Children's Bureau (R. Knee, personal communication, January 26, 2002).

In addition, Albert M. Deutsch's (1937) book *The Mentally Ill in America* brought public attention to the history of the treatment of mentally ill people from colonial times to the present. "This 530 page book covered the entire development of the cure of the mentally ill from colonial times to that time" (Micale & Porter, 1994, p. 56). The second edition of this book, published in 1949, became a reference document to increase public scrutiny on reforms of mental treatment. Federal intervention in health care issues during Franklin Delano Roosevelt's presidency, and the new public awareness for needed improvements in care, were consistent with Deutsch's arguments and gave a supportive historical backdrop to provide federal funds directly to communities (Rossi, 1962).

In addition to this financial support, conceptions of the causes of mental illness were shifting. As a result of the experiences of mental health professionals in WWII, it became more apparent that environmental factors, such as the stresses of battle, were as important as individual factors in producing mental illness. Gerald Grob (1994) summarized these changes in concepts:

> During that conflict military psychiatrists found that neuropsychiatric disorders were far more pervasive and serious than had been previously recognized, that environmental stress associated with combat contributed to mental maladjustment, and that early and purposeful treatment in noninstitutional settings produced favorable outcomes. (p. 191)

Influential psychiatrists, such as Roy R. Grinker, John P. Spiegel, John W. Appel, Leo Bartemeier, Harry Solomon, and others, all addressed the significance of environmental stresses and wrote about them after the war (Grob, 1994, p. 343). Albert J. Glass, a psychiatrist who served in both WWII and the Korean War, was also very influential in pointing out the environmental effects of combat on American troops. He became an advocate for research on social factors in stress and mental illness (Glass, 1953, 1957).

Before and during WWII, the public health-trained mental health professionals in the U.S. Public Health Service (PHS) were assigned to the Coast Guard Academy. It is more than just a historical note that the concepts for the future NIMH were originally discussed and planned informally over a 3-year period (1942–1945) at the Coast Guard Academy. These conversations occurred between Seymour Vestermark and Dale Cameron, two psychiatrists with the PHS; Joseph M. Bobbitt, a PHS psychologist who was to play a future leading role at NIMH; and Robert Felix (A. Miller, personal communication, December 2, 2001). One of the background documents for their conversation was a paper Felix had prepared for a class he was taking while working on his MPH degree at the Johns Hopkins School of Public Health in 1941. This paper outlined Felix's vision for a national public health mental health program. As Alan Miller (personal communication, December 2, 2001), a former staff member at NIMH, recalled in the following:

> The structure they (Vestermark, Cameron, Bobbitt and Felix) proposed for NIMH was very different from any of the other Institutes. Whereas the other Institutes were primarily designed to support and conduct research, they also proposed to include professional education, mental health services and the vital statistics of mental disorders.

In 1946, Surgeon General Thomas Parran requested that Felix draw up a plan for a national agency to deal with mental health issues. The plan that Felix presented to Parran, and that Parran accepted, had its incubation in Felix's paper for the class assignment at Johns Hopkins and those conversations with his three colleagues at the Coast Guard Academy 3 years before. Parran was very supportive of Felix's plan, even though it encompassed more activities than the other parts of the NIH.

JOSEPH M. BOBBITT (1908–1975)

The story of the community movement in psychology cannot be completely told without paying attention to the contributions of Joe Bobbitt. He was born in St. Joseph, Missouri, and spent his boyhood in California. He received his BA and MA from the University of Southern California in 1931 and 1932. He earned his PhD in experimental psychology from Northwestern University in 1937. Bobbitt served in the following leadership roles at NIMH: Chief Psychologist, 1946–1950; Chief, Professional Services Branch, 1950–1956; Assistant Director, 1956–1960; and Associate Director, 1960–1964. He was an informal leader who supported innovation and made it possible for NIMH to identify key topics and commit resources to them. In a talk at the National Symposium on New Trends in Counseling and Psychotherapy at the University of Illinois on February 26, 1949, he outlined a public health approach to the prevention of mental illness that would be timely today. In chairing a symposium on "Implications of Community Mental Health for the Training of Clinical Psychologists" at the 1962 annual convention of the American Psychological Association, he said the following:

> [The community mental health field] should make it clear that a clinical psychologist cannot meet the demands that will be placed upon him if he is only a clinical psychologist. He must be also something of a social psychologist; he must also be something of a cultural anthropologist; he must also be concerned with [what] makes groups and communities

operate, which goes beyond a knowledge of the intrapersonal. (Bobbitt, 1962)

John C. Eberhart, himself an associate director of NIMH, made the following comments at Bobbitt's memorial service: "He was the most honest man I know. He was one whose word was never doubted, who had the courage to deal straight with the world, whose integrity was so strong and so central to his character that he was trusted implicitly by everyone."

NIMH PROGRAMS RELEVANT TO COMMUNITY PSYCHOLOGY, 1946–1965

Members of the mental health professions began to realize that a supportive community could be a powerful force in helping soldiers withstand the stresses of battle conditions. This awareness among psychiatrists and psychologists who had served in WWII influenced how they thought about treatment thereafter (Grob, 1991, 1994, 1996). A new paradigm was emerging as returning mental health professionals advocated for more group approaches and efforts to extend mental health services into the community. This emerging constituency was bolstered by Mary Lasker, a prominent citizen advocate, and Mary E. Switzer, longtime advocate for services to the disabled, who in 1950 became director of the Office of Vocational Rehabilitation (Hughes, 1986). George Stevenson, a psychiatrist and executive director of the National Association for Mental Health, was another powerful advocate. Prestigious groups, such as the President's Scientific Research Board, also advocated for increased federal support of efforts to understand and control disease, including mental illness (Grob, 1991).

Political support was garnered as well. Felix, a consummate organizer and politician, was able to develop excellent working relationships with members of Congress, especially Sen. Lister Hill of Alabama and Rep. John Fogarty of Rhode Island. Through these relationships, Congressional support for revisions in the delivery of mental health services was virtually guaranteed.

NIMH support represented a shift from private to public support and was vital as mental health professionals and social scientists developed community approaches. Before WWII, community research had been funded by private foundations, such as the Milbank Memorial Fund and the Commonwealth Fund. Although private support continued after the war, federal support soon overwhelmed it, as investigators could now apply for and receive peer-reviewed RO1 (regular research) grants from NIMH to pursue community approaches.

Exemplary community approaches began to emerge around the United States. For example, the Wichita Guidance Center in Wichita, Kansas, became known in the 1940s as a model community mental health program in which there was a focus on new and different resources in the community, such as schools and courts. Jerry W. Carter Jr., who later became an influential member of the Community Services Branch of NIMH, was the director. He was one of the first psychologists to be an administrator of a local mental health program. Also in Kansas, psychiatrists and brothers William and Karl Menninger, who were high-ranking psychiatric authorities in the military in WWII, created the multidisciplinary Menninger Clinic in Topeka (Friedman, 1990; Menninger, 1947). They were also tireless in improving the quality of mental health care in state hospitals throughout the United States.

During the immediate post-WWII period, increasing numbers of federal agencies became active in adopting a community perspective. The Office of Vocational Rehabilitation, under the leadership of Mary E. Switzer, was an early host of community approaches. Harold Hildreth, of the Veterans Administration, became another strong voice for community approaches. He later became a staff member with the Community Services Branch at NIMH, where he was an effective advocate for NIMH grant programs in support of community approaches. He was the prime mover for the establishment of the Suicide Prevention Center at the University of California, Los Angeles (R. Knee, personal communication, January 26, 2002).

A number of people in St. Louis, Missouri, came together because of their interest in preventing mental health problems in schoolchildren. The prime mover was psychiatrist Margaret C. L. Gildea, who was convinced that some form of primary prevention was critical to the mental health of schoolchildren. She and A. D. Buchmueller developed a program of education and group therapy for mothers in two school districts (J. C. Glidewell, personal communication, February 4, 2002). Soon after this program began, Herbert A. Domke was appointed health commissioner of St. Louis County. He, too, was convinced of the need for preventive mental health programs in schools. Furthermore, both he and Gildea, with the advice of Ivan N. Mensh, a clinical psychologist, sought to empirically test the effectiveness of programs such as Gildea–Buchmueller's. With NIMH funds (Grant M-592C), including Mental Health Project funds, the landmark St. Louis County Mental Health Project was begun (J. C. Glidewell, personal communication, February 4, 2002). John C. Glidewell, a social psychologist who later became a leading community psychologist, was the research director of the program (Domke, 1959; Gildea, Glidewell, & Kantor, 1967; Glidewell, 1961, 1995; Glidewell, Gildea, & Kaufman, 1973; Glidewell, Mensh,

Domke, Gildea, & Buchmueller, 1957; Glidewell, Mensh, Kantor, Domke, & Gildea, 1959).

Another example of community approaches to the delivery of mental health services is the Community Lodge program founded by George W. Fairweather in Palo Alto, California, in 1960 (Fairweather, 1964, 1967, 1979, 1994; Fairweather, Sanders, Maynard, & Cressler, 1969). For more than 30 years, Fairweather and his colleagues developed and evaluated a program in which mentally ill patients could establish independent living in the community by organizing their own democratic-based organizations. This was a major innovation in the treatment of mental illness and contributed to the emergence of the self-help movement. Fairweather's work was funded by a series of NIMH grants (Nos. 3 R11 MH 01259, 7 RO1 MH 14690, and 7 R12 MN 17888-01). These are just two examples among hundreds of demonstrations of community approaches that were being put into operation with NIMH funds. The St. Louis County project and the Community Lodge program both were begun in the 1950s and became reference points for the later articulation of the field of community psychology.

While the St. Louis County and Community Lodge programs were developing, the profession of psychiatry had already been trying out public health and preventive training efforts. A major resource was Adolf Meyer (1866–1950), an eminent and renowned psychiatrist in the United States and a professor at Johns Hopkins University for more than 30 years (1910–1941; Leys & Evans, 1990). In 1940, he encouraged the newly trained psychiatrist Paul Lemkau (1910–1992) to receive additional training in public health (Zilboorg, 1941). Lemkau did so and became one of the leading public health psychiatrists in the United States. In 1941, he became founding chairperson of the Department of Mental Hygiene in the School of Public Health at Johns Hopkins. The mental hygiene program at Johns Hopkins was the first mental health program in a school of public health and was where Robert Felix received his formal public health training. William G. Hollister, a future chief of the NIMH Community Services Branch, received his MPH in 1948 at Johns Hopkins. Dale Cameron and Alan Miller, both leaders at NIMH in the early years, received their public health training there in 1951 (A. Miller, personal communication, December 2, 2001).

Another major resource for community mental health services was begun in the late 1940s. This was the Human Relations Service of Wellesley, MA, established by Erich Lindemann in 1948. The Human Relations Service was affiliated with the Department of Psychiatry of Massachusetts General Hospital in Boston, where Lindemann was chief psychiatrist (Kelly, 1984; Lindemann, 1953; Satin, 1982). A later resource was the Community Mental Health Program at the Harvard School of Public Health, directed by psychiatrist Gerald Caplan (Caplan, 1964). These two programs began offering postdoctoral training in 1955 supported by NIMH funds and made it possible for the core mental health professions to have postgraduate training opportunities in community mental health consultation and community research. Both of these training efforts received ample NIMH grant support and were largely responsible for training a new cohort of mental health professionals.

In 1954, NIMH staff advocated for a national review of the U.S. mental health delivery system. The American Psychiatric Association and the American Psychological Association were strong supporters of NIMH. In 1955, the 84th Congress passed Public Law 84-182, which established the Mental Health Study Act (1955). This act created the Joint Commission on Mental Illness and Health. Located in Cambridge, Massachusetts, the commission was directed by Jack Ewalt, a Harvard psychiatrist. Fillmore H. Sanford, psychologist and former executive secretary of the American Psychological Association, was the scientific director. The commission published eight books reviewing the status of mental health care in the United States. Although the commission did not emphasize community approaches, two of the books and their authors especially influenced the development of community psychology. The first book, *Concepts of Positive Mental Health*, by Marie Jahoda, advocated for a focus on mental health in contrast to mental illness (Albee, 1996; Jahoda, 1958, 1997). The second book, and the third volume in this series, *Mental Health Manpower*, by George Albee, laid the groundwork for national interests in prevention (Albee, 1959; Goldston, 1994).

Albee became closely identified with the field of community psychology and its prevention emphasis (see chap. 11, this volume). He received the field's award for distinguished contributions in 1981 (Albee, 1982). The final report of the commission, *Action for Mental Health*, was presented to Congress in the spring of 1961 (Action for Mental Health, 1961).

The report provided the background for the development of the National Mental Health program submitted to Congress in 1963, which was subsequently authorized as the Community Mental Health Centers Act (Brand & Sapir, 1964).

NIMH BRANCHES

Before I address the Community Mental Health Centers Act, I will summarize some of the NIMH organizational units. My intent is to illustrate the pervasive impact of NIMH on the creation of community-based research, services, and programs (Rubinstein & Coehlo, 1970). The thesis is that this multiple array of funding programs, established after NIMH was created in

1946, made it possible for a sufficient body of knowledge to be available 20 years later to legitimate the creation of the field of community psychology (Rubinstein, Kelly, & Maines, 1985). The 20-year period after WWII provided sufficient time for knowledge and experience to be established so that community approaches and preventive efforts were plausible, creditable, empirically based, and cost-effective.

The contributions of the different parts of NIMH were essential in establishing the shift in emphasis from individually focused to community-based programming. The NIMH's support of community-based research and services was particularly important. Until the mid-1950s, the Department of Defense was the primary source of research funds in psychology. These funds, which in 1953 totaled $10 million, were largely for basic research in experimental and social psychology. This began to change in 1955, when the Department of Health, Education and Welfare, in which NIH was situated, became the largest source of federal support of psychological research. The Office of Naval Research and the National Science Foundation provided the next levels of support (Capshew, 1999).

In the sections that follow, I briefly sketch several NIMH branches: the Research Grants Branch (a resource for peer reviews of submitted grant proposals), the Professional Services Branch (a consulting group to advise the director), the Biometrics Branch (which conducted nationwide studies of prevalence and incidence of mental illness), the Community Services Branch (which acts as a liaison to the states for staff development and service innovations), and the Training Branch (which is responsible for graduate training in the mental health professions). There also were influential programs developed in the Office of the Director. I also briefly describe the Laboratory of Socio-Environmental Studies, a component of the intramural research program. The significance of these seven units of NIMH is that there was a concentrated source of funds available for different components of the NIMH public health mental health enterprise, each one contributing to a different focus.

Research Grants Branch

This branch was the major resource for funding scholars who applied for research grants through a peer review process (see chap. 4, this volume, for a full description). The philosophy, established early, was that a broad array of topics related to mental health would be salient for funding if an internal review group, composed of peers called *scientific advisors*, judged the proposal to be of the highest quality. The broad definition of mental illness used made it possible for social scientists as well as medical scholars to submit proposals. In 1952, an analysis revealed that over $5 million was allocated for 165 grants. The two largest areas of support during these early years (1948–1955) were research on (a) mental illness and (b) hospitalized mentally ill patients. Substantial support was also received for research on the effects of environmental stress on mental health and illness (Brand & Sapir, 1964, p. 30). Psychiatrists and psychologists received 70% of all funds expended.

Later, Congressional interest in psychopharmacology increased research grants for this purpose. The discovery of chlorpromazine in 1952 led to pharmacological treatments that enabled mental patients to be returned to the community from their previous residences in asylums:

> The introduction of chlorpromazine in 1952 marked a serendipitous breakthrough in the management of severe mental disorders. Within a few years its use, just like that of penicillin before it, had crossed frontiers and continents, regardless of ideological divides, demonstrating vividly how effective techniques propagate themselves in a way that acclaimed ideas, even in this information age, do not. Chlorpromazine crossed frontiers as quickly as few things except new weapons do. It was an engine of war. (Healy, 2002, pp. 164–165)

In 1956, 51% of research projects were awarded to psychologists, and 10% were awarded to social scientists. Later, in 1963, 35% of funds were allocated to support research on the psychological, social, and cultural bases of behavior, and 24% of funds were allocated to support research on the biological bases of behavior (Brand & Sapir, 1964). This affirms that the rationale of awarding grants broadly for mental health, as well as mental illness, was still operative. During this entire period there was substantial support for the sociology and epidemiology of mental illness, including research on race relations, urban poverty, and many other sociocultural projects.

There were a number of leaders in this branch—including John Eberhart (1949–1954, psychologist), Philip Sapir (1954–1967), Louis Wienckowski (1967–1983, psychologist), and Julius Segal (1959–1965, psychologist)— who oversaw the expansion of various grant programs as well as published reviews and analyses of the grant program and specific reports on topics such as refugees and political hostages (Strupp & Parloff, 1996).

Professional Services Branch

This branch, conceived by Robert Felix as a small group involved in program planning, served as consultants to the director. The branch's first chief was public health psychiatrist Dale Cameron. He was succeeded by psychologist Joseph M. Bobbitt (1908–1975), who worked behind the scenes for the support of community-based research. One of the first topics that the branch addressed was the public concern with juvenile delinquency.

The branch arranged contracts with the Institute for Juvenile Research in Chicago and the Bureau of Applied Research at Columbia University, later located at New York University.

The rehabilitation of mentally ill individuals soon became another priority. Richard H. Williams, a sociologist, was a major resource and made it possible for a pioneering study to be carried out by two sociologists at the Harvard School of Public Health, Howard Freeman and Ozzie G. Simmons (Freeman & Simmons, 1963; Wellin, 1999). Mental retardation was also an undeveloped topic. Branch staff made it possible for the now-classic book *Mental Subnormality*, authored by Richard Masland, Thomas Gladwin, and Seymour B. Sarason (Masland, Gladwin, & Sarason, 1958).

Psychiatrist Leonard J. Duhl convened an interdisciplinary team of social scientists outside the branch to consider the impact of the social environment on mental health. This group, known informally as the "Space Cadets," produced an influential book: *The Urban Condition* (Duhl, 1963). The group included such scholars as John B. Calhoun, Herbert J. Gans, Erich Lindemann, Richard L. Meier, John R. Seeley, and Sir Geoffrey Vickers. Three major studies were financed as a result of the work of the Space Cadets: Herb Gans's *Urban Villagers* (1982), Elliot Liebow's *Tally's Corner* (1967), and Lee Rainwater's *Behind Ghetto Walls* (1971); Lemann, 1992). The branch also helped Mobilization for Youth, one of the major antipoverty programs, receive Title V grants.

The Professional Services Branch was a unique organization and served an essential catalytic role. Some of the key persons serving on the staff during this period included John Adair, Antonia Chayes, Joseph H. Douglass, Ray Gould, Matthew Huxley, Dan O'Keefe, and William Soskin (psychologist), in addition to Richard Williams and Len Duhl. The research that the branch stimulated during this period laid the groundwork for clarifying social and environmental factors affecting the expression of mental health and illness. The collective work of branch staff gave legitimacy to the connections between the role of community topics and variables in limiting and enhancing mental health.

Biometrics Branch

Through a variety of data collection and reporting techniques, the Biometrics Branch communicated to Congress the status of mental health in the United States. Morton Kramer directed the branch with assistance from Ben Locke, who focused on mental hospitals, and Anita Bahn, who focused on outpatient clinics. This branch was responsible for identifying the prevalence and incidence of various diagnosed mental conditions. It also became a resource for evaluating various community treatment approaches and played a leading role in research on the epidemiology of mental disease. The branch also helped state mental health authorities develop quality reporting methods. The accuracy, reliability, and uniformity of basic data on mental illness became a high priority for NIMH. National model reporting programs were begun with state hospitals and then extended to outpatient clinics.

Psychiatric case registers were established in three states: Maryland, Hawaii, and New York. The register in Monroe County, New York, was a model comprehensive register for the nation. The branch's leadership in record keeping made possible national research on such topics as migration and mental illness and the role of general practitioners in mental health care. The branch staff served as a resource to the World Health Organization and worked to integrate systematic and comparable reporting mental health systems for the United States and Great Britain. It was the cumulative impact of the branch research that provided the empirical connections between social class and mental illness.

These findings were instrumental in stimulating a number of now-classic investigations that firmly made the connections between social status variables, such as between age and marital status and between community social structure and mental illness (*Community Mental Health and Social Psychiatry,* 1962; Hollingshead & Redlich, 1958; Leighton, 1963, 1967; Myers & Bean, 1968; Srole, Langner, Opler, & Rennie, 1962). These studies helped to establish that community variables were embedded in the expression of mental illness. The topics of race, class, culture, and poverty began to be examined in much more detail as a result of the work of this branch and the work of scholars whom the branch staff stimulated.

Community Services Branch (Research Utilization Branch)

The Community Services Branch, later renamed the *Research Utilization Branch,* was the unit through which NIMH worked to strengthen the states to deliver quality community mental health services. This branch had a unique and major role in helping to transform the delivery of individual mental health services to more community-based mental health services. Through grants-in-aid, demonstrations, and technical assistance, the multi-disciplinary staff had substantial links to the nation through the state mental health authorities.

James Lowry was the first branch chief, followed by Curtis Southard in 1962, William Hollister, and then James W. Osberg; all were public health-trained psychiatrists. The staff included the following psychologists: Carl Anderson, Eli "Mike" Bower, Jerry W. Carter Jr., Howard Davis, Harold Hildreth, William Rhodes, Harold M. Skeels, and Fred Spaner. From the field of social work, there were Ruth Knee and Warren Lamson as well as Thomas Gladwin (an anthropologist). Pearl Shallit and Elsie Ho, public health mental health nurses, were key staffpersons, as were Program Analysis staff members Jack Wiener and Mildred Arrill.

Early in its history the branch was responsible for the Prince George's County Maryland Mental Health Clinic, founded in 1948 (see chap. 8, this volume). The first director was the public health psychiatrist Mabel Ross. The clinic was renamed the *Mental Health Study Center*, with Alan Miller, followed by Stan Yolles and then James W. Osberg, as directors. The Mental Health Study Center remained connected to the branch until 1961. Center staff carried out a variety of studies and demonstrations on the connections between community structures and mental health and illness. One of the early staff members was the psychologist Charles Ullmann, who conducted a study of the socialization of ninth-grade boys and girls in Prince George's County (Ullman, 1957).

The Mental Health Study Center, like all other parts of NIMH, was multidisciplinary. Adele Henderson and Dorothy Boone were public health–psychiatric nurses. Social workers included Herbert Rooney and Fortune V. Mannino. There also were social scientists at the study center; they included John Hartley, Ann C. Maney, Howard J. Ehrlich, and Sheila Feld. I myself, along with community psychologists Robert Shellow and J. R. Newbrough, was at the Mental Health Study Center from 1960 to 1966. Milt Shore, a psychologist and coauthor of chapter 8 of the present volume, was at the study center from 1961 through 1986. Psychiatrists included Fred Hassler; David Michener; and, from 1960 to 1962, Bertram S. Brown, before he moved to the director's office.

In 1955, the Community Services Branch developed Technical Assistance Projects. This mechanism provided an opportunity for national experts to meet with state staff and focus on special topics. From 1956 through 1963, 179 Technical Assistance Projects were held at a total cost of $730,000 (Brand & Sapir, 1964, p. 61).

In 1956, the Mental Health Projects Grant Program (Title V) was established. The purpose of this program was to develop new and improved methods for mental health care. This program supported new services for mentally ill patients, such as halfway houses, day care, and after care, as well as school mental health programs. In the first 5 years of this program, 412 projects were supported for a total amount of $25,310,000 (Knee, 1963). These grants covered the following topics: aging, alcoholism, juvenile delinquency and criminality, manpower, mental hospital programs, mental retardation, schizophrenia, and school mental health. The grant program was important because it provided state and local governments with the means to improve the quality of existing services and, more important, to fund innovative or groundbreaking applied research.

William Hollister, along with Mike Bower, was very active in stimulating school mental health programs throughout the United States (Bower

& Hollister, 1967; Hollister, 1958). In the first 5 years (1957–1962), this grant program funded the St. Louis County Mental Health Project mentioned earlier, as well as Project Re-Ed at Vanderbilt-Peabody University. At Peabody, Nicholas Hobbs and his staff gained national recognition by using nonprofessionals to work in residential settings with children with behavioral disorders (Hobbs, 1968). Another example of the impact of Title V was the funding of projects that enabled eight professional associations to collaborate on improving pupil personnel services for elementary school children throughout the United States. In this way, Title V created a new infrastructure to improve the quality of mental health services in schools throughout the country. A parallel program was the Mental Hospital Improvement and Training Program, headed by Ed Flynn and psychologists Howard Davis and Sam Buker.

The nine NIMH regional offices were affiliated with the Community Services branch from 1946 through 1961. The regional office staff had their fingers on the pulse of the needs of the states and created opportunities to facilitate the translation of community mental health concepts directly to the states. Regional office staff made it possible for investigators in their region to know about each other's work, and through workshops, informal meetings, and conferences, they created networks of community-oriented professionals. The following psychologists, who were already experienced in delivering community programs, were employed in the regional offices: John Bell, Bernard Bloom, Clair Calhoun, J. Wilbert Edgerton, William Hales, Allen Hodges, and Harry McNeill. Bell, who worked at the San Francisco office, was the first psychologist to be an administrator. Edgerton was later an administrator in the Chicago regional office and the recipient of many awards, including the Distinguished Practice Award from the Society for Community Research and Action (Edgerton, 2001). Bloom was one of three key figures in the planning of the 1975 National Conference on Community Psychology (Iscoe, Bloom, & Spielberger, 1977) and received the Distinguished Contribution to Theory and Research Award in 1978 from the Society for Community Research and Action (Bloom, 1978). The Society for Community Research and Action also named an award in honor of Harry McNeill. In 1961, the regional offices became part of the Office of Field Operations, headed by Alan Miller. This office had a major role in developing the community mental health centers program. Key staff members were Dorothea Dolan, Rod Mercker, and psychologist Sam Buker.

Jerry W. Carter, Jr., arranged yearly meetings to take place before the annual American Psychological Association conventions. These 2-day sessions provided opportunities for chief psychologists in state mental health programs to discuss issues directly with NIMH staff. From 1952 through 1968, these joint chiefs–NIMH meetings had a significant role not only in reviewing substantive community mental health goals but also in establishing a reference group for psychologists interested in community approaches. Carter persistently advocated that community mental health services should include more than clinical services.

Training Branch

The National Mental Health Act of 1946 authorized NIMH to award grants to academic institutions for the purposes of training mental health specialists. For more than 30 years, graduate students received stipends and the program received teaching costs (Schneider, 2000). Throughout the early years, there were opportunities for "experimental" training programs also to be funded. These training programs had a collective effect of establishing nontraditional approaches, such as training mental health specialists in public health mental health service delivery. The Training Branch also funded conferences that created opportunities to discuss mental health issues (see chap. 1, this volume).

One such example was an explicit discussion of the future roles of clinical psychology training programs in mental health work that occurred at the Stanford conference in 1955. The report of this NIMH-sponsored conference, edited by Charles Strother of the University of Washington and published in 1956, was an influential resource in raising consciousness about the role of psychologists in community mental health. The report emphasized that more attention should be paid to "cultural and social issues" and to "the concepts, methodologies and data of cultural anthropology and sociology" (Strother, 1956, pp. 128–129; Strother, 1987). Robert Felix, Erich Lindemann, and Jerry Carter all spoke at this conference (Strother, 1956).

The Training Branch psychology staff over these years included Irving Alexander, Ray Balester, Harold Basowitz, Ken Little, C. Scott Moss, Sherman Nelson, Stanley Schneider, Eli Rubinstein, Ralph Simon, Sam Silverstein, Charles Spielberger, Joseph Spiesman, and Forrest Tyler, among others. The Training Branch also included other mental health professionals. Key persons were Esther Garrison (nursing), Milton Wittman (social work), and Ray Feldman (psychiatry).

Office of the Director

Beginning in 1962, there were opportunities for psychologists to be staff assistants in the Office of the Director. Psychologist Stephen E. Goldston, for example, started out as staff assistant to Stanley Yolles (1919–2001), who at the time was Associate Director for Extramural Programs. In this role, Goldston became an NIMH representative for interagency planning following up on the implementation of the recommendations from *Action For Mental Health* (Action for Mental Health, 1961). This work led to the community mental health legislation. In 1967, when Yolles became NIMH director, Goldston became his Special Assistant. In his new role, Goldston was Director for Prevention Programs. It was during this period that Goldston, working with Leonard Duhl, created a series of conferences and training events that enabled mental health professionals to think about prevention more systemically than in the past (Goldston, 1994). In late 1963 and early 1964, Goldston organized regional conferences for the discussion of the concepts of community psychiatry with the faculties of departments of psychiatry. These meetings helped to increase the awareness of community concepts in psychiatry (Goldston, 1965).

Another example was a national conference for deans and faculty in schools of public health to explore how mental health content could be implemented in the schools' curricula (Goldston, 1969). There followed a systematic survey of public health professionals and their attitudes about mental health work (Goldston & Padilla, 1971). The books and conferences developed by Goldston, including *Primary Prevention: An Idea Whose Time Has Come* (Klein & Goldston, 1977), became resources for primary prevention in future years.

Goldston's work was the forerunner of the future Center for Prevention, established in 1981, which has grant-awarding priorities. In chapter 11 of this volume, Albee provides more background on the topic of prevention and Goldston's role in the development of this concept

Laboratory of Socio-Environmental Studies

One of the key components of the intramural research program at NIMH was the Laboratory of Socio-Environmental Studies. John A. Clausen became its chief in 1952. Several years later, Melvin Kohn took over as chief. The goal of the laboratory has been to examine how socially determined environmental conditions, in interaction with psychoneurological processes, affect normal and abnormal psychological functioning in different cultures across the life span. Staff at this laboratory conducted major empirical research on the relationships between class, culture, and mental health and illness (Clausen & Kohn, 1954). Investigators such as psychologist–sociologist Carmi Schooler focused on the connections between a variety of social factors and mental illness. This research contributed to the increasing evidence of how community structures could enable and assist the rehabilitation of mentally ill individuals as well as be a positive force in enabling people's positive mental health (Clausen, 1956).

COMMUNITY MENTAL HEALTH CENTERS LEGISLATION

The community mental health legislation of 1963 and 1965 provided the rationale for an increased federal investment in community approaches. As previously mentioned, with the final report of the Joint Commission on Mental Illness and Health in 1961 (Action for Mental Health, 1961), President John F. Kennedy established an interagency planning committee. The committee was chaired by Boisfeuillet Jones and included Arthur Goldberg, who also was serving as Secretary of Labor, and his assistant, Patrick Moynihan. Anthony Celebreze, Secretary of Health, Education, and Welfare, and John S. Gleason, Administrator of Veterans' Affairs, also were members. Goldston, Joseph H. Douglass, Alan Miller, and Eli Rubinstein (all psychologists) served as NIMH staff assisting the committee. The work of this planning group led to Kennedy's address to Congress on February 5, 1963, regarding the nation's needs in the area of mental health (Bloom, 1984). This message called for a doubling of federal support for clinical, laboratory, and field research. The message also endorsed NIMH's intention to emphasize the treatment of mental illness in community-based mental health centers. Many well-known persons, including Margaret Mead and Benjamin Spock, were involved in encouraging Congress to pass this legislation. Several key organizations also supported the legislation, including the Group for the Advancement of Psychiatry and the American Orthopsychiatric Association. The framing of the legislation also benefited from the open-hospital movement that was active in Great Britain after WWII. This movement was often identified under the concept of "social psychiatry" (Carstairs, 1958; Jones, 1953; Rapoport & Rapoport, 1958; Stanton & Schwartz, 1954; Wing, Denham, & Munro, 1959).

Congress passed this legislation (P.L. 88-164), which clearly represented the vision of 20 years of advocating public health concepts. This philosophy emphasized community involvement in local mental health programs (Smith & Hobbs, 1966). Although some states—for example, Illinois, Ohio, California, and New York—were already going in this direction, this legislation established NIMH as the primary resource for community mental health care for the next 20 years. The Congressional passage of this legislation is a testimony to the organizing talents of Robert H. Felix.

With the participation of federal officials, such as Mary Switzer; citizens, such as Mary Lasker and Mike Gorman; and other prominent persons, such as Margaret Mead and Benjamin Spock, Felix was able to secure full Congressional support. He worked with Sen. Claude Pepper of Florida and Rep. J. Perry Priest of Tennessee (Grob, 1996). Although there were critical appraisals of this new federal legislation, there was also optimism that these proposed services would be a just and equitable solution to address the needs of mentally ill individuals and strengthen the capacities of communities to improve the mental health of citizens (Clausen, 1961; Halleck & Miller, 1963; Mechanic, 1969). (For more detailed discussions of the community mental health centers program, see chap. 10, this volume; Bloom, 1984; Grob, 1994; and Levine, 1981.)

After President Kennedy's assassination in November 1963 and Felix's retirement from NIMH in 1964, the second NIMH Director, Stanley F. Yolles, faced a new political environment. President Lyndon Johnson was articulating the Great Society program. On January 8, 1964, in his first State of the Union address, Johnson said, "The Administration today, here and now, declares unconditional war on poverty in America" (Lemann, 1992, p. 144).

The Great Society program emphasized the use of federal funds to address the unrelenting problems of poverty, racism, and urban dislocation (Beschloss, 2001; Lemann, 1992; O'Connor, 2001). The presidential interest in topics related to social factors in health made it possible for NIMH staff to increase their focus more directly on poverty, urban problems, and substance abuse. Elliot Liebow, Matt Dumont, and others were key NIMH staff in the new Metropolitan Studies Branch, which focused on urban problems and mental health. It became clear, however, that many Great Society programs, outside of NIMH, were not coordinated with the mayors of the larger urban cities or the leaders of the civil rights movement. In addition, there had been growing popular resentment toward federal housing policies that were institutionally racist. In this atmosphere of uncoordinated policy efforts, national public attention became focused on racism and the economic crises facing members of ethnic–minority groups in American cities (Lemann, 1992).

THE SWAMPSCOTT CONFERENCE

It was in this social–political environment—dominated by the Great Society programs, increased U.S. involvement in Vietnam, and major race problems in the South and large northern cities—that the NIMH Training Branch staff considered planning a training conference on the roles of psychologists in community mental health. In late 1964, Joseph Spiesman, chief of the NIMH Training Branch, asked John C. Glidewell of Washington University and the St. Louis Health Department to chair and host such a conference. Glidewell was unable to do it, but he suggested as a replacement the staff of the South Shore Mental Health Center in Quincy, Massachusetts. South Shore was a pioneering community mental health program that was beginning to receive national attention for its innovative work. Saul Cooper, Len Hassol, and Gersh Rosenblum of South Shore agreed to host the conference. At Spiesman's urging, the South Shore staff included the faculty of the clinical psychology program at Boston University (BU). Chester Bennett, director of the BU clinical psychology program, had chaired Rosenblum's doctoral dissertation at BU, and Cooper and Hassol were graduate students at BU. This group then invited Don Klein of BU, former executive director of the Human Relations Service of Wellesley. These five composed the planning group, with Bennett as chair (Klein, 1987, 1995; Rosenblum, 2001). They selected 39 participants, all of whom were active in community mental health research or practice or who were training psychologists in community mental health. NIMH funded the conference, and NIMH psychologists, including Jerry Osterweil, William C. Rhodes, Stanley F. Schneider, Joseph C. Spiesman, and Forrest Tyler, were represented (Bennett et al., 1966).

The conference was held at New Ocean House in Swampscott, Massachusetts, from May 4 through May 8, 1965. While this historic conference was being held, President Johnson was being besieged with criticisms about sending Marines into the Dominican Republic; about his desultory response to civil rights; and about his Gulf of Tonkin resolution, which he believed gave him the mandate for the war in Vietnam (Beschloss, 2001, pp. 308–315).

During the conference, the participants gradually articulated the basic principles that the issues of poverty and the development of communities were broader than community mental health. Thus, there emerged a shared vision for a new field—community psychology. Community psychologists would no doubt work in community mental health centers, but they also would perform broader roles, such as social change agents and community development professionals (Bennett et al., 1966). For a more complete review of the conference, see Kelly (1987), Klein (1995), and Rosenblum (2001). The report of the conference was widely circulated. At the annual meeting of the Council of Representatives of the American Psychological Association in New York City in September 1966, community psychology was approved as the newest division of APA, Division 27.

AFTER SWAMPSCOTT

After the Swampscott conference, initial moves were made to establish the field, and the conference members began to concentrate more on separating the distinctions between community mental health and community psychology. Robert Reiff proposed that the problem with the community mental health emphasis was on the attention to individual pathology, a focus that restricted the field of community psychology and kept it from developing its own unique identity (Reiff, 1971).

Community psychology's emphasis on the community as a unit of analysis and an area of inquiry, combined with its action orientation, established the field as a potential innovation to be defined by its own substantive base of theory and knowledge. (Iscoe & Spielberger, 1970)

Doctoral training in psychology began to include community psychology content, and textbooks for the field began to appear. Two journals were founded: (a) the *American Journal of Community Psychology*, in 1973, and (b) the *Journal of Community Psychology*, in 1974. The first Division 27 award was given to Robert Reiff in 1974. By 1975, 141 university programs offered some content in community psychology, with 15 reporting "distinguishable curricula or specialization in community psychology" (Mann, 1978, p. 296). In late April and early May 1975, the National Conference on Training in Community Psychology was hosted by the University of Texas at Austin. NIMH, the Department of Psychology at the University of Texas, and the Hogg Foundation sponsored the conference. The conference, planned by Ira Iscoe, Bernard Bloom, and Charles Spielberger, was a significant event. It marked increased participation by women and members of ethnic minorities in the field and increased the visibility of younger members. Soon after the conference, the Regional Coordinator System was created, as was the Council of Community Psychology Training Directors. These two related organizations provided more communication opportunities within the now-broader field and more visibility for the training enterprise.

As the field of community psychology was becoming established, the community mental health movement was not living up to its promise. A Canadian observer commented that "the subject of community psychiatry in the United States was, and remains, a kind of grotesque joke" (Shorter, 1997, p. 238). Gerald Grob (1994) gave the following, more balanced, appraisal:

> The new community mental health policy often overlooked the need for supportive services to ensure that severely mentally ill persons would have access to housing, food, social networks, and recreation; it also created a bifurcated system with weak or nonexistent linkages between centers and mental hospitals. (p. 278)

Although the community mental health movement, authorized and facilitated by NIMH, did not reach its potential, the NIMH-stimulated field of community psychology continued to develop in the ensuing years.

CONCLUSION

The creation of the field of community psychology was both directly and indirectly helped by the 20 years of research, professional development, and policies of NIMH prior to 1965. In retrospect, NIMH provided a predictable and known social structure that was an active social and financial support system for psychologists who were interested in pursuing a public health community-oriented perspective. The multiple enterprises of the NIMH gave to community-oriented psychologists encouragement and the wherewithal to pursue their newfound professional objectives. The variety of grant and contract formats made it possible for psychologists with different interests and talents to receive funds for community mental health enterprises. Clinicians who wished to adapt clinical methods in the community had access to federal resources, as did investigators who wanted to carry out epidemiological investigations, and psychologists who hoped to create an entirely new community-based prevention program to test out their vision.

Although the Swampscott conference participants did not directly respond to the NIMH program objectives of clarifying roles for psychologists in community mental health, the conference did set in motion the founding of a new profession. NIMH public policies encouraged and supported psychologists in expanding their roles from individual treatment to community prevention programs. In September 1965, Stanley Yolles, in his role as NIMH director, addressed the Conference of Chief Psychologists, Washington, DC, and reaffirmed the NIMH commitment to the behavioral sciences (Yolles, 1965).

The community public health philosophy underlying NIMH programs helped clinically trained psychologists to focus more directly on social factors and the social structure of communities as resources for mental health. The NIMH was also the major resource in the paradigm shift that enabled community-motivated psychologists to become free of the strict traditions of medical- and psychiatric-oriented individual treatment philosophies.

Robert Felix's early vision was clearly community based, with a strong focus on prevention. His concept of mental illness prevention included an emphasis on mental health that enabled review processes to fund innovative community-based community mental health projects. With the passage of time, the NIMH expanded and became more bureaucratic. This, coupled with increased lobbying efforts from individuals interested in the care of people with severe mental illness, diminished the agency's original public health preventive philosophy. NIMH then became, as some have said, the "National Institute of Mental Illness." It took extra commitment from NIMH staff to continue to advocate for the realization of Felix's vision. Nevertheless, it is clear that the field of community psychology could not have been founded without the support and federal influence of NIMH to create funding opportunities and encouragement to move from inpatient custodial care and outpatient care to community and preventive research and services.

REFERENCES

Action for Mental Health. (1961). *Final report of the Joint Commission on Mental Illness and Health.* New York: Basic Books.

Albee, G. W. (1959). *Mental health manpower trends.* New York: Basic Books.

Albee, G. W. (1982). The politics of nature and nurture. *American Journal of Psychology, 10,* 1–36.

Albee, G. W. (1996). In J. G. Kelly (Ed.). (2003). *Exemplars of community psychology* [DVD]. Edmond, OK: Society for Community Research and Action.

Bennett, C., Anderson, L., Cooper, S., Hassol, L., Klein, D. C., & Rosenblum, G. (1966). *Community psychology: A report of the Boston Conference on the Education of Psychologists for Community Mental Health.* Boston: Boston University Press.

Beschloss, M. (Ed.). (2001). *Reaching for glory: Lyndon Johnson's secret White House tapes, 1964–65.* New York: Simon & Schuster.

Bloom, B. L. (1978). Community psychology: Midstream and middream. *American Journal of Psychology, 6,* 205–217.

Bloom, B. L. (1984). *Community mental health* (2nd ed.). Monterey, CA: Brooks/ Cole.

Bobbitt, J. M. (1962). *Implications of community mental health for the training of clinical psychologists.* Paper presented at the annual meeting of the American Psychological Association, Chicago, IL.

Bower, E. M., & Hollister, W. G. (Eds.). (1967). *Behavioral science frontiers in education.* New York: Wiley.

Brand, J. E., & Sapir, P. (Eds.). (1964). *An historical perspective on the National Institute of Mental Health.* Unpublished manuscript.

Caplan, G. (1964). *Principles of preventive psychiatry.* New York: Basic Books.

Capshew, J. H. (1999). *Psychologists on the march: Science, practice and professional identity in America, 1929–1969.* New York: Cambridge University Press.

Carstairs, G. M. (1958). *The twice born: A study of a community of high-caste Hindus.* Toronto, Ontario, Canada: Clarke-Irwin.

Clausen, J. A. (1956). *Sociology and the field of mental health.* New York: Russell Sage Foundation.

Clausen, J. A. (1961). Mental disorders. In R. Merton & R. Nisbet (Eds.), *Contemporary social problems* (pp. 26–83). New York: Harcourt, Brace & World.

Clausen, J. A., & Kohn, M. L. (1954). The ecological approach in social psychiatry. *American Journal of Sociology, 60,* 140–151.

Community mental health and social psychiatry: A reference guide. (1962). Cambridge, MA: Harvard University Press.

Community Mental Health Centers Act of 1964, Pub. L. No. 88-164.

Deutsch, A. M. (1937). *The mentally ill in America: A history of their care and treatment from colonial times.* Garden City, NY: Doubleday.

Dickson, P. (2001). *Sputnik: The shock of the century*. New York: Walker.

Domke, H. R. (1959). *Progress and problems of community mental health services: Program of the St. Louis County Health Department*. New York: Milbank Memorial Fund.

Duhl, L. J. (Ed.). (1963). *The urban condition*. New York: Basic Books.

Edgerton, J. W. (2001). The community is it! *American Journal of Community Psychology, 29*, 83–95.

Fairweather, G. W. (1964). *Social psychology in treating mental illness: An experimental approach*. New York: Wiley.

Fairweather, G. W. (1967). *Methods for experimental social innovation*. New York: Wiley.

Fairweather, G. W. (1979). Experimental development and dissemination of an alternative to psychiatric hospitalization: Scientific methods for social change. In R. F. Munoz, L. R. Snowden, & J. G. Kelly (Eds.), *Social and psychological research in community settings* (pp. 305–326). San Francisco: Jossey-Bass.

Fairweather, G. W. (1994). In J. G. Kelly (Ed.). (2003). *Exemplars of community psychology* [DVD]. Edmond, OK: Society for Community Research and Action.

Fairweather, G. W., Sanders, D. H., Maynard, H., & Cressler, D. L. (1969). *Community life for the mentally ill: An alternative to institutional care*. Chicago: Aldine.

Freeman, H. E., & Simmons, O. (1963). *When the mental patient comes home*. Cambridge, MA: Harvard University Press.

Freidman, L. J. (1990). *Menninger: The family and the clinic*. New York: Random House.

Gans, H. J. (1982). *Urban villagers: Group and class in the life of Italian-Americans*. Glencoe, IL: Free Press.

Gildea, M. C. L., Glidewell, J. C., & Kantor, M. B. (1967). The St. Louis School Mental Health Project: History and evaluation. In E. L. Cowen, E. A. Gardner, & M. Zax (Eds.), *Emergent approaches to mental health problems* (pp. 290–306). New York: Appleton-Century-Crofts.

Glass, A. J. (1953). Preventive psychiatry in the combat zone. *U.S. Armed Forces Medical Journal, 4*, 683.

Glass, A. J. (1957). Observations upon the epidemiology of mental illness in troops during warfare. In *Symposium on preventive and social psychiatry* (pp. 185–198). Washington, DC: Walter Reed Institute of Research.

Glidewell, J. C. (1961). Mental health discussion groups for parents in St. Louis. *Adult Leadership, 10*, 4–24.

Glidewell, J. C. (1995). In J. G. Kelly (Ed.). (2003). *Exemplars of community psychology* [DVD]. Edmond, OK: Society for Community Research and Action.

Glidewell, J. C., Gildea, M. L., & Kaufman, M. K. (1973). The preventive and therapeutic effects of two school mental health programs. *American Journal of Community Psychology, 1*, 295–329.

Glidewell, J. C., Mensh, I. N., Domke, H. R., Gildea, M. L., & Buchmueller, A. D. (1957). Methods for community mental health research. *American Journal of Orthopsychiatry, 27*, 38–54.

Glidewell, J. C., Mensh, I. N., Kantor, M. B., Domke, H. R., & Gildea, M. L. (1959). Children's behavior symptoms and their relationships to school adjustment, sex and social class. *Journal of Social Issues, 15*, 8–15.

Goldston, S. E. (Ed.). (1965). *Concepts of community psychiatry* (PHS Publication No. 1319). Bethesda, MD: National Institute of Mental Health.

Goldston, S. E. (Ed.). (1969). *Mental health training in public health* (PHS Publication No. 1899). Bethesda, MD: National Institute of Mental Health.

Goldston, S. E. (1994). In J. G. Kelly (Ed.). (2003). *Exemplars of community psychology* [DVD]. Edmond, OK: Society for Community Research and Action.

Goldston, S. E., & Padilla, E. (1971). *Mental health training and public health manpower* (PHS Publication No. 1724-0168). Bethesda MD: National Institute of Mental Health.

Grob, G. N. (1991). *From asylum to community: Mental health policy in modern America.* Princeton, NJ: Princeton University Press.

Grob, G. N. (1994). *The mad among us: A history of the care of America's mentally ill.* New York: Free Press.

Grob, G. N. (1996). Creation of the National Institute of Mental Health. *Public Health Reports, 111*, 178–181.

Halleck, S. L., & Miller, M. (1963). The psychiatric consultation: Questionable social precedents of some current practices. *American Journal of Psychiatry, 120*, 164–169.

Healy, D. (2002). *The creation of psychopharmacology.* Cambridge, MA: Harvard University Press.

Hobbs, N. (1968). Reeducation, reality and community responsibility. In J. W. Carter Jr. (Ed.), *Research contributions from psychology to community mental health* (pp. 7–18). Morningside Heights, NY: Behavioral Publications.

Hollingshead, A. R., & Redlich, F. C. (1958). *Social class and mental illness: A community study.* New York: Wiley.

Hollister, W. G. (1958). Five years' experience with lay discussion leaders in mental health education. *Mental Hygiene, 42*, 106–117.

Hughes, J. (1986). Mary Switzer: Well-mannered juggernaut. In *Vital few: The entrepreneur and American economic progress* (pp. 462–503). New York: Oxford University Press.

Iscoe, I., Bloom, B. L., & Spielberger, C. D. (Eds.). (1977). *Community psychology in transition: Proceedings of the National Conference on Training in Community Psychology.* New York: Hemisphere Publication Services.

Iscoe, I., & Spielberger, C. D. (Eds). (1970). *Community psychology: Perspectives in training and research.* New York: Appleton-Century-Crofts

Jahoda, M. (1958). *Current concepts of positive mental health.* New York: Basic Books.

Jahoda, M. (1997). In J. G. Kelly (Ed.). (2003). *Exemplars of community psychology* [DVD]. Edmond, OK: Society for Community Research and Action.

Jones, M. (1953). *The therapeutic community: New treatment method in psychiatry.* London: Tavistock..

Kelly, J. G. (1984). A tribute to Erich Lindemann. *American Journal of Community Psychology, 12,* 513–514.

Kelly, J. G. (1987). Swampscott anniversary symposium: Reflections and recommendations on the 20th anniversary of Swampscott. *American Journal of Community Psychology, 15,* 511–631.

Kennedy, D. M. (1999). *Freedom from fear: The American people in depression and war, 1929–1945.* New York: Oxford University Press.

Klein, D. C. (1987). The context and times at Swampscott: My story. *American Journal of Community Psychology, 15,* 531–538.

Klein, D. C. (1995). In J. G. Kelly (Ed.). (2003). *Exemplars of community psychology* [DVD]. Edmond, OK: Society for Community Research and Action.

Klein, D. C., & Goldston, S. E. (Eds.). (1977). *Primary prevention: An idea whose time has come.* Proceedings of the Pilot Conference on Primary Prevention, April 24, 1976 (Department of Health, Education and Welfare Publication No. ADM 77-447). Washington, DC: U.S. Government Printing Office.

Knee, R. (1963). *Special report: Project grants program—1957–1962.* Washington, DC: National Institute of Mental Health.

Leavell, H. R., & Clark, E. G. (1953). *Preventive medicine for the doctor in his community: An epidemiologic approach.* New York: McGraw-Hill.

Leighton, A. H. (1963). *The character of danger.* New York: Basic Books.

Leighton, A. H. (1967). Is social environment a cause of psychiatric disorder? *Psychiatric Research Report, 22,* 337–345.

Lemann, N. (1992). *The promised land: The great Black migration and how it changed America.* New York: Vintage Books.

Levine, M. (1981). *The history and politics of community mental health.* New York: Oxford University Press.

Leys, R., & Evans, R. B. (Eds.). (1990). *Defining American psychology: The correspondence between Adolf Meyer and Edward Bradford Titchener.* Baltimore: Johns Hopkins University Press.

Liebow, E. (1967). *Tally's corner: A study of Negro street corner men.* Boston: Little, Brown.

Lindemann, E. (1953). The Wellesley project for the study of certain problems in community mental health. In *Interrelations between the social environment and psychiatric disorders* (pp. 167–188). New York: Milbank Memorial Fund.

Mann, P. A. (1978). *Community psychology: Concepts and applications.* New York: Free Press.

Masland, R. L., Gladwin, T., & Sarason, S. B. (1958). *Mental subnormality.* New York: Basic Books.

Maternity and Infancy Welfare and Hygiene (Sheppard-Towner) Act, 42 U.S.C.A. § 161-175 (1921).

Mechanic, D. (1969). *Mental health and social policy*. Englewood Cliffs, NJ: Prentice Hall.

Menninger, W. C. (1947). Psychiatric experience in the war, 1941–1946. *American Journal of Psychiatry, 103*, 577–586.

The Mental Health Study Act of 1955, Pub. L. No. 84-182.

Meritt, D. M., Greene, G. J., Jopp, D. A., & Kelly, J. G. (1999). A history of Division 27 (Society for Community Research and Action). In D. A. Dewsbury (Ed.), *Unification through division* (Vol. III, pp. 77–79). Washington, DC: American Psychological Association.

Micale, M. S., & Porter, R. (Eds.). (1994). *Discovering the history of psychiatry*. New York: Oxford University Press.

Myers, J. K., & Bean, L. L. (1968). *A decade later: A follow-up of "Social class and mental illness."* New York: Wiley.

National Mental Health Act of 1946, Pub. L. No. 79-487.

O'Connor, A. (2001). *Poverty knowledge: Social science, social policy, and the poor in twentieth-century U.S. history*. Princeton, NJ: Princeton University Press.

Parascandola, J. (1993). *Background report on the organizational history of mental health and substance abuse programs in the PHS*. Unpublished manuscript, U.S. Public Health Service.

Rainwater, L. (1971). *Behind ghetto walls: Black families in a federal slum*. New York: Penguin.

Rapoport, R., & Rapoport, R. (1958). Community as the doctor. *Human Organization, 16*, 28–31.

Reiff, R. (1971, June). From Swampscott to swamp. *The Community Psychologist, 5*, 7–10.

Rosen, G. (1993). *A history of public health*. Baltimore: Johns Hopkins University Press.

Rosenblum, G. (2001). In J. G. Kelly (Ed.). (2003). *Exemplars of community psychology* [DVD]. Edmond, OK: Society for Community Research and Action.

Rossi, A. M. (1962). Some pre-World War II antecedents of community mental health theory and practice. *Mental Hygiene, 46*, 78–94.

Rubinstein, E., & Coehlo, G. (1970). Mental health and behavioral sciences: One federal agency's role in the behavioral sciences. *American Psychologist, 25*, 517–523.

Rubinstein, R. A., Kelly, J. G., & Maines, D. R. (1985). The interdisciplinary background of community psychology: The early roots of an ecological perspective. *Division of Community Psychology Newsletter, 18*, 10–14.

Satin, D. G. (1982). Erich Lindemann: The humanist and the era of community mental health. *Proceedings of the American Philosophical Society, 126*, 327–346.

Schneider, S. F. (2000). Untitled videotape interview. In J. G. Kelly (Ed.), *The history of community psychology: A video presentation of context and exemplars*. Chicago: Society for Community Research and Action.

Shorter, E. (1997). *A history of psychiatry*. New York: Wiley.

Smith, M. B., & Hobbs, N. E. (1966). The community and the community mental health center. *American Psychologist, 21*, 499–509.

Srole, L., Langner, M. S. T., Opler, M. K., & Rennie, T. A. C. (1962). *Mental health in the metropolis*. New York: McGraw-Hill.

Stanton, A. H., & Schwartz, M. S. (1954). *The mental hospital: A study of institutional participation in psychiatric illness and treatment*. New York: Basic Books.

Starr, P. (1982). *The social transformation of American medicine*. New York: Basic Books.

Strickland, S. P. (1972). *Politics, science, and dread diseases: A short history of United States medical research policy*. Cambridge, MA: Harvard University Press.

Strother, C. (Ed.). (1956). *Psychology and mental health*. Washington, DC: American Psychological Association.

Strother, C. (1987). Reflections on the Stanford Conference and subsequent events. *American Journal of Community Psychology, 22*, 519–521.

Strupp, H. H., & Parloff, M. B. (1996). Julius Segal (1924–1994). *American Psychologist, 51*, 263.

Ullman, C. A. (1957). *Identification of maladjusted school children: Comparison of three methods of screening* (PHS Publication No. 211, Public Health Monograph No. 7). Washington, DC: U.S. Public Health Service.

Wellin, C. (1999). *Interview with Professor Benjamin D. Paul*. Unpublished manuscript.

Wing, J. K., Denham, J., & Munro, A. R. (1959). Duration of stay in hospital of patients suffering from schizophrenia. *British Journal of Preventive Social Medicine, 13*, 145–148.

Yolles, S. F. (1965). The role of the psychologist in comprehensive community mental health centers: The NIMH view. *American Psychologist, 20*, 37–41.

Zilboorg, G. (1941). *A history of medical psychology*. New York: Norton.

Zinn, H. (1999). *A people's history of the United States: 1492–present* (20th anniversary ed.). New York: HarperCollins.

10

NATIONAL MENTAL HEALTH POLICY AND THE COMMUNITY MENTAL HEALTH CENTERS, 1963–1981

JAMES W. STOCKDILL

The Mental Health Study Act of 1955 (P.L. 84-182) authorized an "objective, thorough, and nationwide analysis and reevaluation of the human and economic problems of mental illness, and for other purposes" (Joint Commission on Mental Illness and Health, 1961, p. xxv). The Joint Commission on Mental Illness and Health was created under the auspices of the National Institute of Mental Health (NIMH) to carry out this analysis and reevaluation. After more than 6 years of study and debate, the joint commission made its final report, the stated purpose of which was "to arrive at a national program that would approach adequacy in meeting the individual needs of the mentally ill people of America—to develop a plan of action that would satisfy us that we are doing the best we can" (Joint Commission on Mental Illness and Health, 1961, p. xxv). The recommendation of the joint commission that can be seen as most directly influencing federal policy on the funding of community mental health services was stated as follows: "A national mental health program should set as an objective of *one fully staffed, full-time mental health clinic available to each 50,000 of population* [italics added]" (Joint Commission on Mental Illness and Health, 1961, p. xiv). It was the development of this plan of action that in large part led to the passage of the Community Mental Health Centers Construction Act of 1963 (P.L. 88-164), hereinafter the *Community Mental Health Centers Act*. The purpose of this chapter is to review the evolution of national mental health services policy within the context of the development of community mental health centers (CMHCs). (See Foley [1975] for the political history of the development and passage of the Mental Health Study Act of 1955 and the Community Mental Health Centers Act of 1963 and its 1965 amendments.)

In mid-1961, President Kennedy requested the Secretary of the Department of Health, Education and Welfare (DHEW), together with the Secretary of the Department of Labor and the Administrator of Veterans Affairs, to undertake an analysis of the final report of the Joint Commission and suggest possible courses of action (NIMH, 1984). The findings and recommendations of this study group were reported to the President in December 1962 (see chaps. 8 and 9, this volume). One of the five major recommendations indicated that federal funds should be allocated specifically for the construction of CMHCs with the goal of building 2,000 by 1980. In his "Message to the Congress Relative to Mental Illness and Mental Retardation" on February 5, 1963, Kennedy recommended that Congress "authorize grants to the states for the construction of comprehensive community mental health centers, beginning in fiscal year 1965" (Kennedy, 1963, p. 5). This led to the 1963 Community Mental Health Centers Act, which required that each state that wished to take advantage of construction grants must submit a plan setting forth a construction program "which is based on a statewide inventory of existing facilities and survey of need (section 203 [1])." The Secretary of DHEW was given authority to write regulations, and this authority was passed on to NIMH.

It is noteworthy that it was the development of the regulations for implementation of the Community Mental Health Centers Act, rather than the specifics of the legislation, that brought the federal government more directly into the making of national mental health services policy. The drafting of these regulations involved experts within the NIMH bureaucracy and professional associations, and representatives of political interest groups as sources for new policy ideas. NIMH Director Robert Felix began to mobilize the NIMH staff and other experts to identify the substantive content of the regulations and guidelines before Congress passed the legislation (Foley, 1975).

NATIONAL POLICY ESTABLISHED BY THE REGULATIONS AND LEGISLATIVE AMENDMENTS

The initial regulations for the Community Mental Health Centers Act were published in the *Federal Register* on May 6, 1964 ("Regulations," 1964). The two most critical policies established through the initial regulations were the definition of *community* and the identification of the "essential services" that had to be provided in each of those communities. Regulation 54.203(b)(2) required the following:

> The state plan shall provide that every community mental health facility shall: (i) serve a population of not less than 75,000 and not more than 200,000 persons . . . and (ii) be so located as to be near and readily accessible to the community and population to be served, taking into account both political and geographical boundaries.

In relation to the definition of *essential services*, the regulations indicated in section 54.201(g) that "comprehensive mental health services are a complete range of all elements of services . . . in sufficient quantity to meet the needs of persons residing within the community served by a community mental health facility" ("Regulations," 1964, p. 5952). See Exhibit 10.1 for a list of the services in the regulations. The first five of these services were determined to be essential and were required to be included in a construction grant application. In addition, the regulations mandated coordination and linkages across the five essential services to ensure a continuum or system of care in keeping with public health standards (Foley & Sharfstein, 1983).

The first amendments to the Community Mental Health Centers Act came in 1965. In 1963, President Kennedy had requested authority to make grants for the initial staffing of CMHCs. However, Congress did not include this authority in the 1963 legislation. After Kennedy's assassination in November 1963, President Lyndon Johnson, in a "Special Message to the Congress on Advancing the Nation's Health" on January 7, 1965, indicated the following:

EXHIBIT 10.1
List of 10 Services Required in Initial Community
Mental Health Center Regulations

1. Inpatient services	6. Diagnostic services
2. Outpatient services	7. Rehabilitative services
3. Partial hospitalization	8. Pre- and aftercare services
4. Emergency services	9. Training
5. Consultation and education services	10. Research and evaluation

Note. Services 1–5 are essential and must be provided.

An important beginning has been made through legislation enacted by the 88th Congress authorizing aid for construction of community mental health centers. But facilities alone cannot assure services . . . I therefore recommend legislation to authorize a 5 year program of grants for the initial costs of personnel to man community mental health centers which offer comprehensive services. (cited in Spaner, 1984, p. 7)

This time, Congress did respond. On August 4, 1965, Johnson signed into law the Mental Retardation and Community Mental Health Centers Construction Act Amendments of 1965 (P.L. 89-105). The new legislation authorized staffing grants for the "compensation of professional and technical personnel for the initial operation of new community mental health centers or of new services in community mental health centers" (P.L. 89-105, Sec. 220 [a], p. 1). The amendments did not add any new concepts of how to deliver community mental health services, nor was there any expansion of the list of services in the initial legislation. However, this was milestone legislation, not only because it authorized staffing resources but also because it clarified the national policy of movement away from warehousing people with mental illness in state institutions to caring for them in their communities. These initial amendments also allowed staffing grants to be made directly from the federal level of government to the community level—in effect bypassing state government. This last provision resulted in some unintended consequences on the long-range funding of the centers that I discuss later in the chapter.

The 1965 amendments also introduced the "seed money" concept. It was clear that Congress did not want to make any commitment to long-range funding for the staffing of any individual center, so a phase-down funding formula was included. The law provided that federal grant funding would not exceed 75% of the staffing costs for the first 15 months, 60% for the "first year thereafter," 45% for the "second year thereafter," and 30% for the "third year thereafter" (P.L. 89-105, Sec. 220 [b]). The intention was that as the federal funding phased down, state and local funding would replace it. The amendments also required that only public and private nonprofit organizations would be eligible for staffing grants (P.L. 89-105, Sec. 220 [c]). In the 1960s, the success of a center's program was seen as depending largely on the extent to which they could generate state funding, community tax money, charitable contributions, and payment of fees, for there was little private insurance coverage of treatment for mental illness, and Medicaid and Medicare were just being implemented and offered little coverage for mental illness.

In 1967, authorization of CMHC construction and staffing grants was extended through the fiscal year ending June 30, 1970, with no substantive change (P.L. 90-31). However, in 1968 the act was amended to authorize grants for the construction and staffing of community facilities and services for people with alcoholism and narcotic addiction (P.L. 90-574, the "Alcoholic and Narcotic Addict Rehabilitation Amendment"). This amendment was the first to give recognition to the fact that there were substance abuse problems that needed special attention and support.

The Community Mental Health Centers Act Amendments of 1970 (P.L. 91-211) provided the first major policy changes in the basic legislation since 1965. Changes were authorized to meet urgent needs identified during the rapid growth of the CMHC program. The 4 years of experience with the staffing grants indicated that many newly funded mental health centers had been unable to generate funds to replace the federal staffing grant assistance at the previous level and within the period prescribed by the 1965 legislation. Also, it was clear that appropriate services for children and adolescents were not being provided in many service areas. The 1970 amendments included major policy changes.

The duration of all staffing grants was extended from 51 months to 8 years. The amendments required an assurance that funds would be used to "supplement" and not supplant other funds and, if practical, increase the level of third-party health insurance payments that would otherwise be made available for mental health services (Sec. 203 [b]). The 1970 amendments also provided the Secretary of DHEW with the authority to determine whether a service area was a "poverty area"; if so, this area could receive a higher level of federal funding than a nonpoverty area over the 8-year period of a staffing grant (Sec. 201 [b]). This provision was made because NIMH staff had noticed that high-priority poverty service areas designated in state plans were not applying for staffing grants because they could not provide the nonfederal percentage of funds. The 1970 amendments also authorized "Initiation and Development" grants for poverty areas (Sec. 202 [b]). These were 1-year grants, not to exceed $50,000, for purposes of needs assessment, program planning, identification of local funding, and fostering community involvement. The authority to define poverty areas was passed on to the NIMH staff who did so in draft regulations and guidelines that were completed in 1972. However, these regulations were never promulgated in final form, in large part because of the Nixon Administration's intention of phasing out the federal funding of CMHCs (Spaner, 1984, p. 11).

The other major policy change in 1970 was the addition to the Community Mental Health Centers Act of "Part F—Mental Health of Children." This was the first change made in the act for the targeting of a special age group. This program was authorized to assist CMHCs in constructing and staffing treatment facilities and for training and program evaluation related to mental health services for children and adolescents (Sec. 271). The new children's initiative was not part of the executive branch legislative proposals; it had a separate dollar authorization and was therefore very unpopular with the Nixon Administration, which began in January 1969.

In fact, I had a responsibility to work on legislation, and I was investigated by the Office of the Secretary (DHEW) in an attempt to try to link me to this proposed change in the legislation.

The 1970 legislation also amended the Centers Act to include services for drug abuse in addition to drug addiction, which had been authorized earlier (P.L. 91-513). Another new section was added that authorized grants and contracts for the prevention and treatment of alcohol abuse and alcoholism (P.L. 91-616). The Centers Act was again amended in 1972 to direct that CMHCs must provide services to drug abusers living in their service areas, if the Secretary of DHEW determines that such services are "necessary and feasible" (P.L. 92-255). These substance abuse provisions were consistent with the political movement toward making the two substance abuse divisions of NIMH into separate institutes. This was done in 1973 when the Alcohol, Drug Abuse and Mental Health Administration was established with the constituent institutes of NIMH, National Institute on Drug Abuse, and the National Institute on Alcohol Abuse and Alcoholism.

The most comprehensive of all amendments to expand and change the CMHCs program came in the form of Title III of Public Law 94-63, "Community Mental Health Centers Amendments of 1975." This legislation came on the heels of several years of Nixon Administration attempts to impound funds for the CMHC program (and other human service programs), to phase out federal project grant programs, and to move to block grants. With the resignation of President Nixon in 1974, President Gerald Ford used his veto power to block the continuation of several federal project grant programs, in keeping with his predecessor's priorities. There were a variety of views across the mental health constituency groups as to what should and should not be changed in the Community Mental Health Centers Act. In this environment it was necessary to get all of the national mental health stakeholders to coordinate their efforts. To assure political success it had also been necessary for NIMH and the mental health constituency groups to align themselves with other health and human service programs. Therefore, P.L. 94-63 included separate titles for Family Planning Programs, Migrant Health Centers, Community Health Centers, Home Health Services for Communicable Diseases, Hemophilia Programs, National Health Service Corps, and Nurse Training in addition to the amendments to the Community Mental Health Centers Act. Congress passed the act in July and, as expected, President Ford vetoed it on July 26. The Senate overrode the veto the same day and the House did so on July 29, the date it was enacted into law (National Institute of Mental Health, 1980). The difficulties encountered in the passage of this legislation and the complexities of the necessary political strategy used made it clear that using the Community Mental Health Centers Act to set national mental health services policy was increasingly problematic.

The tone of the 1975 amendments to the Community Mental Health Centers Act was a powerful expression of Congressional concern and intent that the CMHC funding be continued and that the changes proposed be implemented. Congressional leaders sought to end the debate between Congress and the executive branch, which had been continuous since 1970, concerning the federal role in improving and expanding community mental health services (NIMH, 1975). The 1975 legislation had a level of detail normally contained in regulations. This was probably due to the fact that the regulations developed by NIMH after the 1970 amendments were prevented from being promulgated in final form by the Nixon Administration.

The new program was now to have 12 essential services, seven grant mechanisms, and many new compliance features and reports to Congress. In addition to the original 5 essential services and the Part F children's program added in 1970, Congress added special services for the elderly, screening services for the courts and other public agencies to link individuals with mental illness to appropriate services, follow-up care for people discharged from inpatient facilities, transitional services through halfway houses to assure appropriate living arrangements and support services to help consumers adjust to community living, and new alcohol and drug abuse services to be provided by the centers. The three screening, follow-up, and transitional services were added because of the growing concerns about deinstitutionalization of people with serious mental illness.

Although the range of new services and grant mechanisms was comprehensive and complex, the compliance requirements of the 1975 amendments were even more daunting. The new major requirements included a stipulation that CMHC services must be coordinated with the services provided by other health and social service agencies in the catchment area and that the governing body of a center must represent the population of the catchment area in terms of employment, age, sex, and place of residence. Other requirements addressed quality control, records management, and needs assessment issues. For the first time, grant approval for CMHC projects was made dependent on the existence of a state mental health plan, and all grant applications had to be submitted to the state mental health authority at the same time they were submitted to NIMH. These last two requirements were intended to help compensate for the bypassing of the states in the 1965 amendments.

After the 1975 renewal and amendments to the legislation, the last significant policy changes in the program came in the Community Mental Health Center Extension Act of 1978 (P.L. 95-622). The 1978 legislation reauthorized the program for 2 years and required CMHCs to provide six services to all age groups immediately after becoming operational: (a) emergency, (b) screening and referral, (c) outpatient, (d) inpatient, (e) follow-up after hospitalization, and (f) consultation and education. The 1978 amendments also authorized up to 5 years, rather than the 3 years provided in the 1975 amendments, for funding of financial distress grants. Thus, the 1978 amendments were significant in the sense that they modified some of the requirements in the 1975 amendments to make them less burdensome on the centers. There were no more significant changes made in national community mental health policy until the 1980 passage of the Mental Health Systems Act (P.L. 96-398), which developed out of President Carter's Commission on Mental Health (for complete CMHC legislation history, see Exhibit 10.2).

IMPACT OF THE NATIONAL MENTAL HEALTH POLICY CHANGES ON MENTAL HEALTH PRACTICES

How successful was the implementation of these sweeping national policy changes in improving the treatment, rehabilitation, and recovery of people with serious mental illness? The 1975 amendments to the Community Mental Health Centers Act contained a statement of Congressional findings that concluded that the centers

> have had a major impact on the improvement of mental health care by fostering coordination and cooperation between various agencies, . . . bringing comprehensive mental health care within a specific geographic area regardless of ability to pay, and developing a system which ensures continuity of care. (P.L. 94-63, Title III, Section 302 [a], p. 5)

These were reasonable general conclusions after the first 10 years of implementation. However, did they stand up to rigorous review?

In the 1968 amendments to the Community Mental Health Centers Act, DHEW was authorized to take up to 1% of CMHC grant funds and use them for studies of the program. The NIMH Office of Program Planning and Evaluation administered the majority of these funds. During 1969 through 1977, NIMH contracted for 45 evaluation projects that related directly to the CMHC program at a total cost of just over $4 million (Stockdill, 1978). In general, the findings of these studies were used for input into legislative renewal and the modification of program policies and procedures. One of the major lessons learned by NIMH staff in relation to applying evaluation findings to program policies was that studies must be directed at specific policies or objectives (Woy, 1978). Any attempt to evaluate a total program in a single study is unrealistic. In the following section, I focus on reporting the findings of some of these studies and their impact on the national mental health services policy changes outlined above.

EXHIBIT 10.2
Legislative Summary Regarding Community Mental Health Centers, 1963–1981

1963: The Community Mental Health Centers Construction Act (P.L. 88-164) authorizes federal grants for the construction of community mental health centers (CMHCs).

1965: The Centers Act is amended (P.L. 89-105) to authorize grants for the staffing of CMHCs.

1967: Authorization of construction and staffing grants is extended (P.L. 90-31) through the fiscal year ending June 30, 1970.

1968: The act is amended (P.L. 90-574) to authorize grants for the construction and staffing of facilities and services for people with alcoholism or narcotic addiction.

1970: The act is amended (P.L. 91-211) to extend authorization for construction and staffing grants to CMHCs for programs for people with alcoholism or narcotic addiction through June 30, 1973. The 1970 amendments also extended the duration of all staffing grants to 8 years, authorized a higher percentage of funds for CMHCs in poverty areas and provided grants to support the development of new programs in poverty areas, authorized additional staffing grants for CMHC consultation and education services, and established a new grant program for child and adolescent mental health services.

1970: The act is amended (P.L. 91-513) to extend drug programs to include services for drug abuse.

1970: The act is amended (P.L. 91-515) by adding a new section on maintenance of effort for staffing grants.

1970: The act is amended (P.L. 91-616) to add a new section authorizing grants and contracts for the prevention and treatment of alcohol abuse.

1972: The act is amended (P.L. 92-255) to require that CMHCs funded after June 30, 1972, must provide services for drug abusers living in their service area. This legislation also authorized additional funds for special project grants for services to narcotic addicts and drug-dependent persons.

1973: Authorization of CMHC construction, staffing, children's services, and alcohol and drug abuse programs is extended (P.L. 93-46) through the fiscal year ending June 30, 1974.

1975: The 1975 amendments expanded the essential CMHC services from 5 to 12, authorized seven grant mechanisms, established many new compliance features, and stipulated certain reports to Congress.

1977: The act is extended through September 30, 1978 (P.L. 95-83).

1978: The act is extended for 2 years (P.L. 95-622). New grantees were now given 3 years in which to phase in services.

1979: A technical amendment (P.L. 96-32) is enacted to correct or clarify items in health and mental health legislation.

1980: The Mental Health Systems Act (P.L. 96-398) is enacted and reauthorizes CMHC initial operations, planning, consultation and education, and financial distress grants through fiscal year 1984 and permits CMHCs to apply for other mental health programs under the new act.

1981: The Omnibus Budget Reconciliation Act of 1981 (P.L. 97-35) consolidates funding for mental health, alcoholism and alcohol abuse, and drug abuse services into a block grant program for the states. This new act repeals the Community Mental Health Centers Act and the Mental Health Systems Act.

The Catchment Area Concept

The catchment area concept can be traced back to the work of the Joint Commission, which was established in 1955 and issued its final report in 1961. The concept was given specificity through the regulations that were approved and published in May 1964. The regulations required that every CMHC must "(i) serve a population of not less than 75,000 and not more than 200,000 persons and (ii) be so located as to be near and readily accessible to the community and population to be served" (Regulation 54.203 [b] [2]). Because it was so central to the philosophy of a CMHC, it was one of the first policy areas to be evaluated. An early evaluation study found the concept to have contributed significantly to improved care (A. D. Little, Inc., 1973). Because each CMHC had to assume responsibility for the mental health of the population in a specified service area, there was greater access to services, population needs were more easily identified, services were more easily tailor made to meet identified needs, and fragmentation of services was reduced. The study found that the population size requirements had been administered flexibly to allow for exceptions as allowed by the regulations. The size of the catchment area populations actually ranged from 6,000 to 350,000 after the first several years of the program. The smallest catchment area was approved for Kodiak Island, Alaska, with a population of 6,000. Waivers were made in special cases where it had been shown that the variations in catchment area boundaries would make services more accessible. The greatest problems in these population parameters seemed to arise when a city or county had to be divided up to meet the NIMH regulatory requirements (Ozarin, 1975). Nevertheless, solutions were found. As a result of what were generally positive evaluations in relation to availability and access of services, the catchment area concept was maintained in all of the extensions of the Community Mental Health Center Act.

Comprehensiveness of Services and Continuity of Care

As outlined above, each CMHC was required to provide inpatient, outpatient, partial hospitalization, emergency, and consultation and education services. This requirement had been based on experience and practice as well as on NIMH research and service demonstrations (Ozarin, 1975). The initial Community Mental Health Centers Act and related regulations required that the five essential services be linked and coordinated into a network of services. A CMHC with coordinated emergency, outpatient, inpatient, partial hospitalization, and consultation and education services provided this continuity of care. In reviewing the findings of the evaluation studies funded between 1969 and 1975 concerning the impact of the requirement for five essential services, Ozarin (1975) found that there was "little reason to doubt that the CMHC program has fostered the elaboration of a wider range of mental health services, available to a greater number of people" (p. 27). Not only were these services available in each of the centers studied, but also each of these services was having an impact on the quality of care.

NIMH evaluation studies and other research found that CMHC emergency services (crisis intervention) reduced both the need for inpatient services and the need for detention in the criminal justice system (Dekker & Stubblebine, 1972; Langsley, Machotka, & Flomenhaft, 1971). Other studies indicated that the expansion of hospital day care and other partial hospitalization services through the CMHCs made it possible for mental health consumers to return sooner to their normal community living and helped reduce future hospital admissions (Glaser, 1969; Herz, Endicott, Spitzer, & Mesnikoff, 1971). These studies confirmed that many consumers who would normally have been admitted to inpatient services could be treated in a partial hospitalization service.

Most mental health centers were established around existing outpatient mental health services. As Ozarin (1975) indicated, this modality was probably "the least innovative of the array of center services" in the first 10 years of the program (p. 32). This was certainly true in relation to clinical practices; however, there was much experimentation with the organization and structure of outpatient services. New group therapies for various client populations were used, and new family therapies were essential because in many centers close to 50% of the outpatient clients had family problems. New intake procedures were experimented with, particularly in multiagency centers that needed a single intake location. Some states, such as Kentucky, established central information and referral services in all centers (Ozarin, 1975). New approaches to providing outpatient services were demonstrated in both urban and rural centers through the development of satellite locations. In 1969, as part of an in-house evaluation, I visited storefront satellite locations in Chicago and remote rural satellites in Mississippi. Both were active and viable programs at that time. In both urban and rural satellite locations, increased involvement of primary-care physicians was necessary and encouraged.

Increase and expansion of mental health inpatient units in community general hospitals was one of the most significant policy impacts of implementation of the 1963 Community Mental Health Centers Act. In many rural areas, the implementation of a mental health center brought inpatient services and staff to communities where none had existed. The increase in general hospital psychiatric inpatient units had begun prior to the centers program (467 units in 1964); however, the expansion was greatly accelerated by implementation of CMHCs (815 units in 1972; Ozarin, 1975). In addition to a great increase in admissions to these community inpatient services, the average length of stay decreased from 17 days in 1968 to 11 days in 1971.

Consultation and Education Services

Consultation and education were originally conceptualized as services to other human service providers in the community, to assist them in identifying and coping with potential mental health problems of their clients and help prevent the need for direct clinical services (NIMH, 1980). These services were also to be provided to assist the general public in understanding and identifying mental health problems to facilitate prevention or early intervention. Data collected by the NIMH Division of Biometry and Epidemiology in 1974 indicated that 5.7% of all staff hours in federally funded CMHCs were allocated to consultation and community education (Ozarin, 1975). Schools received 39% of the time; other mental health agencies, law enforcement, health and medical programs, and social service agencies received over 35% of the staff time; and facilities for the elderly and alcohol and drug abuse each received between 3% and 5% of the time.

The most valid criterion to measure the success of consultation to child and family service agencies was early identification of emotionally disturbed children and reductions in the number of children and adolescents admitted to community emergency services. Mannino, MacLennan, and Shore, of the NIMH Mental Health Study Center, reviewed 35 evaluation research studies concerned with consultation and education services (1975). Positive results were found in 24 of 35 studies. However, because payments for consultation and education services were not covered by insurance and other third-party reimbursement, they were often neglected in the early years of operation. As a result of the identification of this problem, 1975 amendments to the Community Mental Health Centers Act (P.L. 94-63) authorized separate grants for consultation and education services (Sec. 204 [a]).

Continuity of Care

The concept of continuity of care was not well defined in the Community Mental Health Centers Act or the initial regulations and was therefore subject to disagreements in the field. Staff of the NIMH Division of Biometry and Epidemiology took on the task of developing a methodology for measuring continuity of care (Bass, 1971; Bass & Windle, 1972). Using this methodology, the National Opinion Research Center assessed continuity of care by looking at the relationships between CMHCs and other caregiving agencies in Chicago. The researchers found that clinicians had difficulty in providing continuity of care in 38% of the cases in their sample. In over half of the problem cases, consumers or families rejected the prescribed clinical services, missed appointments, or were otherwise uncooperative (National Opinion Research Center, 1971). In another study that examined administrative and organizational relationships in multiagency CMHCs, the National Academy of Public Administration (1971) focused on administrative and clinical continuity as a major concern. The investigators found that organizational and administrative systems to provide the framework for coordination had been created in most of the centers visited. The study's basic conclusion was that the CMHC model of integrating autonomous community programs into a common organizational structure, for the purpose of delivering coordinated mental health services to a specific community, was an effective and viable approach.

The Seed Money Policy

The seed money concept was one of the most controversial policies established by the CMHC program and was subjected to almost continuous review. As a result, this concept was modified 11 times through legislative amendments over the course of the program (Weiner, Woy, Sharfstein, & Bass, 1979). The seed money concept was based on the assumption that mental health centers would generate funding from (a) state and local governments; (b) receipts generated by direct services through client fees, reimbursements from private insurance, and reimbursements from Medicare, Medicaid, and Title 20 Social Services; and (c) other sources, such as consultation and education contracts, fundraising, philanthropy, and, potentially, national health insurance (Stockdill, 1978). Beginning in 1969, with the availability of the 1% evaluation funds, NIMH funded three evaluation studies directed at identifying other sources of funds for mental health centers and measuring the centers' success in garnering these funds as the federal funding declined. The U.S. General Accounting Office also conducted an independent study.

The first study reported on a sample of 16 centers. This study focused on some of the first centers to receive staffing grants and was intended to identify the range of conditions that might be expected to characterize federally funded centers in general (NIMH, Division of Mental Health Service Programs, 1977). The study revealed, as many had feared, that very few of these centers had developed any plans for how they would replace the declining federal dollars (Stanford Research Institute, 1970). In 1972, NIMH contracted for a follow-up evaluation of trends in sources of funds for the new centers (Macro Systems, Inc., 1973). A major objective of this study was to determine whether the findings of the first study were still prevalent. The study sample was composed of 16 centers approaching their 8th year of staffing grant funding. The general findings of this study were that the financial situation of the centers had not changed significantly since the previous study and, most important, that few of these centers had realistic plans for replacing the declining federal funds. These findings were validated in a 1974 study completed by the General Accounting Office (Comptroller General of the United States, 1974). The General Accounting Office study found that the high percentage of low-income clients served directly affected patient fee collection, centers received little or no revenue from consultation and education services, state and local support varied widely from 2% to 70%, and third-party payers primarily covered only inpatient services.

On the basis of findings from these studies, and other indications, Congress included "Financial Distress Grants" in the 1975 amendments to the Community Mental Health Centers Act (Title III, P.L. 94-63, Part B). Up to three 1-year financial distress grants were authorized for centers that would otherwise be forced to significantly reduce services or be unable to provide the services described in new Section 201(b) after their staffing or operating grants ran out. Considerable behind-the-scenes work by NIMH staff to provide supportive data and to educate the staff of supportive members of Congress was the key to this support.

In 1977, there were finally enough "graduate" CMHCs that had completed all federal support for their operations to make possible a study of them as a group in relation to the seed money policy. The study, carried out by Abt Associates, Inc., included a statistical analysis of secondary data on all 99 centers that had been operating for 10 years or more and thus were beyond the initial funding period and discussion and an analysis based on in-depth studies of 28 sample centers (Naierman, Haskins, & Robinson, 1978). The study was undertaken to determine whether centers were able to generate funds from sources other than the federal grants and whether the structure and services of the centers were affected by the termination of the federal funding (NIMH, 1980). This study found that, by the end of the 8 years of funding, most centers had become financially resourceful enough to generate other sources of funds without violating the intent, policies, and objectives of the Community Mental Health Centers Act (Naierman et al., 1978). However, in most centers studied, after the 8th year and termination of the staffing grant, the third-party revenues stabilized in growth while state and local funds increased as they became more essential to the replacement of federal funds. The state and local funds often came with service requirements and state program priorities that could put the centers in conflict with the Community Mental Health Centers Act goals and objectives. For example, consultation and education services were frequently reduced, and there were shifts away from outpatient services in favor of the use of more profitable inpatient services that were covered by insurance. Thus, within a year or two after federal funds ceased, it appeared that the CMHC values and philosophy could be put in jeopardy, despite continued financial viability.

The findings of the evaluation studies outlined above stimulated NIMH staff to reexamine the seed money concept. A second study of "graduate" centers was initiated by the NIMH Division of Mental Health Service Programs in 1978 (Weiner et al., 1979). Under the direction of psychiatrist Steve Sharfstein, then director of the NIMH Division of Mental Health Service Programs, a cohort of 44 centers that had completed their 8 years of staffing grants was selected for study. Data were available for these centers from their 9th year of operation, when they no longer had staffing grant funding. This sample was narrowed down to 29 centers because of incomplete or inaccurate data from 15 centers. The review and analysis of this sample of 29 centers indicated that these centers had growth in revenues through their final 4 years of the staffing grants and through their 9th year of operation. It was found that this continued growth was due to significant increases in third-party reimbursement and in state funds. However, this sample was also divided into two subgroups for review and analysis. One subgroup of 11 centers was given a title of "true graduates" because they had not received any additional grants of any kind from NIMH after completing their staffing grants, and the other group was titled "quasi-graduates" because they had received financial distress grants from NIMH (Weiner et al., 1979). When the financial data were analyzed for each of the subgroups independently, it was discovered that the mix of funding for each subgroup was quite different.

The "true graduates" had been very successful in obtaining state funds and third-party funds in particular. By these centers' 9th year, third-party funds provided 50% of their revenues, and state funds contributed over 36% of the revenue. On the other hand, the revenues of the "quasi-graduates" did not grow as fast as those of the other group, and they were not as successful in garnering third-party funds. By their 9th year of operation, over 40% of the revenues of the quasi-graduate subgroups came from the state level, and about 30% came from third-party revenues. One subgroup was problematic financially, and the other was problematic because of the potential for drifting away from the CMHC model.

Was the seed money concept successfully implemented? Foley and Sharfstein (1983) concluded that it was

> The federal seed money concept primed the pump of a well of state, local and third party funds. In the first two years of federal support, every federal dollar for the average CMHC was matched by 1.5 non-federal dollars, and by the seventh or eighth years, at the point of the CMHCs graduating from federal support, the federal dollar was being matched by four nonfederal dollars. (p. 102)

Poverty Area Funding Policy

The Community Mental Health Center Act amendments of 1970 had not only extended the period for staffing grants from 51 months to 8 years but also provided that catchment areas determined to be "poverty areas" would receive a higher percentage of funding than would nonpoverty areas (P.L. 91-211, Sec. 201 [b]). Poverty area staffing grants were to range from 90% of staffing costs in the first 2 years to 70% in the last 3 years, as compared with nonpoverty area staffing grants, which ranged from 75% in the first 2 years to 30% in the last 4 years of their staffing grants. In addition, the 1970 legislation authorized that new Initiation and Development Grants, which were not to exceed $50,000, be made available to poverty catchment areas (P.L. 91-211, Sec. 202 [b]). It was hoped that these new grants, which were essentially planning grants, and the higher staffing grant funding percentages, would make it possible for poverty areas to participate in the development of CMHCs.

NIMH funded an evaluation project in 1972 to measure the impact of preferential funding in poverty areas (Roy Littlejohn Associates, 1972). The researchers visited 24 centers with designated poverty areas, in 18 states, to identify any improvements in services for low-income clients. These centers had received an average of $66,000 in additional funding because of their designation as poverty areas (Ozarin, 1975). The study found that the CMHCs that were most accessible to impoverished clients were the ones that included a human services orientation and gave priority to quality-of-life issues in addition to clinical issues. The centers that seemed to be most effective in providing services to the poverty area populations used indigenous paraprofessional mental health workers in satellite locations. Differences in language, culture, and transportation were cited as ongoing problems (Roy Littlejohn Associates, 1972). This study, as well as other studies, revealed a lack of effective outreach and low cultural competence of staff in poverty area CMHCs. By 1975, there were 507 operational centers, and 287 of them included designated poverty areas (NIMH, 1978). It seems clear that the poverty area funding policy was a quantitative success, but the quality of care was suffering. It may well have been that populations facing social problems such as poverty, crime, and racism must of necessity see mental health services as a lower priority.

Governance and Citizen Participation

The Community Mental Health Centers Act of 1963 made no mention of citizen participation in governance or other types of involvement with

CMHC operations. However, citizen participation had been an important concept in community mental health planning prior to the advent of CMHCs. In 1963, Congress appropriated funds through Section 314 [c] of the Public Health Services Act for grants-in-aid to states to develop community mental health services plans. NIMH required, as a condition of the planning grants, that the states establish citizen advisory councils to advise state mental health authorities and participate in the planning process (NIMH, 1980). With the passage of the Community Mental Health Centers Act, NIMH continued its support of citizen participation in the development of construction and staffing grants applications (NIMH, 1980). Also, in 1971, NIMH further mandated citizen participation policy by including it in a CMHC Program Operating Handbook with strong language directed at assuring community involvement in the planning and operation of the center's program (Division of Mental Health Service Programs, NIMH, 1971).

However, it was not until 1975 that there was a Congressional mandate for CMHC governing boards with representative citizen participation. Congress prescribed that all federally funded CMHCs (except those centers in operation prior to enactment of this legislation and that were operated by a state or local governmental agency) must have a governing body "composed, where practicable," of individuals who reside in the center's catchment area and who as a group, represent the residents of that area taking into consideration their employment, age, sex, and place of residence and other demographic characteristics of the area (P.L. 94-63, Sec. 201 [c] (1)). The words "where practicable" were put in as a sop to the American Hospital Association because it vowed to oppose the legislation unless the CMHC governing board requirement was made more flexible. Many centers were established under the auspices of community hospitals, which had their own governing boards, and they did not see the necessity of having a separate CMHC governing body. (Here I must confess that I suggested the words "where practicable" as a solution to the problem while meeting in my Silver Spring, Maryland, living room with the American Hospital Association government relations person and a representative of Sen. Kennedy's office.) Before and after the 1975 amendments requiring community participation on governing boards, NIMH used technical assistance funds for ongoing education and training of governing board members concerning their functions and responsibilities.

Deinstitutionalization

Although deinstitutionalization was never a stated goal, objective, or policy in the Community Mental Health Centers Act or its amendments, it became the most written about and discussed issue in relation to the implementation of CMHCs. For the CMHCs, the issue was framed as a question of whether communities and the newly funded CMHCs had the will and the capacity to provide appropriate treatment and rehabilitation for the large numbers of people with serious mental illness being discharged from state mental hospitals during the 1960s and 1970s. The reduction of state mental hospital admissions and costs was always an unstated (in the legislation) but underlying goal of the mental health centers program. President Kennedy, in his 1963 "Message to the Congress On Mental Illness and Retardation," stated that "if we launch a new mental health program now, it will be possible within a decade or two to reduce the number of persons now under custodial care by 50 percent or more" (Kennedy, 1963, pp. 4–5). In fact, during the 15-year period in which CMHCs were funded, the resident population of state mental hospitals declined by more than 50%. Evaluation studies and reports from NIMH regional office staff were indicating that one of the greatest deficits of the program was the inability to meet the needs of individuals with serious and persistent mental illness, particularly those who were discharged from state hospitals in large numbers (Stockdill, 1985).

In the state hospital, patients had a roof over their heads, three square meals a day, transportation, medical services, laundry services, and a routine of daily tasks. In the move from hospital to community, even if the CMHC could provide adequate mental health services for this population, many times they could not and should not have been expected to provide for the other comprehensive health, housing, and social services necessary for community life. However, many centers were criticized for their failure to coordinate their services with state hospitals and with other community programs that might conceivably have worked together to provide the myriad services needed by people with serious mental illness in the community (Stockdill, 1985). NIMH first gave recognition to these problems in early 1974 with the establishment of a Community Support Work Group initiated and chaired by psychiatrist Lucy Ozarin (Turner & TenHoor, 1978). The work group led to two outcomes: (a) a Community Support System, which was designed to describe the network of human services required by people with serious and persistent mental illness, and (b) a new NIMH program, the Community Support Program (CSP), to help states develop community support systems under a variety of circumstances. The CSP effort, with its emphasis on community support systems and psychiatric rehabilitation, was NIMH's answer to the problems identified with deinstitutionalization— but it came too late to prevent the problems (Goldman & Morrissey, 1985). See Turner and TenHoor (1978) for a detailed early history of the CSP.

As many writers would later chronicle, the social, political, and financial resource environment in which the CMHC program was implemented, and in which deinstitutionalization was spawned, was complex and fraught with problems and pitfalls. Barbara Baer (1980) outlined many of the relevant factors in the environment that drove deinstitutionalization beginning in the 1950s: introduction of psychotropic drugs, the goals of state community mental health legislation in the 1950s, the intertwining of federal attention with the civil rights movement and milestone court decisions, increasing hospital expenses, a developing new nursing home and board and care industry, and the fact that state hospital funds were seldom transferred to the community. Braun et al. (1981) pointed out that national deinstitutionalization came at a time of great public dissatisfaction with the conditions in public mental hospitals. They also pointed out that the reduction of state hospital resident populations was "abetted by state governments which saw fiscal advantages in large-scale hospital discharges" (p. 736).

All things considered, the implementation of CMHCs was only one of many factors driving deinstitutionalization. The political environment in the early 1960s was conducive for the passage of major national mental health services legislation. The political activists had to strike while the iron was hot! However, there was another major dilemma emerging in the environment that was not properly accounted for and that would greatly confound deinstitutionalization. At the time of the passage and implementation of the Community Mental Health Centers Act, the early part of the baby boom population was coming into adulthood (18–21 years old) at the age when they were most at risk of schizophrenia and other serious mental illness. By the end of the 1970s, nearly one third of the U.S. population was between the ages of 21 and 36 (Kiesler, Bachrach, Mechanic, McGuire, & Mosher, 1982). This younger group had a much different pattern of service use than the older adults coming back to the community after years of institutionalization. As a result of deinstitutionalization and their attitudes about institutionalization, many of these young adults with serious mental illness often never received any active treatment over a significant period of time (Kiesler et al., 1982). However, they could overwhelm community emergency services with their numbers and co-occurring disorders of mental illness and substance abuse. Bassuk (1980) reported that during one period at a Boston private general hospital, 62% of the emergency visits were made by individuals 20 to 34 years old, even though that group represented only 28% of the general population. Most of the population with mental illness who were part of this demographic bubble in the 1960s and 1970s may never have been in a state mental hospital, but they were part of the responsibility of the growing community mental health system.

THE 1977 PRESIDENT'S COMMISSION ON MENTAL HEALTH
AND THE LAST GASP OF MENTAL HEALTH
POLICY DEVELOPMENT THROUGH THE MENTAL
HEALTH CENTERS ACT

President Carter established the Commission on Mental Health by executive order in his 2nd month in office (Executive Order 11973, February 17, 1977). The President directed the commission to conduct a study of the mental health needs of the nation and to recommend approaches to meet those needs. The commission was composed of 20 individuals, the majority of whom were concerned laypersons (NIMH, 1980). Rosalynn Carter was designated as the honorary chairperson. The work of the commission was assigned to 32 task panels with 450 members, including mental health professionals, mental health advocates, consumers, and family members. The public hearings and research and analysis by task panel and commission members went on for a full year. On the basis of task panel reports and the commission's own review and analysis, the commission completed its final report and submitted it to the President in April 1978 (NIMH, 1980). The final report formed the substance of President Carter's message to Congress submitting the proposed Mental Health Systems Act. Many of the findings and related recommendations of the commission served as a blueprint for the legislation; however, the political process that resulted in the draft Mental Health Systems Act and the legislative process that followed significantly smudged this blueprint.

The Mental Health Systems Act (P.L. 96-398), as finally passed, was one of the most comprehensive and complex pieces of federal human services legislation on record. There was something for everyone. In Title I, the Congress declared that each catchment area designated under the current Community Mental Health Centers Act was to be redesignated as a mental health "service area" and that each service area was to have boundaries

> which conform to or are within the boundaries of a health service area established under Title XV of the Public Health Services Act, and, to the extent practicable, conform to boundaries of one or more school districts or political or other subdivisions in the state. (Sec. 106 [a] [b])

Title II of the Mental Health Systems Act authorized seven new grant mechanisms in addition to reauthorizing CMHC operating grants (see Exhibit 10.3).

The act did indeed incorporate many recommendations of the President's Commission, NIMH, and the national mental health advocacy groups. However, the advocacy groups now represented a much broader range of interests than that of the political oligopoly that existed in 1963. In 1981,

EXHIBIT 10.3
Mental Health Systems Act Title II: New Grant Mechanisms

- Grants for services for chronically mentally ill individuals
- Grants for services for severely mentally disturbed children and adolescents
- Grants for mental health services for elderly individuals and other priority populations
- Grants for non-revenue-producing services
- Grants for mental health services in health care centers
- Grants and contracts for innovative projects
- Grants for the prevention of mental illness and the promotion of mental health (Secs. 202–208).

NIMH staff dutifully began preparing the regulations and guidelines required to implement all nine titles of the Mental Health Systems Act.

President Carter was defeated for reelection in November 1980, and President Reagan took office in January 1981. The final draft of the regulations and guidelines for the Mental Health Systems Act were completed in June 1981 (Memorandum of transmittal from Stockdill to the Acting Assistant Secretary for Health, June 19, 1981). After being reviewed in the Office of the Assistant Secretary for Health and in the Office of the Secretary for Health and Human Services, the regulations received final approval in July 1981. Everything was in place for implementation of the Mental Health Systems Act. However, in the wee hours of a 1981 August morning, after the clocks in the U.S. Capitol had been turned back to keep up the appearances of legality (Stockdill, 1981), Congress passed the Omnibus Budget Reconciliation Act (OBRA) of 1981 (P.L. 97-35). Among other things, OBRA consolidated federal funds for services related to mental health, alcohol abuse, and drug abuse into a state "block grant" program for fiscal years 1982, 1983, and 1984. The size of any single state allotment for 1982 was based on the amount the state received in fiscal year 1981 for mental health services under the Community Mental Health Centers Act and on the amount it received in fiscal year 1980 for alcohol and drug abuse project grants and formula grants (Stockdill, 1981). The block grant legislation also provided that CMHCs initially funded prior to fiscal year 1982 were to receive some portion of each state's block grant allotment for as many years as they would have been eligible for basic staffing or operating grants under the Community Mental Health Centers Act (NIMH, 1981). In addition, OBRA repealed the Community Mental Health Centers Act and the various grant programs authorized by the Mental Health Systems Act. The era of the federal government making national mental health services policy through CMHC legislation was over. We will never know whether the new policy changes contained in the Mental Health Systems Act would have significantly improved community mental health systems.

DISCUSSION AND OBSERVATIONS

The Politics of Mental Health

The implementation of the Community Mental Health Centers Act had a significant impact on the politics of mental health (Brown & Stockdill, 1972). Viewed from the perspective of national politics, the act was about "mobilizing society's scarce resources for the support of mental health programs" (Brown & Stockdill, 1972, p. 669). One could argue that the process of mental health politics in 1963 was more of an elitist model than a pluralist model. However, by the end of the federal funding of CMHCs in 1981, there was very much a pluralistic model of the politics of mental health. In fact, if one looks at the organizational membership of the Joint Commission on Mental Illness and Health (established in 1955), one will note that almost all of the participating organizations were either professional, bureaucratic, or hospital based. The two exceptions were the National Association for Mental Health and the American Legion. The individual members of the commission generally represented these same interests, and the president of the commission, the chairman of the board of trustees, and the staff director were all psychiatrists. There were many factors in the general national social and political environment that influenced the gradual movement toward a pluralistic rather than an elitist model of political involvement in the mental health field. I would like to briefly elaborate on five factors that were most central to the politics of mental health and the determination of national community mental health policy: (a) the establishment of a national organization representing the interests of the CMHCs, (b) more equity of political influence among the four major mental health professional associations, (c) an increase in the influence of the National Mental Health Association, and most important, the beginnings and growth of the (d) consumer and (e) family movements.

After the first funding of staffing grants, the leadership in NIMH encouraged the development of an organization to represent the CMHCs at the national level. It was clear that the CMHC legislation would never have ongoing legislative authority and would have to be renewed and amended continuously. A group of CMHC directors began organizing in the late 1960s. They officially established the National Council of Community Mental Health Centers in 1971 and hired an executive director and a small staff, which included a legislative liaison person. The council became a major influence in the setting of national mental health policy.

Staffing data collected by NIMH on all operating centers in 1973 indicated that across the nation, 8% of the staff were psychiatrists, 6% were psychologists, 10% were social workers, 13% were nursing staff, 14% were other professionals and administrative staff, and 20% were support staff. By

1978, with many more centers operational, the data indicated that, in terms of full-time employees, 4% were psychiatrists and other physicians, 9% were psychologists, 13% were social workers, 10% were registered nurses, and 18% were support staff and other mental health workers. The diminishing presence of psychiatrists in CMHCs was a major issue in 1978, and there was particular concern on the part of some individuals that there was a decreasing percentage of psychiatrists in center director positions. In a political sense, these numbers meant that the other professional associations (psychology, nursing, and social work) came to the national mental health policy bargaining table in a much stronger position than they had in 1963 at the initiation of the CMHC program. Psychiatrists had led the way in the conceptualization of the CMHC program and the passage of the initial legislation, but as the program evolved they lost their privileged position with the other disciplines on the Washington scene.

The National Association for Mental Health, the oldest of the national mental health constituency groups, was given a new cause with the advent of the CMHC program. The National Association of Mental Health was there during lobbying and policy development every step of the way, and its involvement in the passage of the staffing grant amendments was crucial to the movement. It was the one national group made up of citizens who did not have anything to gain as individuals. This set them apart from the professional associations, the CMHC directors, and the state mental health program directors.

The National Alliance for the Mentally Ill was founded in September 1979 in Madison, Wisconsin. Made up predominantly of family members of people with serious mental illness, the founding of NAMI was stimulated by the general concern that the CMHCs and the federally funded research and training programs had not given adequate priority to people with severe and persistent mental illness and their families (Fersh, 1982). With the passage of the Community Mental Health Centers Act and the growth of the movement throughout the 1960s and 1970s, a locus of support was developing in NIMH for improving services for the severely and persistently mentally ill population and their families. As described earlier, in the discussion on deinstitutionalization, the NIMH CSP was implemented in 1978. Many family members played an important part in the conceptualization of the CSP concept, and the CSP provided financial and other support in the early organizing efforts of state and local NAMI chapters, and the staff worked collaboratively with NAMI itself (Parrish, 1991). By 1982, NAMI had 90 family group affiliates in 48 states (Fersh, 1982). NAMI was well on the way to becoming a powerful actor in the politics of mental health.

From its inception in 1978, the CSP also gave stimulus and support to the emerging mental health consumer movement. Working with consumer leaders from around the nation, "CSP championed active roles for people diagnosed with serious mental illness, promoted self help/mutual support approaches, and insisted on empowerment as a basic principle in all aspects of services and supports" (Parrish, 1991, p. 8). The CSP effort also supported the first national Consumer Alternatives conference in 1985. One of the first national consumer organizations grew out of the 1985 conference. Although they did not speak with one voice from one national organization, in the early 1980s mental health consumers and their organizations became very important players in the politics of mental health.

Impact of the CMHC Movement on the Mental Health Professions

In addition to creating new occupational opportunities for mental health professionals in CMHCs and in related evaluation research and education settings, the CMHC movement influenced the mental health professions in several other ways. As the CMHCs were implemented across the country, researchers found a blurring of professional roles. The result was that there were only slight differences in the professional tasks being performed by individuals trained in each of the four disciplines of psychiatry, psychology, nursing, and social work (Bloom & Parad, 1977; Redlich & Kellert, 1978). This was particularly true in outpatient services. In many centers, the only function that remained the exclusive responsibility of the psychiatrist was the prescribing of medications, and by the 1970s, psychologists in some states were considering challenging that. This blurring of professional roles and responsibilities was a stimulus for clinical psychologists, nurses, and social workers to begin to advocate for reimbursement for their services that was equal to that of psychiatrists (Brown & Stockdill, 1972). This advocacy was also reflected in activities of the four professional associations as they lobbied for equal coverage under national health insurance proposals and other third-party funding plans. This competitive activity made collaboration among the professional associations more difficult as the political coalition that was built in the 1960s and 1970s tried to mobilize the support for federal community mental health legislation.

In addition to the blending of mental health professional roles, other changes were also occurring in professional practices. Ozarin (1975) reported that some general hospitals had changed their bylaws to make it possible to add nonpsychiatrist mental health professionals, mainly psychologists and social workers, to their staffs with defined privileges. As well, psychiatric nurses were providing consultation and education services to primary-care nurses and physicians on the management of psychiatric patients receiving primary-care services. About 85% of all federally funded mental health centers were affiliated with general hospitals, and this brought mental health professionals with new skills to their staffs. In many rural areas, the CMHCs brought new psychiatric services and staff to communities where none had existed before; this was a significant change for both the communities and the mental health professionals (Ozarin, 1975). Ozarin (1975) also reported that the CMHC movement influenced the private practice of psychiatry. Private solo and group practices were broadening therapeutic practices to include community mental health principles to make services available to a greater number of clients. Multidisciplinary practice groups and group therapy became more common, as did day-care programs in conjunction with group practice. The CMHC legislation, and the centers themselves, had truly become instruments for influencing community mental health service practices.

Lessons Learned

Was the Community Mental Health Centers Act, and its continuous amendments, an effective instrument for changing national mental health policy? In general, the program policies were successful in improving the organization and delivery of mental health services, increasing the availability of more comprehensiveness services, improving the accessibility of services, increasing community participation in program governance, and increasing the understanding of mental illness and the need for early intervention. However, in looking back at the 18 years of honing and applying the policy instrument, it seems that several hard lessons were learned.

1. Involve All of the Essential Parties in the Systems Change

In 1965, when the initial amendment to the Community Mental Health Centers Act authorizing the staffing grant program was being considered, NIMH, after much disagreement and discussion, made the decision to limit state control of the CMHC program by bypassing the states in the review and approval of staffing grants (Foley, 1975, pp. 104–107). This policy meant that for the first time the U.S. Public Health Service was making grants for health services that did not flow through the states. Some state mental health directors, particularly from the larger population states, strongly objected to this policy.

With hindsight, was this the right policy? Probably not. NIMH staff clearly wanted to expedite the process of getting centers operational through a process of direct federal–community interaction. However, evaluation studies indicated that when the federal grants terminated and states were expected to be the major funding source for continuing the centers, in keeping with the seed money concept, some states did not respond as the federal government had intended. They may have appropriated more money for the centers, but they were not concerned with assuring fidelity to the

CMHC model. Allowing the states more control, and having more federal–state coordination, might have facilitated ongoing fiscal support, generated greater fidelity to CMHC concepts, and averted some of the deinstitutionalization problems.

One could also argue that within the NIMH itself the clinical training programs were not well coordinated with the CMHC program. As the CMHCs proliferated, the supply of professional mental health staff was soon outstripped by the demand, and many of the new staff did not have some of the basic skills or experience needed for working in a treatment team environment in which there was considerable interaction with other human service agencies. NIMH established a Continuing Education Branch, but there did not seem to be a concerted effort to use traditional clinical training grants to encourage university departments in the behavioral sciences to upgrade their curricula and recruitment to meet the needs of the CMHC movement. Without stimulus from the clinical training grant programs, the higher education pipeline could not begin to meet the human resource needs of the centers.

New human resources had to be generated. Early on, the CMHCs recognized that mental health paraprofessionals could be trained to perform a variety of essential tasks in community programs (Ozarin, 1975). Recruitment, selection, and training processes for paraprofessionals were initiated in many centers. To assist in this effort, NIMH established a new paraprofessional training branch. Nevertheless, the fact that the higher education systems were unable to change rapidly was not fully considered at the initiation of the CMHC program. That inflexibility continued to be an issue during the life of the program.

2. Consideration of Demographic Issues

At the initiation of the CMHC program in 1963, the first cohort of the baby boom population was coming to the age (17–21) at which they would be most at risk of serious mental illness. They came into adulthood in waves throughout the 1960s and 1970s. Approximately 64 million babies were born in the United States between 1946 and 1961, and by 1981 they represented almost one third of the nation's population (Stockdill, 1982). The baby boom population came on the scene during the era of deinstitutionalization as a new generation of mental health consumers. In time, the number of young people at risk of developing schizophrenia and other serious mental illness was staggering. By the 1970s, that part of the population with serious and persistent mental illness became a severe strain on many mental health systems across the country. In addition, this population had a much higher rate of substance abuse than earlier populations, and this often confused symptomatology and greatly confounded treatment (Ridgely,

Osher, Goldman, & Talbott, 1987; Stockdill, 1982). The baby boomers were highly mobile and more aggressive than the older adults who had spent much of their lives in state hospitals. Many of this generation of young adults with serious mental illness were periodically homeless. The growing uninstitutionalized population, together with the deinstitutionalized population, greatly complicated the community mental health service delivery process. The initial planners of the CMHC program could not have been expected to have predicted the complications of treating this dual-diagnosis population, but they should have been able to project the size of the child/adolescent/young adult population that would be growing out of the baby boom population.

3. The Social and Political Environment and the Need to Clarify Program Goals

The CMHC movement took place in an era that included the civil rights movement, the "war on poverty," the assassination of a president and two other national leaders, the Vietnam war and the antiwar movement, urban unrest and violence across the country, and impeachment hearings and the eventual resignation of a president. In some urban areas, the CMHC staff and community mental health leaders were active participants in the social and political movements. Panzetta (1971), in his book, *Community Mental Health: Myth and Reality*, described his experience at a CMHC in inner-city Philadelphia, where he was responsible for a crisis intervention service. In 1969, the center had been the "scene of a major confrontation" between management on one side and some staff (mainly paraprofessionals) and local citizens on the other. Panzetta indicated that a failure to clearly identify the goals of the mental health center was at the root of the problem. Were the main goals social, clinical, or both, and to what end? Were the goals directed at family or social disturbances? Although the center staff must be sensitive to community needs, social problems such as crime, racism, and poverty cannot be resolved by the "inadequate tools" of mental health treatment and rehabilitation services (Ozarin, 1975). Foley and Sharfstein (1983) reported on a similar situation in a New York inner-city mental health center where community activists, including paraprofessional mental health workers, had seized the center. This center developed out of a poverty program providing human services through indigenous workers (Ozarin, 1975). The poverty worker activists wanted to continue a socially oriented program directed at resolving poverty conditions rather than a clinically oriented program concerned with the treatment of mental illness (Foley & Sharfstein, 1983). Although these examples were not a common experience with citizen participation in mental health centers, they illustrate the need to clarify program goals, and the scope of program resources and expertise, up front with the community to be served. The lesson learned is that if this does not happen, the center may contribute to conflict within the community, and the quality of mental health services will suffer.

4. The Dilemma of the National Community Mental Health Reformation of 1977–1981

The Community Mental Health Centers Act as a tool for developing national mental health policy could survive the hostile years of the Nixon–Ford administrations, but it could not survive the friendly supportive years of the Carter administration. Why? The only health-related legislative product of the Carter years, the Mental Health Systems Act, was like an overweight and hobbled deer, waiting to be attacked by wolves. And those wolves were waiting just around the corner in the Reagan administration. In a relatively short period of time, President Carter's Commission on Mental Health had done a comprehensive job of identifying some major problems in relation to the implementation of the CMHC program and had identified the mental health service needs of the national population.

However, the drafting of a legislative proposal took over a year to obtain a consensus among all of the bureaucratic layers in DHEW as well as a consensus with the White House staff and the mental health constituency groups (Foley & Sharfstein, 1983). The final administration proposal, which President Carter submitted to Congress on May 15, 1979, contained six major titles, and no final consensus had been reached on major issues dividing some of the mental health constituencies. Thus began the Congressional process. The representatives of the National Council of Community Mental Health Centers testified in hearings that the draft legislation gave the states too much control over the CMHCs. On the other hand, the witnesses from the National Association of State Mental Health Program Directors testified that the first draft of the Systems Act would create a fragmented and uncoordinated "nonsystem" of projects (Foley & Sharfstein, 1983). The act was signed into law by President Carter on October 7, 1980. As outlined above, President Reagan signed OBRA into law, repealing the Systems Act on August 13, 1981.

Why was it so easy to overturn the Mental Health Systems Act? The act contained nine separate titles, each with its own constituency, and as a result it was very vulnerable. Several of the major mental health constituency groups were still having major disagreements about the act. The Congressional staff that had worked on the act viewed the mental health constituency groups as being in disarray and therefore feckless in relation to providing strong political support for the new legislation as a whole. Leadership at NIMH, the National Mental Health Association, or both, was not seen as strong enough to pull the other groups together. Now that the White House leadership was gone, there was no one organization or individual that could pull the mental health field together.

Alas, what irony. Without the continued leadership of President Carter and Rosalynn Carter, the process of the President's Commission on Mental Health left a weakened mental health field and, through the new block grants, the states were given more authority and control over mental health services policy—with far fewer federal resources. The lesson learned for future policymakers at the national level is not to try to initiate a second bold new approach to establishing national community mental health services policy without having broad major constituency and Congressional support. It is hoped that this chapter and the analysis of lessons learned might be of some assistance in guiding future policymakers. As Bert Brown, the Director of NIMH from 1970 to 1978, once said: "Problems beget policy as surely as policies created the problems in the first place. It is in this axis between problem and policy that we must work" (Brown, 1966, p. 18).

REFERENCES

A. D. Little, Inc. (1973). *Report on viability of the catchment area concept* (NIMH Evaluation Contract HSM-42-72-96).

Alcoholic and Narcotic Addict Rehabilitation Amendment of 1968, Pub.L. No. 90-574.

Baer, B. (1980). Deinstitutionalization: Noble solution or tragic failure? *Journal of the Institute for Socioeconomic Studies, 5*, 87–99.

Bass, R. D. (1971). *A method for measuring continuity of care in a community mental health center* (DHEW Publication No. HSM-72-9109). Washington, DC: U.S. Government Printing Office.

Bass, R. D., & Windle, C. (1972). Continuity of care: An approach to measurement. *American Journal of Psychiatry, 129*, 196–201.

Bassuk, E. L. (1980). The impact of deinstitutionalization on the general hospital psychiatric emergency ward. *Hospital and Community Psychiatry, 31*, 623–627.

A bill to amend the Public Works and Economic Development Act of 1965, Pub. L. No. 93-46.

Bloom, B. L., & Parad, H. J. (1977). Professional activities and training needs of community mental health center staff. In B. L. Bloom, I. Iscoe, & C. Spielberger (Eds.), *Community psychology in transition: Proceedings of the National Conference on Training in Community Psychology.* Washington, DC: Hemisphere.

Braun, P., Kochansky, G., Shapiro, R., Greenberg, S., Gudeman, J. E., Johnson, S., & Shore, M. F. (1981). Overview: Deinstitutionalization of psychiatric patients, a critical review of outcome studies. *American Journal of Psychiatry, 138*, 736–749.

Brown, B. (1966, November). *Psychiatric practice and public policy*. Paper presented at the 20th anniversary meeting of the Group for the Advancement of Psychiatry, Philadelphia.

Brown, B., & Stockdill, J. (1972). The politics of mental health. In S. E. Golann & C. Eisdorfer (Eds.), *Handbook of community mental health* (pp. 669–686). New York: Appleton-Century-Crofts.

Community Mental Health Centers Act Amendments of 1967, Pub. L. No. 90-31.

Community Mental Health Centers Act Amendments of 1970, Pub. L. No. 91-211.

Community Mental Health Centers Act Amendments of 1975, Pub. L. No. 94-63.

Community Mental Health Centers Construction Act of 1963, Pub. L. No. 88-164.

Community Mental Health Centers Extension Act of 1978, Pub. L. No. 95-622.

Comprehensive Alcohol Abuse and Alcoholism Prevention, Treatment, and Rehabilitation Act of 1970, Pub. L. No. 91-616.

Comprehensive Drug Abuse Prevention and Control Act of 1970, Pub. L. No. 91-513.

Comptroller General of the United States. (1974). *Need for more effective management of the community mental health centers program: Report to the Congress from the U.S. General Accounting Office*. Washington, DC: U.S. Government Printing Office.

Dekker, B., & Stubblebine, J. (1972). Crisis intervention and prevention of psychiatric disability: A followup study. *American Journal of Psychiatry, 129,* 725–729.

Drug Abuse Office and Treatment Act of 1972, Pub. L. No. 92-255.

Fersh, D. (1982, February 5). A look at a new alliance. *Psychiatric News.*

Foley, H. A. (1975). *Community mental health legislation: The formative process*. Lexington, MA: Heath.

Foley, H. A., & Sharfstein, S. S. (1983). *Madness and government: Who cares for the mentally ill?* Washington, DC: American Psychiatric Press.

Glaser, F. B. (1969). The uses of the Day Program. In L. Bellak & H. H. Barton (Eds.), *Progress in community mental health*. New York: Grune & Stratton.

Goldman, H. H., & Morrissey, J. P. (1985). The alchemy of mental health policy: Homelessness and the fourth cycle of reform. *American Journal of Public Health, 75,* 727–731.

Health Services Extension Act of 1977, Pub. L. No. 95-83.

The Heart Disease, Cancer, Stroke, and Kidney Disease Amendments of 1970, Pub. L. No. 91-515.

Herz, M. I., Endicott, J., Spitzer, R. L., & Mesnikoff, A. (1971). Day versus inpatient hospitalization: A controlled study. *American Journal of Psychiatry, 127,* 1371–1382.

Joint Commission on Mental Illness and Health. (1961). *Action for mental health: Final report of the Joint Commission on Mental Illness and Health*. New York: Wiley.

A Joint Resolution to correct an error made in the printing of Public Law 95-613, 1979, Pub. L. No. 96-32.

Kennedy, J. F. (1963). *Message from the President of the United States to the Congress of the United States relative to mental illness and mental retardation.* Document No. 58, House of Representatives, 88th Congress, 1st session, pp. 4–5.

Kiesler, C., Bachrach, L., Mechanic, D., McGuire, T., & Mosher, L. (1982). *Federal mental health policy making: An assessment of deinstitutionalization.* Paper presented to the National Science Foundation, Office of Special Projects, Washington, DC.

Langsley, D. G., Machotka, P., & Flomenhaft, K. (1971). Avoiding mental hospital admission: A followup study. *American Journal of Psychiatry, 127,* 1391–1394.

Macro Systems, Inc. (1973). *Trends in sources of funds for community mental health centers.* Silver Spring, MD: Author.

Mannino, F. V., MacLennan, B. W., & Shore, M. F. (1975). *The practice of mental health consultation* (DHEW Publication No. ADM-74-112). Washington, DC: U.S. Government Printing Office.

Mental Health Study Act of 1955, Pub. L. No. 84-182.

Mental Health Systems Act of 1980, Pub. L. No. 96-398.

Mental Retardation and Community Mental Health Centers Construction Act Amendments of 1965, Pub. L. No. 89-105.

Naierman, N., Haskins, B., & Robinson, G. (1978). *Community mental health centers: A decade later.* Cambridge, MA: Abt Books.

National Academy of Public Administration. (1971). *The multiagency community mental health center: Administrative and organizational relationships* (NIMH Evaluation Contract No. HSM 42-70-55).

National Institute of Mental Health. (1975). *Briefing paper on Pub. L. 94-63, The Health Services and Nurse Training Act of 1975, the tone of Title III,* p. 2. Unpublished document.

National Institute of Mental Health. (1978). *Briefing Paper No. 3 on the catchment area concept.* Unpublished document.

National Institute of Mental Health. (1980). *History of the community mental health centers program.* Unpublished document.

National Institute of Mental Health. (1981). *Directory of federally funded community mental health centers.* Washington, DC: U.S. Government Printing Office.

National Institute of Mental Health. (1984). *Review of legislative activities.* Unpublished document.

National Institute of Mental Health, Division of Mental Health Service Programs. (1971). *Community mental health center operating handbook.* Washington, DC: U.S. Government Printing Office.

National Institute of Mental Health, Division of Mental Health Service Programs (1977). Unpublished CMHC status report #27: CMHC *alumni (Funding Terminees).*

National Opinion Research Center. (1971). *Relationship between CMHC and other caregiving agencies* (Evaluation Contract No. HSM-42-71-7). Chicago: University of Chicago Press.

Omnibus Budget Reconciliation Act of 1981, Pub. L. No. 97-35.

Ozarin, L. D. (1975, September). *Community mental health: Does it work? Review of the evaluation literature.* Presentation at the Fall Institute of the Department of Psychiatry, Dartmouth Medical School, Hanover, NH.

Panzetta, A. F. (1971). *Community mental health: Myth and reality.* Philadelphia: Lea & Febiger.

Parrish, J. (1991). CSP: Program of firsts. *Innovations and Research, 1,* 8–9.

Redlich, F., & Kellert, S. R. (1978). Trends in American mental health. *American Journal of Psychiatry, 135,* 22–28.

Regulations for the Community Mental Health Center's Act of 1963. (1964). *Federal Register,* U.S. Department of Health, Education and Welfare, Public Health Service.

Ridgely, M. S., Osher, F. C., Goldman, H. H., & Talbott, J. A. (1987, December). *Chronically mentally ill young adults with substance abuse problems: A review of research, treatment and training issues.* Report submitted to the Alcohol, Drug Abuse and Mental Health Administration of the U.S. Department of Health and Human Services by the University of Maryland School of Medicine.

Roy Littlejohn Associates. (1972, May). *The impact of preferential poverty funding on the operations of community mental health centers* (NIMH Contract No. HSM-42-72-89).

Spaner, F. E. (1984, December). *A brief history of the community mental health centers program, with attention to the development of services for the elderly.* Report submitted to the National Institute of Mental Health under Purchase Order No. 84MO29501901D.

Stanford Research Institute. (1970). *Sources of funds in community mental health centers* (NIMH Evaluation Contract No. HSM-42-69-101).

Stockdill, J. (1978, February). *The history of community mental health center program evaluation efforts at NIMH.* Paper presented at the annual meeting of the National Council of Community Mental Health Centers, Kansas City, MO.

Stockdill, J. (1981, June 19). Memorandum of transmittal of draft final regulations for the Mental Health Systems Act to the DHHS Assistant Secretary of Health through the Acting Administrator, ADAMHA.

Stockdill, J. (1981, October). *History of the community mental health centers program and implementation of the new block grant legislation.* Paper presented at a seminar on the Omnibus Budget Reconciliation Act (P.L. 97-35), Montgomery County, MD.

Stockdill, J. (1982, May). *Mental health services and the new federalism.* Paper presented at the New Federalism in Action Block Grant Conference, Atlanta, GA.

Stockdill, J., (1985, July). *Alternative mental health resources in the United States.* Paper presented at the World Congress on Mental Health, Sussex, England.

Turner, J. C., & TenHoor, W. J. (1978). The NIMH Community Support Program: Pilot approach to needed social reform. *Schizophrenia Bulletin, 4,* 319–348.

Weiner, R. S., Woy, J. R., Sharfstein, S. S., & Bass, R. D. (1979). Community mental health centers and the "seed money concept": Effects of terminating federal funds. *Community Mental Health Journal, 15,* 129–138.

Woy, R. J. (1978, November). *Policy-making for mental health: The role of program evaluation.* Paper presented as part of a panel at the 2nd annual meeting of the Evaluation Research Society, Washington, DC.

11

PREVENTION OF MENTAL DISORDERS

GEORGE W. ALBEE

In this chapter I make no pretense of objectivity. I have written elsewhere about the role of personal values in influencing "scientific" perceptions (Albee, 1983). There exists a clear dividing line in approaches to the prevention of mental disorders. On one side, and I find myself here, is the position that social–environmental sources of stress often produce mental–emotional problems. These are not diseases in the usual sense of identifiable physical pathology—rather, people learn to be mentally disordered with normal nervous systems. Prevention requires efforts at social justice. On the other side, and this view is currently ascendant in the United States, is

In preparing this chapter, I have relied on the published record of two Presidential Commissions and one nongovernmental organization (NGO) group, the final report of the Joint Commission on Mental Illness and Health entitled *Action for Mental Health* (1961), published with a grant from the American Legion. I thank the copyright owner for permission to use excerpts from this volume. I have used material from the report of the President's Commission on Mental Health (1977–1978) and from the report of the Task Panel on Prevention (1978) of this commission. I also have used material from the Report of the National Mental Health Association's (NMHA) Commission on the Prevention of Mental/Emotional Disabilities, published in 1987. I have drawn on chapters I have written for volumes in the series of books copyrighted by the Vermont Conference on the Primary Prevention of Psychopathology, which generously gave me blanket permission to use this material. Also, I have used materials from articles I have written in the journal *American Psychologist* with permission of the American Psychological Association, as well as from the reward acceptance address of Stephen E. Goldston (1986) in *American Psychologist* with the permission of both Goldston and the American Psychological Association.

the view that all mental "illnesses" are due to brain disorders and related physical pathology.

The field of public health has traditionally taught us much of what we need to know to prevent plagues effectively. It is well established that no mass disorder afflicting humankind has ever been eliminated by attempts at treating only infected individuals. Incidence (the number of new cases in a time period) can be reduced only through successful *primary prevention*: proactive steps to reduce or eliminate the undesirable condition in unaffected populations. Primary prevention nearly always involves the reduction of risk to populations or to specific large groups at high risk.

In the case of prevention of mental disorders, it has long been argued that a major noxious agent is stress, which must be reduced. Resistance to stress can be developed through ensuring secure employment and preventing poverty and homelessness. A secure, loving early life experience strengthens resistance to stress, as do reduction of child abuse, neglect, and insecure life circumstances. Psychological factors can also reduce the risk of somatic ailments.

The National Institute of Mental Health (NIMH), under the National Institutes of Health (NIH), is part of the United States Public Health Service (USPHS) and reports to the U.S. Surgeon General. A major role of the USPHS is prevention, so by administrative placement and definition, NIMH has an implied prevention mission. A basic tenet of public health is that prevention programs are only effective if applied at a nationwide level. The first three directors of NIMH, Robert Felix, Bert Brown, and Stanley Yolles, were all psychiatrists with training in public health.

NIMH, COMMUNITY MENTAL HEALTH, AND PREVENTION

Washington's "Noble Conspirators" (see below) struggled for years after World War II to expand the amount of federal support of medical research, to get federal money into the care of people with mental disorders, and to obtain federal support for the training of mental health personnel and for mental health research.

All of the characters in this struggle, including lobbyists like Mike Gorman, Mary Lasker, and Florence Mahoney, and especially the psychiatric-warrior Robert Felix, as well as the medical administrator, Boisfeuillet Jones, felt an overpowering revulsion toward the overcrowded, hopeless state hospitals, and they set out after World War II to "break the back" of these institutions. Their Congressional allies included Senator Lister Hill and Representative John Fogarty. Their efforts achieved limited success and have not been fully realized. Large numbers of elderly state hospital inmates were transferred to equally oppressive nursing homes, and patients on the back wards of mental hospitals were often dumped into inhospitable communities.

What the "Noble Conspirators" achieved was the establishment of NIMH and a greatly expanded training of NIMH-supported professional mental health workers between 1948 and 1980, with the largest increase occurring in psychology. The story of their efforts to get the Congress to reverse its historic reluctance to put federal funds into caring for the mentally ill is told with great clarity and interest by Foley and Sharfstein (1983). The development of the projected 2,000 community mental health centers (CMHCs) was not (and will not be) realized, despite the support of John F. Kennedy and Lyndon B. Johnson. Each period of increase in CMHC development has been followed by efforts of more conservative administrations to get the federal government out of these programs and to return the care of the mentally ill to state and local communities.

Psychiatry played a prominent role in the NIMH effort to develop CMHCs, and its parent group, the American Medical Association (AMA), often opposed it. The AMA had long been opposed to the use of federal funds for the care of the mentally ill because of their members' fears that doing so would open the doors to socialized medicine. Although the AMA supported the construction of the CMHCs, it strongly opposed the use of federal funds to staff them (see Williams, 1964).

Foley and Sharfstein (1983) clearly described the failure of society to provide for the continuing care of chronically disturbed people discharged from the state hospitals. The CMHCs were typically understaffed and too few in number to take up the burden of care for the seriously mentally ill. Many of these individuals became homeless and could not secure welfare entitlements because of the regulation that no one was eligible for such benefits who lacks a home address. This peculiar *Catch-22* situation still holds. The bag ladies and the homeless men cannot afford permanent residences, and so they are ineligible for the welfare payments that would allow them to obtain a permanent address. Many wind up in jails and prisons.

The 1950s

In the 1950s, not long after the establishment of NIMH, the national psychiatric leadership urged the development of a new major plan for the care and treatment of the large and growing number of persons with mental illnesses. A national commission to study the nation's needs and resources in the field of mental illness and health was established by an act of Congress in 1955. The Mental Health Study Act (P.L. 84-182) directed that a Joint Commission on Mental Illness and Health (JCMIH), as chosen by NIMH, analyze and evaluate these needs and resources and make recommendations for a national mental health program.

The final report was delivered to the Congress on December 30, 1960, after 3 years of intense work by a number of task forces. This final report, *Action for Mental Health* (JCMIH, 1961), contained a lengthy and detailed set of recommendations for major changes in the delivery of mental health services, including the transformation of the traditional state mental hospital.

Except for the consultation and education requirements in the CMHCs, the final report of the JCMIH is sparse in its expressed concern for prevention. There is note of the possible importance of "social forces" as prevention:

> Primary prevention is an important area for applied research. Many of the specific studies in this area reflect our growing interest in and understanding of the effects of social forces. It must be said that systematic studies are still infrequent but topics such as the following are now among the serious interests of applied researchers: the evaluation of mental health education programs, particularly those directed at parents; the influence of various school curricula, different educational policies, and teaching procedures on the adjustment and mental health of children; the effects of large-scale readjustments and changes in the society such as the introduction of automation in industry, the desegregation of our schools, and the relocation through urban renewal projects of large numbers of persons. (JCMIH, 1961, p. 208)

One further quotation from the report of the JCMIH has relevance to the current question of preventing mental disorder versus fostering improved positive mental health:

> The primary prevention of mental illness presents a twofold problem. First, no program of prevention through public education or other means should be undertaken without a thorough assessment of the available scientific knowledge and a grounding of the program in such knowledge. Second, advances in prevention of mental illness, as in its cure, depend on the development of the extensive research program proposed above.
>
> It is our purpose to redirect attention to the possibilities of improving the mental health of the mentally ill. It is not our purpose, however, to dismiss the many measures of public information, mental health education, and child and adult guidance that may enhance an understanding of one's own and others' behavior and so build self-confidence, reduce anxiety, and result in better social adjustment and greater personal satisfaction. But our main concern here, in recommendations for a program attacking mental illness, is with various levels of service beginning with secondary prevention—early treatment of beginning disturbances to ward off more serious illness, if possible—and continuing through intensive and protracted treatment of the acutely and chronically ill. (JCMIH, 1961, pp. 242–243)

My own work for the JCMIH (Albee, 1959) involved a detailed study of professional manpower (as it was called then) available and needed to realize the program aspirations of the JCMIH. My conclusion, with supportive details on the shortage of professionals in every field concerned with mental health, was that "Our country will continue to be faced with serious personnel shortages in all fields related to mental illness and mental health for many years to come" (Albee, 1959, p. 259). The implications of my study were widely discussed and led to major efforts by NIMH to support the training of many more mental health professionals in succeeding decades.

During the year I spent in Cambridge, Massachusetts (1956), writing the report on manpower, frequent conversations with other JCMIH task force directors had major influences on my own conversion to the critical importance of primary prevention in a public health context. Marie Jahoda (1958) convinced me that most mental disorders were interpersonal and learned, and that they often could be unlearned (through psychotherapy) and eventually prevented (through good child rearing by emotionally secure parents). John Gordon, professor of epidemiology at the Harvard School of Public Health, convinced me that "no mass disorder has ever been brought under control by attempts at treating the affected individual nor by training large numbers of practitioners" (personal communication, November, 10, 1956)

The 1960s and 1970s

The JCMIH report initiated, during the early and mid-1960s, a period of interest, growth, and modernization of the mental health intervention system. In 1965, the new Commission on the Mental Health of Children had less impact. The Nixon–Agnew–Ford Administration had little interest in mental health and, indeed, sought actively to reduce and dismantle the research and training budgets in this field and to reduce the power and visibility of NIMH.

A review and discussion of prevention efforts at NIMH cannot be told without noting the contributions of a central character in this history: Stephen E. Goldston. Goldston's NIMH career began in 1962–1963, when he provided staff support for a training program in special projects in mental health. His advisory committee included Erich Lindemann, Herman Stein, myself, and others heavily interested in prevention. Goldston was trained in psychology and also held a graduate degree in public health.

In 1967, he suggested to Stanley Yolles, director of NIMH, that he be allowed to develop a program in the area of primary prevention. A few NIMH staffers had been active in relating public education to positive mental health (e.g., William Hollister, Mike Bower, and Bill Rhodes), but there was no clear prevention initiative. With cautionary warnings to him that prevention was unlikely to acquire major significance, Yolles appointed Goldston Special Assistant to the Director (of NIMH) for Prevention.

For the next 19 years, Goldston struggled to get a significant NIMH commitment to efforts at prevention. His efforts were aided by the interest and support of psychiatrists such as Ernest Gruenberg, Reginald Lourie, Gerald Caplan, and Erich Lindemann and psychologists such as Emory Cowen and Bernard Bloom. Goldston provided advice and NIMH financial support for many in the series of annual Vermont Conferences on the Primary Prevention of Psychopathology, which began in 1975 and continued for more than 20 years. Many NIMH professionals were active participants in these Vermont Conferences. In addition to Goldston, presenters and discussants included Mike Bower, Luis Laosa, Ed Kelty, Juan Ramos, Joyce Lazar, and others. Dozens of the presenters, over the years, reported on prevention research funded by NIMH.

In 1977, the first volume of the Vermont series of books on primary prevention (Albee & Joffe, 1977) was published. Klein and Goldston (1977) published *Primary Prevention: An Idea Whose Time Has Come*, and President Carter established, that same year, the President's Commission on Mental Health.

LaLonde's (1975) report on the health of Canadians was a major review of research on the importance of lifestyle in the development, maintenance, and preservation of health. Since then, numerous research studies have shown the critical importance of life experiences and lifestyles in fostering good health, including mental health.

THE CARTER COMMISSION

President Jimmy Carter established the President's Commission on Mental Health (PCMH) in February 1977. This action was the fulfillment of a campaign promise and also a reflection of First Lady Rosalynn Carter's clear interest in mental health. The charge to the commission was to review the mental health needs of the nation and to come back to the President some 13 months later with recommendations about how these needs might best be met.

The PCMH itself was an interesting group. Chosen by a committee headed by John Gardner with even greater care than a New York City election slate, it included representatives of the major professions, of each large minority group and major religion, a member of Alcoholics Anonymous, and an articulate "ex-patient" spokeswoman. It is curious that Volume 1, although it lists the names of the PCMH members, does not identify any of them by profession, degree, or work setting. Two psychologists served on the commission: Beverly B. Long and John J. Conger (who was recording secretary and later president of the American Psychological Association). Three members of the commission were psychiatrists; social work, law, education, and nursing were also represented.

The work of the commission was helped along enormously by a skilled and dedicated staff of professionals, many of them on loan from other federal agencies, including NIMH. Finally, there was a large number of task panels reviewing and summarizing knowledge in a wide range of areas, including various aspects of service delivery; the family; special populations, including minorities, women, and the physically handicapped; and specialist groups concerned with a range of topics, including legal and ethical issues, Vietnam-era veterans, migrant and seasonal farm workers, the role of the arts, the use of the public media, and prevention. Liaison task panels were set up in the areas of mental retardation, alcohol-related problems, and psychoactive drug misuse. Altogether, several hundred people played an active role in the development of reports to the commission, including drafts of proposed recommendations.

The report suggests that at any given time "ten percent of the population needs some form of mental health services" (PCMH, 1977–1978, p. 8) and goes on to state "there is new evidence that this figure may be nearer 15 percent of the population" (PCMH, 1977–1978, p. 8). According to the commission's own figures, fewer than 7 million people were seen by mental health professionals in 1975. This means that less than one-fifth of those needing help actually received it—in formal professional settings, at least. It is clear that the commission favored getting more help to the unserved and underserved, a formidable task. The report pointed out that "high quality mental health care should be available to all who need it at reasonable cost" (PCMH, 1977–1978, p. 9).

Who are the underserved and unserved? They are described in several different places in the commission's report. Children, adolescents, and the elderly were identified repeatedly as underserved. These three groups together represent more than half the U.S. population. Then there are the under-served minority groups, which included 22 million African Americans, 12 million Hispanic Americans, 3 million Asian and Pacific Island Americans, and 1 million American Indians and Alaska Natives. All of these groups were underserved or, in many instances, inappropriately served by persons insensitive to cultural differences or incompetent in appropriate languages. Although these identified groups of 38 million people clearly overlap some-what with the earlier groups identified as underserved, that is not the end of the statistical complexities. Five million seasonal and migrant farm workers were largely excluded from mental health care. Elsewhere in the report one discovers that women also often did not receive appropriate care in the mental health system. Neither did people who live in rural America, in small towns, or in the poor sections of American cities. Neither did 10 million people with alcohol-related problems, nor an unspecified number of people who misuse psychoactive drugs, nor the very large number of children and parents involved in child abuse, nor 2 million children with severe learning disabilities, nor 40 million physically disabled Americans, nor 6 million mentally retarded persons. Although the commission made some very brave statements about the recent improvements in the availability of mental health care in American society, it seems clear that this improved care must have been available largely to those groups not identified as being underserved—they could only be White, educated males living in the affluent sections and suburbs of major American cities.

There was a heartening section in the report on the importance of primary prevention, the first time a national commission had recognized the position that secondary and tertiary prevention, though humane, never eliminate the major plagues and distresses afflicting humankind. A "Center for Primary Prevention" was proposed at NIMH with convening and lead authority (important bureaucratese) to involve all of the other federal agencies that could contribute. States were encouraged to set up special offices responsible for stimulating prevention activities. The report proposed a $10 million annual budget for training and research in prevention and that ultimately 10% of the NIMH budget be specifically earmarked for prevention.

The Task Panel on Prevention (PCMH)

The establishment of the President's Commission of the Task Panel on Prevention (1978) was largely a consequence of Beverly B. Long's persuasive efforts. She was president of the National Association for Mental Health (a citizen's nongovernment organization) and was supported in her efforts by Rosalynn Carter, honorary chair of the commission. Both Beverly B. Long and Rosalynn Carter attended meetings of the Task Panel on Prevention and defended the critical importance of federal prevention efforts when other members of the commission questioned its value. Steve Goldston, at my invitation as chair, became an official consultant to the task panel and presented in 1977 a detailed fact sheet on NIMH prevention activities.

The fact sheet indicated that NIMH was not appropriately developing prevention efforts. There was no specified administrative entity or programmatic effort within NIMH for primary prevention, and only one full-time NIMH mental health professional was assigned to primary prevention. It is telling that NIMH specifically allocated no research funds for prevention activities.

To a considerable extent, the Task Panel on Prevention was persuaded that the shortfalls and gaps reflected in these facts had to be addressed. As a result of the report of the Task Panel on Prevention (which included among its members myself, psychologists Bernard Bloom, Emory Cowen, Nikki Erlenmeyer-Kimling, Donald Klein, and Vera Paster), the commission made the following statement in its report to the President:

> At present, our efforts to prevent mental illness or to promote mental health are unstructured, unfocused, and uncoordinated. They command few dollars, limited personnel and little interest at levels where resources are sufficient to achieve results. If we are to change this state of affairs, as we believe we must, the prevention of mental illness and the promotion of mental health must become a visible part of national policy. (President's Commission on Mental Health, 1977–1978, p. 53)

In response to the report of its Task Panel on Prevention, the President's Commission made a number of urgent recommendations about strengthening prevention efforts at NIMH. The changes suggested by the PCMH actually occurred at NIMH. Among the most significant changes were the establishment of the Office of Prevention and the Center for Prevention Research; also, an ongoing prevention research grants program was established; a prevention publication series was established and produced 10 issues; a national prevention constituency was developed that was composed of senior researchers, service providers, and all major mental health organizations; and prevention efforts were legally mandated in Section 455(d) of the Public Health Services Act.

The commission recommended that a Center for Prevention be established in NIMH and that primary prevention be the major priority of this center. The commission also recommended that $10 million be allocated during the 1st year (with a funding level of no less than 10% of the NIMH budget within 10 years) to support epidemiological, biomedical, behavioral, and clinical research aimed at prevention; to assess and evaluate existing programs of prevention; to replicate effective preventive programs, including those related to community support systems; and to engage in other appropriate activities.

PREVENTION IN THE 1980s

The 1986 Commission of the National Mental Health Association (NMHA) was a last effort of the traditional (social change) prevention forces. With the Carter Commission report shelved, and with a new NIMH agenda (mental disorders are biological, due to a brain defect, genetic, or some combination of these), and with organic-minded psychiatric leaders in control focused on treatment, a new commission was formed with the National Mental Health Association (an NGO citizen's group) as the sponsor. (This was the most scientific, and carefully planned, of all prevention commissions because it relied on input from national experts rather than on opinions of people with a separate agenda.)

In the spring of 1986, after 2 years of work, this Commission on the Prevention of Mental–Emotional Disabilities presented its final report at a press conference at the National Press Club in Washington, DC. The NMHA commission's report was expected by many to go a long way toward shifting the nation's priorities in the direction of greater efforts away from a focus on treatment and in the direction of prevention of mental and emotional disabilities.

The commission was inspired by the enthusiasm and leadership of Beverly Long, who was a past NMHA president and who had served as a member of the President's Commission on Mental Health. (Long had also just completed her term as president of the World Federation for Mental Health.) She had long been active in NIMH in various advisory roles. In addition to Beverly B. Long (Chair), other commission members were Paul Ahr, myself (George Albee), Willis Goldbeck, Thomas Leonard, Betty Tableman, and George Tarjan. Members of the NMHA commission heard from a carefully selected group of prevention experts who made oral presentations at commission hearings and whose written comprehensive reviews of specific areas of prevention research were published as a separate volume by NMHA.

The guiding principles for the Long/NMHA report were the development of preventive interventions aimed at the reduction of undue stressors and the development of competencies and support systems for people at risk. The commission defined four organizing principles as the framework for considering prevention efforts: (a) biological integrity, (b) psychosocial competence, (c) social support systems, and (d) new societal policies and attitudes (see NMHA, 1986, pp. 13–16; the final report also appears as a separate issue of the *Journal of Primary Prevention* [Commission on the Prevention of Mental–Emotional Disabilities, 1987]).

Two aspects of the development of mental–emotional disabilities were held to be especially relevant to prevention efforts:

1. Disability more often than not develops along a continuum from barely identifiable behavior to disabling symptoms and breakdown.
2. Research points to a commonality of antecedent stressors in many mental–emotional and physical disorders; thus, successful interventions may well affect a range of disorders (NMHA, 1986, pp. 1–2). (The current NIMH leadership would now challenge both statements.)

The NMHA commission noted that successful prevention interventions have been possible when directed at some of the organic causes of mental–emotional disabilities. More recently, it added, major research efforts have been devoted to the relationship between stressful life events or circumstances and the onset of mental and physical disorders. It is known that stressors of various kinds, especially multiple stressors, can lead to damaging mental and physical symptoms in vulnerable persons.

According to the NMHA commission, research has identified groups of individuals at increased risk for developing mental–emotional disorders. These risk factors include genetic and physical vulnerability; economic deprivation; negative family circumstances; disruption of family stability; poor child nurturing; physical, verbal, and sexual abuse; and critical events such as sexual assault, parental death, bereavement, marital disruption, and involuntary unemployment. Particularly at risk are individuals who experience multiple stressors (NMHA, 1986, p. 2). The identification of at-risk populations has provided opportunities for increasing knowledge about the development of mental disorders and possible prevention interventions.

Research has indicated ways to offset some of these identified risks. We know the importance of family planning and genetic counseling, learning how to cope with frustrations and stress, having realistic expectations and perceptions, developing early trusting relationships, and having access to community resources designed to facilitate the management of life crises or transitions. People coming together in self-help networks to share their problems have demonstrated the benefits of social support in times of stress. The prevention knowledge base in some areas, such as social support and the importance of prenatal care, is firm and solid. In other areas, such as the development of interpersonal competencies, there is sound knowledge of relevant factors and growing evidence of effective interventions. In some areas, there is as-yet-limited research to test speculations and plausible theory.

On the basis of consideration of then-current knowledge, availability of existing organizational structure, and urgency of need, the NMHA commission identified the following four specific areas (NMHA, 1986, p. 3) to have immediate potential for preventing mental–emotional disabilities:

1. *Wanted and healthy babies*. Interventions to help ensure wanted, healthy, full-term babies, including programs of health and parenting education, family planning, comprehensive prenatal care services, and social support of high-risk families.
2. *Prevention of adolescent pregnancy*. Cooperative efforts by parents, schools, and other social service agencies to prevent adolescent pregnancy, through programs to develop responsible decision making, provide health and sex education programs that emphasize the consequences of sexual activity, and

ensure access to counseling about contraception and health services.

3. *School programs.* Programs in preschool through high school that incorporate validated mental health strategies and competence building as an integral part of the curriculum. The commission emphasized the importance of academic mastery and the development of psychosocial skills, especially in kindergarten and the early elementary grades.

4. *Support, information, and training for individuals in situations of extreme stress.* Programs that help children and adults to anticipate and manage adverse life circumstances or critical life events—such as home visits to high-risk families with infants, training in coping skills, and mutual support groups.

The NMHA commission made it clear that the term *mental–emotional disability* refers to a *spectrum* of mental and emotional disorders (NMHA, 1986, p. 9):

> We are addressing the spectrum of mental–emotional disorders, including schizophrenia, affective disorders, anxiety, substance abuse and other cognitive, emotional or behavioral disorders which seriously interfere with an individual's life and productivity whether in work, school, relationships or general ability to "carry on."

It is not hard to understand why the report failed to influence NIMH. It strongly supported competence promotion as prevention and the idea that mental disorders can be shown to exist on a continuum from mild to severe. This *spectrum hypothesis* was characterized in a book by conservative psychiatrist E. F. Torrey (1997) as "socialist dogma." Indeed, Torrey sees the whole mental hygiene movement (i.e., the belief that mental disorders can be prevented by better child rearing in a wholesome social environment) as a left-wing, even Marxist, movement long opposed by conservative forces, including the American Legion and the Daughters of the American Revolution (see Albee, 1997).

Both the Carter Commission and the Long/NMHA Commission stressed the benefits of competency training in the prevention of mental disorders. The latest official criticism of this view is that such programs are not "disease specific." But if mental disorders are *not* specific diseases, and if programs to improve social competencies, self-esteem, and mutual support systems reduce rates of mental disorders, then the disease-specific model is weakened beyond repair, and if mental disorders exist on a continuum (as both the Carter Commission and the Long/NMHA Commissions argued) then the disease-specific model is threatened.

A CHANGE IN PREVENTION MODELS

Since the early 1980s, the psychiatric leadership at NIMH has emphasized the biological–brain defect–genetic theory of the origins of mental illness and has deemphasized the effects of environmental stresses such as poverty, social stress, and exploitation. Primary prevention has been blended with secondary prevention (treatment) and tertiary prevention (rehabilitation).

Herbert Pardes was NIMH director at the time of the change in direction (1978–1984). He was slow to pursue the recommendations of President Carter's Commission (1977–1978) that had suggested that prevention efforts be aimed at reduction in poverty and in the stresses of social injustice. Pardes favored a biological model of causation that did not emphasize social change.

Lewis Judd became NIMH director from 1988 to 1992. His major contribution to NIMH policy was his edict declaring that the 1990s were to be the "Decade of the Brain," during which a major focus on brain research would lead to important breakthroughs in the understanding of mental disorders. At the conclusion of the Decade of the Brain, no major breakthrough had been made, but the new post-Judd directors of NIMH have continued to emphasize the importance of further brain research.

Following Judd, the director of NIMH from 1992 to 1994 was Fred Goodwin. Goodwin evoked a storm of controversy by remarks made about the hypersexuality and violence of inner-city males while he was director of the Alcohol, Drug Abuse and Mental Health Administration. He proposed, in the context of these remarks, the study of a large number of inner-city males at risk for violence, paying special attention to genetic and biochemical determinants. He added that there was not time to unravel the social causes of inner-city violence.

Steven E. Hyman became NIMH director in April 1996. He continued to work in his own laboratory on the National Institutes of Health campus on molecular neurobiology, focusing on how neurotransmitters alter the expression of genes in the brain and thereby produce long-term changes in neural function that can alter behavior. Hyman put his own stamp on NIMH's mission with an emphasis on "the underlying basic science of brain and behavior . . . on the causes and treatment of mental disorders . . . on genes . . . molecular and cellular level events . . . brain circuits . . . brain imaging, molecular genetics and computer modeling" (*Facts About NIMH*, n.d.). Hyman broadened the NIMH prevention initiative to include interventions at different points in the course of individual illness to prevent recurrence. This means that primary prevention has been married to secondary and tertiary efforts. (See "Prevention Research Initiative" in *Schizophrenia Research at NIMH*, n.d.)

The Decade of the Brain

Since 1991, the Decade of the Brain project has offered members of Congress opportunities to learn about some of the most exciting and significant research underway in the fields of molecular biology, neuropsychology, developmental neurobiology, behavioral genetics, molecular genetics, biophysics, chemistry, anatomy, cognitive psychology, cognitive neuroscience, neuroimaging, artificial intelligence, and linguistics—all fields in which the brain is being studied. The brain's complexity demands this kind of cross-disciplinary, cross-fertilizing approach.

There has been no formal written report on the results of the Decade of the Brain. In a briefing over breakfast for members of Congress on September 25, 1998, Hyman talked about schizophrenia as "clearly a brain disease" with exactly the same incidence—1%—throughout the world. It is "caused by genes; something happens during brain development that converts this genetic vulnerability into disease. Exactly what happens is the subject of neuroscientific research" (Hyman, 1998). Hyman's conclusions are not in agreement with other views on schizophrenia (see Boyle, 1990, for an opposite view).

A NEW NIMH APPROACH TO PREVENTION

In 1996, Hyman commissioned a National Advisory Mental Health Council Workgroup on Mental Disorders Prevention Research with this charge: to review the institute's current prevention research portfolio and, of particular importance, to identify gaps and opportunities for future research. At least two major issues gave rise to this process: (a) recognition of the value of the prevention research perspective (including its developmental approach and its focus on nonclinical as well as clinical settings) and (b) a growing realization that severe mental disorders, which are now underrepresented in the NIMH prevention research portfolio, are not likely to be amenable to primary prevention interventions with our current knowledge base.

The workgroup's recommendation included a significant change in historic NIMH policy. Prevention was extended beyond primary prevention to include treatment and relapse prevention. In effect, under Hyman's regime, little remained of primary prevention. Research on social causes of emotional disorders largely disappeared.

EXPLANATORY MODELS AND PREVENTION

In the history of modern medicine, it has been common for some observed physical pathology to cause physical symptoms; a diagnostic name is then attached to the "disease." Sometimes the cause of the observed physical problem must be sought in microbiology or physiology. Disturbed behavior is exhibited in most mental disorders, but few reliable underlying physical correlates or markers have been discovered. However, the search goes on. If, as some suspect, most mental disorders are *learned* in pathological social environments (child abuse and neglect; exploitation of the powerless; discrimination against women, gays and lesbians, the elderly, and the physically disabled, all of whom are at high risk), then no underlying physical pathology will be found that needs to be corrected. Instead, primary prevention will require successful efforts at reducing stresses in these at-risk groups through social change. This view, common before 1980 and widely shared in present-day United Kingdom, Canada, and elsewhere, is much more conducive to prevention efforts that involve reducing the stresses of poverty; the stresses of racism; and discrimination against women, the aged, the physically disabled, and other victims of social injustice.

However, recent NIMH-funded proposals for "prevention science" have been largely silent on these social issues and have stressed experimental-control studies aimed at reducing risk for *Diagnostic and Statistical Manual of Mental Disorders* (DSM–IV; American Psychiatric Association, 1994) conditions (see Perry & Albee, 1994).

A new prevention science was put forward by NIMH and the Institute of Medicine (IOM) that advocated strict experimental interventions with controls to reduce risks for psychiatric disorders. Articles by Muñoz, Mrazek, and Haggerty (1996); Heller (1996); and Reiss and Price (1996) support, elaborate, and discuss this agenda. Controversial issues included (a) the use of risk reduction of *DSM* psychiatric disorders as the criteria for acceptable research; (b) rejection of studies of competence promotion as not aimed at specific disorders; and (c) rejection of prevention studies, done before the counterrevolution that occurred in 1980 and thereafter, which advocated social and political change aimed at achieving social equality for disadvantaged groups. Arguments against the restricted new approach were presented by me (Albee, 1996).

One of the core issues for the new preventionists was whether to include mental health promotion efforts as part of the overall strategy. This issue, perhaps more than any other, separates the new from the old. Muñoz et al. (1996), in opposition to promotion efforts, echoed the theme: "The major focus of promotion programs is to achieve optimal states of wellness" (p. 1121). But is immunization designed to achieve more robust health? Is finding social support for the frail elderly aimed at reaching optimal wellness? The IOM report specifically and deliberately "has chosen not to include mental health promotion within the spectrum of interventions focused on mental disorders. [The reason:] health promotion is not driven by a focus on illness but rather a focus on the enhancement of well-being" (Mrazek

& Haggerty, 1994, p. 27). Promotion does not have "a disorder orientation," claimed Muñoz et al. But does not a feeling of well-being, of positive self-esteem, of enhanced social competence, strengthen resistance to stress? Are these not protective factors in another guise? However, evidence for competence-enhancing strategies does not fit the IOM's and NIMH's focus on reducing risk factors for specific DSM categories.

If prevention science is defined exclusively as the search for, and reduction of, risk factors for DSM–IV disorders through experimental and control-group research in a developmental context, then anything done before 1980 does not count. This judgment occurred frequently in the preceding articles and in the IOM (Mrazek & Haggerty, 1994) and NIMH (1993) publications. It is hard for some of us to turn our back on major early prevention studies, such as Skodak's (1984) study of the effects of growing up in a caring family rather than in an orphanage, Harlow and Harlow's (1966) careful experimental work on the social world of infant monkeys and their later adjustment, Bowlby's (1969) study of attachment, Broussard's (1976) continued study of the consequences of mother–neonatal perceptions, Cowen's (1994) work on competence enhancement, Dooley and Catalano's (1979) work on economic change and behavior disorder, Fryer's (1995) detailed review of the mental health consequences of unemployment, or David's (1992) "Born Unwanted: Long-Term Developmental Effects of Denied Abortion." This list could be extended for pages; however, all of these studies occurred before the creation of scientific prevention research.

Perry and Albee (1994) expressed the view that effective prevention will require societal change and political action to achieve equal rights and to reduce the stresses of discrimination and exploitation. Heller's (1996) ambivalent response to this view was as follows: "articulating a moral position without evidence of intervention effectiveness is not enough, because an equally (sic) compelling morality for many citizens is one that champions individual initiative and responsibility as the primary ingredients needed to overcome social adversity" (p. 1124). This statement hearkens back to a time when many Americans embraced the romanticized Horatio Alger myth that anyone could pull themselves up by their bootstraps. Environmental factors were largely ignored, and factors located inside the individual were heavily weighted. This worldview means, in effect, that 5 million migrant farm laborers (with the highest rate of schizophrenia and alcoholism) should show more individual initiative and hurtle over the environmental barriers they confront, as should unemployed workers who lost their jobs as the result of corporate downsizing, unemployed inner-city teenagers, and poverty-stricken elderly women, as well as all of the other groups known to be at high risk. Because we have more knowledge of the effects of structural obstacles and their effects on individuals and groups than we did half a century ago, the myth is no longer credible.

Shore (1994), a former president of the American Orthopsychiatric Association and former editor of its journal (and retired NIMH officer) was an active researcher before prevention science was discovered. According to Shore:

> We must always remember that the prevention initiatives that have had the most profound effects on mental health have been the women's movement, Social Security, Medicare, the Civil Rights Laws, and PL-94-142, The Right to Education for All Handicapped Act. (1994, p. 16)

It is not necessary to search the scientific literature for evidence that water runs downhill. Nor do we require elaborate epidemiological studies to validate the observation that economically exploited groups are regarded as inferior, even subhuman, by the exploiters. And it is clear that these groups have higher rates of both physical illness and mental and emotional disorders. It is logical that prevention programs should include efforts at achieving social equality for all (Albee, 1995), but such efforts threaten the status quo and so are not part of the prevention agenda.

WHO WILL BELL THE CAT?

NIMH does not have many critics. With a budget approaching $1 billion and more than 2,000 grants and contracts awarded to researchers and training programs at universities and other institutions across the United States (and overseas), it is the major source of financial support for the mental health research and training system. Many studies evaluating its prevention programs, like that of the IOM (chartered in 1970 by the National Academy of Sciences)—*Reducing Risks for Mental Disorders: Frontiers for Preventive Intervention Research* (Mrazek & Haggerty, 1994)—are funded by NIMH. Some of the people on the IOM committee who oversaw this report were funded by NIMH. Few are willing to bite the hand that feeds them.

Back in the early 1970s, Ralph Nader's Center for the Study of Responsive Law published *The Madness Establishment: Ralph Nader's Study Group Report on the National Institute of Mental Health* (Chu & Trotter, 1974). Chu and Trotter (1974) spent 2½ years studying the NIMH's CMHC program and concluded that it was largely a failure and that it perpetuated a two-tiered program of treatment: one for the rich, one for the poor. According to Chu and Trotter (1974), efforts at prevention through consultation and education, in "recognition of the large role played by the environment in emotional disturbance and the realization that an individual's inner conflicts cannot be understood apart from social and political realities" (p. 64) were assigned low priority and were "least practiced" (p. 65).

NIMH must be ever conscious of and sensitive to the watchful eye of the National Alliance for the Mentally Ill (NAMI), a well-funded, politically effective NGO composed largely of middle- and upper-class parents of severely disturbed children, adolescents, and young adults. NAMI wants more money spent on the treatment (drug-based, mostly) and care of young people who are severely disturbed, suffering (NAMI insists) from brain disorders. NAMI resists with passion the possibility that some severe mental disorders might be socioenvironmental in etiology. They support involuntary commitment for involuntary treatment if necessary. They strongly oppose many basic (mostly animal) research studies funded by NIMH that do not bear directly on their brain-defect model.

Psychoanalysis has been gradually excluded from psychiatric teaching in medical schools and residencies that now focus on psychopharmacology. The neuroses, long a centerpiece of psychiatric diagnosis, were downgraded and converted into peripheral symptoms of more biological disorders in DSM–IV, and the childhood origins of neurotic symptoms are expunged from the new model. Treatment and research now focus on biological–genetic–brain defects to be reduced by a growing cornucopia of drugs produced by the major pharmaceutical companies.

It is interesting and illuminating to see the changes in the explanatory model put forth by lay leaders in the field after the conservative takeover. Illustrative of many is the change in Rosalynn Carter, once the leading advocate for prevention. In 1981, Rosalynn Carter, who had been Honorary Chair of the President's Commission on Mental Health, supported a social model:

> It is clear that the impact of poverty, racism, and discrimination in all its forms adversely affects the mental health of millions . . . Too often, the pressing need for services distracts our efforts from those primary prevention activities which in the long run can have far greater impact on the mental health of our people. (Carter, 1981)

Seventeen years later, on July 17, 1998, on the NBC Evening News, Rosalynn Carter was asked about her long-standing interest in the field of mental health. She now lined up with the new position of the national mental health leadership: "We now know that mental illnesses are due to problems in the brain. We can treat brain disease."

A LAST WORD

NIMH, as part of the U.S. Public Health Service, is the logical place for the support of prevention efforts to reduce the number and severity of mental disorders. Prevention is the core of public health. It is well-known that diseases and disorders cannot be treated out of existence. No amount of research on treatment, even if resulting in success, can reduce incidence (the rate of new cases). However, NIMH has long focused its programs on treatment and on training treatment professionals. Resistance to prevention efforts has existed from the beginning. The reason usually given—nothing can be prevented if the cause is unknown—is clearly invalid. NIMH has resisted the clear finding that social–environmental induced stresses are responsible, to a significant degree, for most mental disorders, and that effective efforts at prevention have clearly been demonstrated by reducing these stresses and by fostering improved competence and social skills.

So long as NIMH insists that most mental disorders are due to as-yet-unknown organic defects, there will be little effective prevention. And so long as NIMH blends primary prevention with secondary and tertiary prevention, its efforts will be meaningless.

REFERENCES

Albee, G. W. (1959). *Mental health manpower trends*. New York: Basic Books.

Albee, G. W. (1983). Political ideology and science: A reply to Eysenck. *American Psychologist, 38*, 965–966.

Albee, G. W. (1995). Ann and me. *Journal of Primary Prevention, 15*(4), 331–349.

Albee, G. W. (1996). Revolutions and counterrevolutions in prevention. *American Psychologist, 51*, 1130–1133.

Albee, G. W. (1997). The radicals made us do it! Or is mental health a socialist plot? Review of E. F. Torrey, *Out of the shadows: Confronting America's mental health crisis.Contemporary Psychology, 42*, 891–892.

Albee, G. W., & Joffe, J. M. (Eds.). (1977). *Primary prevention of psychopathology: The issues* (Vol. 1). Hanover, NH: University Press of New England.

American Psychiatric Association. (1994). *Diagnostic and statistical manual of mental disorders* (4th ed.). Washington, DC: Author.

Bowlby, J. (1969). *Attachment and loss: Vol. 1. Attachment*. New York: Basic Books.

Boyle, M. (1990). *Schizophrenia: A scientific delusion?* London: Routledge.

Broussard, E. R. (1976). Neonatal prediction and outcome at 10/11 years. *Child Psychiatry and Human Development, 7*, 85–93.

Carter, R. (1981). Quotation from the dust jacket of J. M. Jofee & G. W. Albee (Eds.), *Prevention through political action and social change*. Hanover, NH: University Press of New England.

Chu, F. D., & Trotter, S. (1974). *The madness establishment: Ralph Nader's study group report on the National Institute of Mental Health*. New York: Grossman.

Commission on the Prevention of Mental/Emotional Disabilities. (1986). *Report of the Commission*. Alexandria, VA: National Mental Health Association.

Commission on the Prevention of Mental/Emotional Disabilities. (1987). The Commission on the Prevention of Mental–Emotional Disabilities, *Journal of Primary Prevention, 7*(4), 175–241.

Cowen, E. (1994). The enhancement of competence: Challenges and opportunities. *American Journal of Community Psychology, 22,* 149–179.

David, H. P. (1992). Born unwanted: Long-term development effects of denied abortion. *Journal of Social Issues, 48,* 163–191.

Dooley, D., & Catalano, R. (1979). Economic, life, and disorder changes: Time-series analyses. *American Journal of Community Psychology, 7,* 381–396.

Facts About NIMH. (n.d.). Retrieved June, 2000, from http://www.nimh.nih.gov/about/nimh.cfm

Foley, H. A., & Sharfstein, S. S. (1983). *Madness and government: Who cares for the mentally ill?* Washington, DC: American Psychiatric Press.

Fryer, D. (1995, June). Labour market disadvantage, deprivation and mental health: The 1994 C. S. Myers Lecture. *The Psychologist,* 265–272.

Goldston, S. E. (1986). Primary prevention: Historical perspective and a blueprint for action. *American Psychologist, 41,* 453–460.

Harlow, H., & Harlow, M. (1966). Learning to love. *American Scientist, 54,* 244–272.

Heller, K. (1996). Coming of age of prevention science: Comments on the 1994 National Institute of Mental Health—Institute of Medicine prevention reports. *American Psychologist, 51,* 1123–1127.

Hyman, S. (1998, September 25). *Schizophrenia: Understanding it, treating it, living with it: NIMH and the Library of Congress project on the decade of the brain—Congressional breakfast.* Retrieved from http://www.loc.gov/loc/brain/brkfast.html

Jahoda, M. (1958). *Current concepts of positive mental health.* New York: Basic Books.

Joint Commission on Mental Illness and Health. (1961). *Action for mental health.* New York: Basic Books.

Klein, D., & Goldston, S. (1977). *Primary prevention: An idea whose time has come* (DHEW Publication No. ADM-77-447). Washington, DC: U.S. Government Printing Office.

LaLonde, M. (1975). *A new perspective on the health of Canadians: A working document.* Ottawa, Ontario, Canada: Information Canada.

Muñoz, R. F., Mrazek, P. J., & Haggerty, R. J. (1996). Institute of Medicine report on prevention of mental disorders: Summary and commentary. *American Psychologist, 51,* 1116–1122.

Mrazek, P. J., & Haggerty, R. J. (Eds.). (1994). *Reducing risks for mental disorders: Frontiers for preventive intervention research.* Washington, DC: National Academy Press.

National Institute of Mental Health, Prevention Research Steering Committee. (1993, March 9). *The prevention of mental disorders: A national research agenda: Executive summary.* Rockville, MD: Author.

National Mental Health Association. (1986). Commission on the Prevention of Mental/Emotional Disabilities. *Journal of Primary Prevention, 7*(4).

Perry, M., & Albee, G. W. (1994). On "The Science of Prevention." *American Psychologist, 49,* 1087–1088.

President's Commission on Mental Health. (1977–1978). *Report to the President.* Washington, DC: U.S. Government Printing Office.

Reiss, D., & Price, R. H. (1996). National research agenda for prevention research: The National Institute of Mental Health Report. *American Psychologist, 51,* 1109–1115.

Schizophrenia Research at NIMH. (n.d.). Retrieved May 2000, from http://www.nimh.nih.gov/publicat/schizresfact.cfm

Shore, M. F. (1994, September). Narrowing prevention. *Readings: A Journal of Reviews and Commentary in Mental Health, ix,* 13–17.

Skodak, M. (1984). Prevention in retrospect: Adoption follow-up. In J. M. Joffe, G. W. Albee, & L. D. Kelly (Eds.), *Readings in primary prevention: Basic concepts* (pp. 348–361). Hanover, NH: University Press of New England.

Task Panel on Prevention. (1978). *Vol. IV: Report to the President's Commission on Mental Health.* Washington, DC: U.S. Government Printing Office.

Torrey, E. F. (1997). *Out of the shadows: Confronting America's mental illness crisis.* New York: Wiley.

Williams, G. (1964). The help we need. *Atlantic Monthly, 214,* 112–114.

INDEX

Authoritarian culture of psychoanalysis, film analysis as antidote to, 119
Authoritarian personality, and Custodial Mental Illness Ideology Scale, 72
Axline, Virginia M., 90

Baby boom, 7, 279, 287
Baer, Barbara, 279
Bahn, Anita, 243
Bales, Robert F., 69, 71
Balester, Ray, 247
Bandura, Albert, 91, 93
Banks, Edwin M., 46
Banta, Thomas J., 98
Bardach, John E., 49
Barker, Roger, 188
Barlow, George W., 49
Bartemeier, Leo, 235
Basowitz, Harold, 13, 18, 247
Bates, Marston, 54
Bayley, Nancy, 76, 77
Beach, Frank A., 35, 40, 41, 42, 43, 54, 77, 78, 81, 82, 103
Beck, Lloyd H., 73
Beck, Samuel J., 84, 86
Becker, Joseph, 89
Becker, Wesley C., 88
Behavior (journal), 37
Behavioral neuroscience, 36
Behavioral Neuroscience (journal), 36
Behavior theory, 102, 134–135
Behind Ghetto Walls (Rainwater), 243
Beier, Delton C., 192
Bell, John, 246
Bender, Morris B., 90
Bennett, Chester C., 192, 251
Bennett, E. L., 77
Benton, Arthur L., 192
Bergin, Allen, 133, 138
Bergman, Paul, 119, 125, 127
Berkeley Growth Study, 76
Berkeley Guidance Study, 76, 77
Berkowitz, Leonard, 97, 98, 102
Berlyne, Daniel E., 41
Bernreuter, Robert G., 192
Bernstein, Irwin S., 41, 43, 47, 54, 55
Best, Jay Boyd, 41
Bettelheim, Bruno, 84, 86, 188
Bever, Thomas, 99
Bice, Harry V., 200

Bieri, James, 70, 95
Big Science, 100–101
Bingham, Walter V., 156
Biological–brain defect–genetic theory of origins of mental illness, 307
Biomedical model, 136–137
Biometrics branch of NIMH, 241, 243–244
Birch, Jack W., 200
Birdwhistell, Ray, 124
Bishop, Alison (Jolly), 40
Bitterman, Morton E., 41, 42, 43
Bivens, Lyle, 13
Blain, Daniel, 168
Blake, Robert, 192
Bleach, Gail, 215
Blehar, Mary, 215
Block, Jack, 13, 77, 79
Block grant program, for community mental health, 281
Blocksma, Douglas, 73
Bloom, Bernard, 246, 252, 300, 303
Blum, Gerald S., 73, 74
Bobbitt, Joseph M., 17, 183, 192, 196, 200, 235, 236, 236–237, 242
Boone, Dorothy, 245
Bordin, Edward S., 68, 73, 74, 75, 133–134, 135, 192, 195, 196, 199, 200
Borgatta, Edgar F. 98
Boring, E. G., 68
Boston, Opal, 200
Boston University, 251
Boulder conference, 153–154, 171, 171–172, 174, 191–194, 203
  and APA, 153, 171, 199
  and Committee on Training, 184
  and PhD degree, 172, 196
  and Shakow report, 186
  and subdoctoral training, 202
  and Thayer conference, 199
Boulder (scientist-practitioner) model of training, 154, 171, 172–174, 197, 204
Bourne, Geoffrey, 51
Brower, Eli "Mike," 244, 245, 299, 300
Bower, Gordon H., 91, 93
Bower, Lincoln P., 49
Bowman, Karl M., 183, 189
Bowman, Paul H., 84
Boyer, Paul, 9

National Institute of Mental Health
(NIMH), *continued*
   and Mental Health Systems Act,
     288–289
   prehistory of, 234–236
   and Swampscott conference,
     250–252, 253
  and Community Support Program
    (CSP), 278, 283–284
  comparative psychology support
    from, 31–32, 38–43, 55–57,
    58–59
   and other animal behaviorists,
     39, 45, 46
   research topics supported, 43–45
  and conferences, 203–204
  in consultation and education
    research, 224
  contributions of, 227
  and counseling or guidance
    professionals, 197
  and counseling psychology, 195
  demonstration clinics of, 212 (*see
    also* Mental Health Study Center
    of Prince George's County)
  establishment of, 5, 7, 17, 32, 153,
    211, 233, 297
  as funding agency, 20–21, 33, 61,
    62–64, 66–67, 97, 99, 100–104,
    312
   at California Institute of
     Technology, 99
   and cognitive movement, 99
   at Columbia University, 92,
     95–96
   in community mental health,
     234, 239, 240–241, 253
   for comparative psychology, 38,
     39–40, 41–42, 43, 44, 46, 56
   at Harvard University, 67–72
   at McGill University, 99–100
   at New York University, 87,
     90–91
   and psychologists, 18–19
   and psychotherapy research, 115
   at Stanford University, 91–92,
     93–94
   at University of California, 76–
     77, 78–79
   at University of Chicago, 81,
     84–86

   at University of Illinois, 87,
     88–89
   at University of Michigan, 72–76
   at University of Wisconsin, 92,
     97, 98
   at Yale University, 77, 80–81,
     82–83
   at Yerkes Laboratories, 52
  hindrances to success of, 225–226
  Intramural Psychology Laboratory at,
    18, 116, 122
  Intramural Research Program at, 6,
    12, 132
  JCPP articles acknowledging support
    from, 58
  and Joint Commission on Mental
    Illness and Health, 261
  Laboratory of Socio-Environmental
    Studies at, 248
  and mental health family, 204
  and Mental Health Study Center,
    212, 225, 245 (*see also* Mental
    Health Study Center of Prince
    George's County)
  mission of, 32–33
  and Nebraska Symposium, 188
  nursing supported by, 20–21
  Office of Director of, 241, 247–248
  and prevention, 296, 302, 312–313
   and biological–brain defect–
     genetic theory of origins of
     mental illness, 307
   Center for Prevention at, 303
   and Goldston, 299–300
   and Hyman's changes, 308
   Hyman's joining of primary and
     secondary prevention, 307, 308
   rejection of environmental and
     political factors, 309–311
   and Task Panel of PCMH,
     302–303
  psychiatry supported by, 20–21
  psychoanalysis less supported by, 134
  and psychology or psychologists, 3,
    17–19, 20–21, 226
   and evaluation research, 22
   and graduate training in clinical
     psychology, 153
   history of relationship between,
     4–6
   and self-help by public, 22–23

ABOUT THE EDITORS

Wade E. Pickren, PhD, grew up with his 11 siblings in then-rural central Florida, where he roamed the forests and orange groves. After an early adulthood marked by Cowperian variety, Dr. Pickren returned to college and completed his BS in psychology at the University of Central Florida. He entered the University of Florida's Graduate Program in Clinical and Health Psychology, intending to become a clinical psychologist. However, after he completed his MA in clinical health psychology, he enrolled in a history of psychology course taught by Don Dewsbury and there found his true intellectual interest. Dr. Pickren switched programs and earned his PhD in the history of psychology with a minor in the history of science from the University of Florida. He now serves as the American Psychological Association's historian and director of archives and library services. He is also the editor of the history of psychology and obituaries section of the *American Psychologist*. Dr. Pickren's scholarly interests include the history of post-World War II American psychology, the history of medicine and psychology, and psychology and the public imagination.

Stanley F. Schneider, PhD, (1922–2002) grew up in New York City. He earned his bachelor's degree in absentia from Cornell (1943), as he had already entered the U. S. Army. It was during World War II that he first found his interest in clinical psychology. After the war, he earned his master's (1950) and doctoral (1953) degrees at the University of Michigan. In 1963, Dr. Schneider accepted a position at the National Institute for Mental Health in the training branch. In 1969, he became chief of the Psychology Education Program. He remained chief until the Training Division was eliminated in 1985. Under his leadership, psychology training at the

National Institute of Mental Health became more focused on increasing diversity, strengthened psychology at historically Black colleges and universities, supported rural psychology, and stimulated new fields like community and health psychology. Dr. Schneider was a *bon vivant*, a lover of life, and he was loved by all who knew him.